HIGHLAND
THE STORY OF THE FAR NORTH LINE
SURVIVOR

Dedicated to my father, the late Frank Spaven,
who helped to save the Far North Line in 1963-64, and then spent many
years promoting its development, as well as recording its life on camera.

HIGHLAND SURVIVOR
THE STORY OF THE FAR NORTH LINE

DAVID SPAVEN

KESSOCK BOOKS

First published in Great Britain
by Kessock Books 2016

Copyright © David Spaven 2016

The right of David Spaven to be considered as author of this work
has been asserted by him in accordance with the Copyright, Designs and
Patents Act 1988.

A CIP catalogue record for this book is available from the British Library
ISBN 978-0-9930296-4-6

Designed by Audiografix

Printed and bound in Great Britain
by CPI Group (UK), Croydon, CR40 4YY

CONTENTS

'The day shall come when long strings of carriages without horses shall run between Dingwall and Inverness.'

Coinneach Odhar ('The Brahan Seer'), 16th/17th century

'I am today announcing my decision that the through [rail] services to Kyle of Lochalsh and to Wick and Thurso must be retained in present circumstances. The evidence that the alternatives now available or likely to be available in the next few years are inadequate is very strong, and the Consultative Committee, Highland Transport Board and Highland Panel are unanimous that the service should be retained for the present.'

Ernest Marples MP, Minister of Transport, 16 April 1964

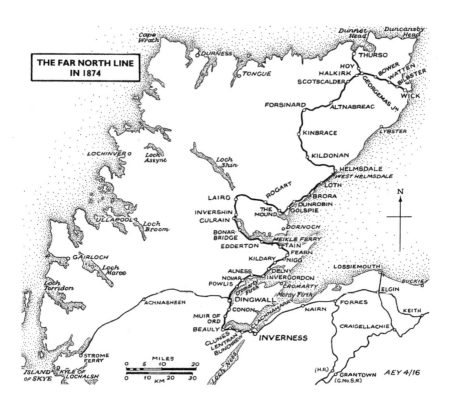

The Far North Line and its stations, on opening through to Wick and Thurso in 1874. (Only principal stations are shown on other lines.)
Alan Young

INTRODUCTION

When Dr Richard Beeching published on 27 March 1963 his infamous report *The Reshaping of British Railways*, the 425-mile Highland rail network – which had served the region since Victorian times – faced savage surgery.

All 232 miles of railway north and west of Inverness – the Far North Line to Wick and Thurso and the Kyle of Lochalsh line – were proposed for closure, leaving a vast tract of northern Scotland entirely dependent on road transport.

But Highlanders were quick to respond to the threat. On 29 March, the *Inverness Courier* thundered: 'Today this country is facing the greatest crisis it has ever had to face in peace.' Just 15 days after Beeching unveiled his report, a conference held in Inverness by the Highland Transport Committee unanimously passed a resolution deploring and opposing the proposed withdrawal of passenger services.

This soon grew into wide-ranging opposition – including the memorable 'MacPuff' campaign – which was instrumental in securing a ministerial reprieve in 1964 for the entire network north and west of Inverness. It was by far the biggest reprieve of the Beeching era, and ensured the survival of what was then, and remains today, Britain's longest rural railway (and longest single-track railway), over the 168 route miles of the Far North Line from Inverness to Wick and Thurso, Britain's most northerly railway station.

While the railway from Dingwall to Kyle, with its romantic and long-acknowledged scenic qualities, has been written about many times, its longer sister has attracted less attention: surprisingly so, for a railway of such great character, scenic diversity and challenging terrain.

In *Highland Survivor*, I relate the remarkable story of the Far North Line: its origins, heyday, stunning escape from the Beeching Axe, and subsequent chequered history. I have been aided in this engrossing research and writing task by a wide range of public and private archive sources, eye-witness accounts and anecdotes from railway staff, as well as access to a unique selection of previously unpublished photographs.

The story certainly did not end with the 1964 reprieve. During the 1970s the Far North Line enjoyed a major freight boom, following the establishment of new industries along the Cromarty Firth. The political spotlight returned in the 1980s when a bold plan to re-route the railway over the Dornoch Firth was scrapped in controversial circumstances, and at the close of that decade the line was severed by the collapse of the Ness Viaduct in Inverness, leaving trains marooned until the bridge was replaced and re-opened in 1990.

I then trace the ups and downs of this unique railway through to the present day, and conclude with an assessment of where Britain's most northerly railway now stands. Buoyed by plans for the new ScotRail franchise to promote the scenic qualities of the line, it nevertheless faces uncertainty over the investment needed to make journey times and service reliability much more competitive with road transport.

My motivation

I first travelled on the Far North Line at the age of 14 in late 1966, shortly after our family moved home from Edinburgh to Inverness, following the appointment of my father Frank as the Planning & Research Officer of the new Highlands & Islands Development Board (HIDB). Thereafter, until leaving for University in Edinburgh in 1970, I would enjoy many leisure trips on the line and would often watch (and photograph) from two handy elevated viewpoints on Crown Drive and Auldcastle Road, its southbound passenger trains slowing past Welsh's Bridge signal box, prior to reversing into the main platforms of Inverness station.

But my real attachment to the railway began in the summer of 1973. Following the HIDB's prolonged promotion of major inward investment, in 1971 the British Aluminium Company (which already had Highland operations at Fort William and Kinlochleven) opened an aluminium smelter at Invergordon, convenient for rail access and the deep water of the Cromarty Firth. The smelter had a big impact on the Far North Line, generating an unprecedented freight boom: but its high wages attracted staff away from the railway.

As a youthful rail campaigner (and also a student, inevitably seeking summer work) I heard from Adrian Varwell, the Invergordon-based Highland Area Secretary of the Scottish Association for Public Transport (SAPT), that the British Rail (BR) Area Manager's office at Invergordon was on the lookout for temporary staff. I jumped at the opportunity to work on the railway, and spent the summers of 1973 and 1974 employed by BR at Invergordon and Tain.

In hindsight, I can see that my experience on the Far North Line was life-changing, diverting my interest from a career in town and country planning, and leading within three years to the start of a working life which has been spent entirely in and around the rail industry. As a BR marketing manager, most of the freight traffics I controlled were well to the south of the Far North Line, but I did find myself playing a key part in two very unusual traffic flows on the line in the 1980s: coal from Invergordon, and peat from Scotscalder. And, in a fortuitous turn of events, in late 2015 and early 2016 I was busy as a consultant in efforts to secure timber traffic from the Flow Country to Inverness via a new railhead at Kinbrace.

Four decades on from my first working experience on the railway, and coming late to a parallel career as an author, I wrote my first book, *Mapping the Railways* (2011). *Britain's Scenic Railways* and *Waverley Route: the life, death and rebirth of the Borders Railway* followed in 2012. Then in 2015 I produced a revised edition, *Waverley Route: the battle for the Borders Railway*, to coincide with the completion of the new line, as well as authoring *The Railway Atlas of Scotland*. So what would be next?

In February 2015, I was contacted by Richard Ardern, long-time activist with Friends of the Far North Line (and a former colleague of my father's in the HIDB). He in turn had just been approached by BBC Alba, who were planning a documentary about the 150th anniversary of the Highland Railway and wanted to find out more about the 1963-64 MacPuff campaign. As Richard said: 'It seems to me to be a story which could do with being written up'.

Coincidentally, only the previous day I had re-established contact with Rab MacWilliam, a former school chum at Inverness Royal Academy, with whom I briefly shared a house in London in the early 1980s. After a lifetime in London-based publishing and writing, Rab had helped to establish Kessock Books in Inverness: and did I have any railway book ideas? I wasted no time in replying that 'there's a great story to be told' about the Far North Line in general and MacPuff in particular. So, when research confirmed that a dedicated history of the line had never been written, the *Highland Survivor* project began.

Over and above its unique fascination as Britain's longest rural railway, it seemed to me that there were two key reasons for researching and writing the story of the Far North Line.

First, what was the secret of the remarkable success of the 1963-64 campaign, culminating in the biggest reprieve of the Beeching era? One of the key drivers here was the fact that, in the early to mid-1960s, my father was a Scottish Office civil servant advising on the regional development implications of the Beeching proposals, and in his obituary in the *Scotsman* in 2003, he was credited with being 'instrumental in saving the bulk of the Highland rail network'. Would my own research support this conclusion? Was there some other 'silver bullet'? Or were there, as I found in my researches for *Waverley Route*, a wide range of factors which determined the ultimate Ministerial decision?

My second motivation was to understand how the railway has managed to survive over the subsequent five decades of much more intensive bus, car and lorry competition on vastly improved roads, and what its future prospects might be in an anticipated era of 'austerity'. The Far North Line's place in the economic and social life of the North of Scotland has clearly shrunk significantly since 1963. But is there a new enhanced role for it to play?

Reflecting these research priorities, much of the book (the final nine chapters) focuses on the period from the 1950s to the present day, paying special attention to the pivotal years 1960 to 1964. However, I do not neglect the earlier eras, with the story of the origins and construction of the railway, in particular, and the subsequent phases of its history, including a mammoth war effort from 1914 to 1919. I then consider the early years of nationalisation, setting the scene for the first of many subsequent clouds on the railway horizon. The book follows a generally chronological sequence, but the two thematic chapters – Chapter 2 on 'Operating the railway' and Chapter 3 on 'The impact of the railway' – embrace a broader sweep of history.

Highland Survivor is not a typical railway history, in that I deliberately do not explore the technical and performance details of locomotives or the engineering of the Far North Line. These are well catered for in books by, among others, HA Vallance and David Ross, as set out in the Bibliography at the end of the book. While I touch on a number of aspects of rail operations (including specific trains and locomotive types which played a central role in key eras and episodes), this is firmly in the context of a history written primarily from a political, social and business perspective.

A minor stylistic point which should be mentioned is that, when referring to my experiences, opinions, etc, throughout the book I use the form 'I' or 'me' rather than the more formal 'the author': this was suggested by my publishing editor, Rab MacWilliam, and it does seem appropriate for a book about a railway with which I have many personal and professional connections. Kessock Books is the fourth publisher with whom I have worked, and Rab has proved to be – by far – the most hands-on editor to date in terms of advice on English style and usage: this has been very much to my advantage.

Sources and acknowledgements

My primary research for *Highland Survivor* has focused particularly on the core period surrounding the Beeching closure threat and its sequel: the 1960s and 1970s. Here my key sources were Highland Council's Highland Archive in

Inverness, the Council's public libraries in Dingwall, Inverness and Wick, and the National Records of Scotland in Edinburgh.

I was initially pointed towards the Highland Archive by Richard Durham, who had donated the personal archives of his father, the late Phil Durham (a leading light in the MacPuff campaign, and of whom more later). I am also grateful to Richard for subsequent discussions and a period photo of his father. On seven visits to the Highland Archive, I was well advised by its enthusiastic team of archivists, and was able to uncover a wealth of material: not only the Durham papers but also those of my late father, Frank Spaven, encompassing both his time in Inverness and his earlier work as a Scottish Office civil servant advising on the regional development implications of the Beeching Report.

Microfiche reproductions of the news and editorial columns of the *Inverness Courier, John O'Groat Journal and Ross-shire Journal*, in Inverness, Dingwall and Wick libraries, brought to life much of the drama of the short, but intense, 1963-64 struggle to combat the proposed closure of both the Far North and Kyle lines. I am grateful to staff at all three libraries, and for the Council's excellent newspaper micro-fiche scanning service at the Inverness and Wick branches. This saved me many laborious hours of note-taking. Scottish Provincial Press (owner of all three titles) kindly permitted me to quote extensively from the editorials and news columns of these newspapers.

Richard Ardern provided me with a unique insight into the modern history of the Far North Line, not least through his dedicated campaigning work for the Friends of the Far North Line over the last two decades. He also pointed me towards countless archive sources (including his own) which were crucial to the telling of the story, including correspondence, press cuttings and BR 'Working Timetables'. His invaluable help extended to the not insignificant task of proof-reading the entire (un-edited) draft text and pointing out a variety of errors and omissions, both in terms of content and language. The book would undoubtedly not have been as authoritative as I hope it now is without Richard's critical input.

My old railway colleague, David Prescott, also read the entire draft and tightened up my textual analysis. Both he and Jim Summers, formerly Regional Operations Manager for ScotRail, brought to bear their long experience of railway management to shed light on some key aspects of the unusual challenge presented by the Far North Line. Other friends and colleagues from the 'railway family' who checked various sections of the text and provided comments include Hamish Baillie, John Holwell and John

Yellowlees. I am most grateful to them all, as indeed I am for the quoted thoughts of a number of other existing and former railway managers who preferred – for good reasons – to remain anonymous.

The memories and knowledge of two former railwaymen particularly connected with the Far North Line provided an additional dimension to the story. Iain MacDonald brought tales of his 50 years on the railway, much of it as a signalman on the Far North Line, including those halcyon (for me) summers of 1973 and 1974 at Invergordon where I began my life on the railway. My ex-BR management colleague, Rae Montgomery, had insightful memories of his 1963-65 sojourn on the railway in the Inverness area, and he also assiduously checked my text on the Beeching period.

Adrian Varwell provided his recollections of the SAPT's lobbying for improved passenger services, including the successful re-openings of Alness and Muir of Ord stations in the 1970s. Partly overcoming the unfortunate loss of all the SAPT Highland archive in a later era, Tom Hart, an SAPT stalwart since its 1962 establishment (as the Scottish Railway Development Association), was able to provide me with some key campaigning documents which help to tell the story leading up to the controversial Dornoch Bridge saga of the 1980s.

Long-standing railway campaigning colleagues, Andrew Boyd and Bill Jamieson, supplied me – from their personal collections of Working Timetables for rail staff – with enough detail of the scale of freight train operations on the Far North Line in the 1960s, 1970s and 1980s to fill the gaps in my own memory. To these I was able to add much material from my own archives and those of my father's which I have inherited.

I am also most grateful to former BBC reporter, Bill Hamilton, for permission to reproduce much of his fascinating account of 1978's headline-grabbing snowbound train at Altnabreac, from his autobiography, *Man on the spot: a broadcaster's story* (2010).

During the course of my research, I was privileged to meet up with former farmer and Highland development advocate Reay Clarke at his Edderton home. Although not directly involved in the MacPuff campaign, he knew well most of the protagonists (many of whom were farmers) and was able to provide me with some very useful insights into the dynamics of that period.

I also owe thanks to Reay for opening my eyes to a hitherto (to me) unknown, but crucial, aspect of changing Highland land use, namely the long-term loss of fertility through the switch from 'transhumance' farming (as still practiced in upland Switzerland) to large-scale sheep farming. Reay's family's story and the wider lessons of history are well described in his very readable *Two Hundred Years of Farming in Sutherland* (2014).

Many of the photographs in the book come from my own archive and that of my father, mostly taken from the 1970s to the 1990s. Gaps in the collection have been admirably filled by a dozen other photographers, all acknowledged in the photo captions. Particular thanks go to Ewan Crawford of the Railscot web site –www.railscot.co.uk – for his technical wizardry in sorting out some key shots where I, unforgivably, managed to lose my original slides. No book on the history of a railway could be complete without maps and, as in three of my previous publications, I have been fortunate to benefit from the considered craft of Alan Young's delightful hand-drawn maps.

Last, but not least, this book could not have been written without tapping into the 23-year experience of Frank Roach, Partnership Manager of HITRANS, the regional transport partnership. He was also a founder member of Friends of the Far North Line, and it can safely be asserted that many of the significant developments on the Far North Line over the last two decades could not have happened without Frank's assiduous networking, lobbying – and lateral thinking.

David Spaven, Edinburgh, July 2016

PART 1

Highland Railway Glenbarry class 2-2-2 No. 55 at Thurso, around 1900. Built by Neilson & Co in Glasgow in 1864, it was originally used on passenger duties on the Highland Main Line, then the Far North Line, and latterly as the Thurso branch locomotive, before being sold in 1906 for breaking up. Vintage postcard, from the Ewan Crawford collection.

BEFORE BEECHING

CHAPTER 1: HOW THE RAILWAY REACHED CAITHNESS

In the first half of the 19th century, the extensive territory of the Highland mainland – Ross-shire, Sutherland and Caithness – north of the region's largest town, Inverness, was still experiencing fundamental economic and social change in the aftermath of the 1745 Jacobite Rebellion. The clan system was eroding, and landowners (a combination of Highland clan chiefs and an increasing number of southern incomers) were seeking to realise greater profit from their holdings through large-scale sheep farming.

Traditional subsistence farming in the Highlands had been based on 'transhumance', the practice of moving livestock from one grazing ground to another in a seasonal cycle. In winter, cattle remained on low-lying land, where arable crops would be cultivated in summer in strips or rigs ('run rigs'), and in summer the cattle were moved to higher-lying 'shielings'.

The combination of land 'improvement', the elimination of transhumance and the frequently enforced clearance of the native population from the land (to coastal villages, or abroad, generally to North America) permitted widespread exploitation of the new cash crop, wool, and brought unprecedented prosperity to landowners.

Communication within the region had traditionally been by horse tracks, drove roads (for cattle) or sea. The first metalled roads were built by the military following the Jacobite Rebellion of 1715, almost all of them to the south and east of Inverness.

Railways and the era of Jacobite rebellions are rarely mentioned in the same breath, but the earliest Scottish developments which led to what we now know as railways arrived in the third decade of the 18th century. As Christopher Harvie records in *Deep Fried Hillman Imp* (2001):

> Hanoverian infantrymen must have wondered, while dodging claymores, what the rails and little trucks were doing there, in the fields by Prestonpans. On 21 September, 1745 General John Cope positioned his cannon along the embankment of Scotland's first railway, the Tranent & Cockenzie Waggonway – only to be overwhelmed by the ferocity of the Jacobite charge which installed Charles Edward at Holyroodhouse. The wagonway had already been there for

twenty-three years to carry coal to the harbour and saltpans, built as part of a South-Sea Bubble speculation called the York Buildings Company.

It would, however, be another 110 years before the arrival of the railway began the transformation of Inverness, *Bradshaw's Descriptive Railway Handbook* of 1863 describing its humble earlier circumstances thus:

> Inverness lies as it were at the back of Scotland, in a part formerly little visited or accessible. About the year 1770, it had no banks, lamps or tiled houses, and one cargo of coals (called "blackstones") a year was enough to supply the demand; but smuggled tea, brandy, fish and game were plentiful.

By the end of the 18th century, when the possibility of a further Jacobite rebellion had disappeared, the maintenance of the military roads was handed over to civilian labour. Their subsequent rapid deterioration led, in 1803, to the establishment of the Commission for Roads and Bridges in the Highlands. The Caledonian Canal Commission was established the same year to build a waterway linking the east and west coasts through Lochs Ness, Oich and Lochy. The engineer for both Commissions was Thomas Telford, one of Britain's leading civil engineers.[1]

In 1824, Joseph Mitchell of Forres, who had been a pupil of Telford's in London, was appointed as Chief Inspector of Roads. Mitchell and his partners Murdoch and William Paterson would engineer virtually the entire Highland Railway system. Neil T Sinclair noted that: 'Between 1803 and 1898 Telford, Mitchell and the Patersons were therefore responsible for almost all the new canal, road and railway infrastructure in the Central and Northern Highlands.'[2]

Despite significant improvements in communications in the first decades of the 19th century, including completion by 1813 of the Inverness to Thurso toll road, the region still lagged far behind the level of economic development being experienced in Central Scotland. As HA Vallance records:

> In the years following the Industrial Revolution, when many parts of the country were experiencing a trade boom, with its consequent increase of wealth, the Highlands of Scotland were plunged in the depths of financial depression, and poverty was rife... The absence of mineral wealth retarded, to a great extent, the development of the country; but the chief obstacle was the lack of good transport, which prevented such industries as did exist from securing a wide market and a ready outlet for their wares.[3]

The physical barrier of the Grampian Mountains checked the direct advance of the rail network to the Highlands. However, a train journey from the Central Belt to Inverness, albeit a circuitous one via lower-lying country along the east coast, first became possible in August 1858 when the Inverness & Aberdeen

Junction Railway completed the final link, from Elgin to the Great North of Scotland Railway's line from Aberdeen at Keith. This followed the opening in 1855 of the first railway in the Highlands – from Inverness to Nairn – and its extension in March 1858 through to Forres and Elgin.

The earlier great British 'railway mania' of the mid-1840s had been the biggest of five railway promotional booms of the Victorian years. Parliamentary powers were obtained for over 9,000 route miles of new railways between 1844 and 1847 – but over a third of the mileage authorised was never built. Scotland was not exempt from this speculative frenzy, PJG Ransom[4] noting that most of the 112 railways north of the Border proposed in this period were not built – at least at that time – and recording Lord Cockburn's comment that 'The country is an asylum of railway lunatics'.

The frenzy extended as far as Britain's most northerly mainland county, Caithness, when in 1845 a preliminary survey of the 20 relatively level miles of the proposed 'Wick and Thurso Railway' was undertaken for local interests. This was to have been an isolated outlier of the emerging rail network, with no southward link – not even Inverness was rail-connected at the time – and, as recorded by David McConnell[5], this disconnection, 'together with it having been proposed at a time when there was so much reckless railway speculation and investment, inevitably led to its failure to materialise'.

At the time, the small town of Thurso, whose origins go back to trading activities during 11th-century Norse occupation, was busy with fishing, weaving, tanning and the production of flagstones (sandstone split to form large flat slabs for building works). These flagstones even led to the construction in 1824 of a five-kilometre tramway from Weydale quarry to the River Thurso. It was also (and remains) the closest mainland town to the Orkney Islands. The Inverness to Thurso mail-coach first ran in 1819, initially taking a dog-leg route via Wick. In the 1840s stage-coaches took 89 hours to reach London from Thurso's *Royal Hotel,* averaging about 7½mph[6]. Ironically, nearly 200 years after the first mail-coach, trains from Inverness would only be reaching Wick after an even wider dog-leg route, via Thurso.

While Thurso overlooks the Pentland Firth to the north, Wick faces east to the North Sea, and shares Thurso's Norse origins. With a quickly growing population (7,475 by 1864), in part stimulated by the late 18th century development of cod and herring fisheries and subsequent harbour expansion, Wick was, with the exception of Inverness, the largest town in the north of Scotland. It was to become the county town of the new elected Caithness County Council in 1890, and was not to be overtaken in population terms by Thurso until the latter's expansion in the 1950s and 1960s due to the establishment of the nearby Dounreay nuclear plant. Both towns were key targets for rail network expansion in the mid-19th century, although their interests in terms of prospective routes to the south were to diverge when enthusiasm for rail connection heightened.

It was to be 1874 before the railway reached Thurso and Wick from Inverness, requiring no less than five private Acts of Parliament for five different stretches of railway. As with most railways in Britain, the Far North Line was not the outcome of a strategic plan but rather the end-result of a sequence of separate initiatives, each with its own private vested interests. This pattern of history created what is still a railway of fascinating scenic contrasts but, regrettably for many everyday transport purposes, one which is now poorly placed to compete with the car (in particular) and the bus.

Northwards from Inverness

In 1845, the same year as the putative Wick and Thurso Railway was surveyed, Joseph Mitchell had overcome logistical difficulties to survey a direct rail route over tough terrain from Perth to Inverness. Mitchell was by then Government engineer for construction of roads, bridges, harbours and buildings in the Highlands, and would eventually become Chief Engineer of the Highland Railway.

It took nearly 20 years before the Grampians were crossed to reach Inverness direct from Perth and, soon after the Inverness & Nairn Railway opened in 1855, the attention of prospective railway promoters turned to the possibility of an extension northwards from Inverness. There was initial uncertainty about the best route, with one scheme proposing to establish a steamer service between Nairn and the north side of the Cromarty Firth, connecting with onward rail services. The reason for the uncertainty was the perceived heavy expense of an Inverness-Dingwall railway bridging the River Ness and the Caledonian Canal, and the Rivers Beauly and Conon.

In 1859, Murdoch Paterson, who had been assistant to Joseph Mitchell on the construction of the railway from Inverness to Nairn and onward to Keith, undertook, together with his brother William Paterson and Mitchell, a survey of the landward route from Inverness to Invergordon via Beauly and Dingwall. The Inverness & Ross-shire Railway Act was then passed unopposed at Westminster in 1860, and the directors, who were primarily local and regional landowners led by Sir Alexander Matheson of Ardross, raised sufficient capital to meet the estimated cost of £215,000 for 31 miles of single-track railway.

On 19 September 1860, the first sod was cut in Inverness by Lady Matheson. David Ross in *The Highland Railway* described an appropriately festive occasion on a day which was observed as a general holiday in the town:

> A public gathering in the Academy Park in Inverness, and a procession through the town, marked the start of work. The navvies were entertained to beef, bread and ale in "a specially erected booth", while the quality went to the Station Hotel for a lunch that lasted from 1 p.m. to shortly after 10 p.m.[7]

The construction of the railway was pushed forward rapidly by Scottish 'navvies' (derived from the 'navigators' who built the first 'navigation canals' in the 18th century), unlike many lines further south where Irish labour dominated. Ross related labour-management confrontations which were a symptom of the harsh circumstances of railway construction for much of the 19th century:

> Many west-coasters, from Applecross, Ullapool and Gairloch, worked on the Ross-shire line. Their inexperience and *[Joseph]* Mitchell's keen contract price combined to make their pay low, and there was some trouble. Work stopped for a day on the Ness Viaduct on 20 November 1860, when they struck to get a rise from 3*d* to 4*d* a day; and the *Inverness Advertiser* of 21 June 1861 reported "a day of turmoil" at Alness, when some of the workmen were charged with intimidating their fellows.

Rails reach Ross-shire

The section of railway from Inverness to the burgh of Dingwall was opened in June 1862, thus fulfilling the Brahan Seer's ancient prophecy about 'long strings of carriages without horses' running between Dingwall and Inverness. David Ross *(ibid)* relates that, at a celebratory lunch in Dingwall two days after the opening, Provost Falconer of Dingwall:

> …described the arrival of the railway as "…beyond all comparison the most momentous event that has ever occurred in its annals since the title of 'royal' was conferred upon it by Alexander 1 in 1226". Inverness to Dingwall by coach (inside rate) had been 7*s* 6*d*; now by train the first class return was 4*s* 6*d*, and a third class return only 1*s* 6½*d*.

The existing Inverness & Nairn terminus at Inverness could not be adapted for conversion to a through station, as it faced south with a frontage to Academy Street (giving the town, ever since, one of the most central station locations anywhere in Scotland), while the Inverness & Ross-shire approached the town from the west. It was therefore decided to enlarge the station by building two additional terminal platforms to the west to accommodate the new train service. Eventually there would be three (as there are today: Platforms 5, 6 and 7), accommodating Far North and Kyle line trains.

The two railways diverged immediately beyond the covered area of the station, passing on either side of the 'Lochgorm Works' locomotive shops. The third side of the triangle, which provided a physical connection from east to west, was formed by part of the Inverness Harbour branch line and subsequently became known (and remains known to this day) as the 'Rose Street Curve'.

The curve was to be used not only for Far North and Kyle freight trains to and from Millburn Yard (to the east) and occasional non-stop passenger trains avoiding Inverness station, but also for regular passenger trains from the Far North and Kyle which, in the southbound direction only, ran east to beyond Welsh's Bridge signal box before reversing into the main platforms (1 to 4) of Inverness station. This practice – which survived until the early 1980s – facilitated both the release of locomotives (which would otherwise be 'trapped' at the buffer stops of Platforms 5 to 7) and easy cross-platform passenger transfer to Aberdeen-bound and Highland Main Line trains, but it did add several minutes to journey times.

Trains over the new railway to Dingwall were worked by the Inverness & Aberdeen Junction Railway, which had merged with the Inverness & Nairn Railway in 1861. The independent existence of the Inverness & Ross-shire was even more short-lived, merging with the former by Act of Parliament in June 1862, the same month as the railway reached Dingwall. The last stretch of the new railway, through to Invergordon, was opened in March 1963, the final cost of construction being £285,000, a third higher than the original estimate.

In part, this reflected the opposition of a landowner, Colin Mackenzie of Findon, who claimed that his tenants would be endangered if they had to use a proposed road level crossing between Dingwall and Invergordon. The fact that Mackenzie was also a shareholder in the railway may have contributed to bridge construction being conceded.

Meanwhile, far to the south but with eventual implications for the Inverness & Ross-shire Railway, in 1856 the independent Perth & Dunkeld Railway had opened north from Stanley Junction, on the Scottish Midland line from Perth to Forfar, to the small town of Dunkeld in 1856. Then, in order to improve on the lengthy route from Inverness to the south via Aberdeen, construction work on the Inverness & Perth Junction Railway – linking the existing railways at Forres and Dunkeld – began in 1861, and was completed just two years later, despite the terrain involved.

The Duke of Sutherland intervenes

In May 1863, just two months after the railway had opened to Invergordon, the Ross-shire Extension Act was passed in Parliament, providing powers to extend the line to Bonar Bridge (actually Ardgay, on the south bank of the Kyle of Sutherland), 26½ miles from Invergordon, and 58 miles from Inverness.

The prime mover was the third Duke of Sutherland who contributed £30,000 to the estimated £213,000 cost for this section, as part of his endeavours to open up to development his extensive landholdings west and north west of Bonar Bridge. While the third Duke's forebears (in particular his grandfather, the first Duke) have long attracted opprobrium for 'the Clearances':

> Since the creation of the title in 1833, successive Dukes had done much to better conditions in the county and expended considerable sums on various improvement schemes. Large tracts of moorland were reclaimed and turned into fertile farm lands *[although large-scale sheep farming and then creation of deer forest would in due course result in substantial degradation of fertility]*, while in the west and north of the county new roads were made in the neighbourhoods of Durness and Lochinver.[8] *(my italics)*

The railway extension was opened to a temporary terminus at Meikle Ferry, 2½ miles north of Tain, in June 1864, and reached Bonar Bridge in October of that year. The choice of route beyond Meikle Ferry, where a tongue of land juts out into the Dornoch Firth, was to prove decisive just over a century later, in terms of the railway's (in)ability to compete with the upgraded A9 road to East Sutherland and Caithness.

Proponents of a direct line to Wick and Thurso envisaged bridging the Dornoch Firth, whose waters are relatively shallow at this point, to take the railway through the significant settlement of Dornoch and onwards up the coast to Golspie. The Duke had different priorities. His requirements and his financial contribution ensured that the next stage of railway extension – the Sutherland Railway – would instead take a wide sweep inland, north west to the village of Lairg, then turn south east through Strath Fleet to reach the coast near Golspie before terminating at Brora.

From Meikle Ferry via Lairg to Golspie, a rail distance of over 37 miles would have to be travelled, with many stretches of severe gradients of up to 1 in 70. Fewer than 20 miles of construction would have been required to take a predominantly level railway from Meikle Ferry via Dornoch to Golspie. The circuitous railway to Thurso and Wick would eventually prove to be severely handicapped by the Duke's diversion, once the bus and the car arrived to challenge the railway's dominance of land transport.

In the same year as the Ross-shire Extension reached Bonar Bridge, a committee was formed to promote the continuation of this railway through Sutherland to Caithness. Joseph Mitchell intimated to the committee that he could take the railway along the coast as far north as Helmsdale, but he thought it virtually impossible to continue it by the coast because of the precipitous nature of the Ord of Caithness, where the hills ended sharply at the sea. Mitchell therefore concluded that the only way to reach Caithness was by taking a long detour inland, avoiding the Ord altogether.[9]

The inland alignment surveyed by Mitchell that year did not go down well with the committee, as the route along the coast followed by the Parliamentary road, which served coastal villages and the fishing industry, was the accepted corridor of communication with the south. Progress on the project stalled but significant developments were taking place further south.

On 1 February 1865, the Inverness & Perth Junction Railway amalgamated with the Inverness & Aberdeen Junction Railway, and on 29 June of the same year became the Highland Railway. The latter was one of the five companies which dominated the Scottish railway system until the Government-directed 'Grouping' of 1923 consolidated over 100 companies across Britain into just four: the Great Western; London & North Eastern; London, Midland & Scottish; and Southern. The Highland Railway's impact on the development of the region was to be profound. David Ross (ibid) noted that, 'The railway company was by far the single biggest commercial concern in the Highlands from the 1860s into the 1920s.'

29 June 1865 also saw the authorisation of the Sutherland Railway from Bonar Bridge via Lairg to Brora, a distance of just under 33 miles. The company chair and principal shareholder was the third Duke of Sutherland, one of the biggest landowners in Western Europe. 'George Granville William Sutherland-Leveson-Gower' inherited estates totalling 1,200,000 acres in Sutherland alone – managed from his palatial Highland residence at Dunrobin Castle, on the route of the Sutherland Railway – plus 32,000 acres of coal-rich land in Staffordshire.

It has been recorded that 'the Duke was a well-liked, benevolent man with a sincere interest in his own county of Sutherland, its people and the Highlands generally. He was eager to develop the far north of Scotland by means of the railway.'[10] He had 'spent some time learning engineering at the London & North Western Railway works at Wolverton in Buckinghamshire', and was an enthusiast for railways, but 'was more interested in engines than civil engineering, and, though he wanted his railway, he did not want to pay a penny more than he had to'.[11]

This led to disputes with Joseph Mitchell & Company, who had been appointed as engineers for the line. The Duke was adamant that Mitchell's railways had cost more than they should, a view he reportedly shared with his fellow Directors of the Highland Railway. Nevertheless, Ross (ibid) concludes that:

Mitchell's reputation as a creator of well-surveyed, excellently-engineered and soundly-built lines through difficult country is safe enough for it to be noted that he had no special formula on cost beyond keeping his estimates low, driving a hard bargain with contractors, and maintaining a close watch on their activity. In addition, the lines were single track, the extent of sidings very small, and buildings normally of wood. Some stations were not built until after the line was opened. But Mitchell still took the American railroad as his model – get the track down and the line in business, and refinements can follow; if he had not adopted this philosophy, the lines might never have been completed.

Works commenced on the Sutherland Railway in the second half of 1865, but the company soon encountered financial difficulties which were not resolved until October 1866 when the Highland Railway finally agreed to an offer from its largest shareholder (the Duke) to take up £30,000 of its unissued stock 'to put the company in funds to invest £30,000 in the Sutherland Railway': provided that the latter continued its line to Golspie at once and completed it to Brora within the time prescribed by the Act.

The new railway was opened as far as Golspie in 1868, its two trains daily in each direction to and from Inverness worked by the Highland Railway as an extension of the southern lines, with connecting horse-drawn road-coaches for Wick and Thurso at Golspie.

Onwards to Caithness

The Act authorising the transfer to the new undertaking of the six uncompleted miles of the Sutherland Railway from Golspie to Brora, and the extension of the railway to Helmsdale – 'the Duke of Sutherland's Railway' – was passed in 1870, although construction had begun earlier. The section from a temporary terminus at Dunrobin to another just south of Helmsdale opened on 1 November 1870, and an interim twice-daily service was operated by the Duke's own steam locomotive and coaches until the works were completed in 1871 and the Highland Railway took over operations.

While the railway was being pushed up the East Sutherland coast, options for its extension to Wick and Thurso continued to be debated. Caithness had a population of 41,100 in 1864, with significantly improved farming lands, major flagstone quarries and an extensive fishing industry. In 1856 Scrabster had become a key steamer port on the Leith-Aberdeen-Orkney-Shetland route. Potential traffics for a railway – and the economic benefits it could provide – were clear, justifying the push north from Sutherland's generally modest opportunities.

The Caithness Railway – linking Thurso and Wick – was authorised in 1866 but funding was not forthcoming for this purely local undertaking, and it was not until 1871 that the Sutherland & Caithness Railway (S&CR) was authorised. This took over the Caithness Railway, connecting it at Georgemas Junction via Joseph Mitchell's 1864-surveyed route over the hills to Forsinard and down sparsely-populated Strath Ullie and the Strath of Kildonan to Helmsdale. Construction began in 1871, with the Highland Railway subscribing £50,000 and the Duke of Sutherland £60,000.

The authorised railway was to terminate at the Wick town boundary and at the edge of Thurso. The failure to penetrate through to Wick harbour and Scrabster pier was castigated in a letter from Joseph Mitchell to the *Inverness Courier* of 28 November 1865 as 'a fatal and unaccountable error'. Reflecting on these omissions, David Ross *(ibid)* comments:

> In the case of Wick, there might have been a difficulty in passing through the town to reach the quays; the reason for not going to Scrabster is less obvious, but it is likely that in both cases it was felt sensible to wait and see what traffic developed, before extending the line. The S&CR shareholders, led by the economical Duke, would not have wanted to inject any further capital until a return was safely predictable.

Nevertheless, the failure to connect directly with steamers at Scrabster – together with the Duke's circuitous diversion of the line via Lairg – can be seen from a 21st-century perspective as the main obstacles to today's railway's ability to compete with the car and the bus for most Inverness to Caithness journeys.

The construction of the line was undertaken by between 400 and 560 men in each of two sections: a Caithness section under Murdoch Paterson, who had helped to survey the Inverness-Invergordon stretch (and whose greatest achievement, as Chief Engineer of the Highland Railway from 1874 to 1898, would be the direct Inverness-Aviemore line built in the 1890s), and a Sutherland section under William Baxter, the Brora engineer who had built the Duke of Sutherland's Railway. Many of the navvies were local or from elsewhere in Sutherland, and 'departed so far from the conventional image of the railway navvy as to combine among themselves to pay for a preacher to come on a Sunday'.[12]

A greater degree of material comfort than would have been expected was provided through the construction of planned houses for the railway's isolated surfacemen. Additionally, wooden huts – double-walled with moss insulation – were built where necessary. According to Ross, the Duke detested the traditional 'truck' system by which contractors paid their men in tokens which could only be exchanged for goods at the contractor's own store, so the men were paid for their labour in cash and could then purchase provisions and clothing from 'approved' merchants.

John Thomas and David Turnock also allude to relatively benign conditions, and a most unusual pastime:

> At the end of each day's work a locomotive went along the line picking up the navvies and conveying them to what a reporter on the *Northern Ensign* described as smart, yellow-painted wooden houses. To pass their hours of leisure in the long summer evenings the navvies would often engage in a pursuit that their far-flung contemporaries *[in the USA]* were keenly following: the search for gold, with some little success along the burns of Torrish, Kildonan, Suisgill and Kinbrace.[13]

At work, these men were pushing the new railway over wild country, including the exposed section around Altnabreac (still isolated in 2016, as one of just four stations in Britain with no tarred road access) and the 708-feet-high County March Summit. Bad weather was not the only obstacle to smooth progress of construction. Ross *(ibid)* quoted a letter from Murdoch Paterson to the company's directors on 23 October 1871, which noted that:

> We have immense tracts of peat moss to contend with from the County March to Dorrery *[Scotscalder]* – a distance of twelve miles, and I have sounded the depth of it every fifty feet. There are many parts where the peat is very soft, and is termed "flow" moss and we have done all in our power to escape it with the line, as, from its softness, it can not be properly drained…

According to Ross, not one shareholder of the company came from Wick, which 'with its seaborne export trade of salted herring to Danzig, Königsberg and other Baltic ports, had no enthusiasm for being at the end of a railway that wound through the empty wastes of Sutherland'. This contributed to an amusing incident just two days after the last rails had been laid. The first train to traverse the entire length of the new railway was the Duke's, with the Duke himself at the controls of his locomotive, *Dunrobin*, when it pulled into the new Wick station, around 90 minutes early, at 3pm on 9 July 1874:

> On the news of his arrival, the provost and a few local worthies hastily turned out to greet him, but it was a somewhat constrained reception for, as the *Groat [John O'Groat Journal]* caustically observed, "they do not in their corporate or personal capacity hold a single £10 share in the company among them".[14]

In contrast, at Thurso:

> …a crowd estimated at 3,000 was waiting, with two bands. A banquet had been prepared, with the duke as a somewhat reluctant guest of honour. Sir Tollemache Sinclair *[a landowner and Liberal MP for Caithness]* had organised a collection to make him a presentation, but the duke deprecated the notion, saying he had enough silver plate already, and asked that Sir Tollemache's collection be distributed among "those poor fellows who have borne the burden and the heat of the day in pushing on the works as they have done. I refer to the workmen on the line".[15]

CHAPTER 2: OPERATING THE RAILWAY

The Far North Line opened to the public on 28 July 1874. It had taken 14 years and five separate railway company developments to extend the railway the 161½ miles from Inverness to Wick, together with the six and a half mile branch from Georgemas to Thurso.

There had been no grand plan – rather, a collection of disparate initiatives with different motivations – but the British rail network had finally reached its most northerly outposts, and large tracts of Highland countryside had been opened up to potential development. The Far North Line began operations after much of the Scottish rail network had been established. The only other long-distance route yet to be built was the West Highland Line from Glasgow to Fort William and Mallaig.

The distance from Inverness to Wick as the crow flies is just 80 miles, but eight decades were to elapse before the meandering nature of the Far North Line began to threaten the railway's existence. From the start, the Highland Railway operated the whole line, not just on its own metals to Bonar Bridge but also over the Sutherland Railway, the Duke of Sutherland's Railway and the Sutherland & Caithness Railway. These companies eventually merged with the Highland in 1884.

Due to its length and two major inland diversions, the route of the Far North Line fell into six distinct geographical sections, which in turn have had their impact on the nature of railway operations. Interestingly, the first three of these sections largely match the territories of three of the original railway companies (Inverness & Ross-shire, Sutherland and Duke of Sutherland's). The six sections were (and are):

- 58 miles of generally well-aligned route from Inverness to Bonar Bridge, through lands predominantly close to the coast, skirting the Beauly, Cromarty and Dornoch Firths – with no gradient steeper than 1 in 100

- 23 miles of mostly steeply-graded (and in places sharply-curved) railway, striking inland from near sea level at Bonar Bridge, up Strath Oykel and the valley of the River Shin to Lairg Summit (488 feet), then dropping down Strath Fleet to reach the coast at The Mound – with much of the central section at gradients of 1 in 70 to 80

- another generally well-aligned section, close to the North Sea coast, over the 21 miles from The Mound to Helmsdale – with gradients mostly from

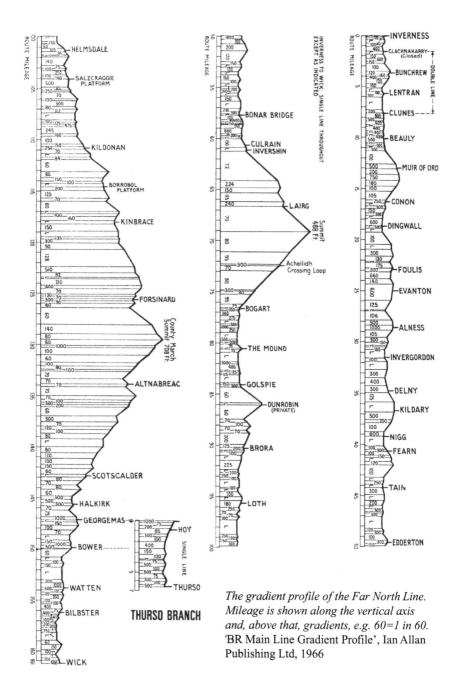

The gradient profile of the Far North Line. Mileage is shown along the vertical axis and, above that, gradients, e.g. 60=1 in 60. 'BR Main Line Gradient Profile', Ian Allan Publishing Ltd, 1966

1 in 100 to level, a notable exception being the short but stiff climb at 1 in 60 (in both directions) to Dunrobin, a seemingly deliberate diversion of the Duke of Sutherland's Railway away from the coast in order to minimise noise or visual intrusion at his castle

- the start of the second great sweep inland, steadily climbing over the 24 miles from Helmsdale to Forsinard, through Strath Ullie and the Strath of Kildonan beside the River Helmsdale and eventually its Bannock Burn tributary – relatively hemmed in by hill and mountain, but with gradients mostly 1 in 100 or easier along the valley floor, the stiffest climbs being (northbound) two sections of 1 in 60 between Kildonan and Kinbrace

- the dramatic strike north eastwards from Forsinard, leaving river valleys behind to climb through largely uninhabited country and reach Caithness at the County March Summit (708 feet), then dropping at gradients typically 1 in 80 or steeper to the level terrain at Georgemas Junction – a distance of 21½ miles , with the steepest climb being two miles at 1 in 60 between Forsinard and the summit

- 14 miles of mainly easy gradients, dropping gradually down from Georgemas to the terminus at Wick, plus similar terrain over the six and a half miles of the branch from Georgemas to the railway's other terminus at Thurso – the steepest gradients being short stretches of 1 in 60 on the former, the maximum across the 168 miles of the Far North Line

Infrastructure and train services

Many earthworks and structures were needed to take the railway across natural and man-made barriers, the most significant crossing of the latter type being the swing bridge over the 1822 Caledonian Canal at Clachnaharry by Inverness.

The large mountain-fed rivers which drain into the Beauly, Cromarty and Dornoch Firths are crossed by the railway close to the sea, and substantial bridges were therefore required – notably the Ness Viaduct in Inverness, the viaducts over the Rivers Beauly and Conon and, most dramatically, the imposing 230-feet lattice girder span of the Oykel (or Shin) Viaduct over the Kyle of Sutherland between Culrain and Invershin.

After the completion of the last section to Caithness, the southern part of the line was gradually developed to meet increasing demand. Stations facilities were expanded and, as recorded by Keith Fenwick in *Inverness & Ross-shire Railway* (2012):

Passing places were added at most of the stations, initially where needed to handle the gradually increasing train service; after the regulations changed in 1889 the line was completely resignalled with interlocked points and signals and tablet working *[see below]* and several new loops were put in. Most crossing points were provided with two signal boxes with the single line token instruments placed in the booking office.

Given the relative sparse density of population and potential traffic over most of the route, the line was single-track throughout. Indeed, the Highland Railway as a whole was different from most British railways, in that a high proportion of its network was single-track. However, the Far North Line had no fewer than 31 intermediate crossing loops immediately prior to the doubling of the Clachnaharry to Clunes section (a distance of six miles) in 1913-14, all bar one (Acheilidh, between Lairg and Rogart) being located at stations.

Six of these loops were constructed between 1902 and 1911, and a final further loop was added at Foulis (between Dingwall and Invergordon) in 1916 as part of the war effort. The section between Inverness and Clachnaharry was never double-tracked, as this would have necessitated widening both the Ness Viaduct and the Caledonian Canal swing bridge.

Single-track railways require particular signalling arrangements to avoid train collisions, and for a long time the Highland Railway used the early method of telegraphing passing orders between signal boxes. From the 1890s, the safer 'Tyer' electric tablet or token system was introduced, as described in *The Oxford Companion to British Railway History* (2003):

> [Train tablets] were held in two instruments, one located at each end of the section, electrically interlocked so that only one tablet could be released at any one time. Tablets were made in different shapes so that a tablet for one section could not be put into an instrument for an adjacent section.

Train crews exchanged tablets or tokens (in carrying hoops) with signalmen, a potentially dangerous practice for non-stopping trains, and one which was eventually replaced at some locations by the 'Manson' automatic token exchange apparatus. The latter involved fixed trackside equipment and a catcher device which was extended from the side of the locomotive cab just before the train passed the exchange point and automatically retracted after the exchange.

For most of the Far North Line's first 90 years, the passenger service in winter was based on two trains a day in each direction along the entire length of the railway, with 'short workings' (ie not running all the way to Wick/Thurso) from Inverness to Tain and Helmsdale, and back. The fastest train between Inverness and Wick in August 1874 took 7 hours 5 minutes – an average speed of just

32mph – in part reflecting some difficult terrain (both gradients and curvature) and the constraints of single-line working, but more so because of the need to call at up to 39 intermediate station, although some were only 'request' stops.

Two additional request halts were opened to serve 'hunting, shooting and fishing' customers between Helmsdale and Kinbrace: at Borrobol Platform (in 1878) and Salzcraggie Platform (in 1908). Alan Young's hand-drawn map of the line and branches at their zenith in 1916 *[see end of Chapter 4]* shows all the passenger stations served at the time.

The temporary terminus at Meikle Ferry had closed in 1869 after just five years' life, while Clachnaharry station closed in 1913: both through lack of custom. The temporary terminus at Dunrobin had become a private station serving the Duke's nearby castle when the through line from Golspie to Helmsdale was opened in its entirety in 1871, and in 1902 the station buildings were reconstructed to an attractive rustic Arts & Crafts design of the estate architect.

The Dukes of Sutherland retained the right to operate their 'Dunrobin' locomotive and two saloon coaches over the railway. By the 1890s these trips were primarily to Inverness for meetings of the Board of Directors of the Highland Railway. Remarkably, this arrangement, and the right to attach the saloon to the overnight sleeper from Inverness to London, remained in place until nationalisation in 1948.

As the decades passed, so the steady improvement of steam engine design led to the introduction of more powerful locomotives on the Far North Line, initially built by the Highland Railway in Inverness but later increasingly at the various world-leading works in Glasgow. However, it was the omission of a number of intermediate stops which allowed the timing of the fastest train from Inverness to Wick in July 1885 to be cut to 6 hours from 1874's 7 hours 5 minutes. At various periods in the line's history up until the 1960s, the fastest trains were promoted with distinctive names: the *Further North Express*, the *John O'Groat* and the *Orcadian*. And in 1905 the *Further North Express* was running non-stop from Inverness to The Mound (81 miles) on Fridays in June: the longest non-stop run on the Highland at that time.

Around six hours would remain the norm until as late as the 1930s, when the introduction of the London, Midland & Scottish Railway's 'Black 5' locomotives – soon to be known as 'Hikers' – brought down the fastest journey time from Inverness to Wick (in the August 1939 timetable) to just 4 hours 49 minutes, only half an hour slower than 2016's fastest journey of

4 hours 18 minutes by modern diesel unit. The slowest Inverness to Wick trains, calling at most or all of the 41 (later 40, after Clachnaharry closed) intermediate stations, took two hours longer than the fastest in 1885, and 1 hour 20 minutes longer in 1939.

As well as the end-to-end passenger services and the short workings from Inverness, the Highland Railway operated two passenger trains daily from Wick to Thurso and return (some of these being 'mixed' passenger and goods services) and, of course, goods services over the entire length of the Far North Line. Thomas & Turnock *(ibid)* record that in the 1880s around half of all the timetabled Highland trains were mixed: a sensible consolidation of traffic on lightly-populated routes where the total traffic on offer was not substantial.

There were operational dangers, however, where, as in Highland Railway custom, in order to simplify shunting of goods wagons at intermediate stations, the wagons were marshalled immediately behind the locomotive. As a result, there was no continuous braking system linking the locomotive and the passenger coaches which enabled all their wheels to be braked simultaneously. But by the turn of the century the Highland was belatedly complying with Board of Trade regulations requiring continuous braking systems and passenger coaches marshalled next to the locomotive. As we shall see in Chapter 9, mixed trains would briefly again be a feature of the Far North Line as late as the mid-1980s.

In the Victorian era, there were typically two good trains daily from Inverness to Wick and return (with connections to Thurso), plus short workings from Inverness to Tain and Helmsdale, which was a broadly similar pattern to passenger services. And it was in goods transport and the creation of new 'export' and 'import' markets for the Far North that the railway would have some of its most dramatic economic impacts.

Keeping this dispersed transport enterprise operational involved a large complement of staff for a rural area, with many working at relatively isolated locations to maintain the track, as well as the required signalmen and staff at scores of stations. And they all had to live somewhere. In *Highland Railway: People and Places* (2005), Neil T Sinclair records that:

> One advantage of working for the Highland Railway was the housing it provided for staff in rural areas. The Perth, Kyle and Wick lines ran through sparsely populated country. In these areas the HR had to build houses for their staff and this was the major reason why the HR had more houses per employee than any other British railway. By 1921 the company owned 482 dwellings.

Problems of operation

The combination of difficult terrain, a northern climate and the constraints of working over a single-track railway meant that there would often be operating difficulties to disrupt the Far North Line's timetable. Thomas & Turnock *(ibid)* record that the reality of time-keeping was very different from the timetable:

> Drivers were informed that most of the times shown against stations were departure times and they were exhorted to regulate their arrival times to allow ample time for the discharge of station duties and still ensure departure according to the timetable. With forty stations on the line and with station duties involving everything from live calves trussed in canvas travelling as parcels to occupied coffins, there were days when the exigencies of the traffic made a mockery of the timetable. Train paths were irretrievably lost, and there were long delays at stations waiting for opposing traffic to clear the single line, and spectacularly late arrivals at the northern termini.

A further distinctive aspect of Far North operation was the occasional disruptive impact of maintaining connections at Inverness out of train services from the south. If trains presented by the Caledonian or North British Railways to the Highland at Perth were late, then train paths on the largely single-track Highland Main Line to Inverness would be disrupted, and late arrivals in Inverness would then delay trains to Wick and Thurso. This was not only for passenger connections, but also in some cases for through parcels and/or passenger coaches to be shunted from one train to the other. The late departures from Inverness would in turn upset planned crossing points with trains from the Far North to Inverness, and so the timetable could fairly quickly fall apart.

Such are the handicaps of operating over a single-track railway, still today at the heart of timetable constraints on the Far North Line. More surprisingly, this is also the case on the Highland Main Line, where a two-thirds single-track railway tries to compete with an entirely dual-lane or dual-carriageway A9 road, completely rebuilt in the 1970s and 80s.

Major operational incidents – involving danger to life and limb – did occur on the railway, but HA Vallance *(ibid)* observes that: 'Throughout its history, the Highland Railway enjoyed an exceptional freedom from serious accidents.' Although staff casualties were incurred during the early years, the first passenger fatality was not until 1894 when a defective signal at Newtonmore led to a collision between two trains, in which one passenger was killed and eight were seriously injured.

Vallance refers to an earlier accident on the Far North Line on 26 November 1885, which could have had very serious results and did appear to have an eventual impact on operational safety regulations – very much the pattern on Britain's railways where, over a period of nearly 200 years, lessons have been carefully learnt from accidents. In this particular case, just north of The Mound where the railway runs close to the shore for some distance, an 'Up' [to Inverness] mixed train, comprising 11 wagons and seven passenger vehicles, was approaching the station, when an axle on one of the leading wagons broke and the whole train was derailed. The engine and several wagons ploughed along the track for some 500 yards before coming to rest, but the remainder of the train, including the passenger coaches, ran down the embankment and fell in the sea.

The accident occurred on a 30 chain curve near the foot of a 1 in 70 stretch of gradient.[16] One of the passengers – a Mr Alexander Watson from Wick, who was travelling with the remains of one of his children for interment in Forres – was badly injured. He subsequently raised an action against the Highland Railway, with a jury trial being held before Lord Shand in Edinburgh on 27 and 28 July, the question being:

> Whether, on or about the 26th day of November, at or near the Mound station, on the Sutherland and Caithness section of the defenders' line of railway, the pursuer, while travelling as a passenger thereon, was injured in his person, through the fault of the defenders, to his loss, injury and damage?

The proceedings of the trial[17] reveal that some very senior witnesses were called. In the case of the pursuer, these included Major Marindin, Board of Trade Railway Inspecting Officer; Dugald Drummond, Locomotive Superintendent of the Caledonian Railway; and Joseph Bell, Lecturer in Clinical Surgery at Edinburgh Royal Infirmary (said to be the person on whom Sir Arthur Conon Doyle based his character, Sherlock Holmes).

For the defenders, an impressive array of witnesses called to defend, *inter alia,* the Highland Railway's mixed train practices, included not just Andrew Dougall, General Manager of the Highland, but also William Moffatt, General Manager of its big rival, the Great North of Scotland Railway, plus a range of Superintendents from the Caledonian, Glasgow & South Western, Great Western, London & North Western and North Bridge Railways – further supported by Benjamin Baker, Engineer to the Forth Bridge, then under construction. The presence of Caledonian Railway representatives on both sides of the action must have made for some interesting dynamics.

The trial lasted two days, but the jury took just three quarters of an hour to find unanimously that 'the Highland Railway Company were not responsible for the injury to the pursuer'. The deciding factor was that the wagon on which an axle broke was owned by the Caledonian Railway, and the Highland was deemed to have carried out all the checks which could reasonably have been expected once the wagon had come into their original possession at Perth. It would not have been any consolation to Alexander Watson that, under the Regulation of Railways Act 1889, the Board of Trade issued an order in February 1891 to the Highland Railway, requiring all passenger vehicles on mixed trains to be marshalled next to the locomotive so that the continuous brake could work on them, an order with which the Highland, eventually, complied.

The snow fiend

Operating in a northern and often upland climate, the Highland Railway was vulnerable to snow, particularly in the colder east where the Far North Line runs:

> A snowfall of quite moderate depth, if accompanied by a high wind, can pile up in drifts several feet thick. And the wind frequently blows the already deposited snow across open country until it encounters some obstacle – such as the side of a railway cutting – against which it can accumulate.[18]

Following serious snow blockages in the years immediately following the opening of the Highland Main Line in 1863, it was decided to erect artificial barriers, known as 'snow fences', at the most vulnerable points throughout the system. These were constructed of old railway sleepers – and their remains can still be seen in places today, long after their maintenance and renewal ceased. The exposed moors by the Caithness-Sutherland boundary were particularly vulnerable to drifting, and more dramatic measures were required.

A Lancashire man named Howie, the resident engineer of the Caledonian Canal works, invented a snow 'blower', which was a close-boarded, large and wide 'fence' erected above and broadly parallel to cutting slopes. The bottom edge of the blower almost touched the ground, but the top (or outer) edge was raised some eight or ten feet. These artificial troughs deflected wind currents away from the railway away so that the snow was swept up and deposited elsewhere – a phenomenon known as the 'Venturi effect' – an arrangement that survived until the 1960s.

Drifting also called for the use of snow ploughs. These were either attached to the buffer beam of the locomotive, or were large independent ploughs pushed by the loco or several locos. This practice, begun in steam days, continues in the modern railway with diesel traction.

Sometimes, however, weather conditions have been too extreme to counteract even all these man-made measures and the hard physical labour of men with shovels. A severe blizzard in late December 1894 was followed by heavy snow storms in January and February of 1895, and the last of the drifts on the Highland Railway was not cleared away until March. During some of this period, all sections of the main line from Perth to Wick were snowbound, except the 101 miles from Inverness to Helmsdale. It was north of the latter that an unexpected silver lining followed the cloud:

> The winter herring season was in full swing, and serious delays were experienced in getting the fish through from Wick to the south. One of the first trains to be snowed up was a fish special, which was completely buried near the Fairy Hillocks (by Altnabreac), after being hastily abandoned. When it was relieved, ten days later, the contents were delivered to their destinations in perfect condition. The snow had acted as a gigantic refrigerator.[19]

In January 1918, a snow plough locomotive, which had been sent to clear the line for a London (Euston) to Thurso naval special, itself became completely stuck near Scotscalder, with the special also being snowed up a few hours later a short distance to the south. The train was abandoned by its 300 passengers, who tramped across the moor to Thurso. A relief train, carrying a party of 100 men, was quickly despatched to the scene of the blockage, but so severe was the weather that a week elapsed before the line was sufficiently cleared for the full service to be resumed.[20]

Snow has continued – sporadically, but at times dramatically – to dog the winter operations of the Far North Line through to the present day. In 1978, as we shall see, the railway featured in headlines across the world when an Inverness to Wick train came to grief near Altnabreac and its passengers had to be helicoptered to safety.

One of the distinctive 'Venturi snow blowers', looking south beside Loch an Ruathair, between Forsinard and Kinbrace, on 23 April 1952. HC Casserley

CHAPTER 3: THE IMPACT OF THE RAILWAY

The new railway had an immediate transport impact, cutting the overland journey time from Caithness to Inverness by half. The wider economic and social impacts were also dramatic, and led to the Highland Railway (HR), formed in 1865, becoming the largest single employer in the region.[21] Thomas and Turnock *(ibid)* reflect that:

> One of the most intriguing questions about the effect of railways concerns their impact on the settlement pattern, for some places seemed to blossom with the arrival of the railway while others were adversely affected . . . the railway tended to encourage centralisation on the regional centres and other towns which could now be reached by many more people taking day trips than had ever been the case before. The larger places developed their industries and service functions at the expense of the weaker centres as people found themselves able to leapfrog the nearest market in favour of the more distant places if the latter were more competitive. Without exception the main regional centres grew rapidly during the railway age.

This was undoubtedly true of Inverness, whose population grew from 9,969 in 1851 to 22,216 in 1911, the town emerging as the undisputed capital of the Highlands. It housed not only the Highland Railway headquarters in Station Square and the busy station with its seven platforms and nearby goods yards serving lines running north, west, south and east, but also a large 'roundhouse' where locomotives were stabled and coaled, and the Lochgorm Works where locomotives, carriages and wagons were built and maintained. These activities stimulated all kinds of demands for supporting goods and services.

Historical population records for the other towns served by the Far North Line are incomplete, but the most striking figures available are for Wick, which grew from 7,475 in 1864 to 9,086 in 1911. However, Thurso fell from 4,679 in 1831 to 3,335 in 1911. Tain's population also dropped significantly, from 2,588 in 1851 to 1,599 in 1911, while Dingwall showed an increase from 1,990 to 2,639 over the same period. One may conclude that, at least in part, the Far North Line experience supports Thomas & Turnock's thesis on differential development impacts, with the main regional centres growing at the expense of other towns.

In terms of impacts on the Highland economy, there were limits to what the railway could do for the region: the population continued to decline, while the rest of the country's had been growing very fast; the economic base was not strong enough to provide a general standard of living comparable with other regions; and virtually all the land in the region continued to be held in large estates.[22]

However, wool prices rose by a third and cattle prices doubled between 1850 and 1882. Referring to the growth in the sheep population in the mid-19th century (some time after the main thrust of the population clearances and associated establishment of large-scale sheep farming), David Ross *(ibid)* comments that: 'The railways were beneficiaries but also in part creators of this growth, as they were for other market-aimed produce.' Of course, landowners had been key backers of the constituent companies of the Far North Line, and 'they saw the potential benefits of the railway for themselves, but it had to be a sufficiently convincing investment in its own right...The economic stimulus provided by the railway would eventually provide thoughtful investors with their reward.'

Transport of live cattle and sheep was a key element of railway goods traffic on the Far North Line from the early days, right through to the 1960s: principally associated with the annual sheep sales at Lairg. The railway revolutionised the cattle trade in the Highlands. Beasts had previously been driven to the great southern markets, such as the Falkirk 'trysts', along a system of drove roads, over which a journey could take several weeks, with the cattle arriving at market in poor condition. By contrast, rail could deliver beasts to market in a few days or less, and in good condition.[23]

But mass transportation by rail was not without its problems. For instance, animals crammed together in wagons were very susceptible to cattle plague. The first Royal Highland & Agricultural Show to be held in Inverness since the coming of the railway, with an extensive programme of passenger and livestock trains planned, had to be cancelled at short notice due to an outbreak of cattle plague in Inverness.[24]

The arrival of the railway also gave the established whisky distilling industry a major boost, transforming the cost of transporting inwards raw materials (barley, grain and coal) and sending the finished product to increasingly distant markets. Although the territory north of Inverness has never seen a major concentration of commercial distilling such as on Speyside, the Far North Line served nine malt distilleries from the Victorian era onwards – a few rail connections even surviving until the early 1970s – either via their own private rail sidings (Balblair at Edderton, and Glenmorangie near Tain), a short branch line (Dalmore at Alness, and Glen Albyn in Inverness) or located a short horse-and-cart ride away from a railway goods yard (Brora, Glen Mhor in Inverness, Ord at Muir of Ord, Pulteney in Wick, and Teaninich at Alness). And, as we shall see in Chapter 6, in the early 1960s the largest grain distillery in Europe was deliberately sited straddling the Far North Line in Invergordon.

The fishing industry was also transformed by the arrival of the Far North Line, opening up new markets for fresh fish in the south, notably sea fish from Wick and salmon caught inland. The latter would be increasingly associated with the 'hunting, shooting and fishing' economy which developed over large tracts of land devoted to 'deer forest' rather than sheep – a response to falling wool prices and the development of refrigerated transport from Australia in the mid-1870s.

This new facet of the rural economy contributed to the growth of tourist passenger traffic on the railway, but it was not only the 'shooting box' economy which was opened up by the railway. *The Oxford Companion to British Railway History (ibid)* records that: 'The railways of Britain played a central role of converting tourism from an elite experience which had been enjoyed only by the monied few, into a mass phenomenon in which all classes and sections of society participated.' Far North Line trains would typically operate to a greater frequency over the summer months and, although the line has, surprisingly, never attained the cachet of the West Highland and Kyle routes, it has a remarkable diversity of scenery which, arguably, has been under-promoted throughout its history.

Like railways the length and breadth of Britain, the line to Caithness soon developed staple non-passenger markets in the transport of coal (both domestic and industrial) and Royal Mail traffic. While further from coal fields than almost any other part of Britain – apart from the small mine at Brora – the Far North Line needed this fuel for its locomotives, and coal was to remain a core goods traffic until the mid-1980s, as were Royal Mail letters and parcels. Goods and parcels traffic were handled at the large majority of stations along the line, even at lonely Forsinard where in the railway's heyday some unusual consignments were regularly loaded: for instance, peat for transport south to various distilleries, crates of rabbits, and sphagnum mosses for use as wound dressings during the two World Wars.[25]

Such were some prosaic aspects of the role of the Far North Line in facilitating new trade flows. Reflecting on the profound impact of the Highland Railway in general, David Ross *(ibid)* concludes that:

> ...the railway was the first large Highland industrial enterprise to establish a permanent presence. By providing its services, staying independent and solvent, and paying its wages and dividends, the Highland Railway made a long-term contribution to the regional economy. As the biggest business, it kept a large amount of money in circulation.

But Ross also quotes a voice of dissent about one consequence of the railway, from John Stuart Blackie, a celebrated advocate of crofters' land rights:

…the class of Highlanders who hang upon the skirts of professional tourists in the Highlands, as in other countries, is both morally and physically an inferior type to the sturdy rural population whom the big farm mania has displaced.

The railway had brought big changes, or better or worse. And a significant part of that change was in the working lives of the men and women who left behind traditional rural-agricultural jobs to staff this new, essentially urban-industrial mode of transport. However, working for the Highland Railway was usually a lifelong career, with railway employment often passing from one generation o a amily to the next. I staff did leave, it tended to be or a non-railway job in the area. Very few moved to posts with other railway companies. It was the officials who were the exception: 'Many o the staff who let the Highlands went to another part of the Empire, particularly Canada, or a country in the British sphere of influence.'[26]

The terminus of the Wick-Lybster branch line was the farthest one could travel from London Euston on the London, Midland & Scottish Railway (LMS) at 743 miles. LMS No. 15053 (ex-Highland Railway) waits to depart with the 2.20pm train to Wick on 18 July 1931. The branch closed completely in 1944. HC Casserley

CHAPTER 4: EXPANSION AND WAR SERVICE

The 1874 completion of the Far North Line had been preceded in 1870 by the opening of the Dingwall & Skye Railway, from Dingwall to Strome Ferry. This was to be amalgamated with the Highland Railway in 1880 and extended through to Kyle of Lochalsh in 1897. The Kyle line has had a fascinating and turbulent history, and has not lacked the attention of railway historians and enthusiasts.[27]

The completion of the railway to Strome Ferry was followed in 1877 by a much more modest extension of the rail network north of Inverness: the construction of a branch goods line of less than a mile from Canal Junction (between Inverness and Clachnaharry) to Muirtown Basin on the Caledonian Canal. This was eventually to be the location of two distilleries: Glen Albyn (immediately beside the railway) and Glen Mhor (nearby, but separated from the branch line by the A9 road).

Not far to the north, the Black Isle peninsula lying between the Beauly and Cromarty Firths found itself bypassed by both railway and main road. Short of building an expensive bridge across the Beauly Firth at Kessock Ferry and constructing heavy earthworks heading east towards the largest towns, Fortrose and Rosemarkie, the only realistic rail route was a branch line from Muir of Ord. This was authorised in 1890 but the railway only ever reached as far as Fortrose (13½ miles), in 1894.

Much further north, due to the Duke of Sutherland's resistance to a coastal route from Ross-shire to Sutherland, the county town of Dornoch had been completely bypassed by the Far North Line. Pressure grew for a local connection to the national network, and the Highland Railway eventually backed the promotion of a 'light railway' over the eight miles from The Mound to Dornoch.

Prior to the Light Railways Act of 1896, all new railway lines in Britain had required a specific Act of Parliament before they could be built. This was an expensive and time-consuming process, and the severe economic recession and associated high interest rates of the 1870s and 1880s had brought a halt to many new railway schemes in Britain.

With the Light Railways Act in place, railway companies could build new railways in sparsely populated regions of the country without requiring a specific Act of Parliament. While cutting out much of the 'red tape' and expensive legislation, it did impose severe limitations, including a weight limit of 12 tons per axle and a speed limit of 25mph. Cost-cutting measures included modest earthworks, bridges and stations, lightly laid track spiked directly onto sleepers (ie without the usual metal 'chairs' to hold the rails in place), the absence of level crossing gates, minimal signalling and the operation of 'one engine in steam' (i.e. with only one locomotive being allowed to work on the line at any given time).

The Dornoch branch was opened in 1902 and worked by the Highland Railway, although the local railway company remained nominally independent until the 1923 'Grouping'. While theoretically a light railway, the line was substantially built, the Board of Trade having imposed many restrictions which resulted in a much heavier expenditure than otherwise would have been necessary. The line was fenced throughout, and gates were provided at the numerous level crossings, but the permanent way was lighter than that on the main line and the rails were spiked direct to the sleepers.[28]

Dornoch and Fortrose were not the only settlements to be reached by a highly circuitous rail route from the south. With Government assistance, a light railway of 14 miles length was opened from Wick to the coastal fishing village of Lybster in 1903. All three branches would prove vulnerable to road competition, and as such were fated to have short lives, closing completely in 1960, 1960 and 1944 respectively. In 1903, the opening of the Wick & Lybster Light Railway – nominally independent like the Dornoch line – marked the limit of growth of the Highland Railway.

But it certainly did not bring an end to many disparate (and all ultimately unsuccessful) ambitions to push railways even further into sparsely populated territory in the north.

Some might-have-beens

Prior to the rise in road competition in the aftermath of World War One, Highland rail network extension schemes continued to be promoted, many of them immediately encouraged by the 1896 Light Railways Act. David Ross *(ibid)* records that:

> The promoters invariably came to see the Highland company, which, carefully keeping its financial distance, gave them fair words and few promises… the Highland had no intention of investing any of its own money in these enterprises, and therefore had nothing to lose; and chiefly wanted to ensure that no other company should have the chance to act as a patron. The embrace was a smothering one…

No fewer than eight standard-gauge schemes (ie with 4 feet 8½ inches between the rails) were proposed to branch off the Far North Line, but seven were never built and the eighth was uncompleted. Three would have been of a remarkably long distance, and shared the characteristic of passing through sparsely-populated and largely unproductive terrain for a railway. Lairg to Laxford Bridge and Kinlochbervie represented a distance of 53 miles, while the rival Culrain & Lochinver and Invershin & Lochinver schemes would each have covered around 40 miles. According to Ross, the former seemed more likely to succeed:

> ...but the proposal languished when in the following year Sutherland County Council backed the alternative Invershin-Lochinver line, and the Highland Railway switched its limp-wristed support to the rival. Had there been a united effort behind the Culrain & Lochinver, it might have been built.

Perhaps, but it would certainly have struggled to survive road competition, well before the Beeching era. Other schemes which failed to attract the necessary capital (or Government funding) were relatively short lines from Fearn to Portmahomack, Thurso or Wick to Gills Bay, and Forsinard to Melvich and Portskerra. Apparently, the last route was fully surveyed and one or two bridges constructed before the scheme failed, but another route much further south would come even closer to fruition.

This belatedly planned line was the 18-mile Cromarty & Dingwall Railway (actually a misnomer, as the eventual junction with the Far North Line was planned to be at Conon), on which construction work began in early 1914, but was slowed by the start of World War One later that year. Nevertheless, by late 1916 earthworks had been completed over 12 miles, and rails laid along the first four miles from Cromarty (with a locomotive and works train operating over the line). Early 1917 saw an abrupt end to construction when, as recorded by Eric H Malcolm in *The Cromarty & Dingwall Light Railway* (1993), 'the permanent way material – both that which was laid and in stock, which was practically everything needed to finish the job – was commandeered and removed by the Ministry of Munitions for use in France'. That was the end of the Cromarty & Dingwall Railway.

Of all the failed schemes, probably the only one which can be viewed from a 21st century perspective as a regrettable omission was the link from Thurso to Scrabster. Joseph Mitchell's 1864 survey suggested Scrabster as the northernmost branch terminal of the proposed railway from Helmsdale, but it was not included in the 1871 Sutherland & Caithness Railway Act. David Ross *(ibid)* records that:

> In April 1896 the Harbour Board wrote to the Highland Railway to say it had a light railway in mind: would the Highland Railway build it for them? The Highland Railway Traffic Committee felt that the company might like to build it for itself.

A report in the *John o'Groat Journal* on 15 May 1896 indicated that a survey was under way, but no further action was ever taken. At less than three miles in length, it was by far the shortest of all the failed schemes – and hence the cheapest, albeit that the drop down to sea level at Scrabster would not have been straightforward – and if built would surely have survived until the present day. While not enough to overcome the disadvantages of the circuitous overall route of the Far North Line in the era of the car and the lorry, a Scrabster extension would have given the railway an important additional direct market.

A massive war role for a modest railway

As Christian Wolmar records[29], the strategic importance of the railways in wartime had been realised as early as 1855 in the Crimean War when the army shipped out 900 navvies to build the Balaclava Railway. Government provision for control of the railways in the event of war was made through the 1871 Regulation of the Forces Act, and in 1912 – as the situation across Europe worsened – so the Government formed the Railway Executive Committee (comprising General Managers of the largest railway companies) to run the system if war was declared. When this came to pass on 4 August 1914, the Committee took immediate charge.

The first – and huge – task was the successful passage of the tens of thousands of troops and associated *materiel* of the British Expeditionary Force over the metals of the London & South Western Railway to Southampton Docks. However, attention soon turned to the opposite end of the country, since Britain's Grand Fleet, consisting of 96 ships and 70,000 men, was based at Scapa Flow in Orkney, and a large repair port was established at Invergordon. As PJG Ransom records in *Iron Road*, 'For the Highland Railway, the effect was as though a new city had materialised at its northernmost terminus.'

Wolmar *(ibid)* rightly comments that: 'The railway credited with playing the second most important role in the war could not have been more different in every respect from the South Western', but he overplays the contrast when referring to three quarters of the Perth-Thurso railway being single-track 'with few passing points or sidings'. There was, on average, a passing loop every five miles between Thurso and Inverness, and every four miles on the single-track sections between Inverness and Perth (just over a third of the route had been double-tracked by 1909).

Nevertheless, the Highland faced a massive task. During the period of major works at Invergordon (including a new pier, oil-fuel tanks, housing for 4,000 workers and three military camps accommodating 7,000 men), 'every siding north of Perth was choked with wagons consigned to Invergordon which the main line of the Highland Railway was unable to accommodate'.[30]

Movement of timber – northbound for sea defences at Scapa Flow, southbound as pit-props – increased tenfold during the War, while domestic and industrial coal for the Far North was switched from sea to rail, over and above the increased supplies needed for the railway's locomotives. Vallance *(ibid)* records a situation in which 'there were occasions when the sidings of nearly all the stations between Inverness and Wick were blocked with coal wagons which could not be moved because of the congested state of the lines'. Fortunately, supplies were sent by rail to Grangemouth Docks and thence by sea.

The heroic task of goods movement faced by the line was exacerbated by the fact that the outbreak of war came at a time of year when the Highland would normally have been winding down its services after the busy tourist season, releasing heavily used engines for overhaul. Instead, this modest railway company faced four continuous years of unprecedentedly intensive working.

Much track work was also normally undertaken in the off-season, so the Highland soon came under excessive strain in its efforts to handle these vastly increased train operations. By the summer of 1915, out of 152 locomotives owned by the company, 50 had to be withdrawn from service and 50 others were in urgent need of repair. The unified railway came partly to the rescue, however, when the Railway Executive arranged for the loan of 20 locomotives from other companies – and more arrived in due course.

The wartime role of the railway also had major staffing implications. The Highland had to manage greatly increased traffic at the same time as losing many of its experienced staff to the armed forces: 756 individuals, some 25 per cent of the Highland workforce, of whom 87 were killed. As Neil T Sinclair records:

> Women were employed in significant numbers to replace the men. The total of female workers rose from 15 to 138 during World War One. At a large meeting of employees in Inverness in August 1915, A. Bellamy, NUR president, expressed concern that women were being used as "cheap labour", a reminder that women were generally paid less than their male counterparts.[31]

To add to the Highland Railway's importance to the war effort, Inverness became a centre for the distribution of ammunition to the Grand Fleet, routed over a new branch line to the harbour from 1915. Another heavy traffic, albeit non-hazardous, focused on Inverness was the distribution of letters and parcels for the fleet. Reviewing the cumulative effect of all these military developments in the north, it can be seen that the entire region was becoming of the greatest strategic importance to the country.

Two enemy spies were apprehended in the Station Hotel in Inverness, taken to London for trial, and convicted. Then, in August 1916, Inverness and the whole of the country to the north and west were declared a special military area. According to Vallance, 'naval ratings or civilians proceeding to the Grand Fleet had to be identified by the senior naval officer's staff before they were allowed to go further'.

This set the scene for probably the best-known aspect of the Far North Line's role in the war effort: 'the Jellicoe Specials', named after Admiral Sir John Jellicoe, commander-in-chief of the Grand Fleet until 1916. The increasing military importance of the north of Scotland and Orkney inevitably created significant demands for movement of officers and men from London and elsewhere, and it was eventually decided to run a special naval train every weekday in each direction between Euston and Thurso.

The first train ran on 15 February 1917 and services continued until 30 April 1919. Initially, the service ran non-stop from Carlisle to Perth via the Caledonian Railway, but after May 1917 was routed via the North British Railway's Waverley Route through the Borders, then Edinburgh and Fife, so that men for Rosyth Dockyard on the Forth could reach their destination without changing trains.

It was a 21½ hour journey for the 717 miles from London to Thurso – an average speed of 33mph – and 22 hrs 20 mins southbound. The train ran 272 miles over the Highland Railway in around 10½ hours, including a wait of 30 minutes at Inverness. North of Inverness, stops were made at Alness and Invergordon for passengers, and at Helmsdale and Forsinard for locomotive purposes.[32]

The train usually consisted of 14 vehicles, including sleeping accommodation for officers, and some compartments converted into cells for naval prisoners. Despite the complexities of the routing and the severe congestion on the Highland Railway, Vallance concludes: 'When the length of the journey is taken into consideration, the record of punctuality is high'.

Vallance also records that, in addition to these Jellicoe Specials, at Invergordon alone 1,020 other special trains, as well as naval ambulance services, were dealt with between August 1914 and August 1919.

Following the entry of the USA into the war on 6 April 1917, the Allies decided to lay a minefield over the 230 miles from Orkney to Norway. The materials were manufactured in the USA and shipped to the west coast of Scotland at Corpach and Kyle of Lochalsh, for assembly at two US naval bases, in Inverness and at Dalmore, just south of Invergordon.

'U.S. Naval Base 18' was located close to the Muirtown Basin of the Caledonian Canal, and as a result the Highland Railway's goods branch line was commandeered by the Admiralty; it was, according to Vallance, 'greatly extended', although the nature of this extension is not clear. The components from the USA reached Muirtown via the Caledonian Canal from Corpach, on lighters. He also records that: 'The American staff was housed in the adjacent Glen Albyn Distillery', no doubt an interesting (and welcome) juxtaposition.

The other location, 'U.S. Naval base 17', also involved the acquisition of a distillery, at Dalmore, presumably because it had its own private rail siding, a short branch line from Alness. Materials for this base were landed at Kyle of Lochalsh and then transported by three or four special trains daily for around a week after the arrival of the fortnightly ships. The Admiralty commandeered the entire railway west of Dingwall, with the Highland Railway allowed to run just one train daily in each direction for passengers and mails. All goods traffic for the islands was re-routed by ship from Glasgow. Reviewing the war effort, Vallance concludes that:

> Had it not been for the Government control, and the existence of the powerful Railway Executive Committee, the Highland Railway would have been faced with an impossible task during the war years. Fortunately, as part of a temporarily unified national railway system, it was able to rely for help on its larger partners. It was this fact alone that enabled the Company to avoid the complete breakdown that would have been little short of a disaster.

A profound verdict, but the crucial national role of the Far North Line between 1914 and 1919 also had its prosaic aspects, with a plaque at Dingwall station recording that 134,864 servicemen were given a cup of tea there during the war.

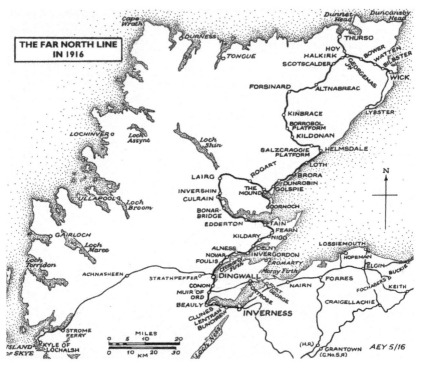

The Far North Line and its stations in the railway's heyday in 1916. (Only principal stations are shown on branch lines and other routes.) Alan Young

CHAPTER 5: THE GROUPING AND NATIONALISATION

By the end of the War, the unified railway had proved its capabilities, and it seemed unlikely that the system would revert to its former structure of more than 100 separate companies. Also, as PJG Ransom *(ibid)* records, 'at the end of the First World War, railways were physically in a bad state', and 'the Highland Railway was in a particularly bad way'.

Nationally, the possibility of state ownership had been mooted for many years. Within the Highlands, Joseph Mitchell had produced in 1862 a pamphlet advocating that railways should be built and owned by the state, in order to eliminate wasteful competition, in the hope that the state's resultant profits would reduce taxation.

A traditional scene at Golspie, viewed from a northbound train on 17 July 1931, with a Highland Railway water tower at the end of the platform. Henry Casserley (1903-1991) was a prolific photographer of steam railways from the 1920s to the 1970s and provided a vast source of illustrations for books and magazines. HC Casserley

Various schemes were proposed for amalgamation on a large scale – short of nationalisation – and there was an early intention to set up a separate railway company for Scotland. However, this was opposed in Scotland because of concerns that the new national standard wage rate would raise the costs of a Scottish company disproportionately. If costs were to be raised to English levels, then the support of English traffic receipts would be needed through a financial link with the railways south of the border.[33]

In due course, the 1921 Railways Act provided for the grouping of all Britain's railways into four companies, the largest of these being the London, Midland & Scottish Railway (LMS), incorporating the Highland, Caledonian and Glasgow & South Western within Scotland – with the North British and Great North of Scotland going to the London & North Eastern Railway (LNER). The LMS would extend over 7,500 route miles, of which the Highland contributed just 500 miles, but it did at least provide one Board member, AE Pullar (of the family which created the 'Pullars of Perth' dyeing company and, later, dry-cleaning shops), its deputy chairman, to the new company which began business on 1 January 1923. At the time, in terms of paid-up capital, the LMS was the largest railway company in the world.

Not quite the farthest-flung outpost of the London, Midland & Scottish Railway (LMS): a mileage sign at Wick station photographed on 18 July 1931. HC Casserley

The economics of overland transport had also changed since pre-war days. PJG Ransom observes that 'motoring had been the province of the wealthy. In the 1920s mass-produced motor cars brought motor cars to the middle classes. They embraced it enthusiastically.' Bus services also expanded greatly during the 1920s, taking advantage of their greater flexibility, and war-surplus lorries contributed to a growing challenge to the railway's dominance in goods transport. The railway was constrained by a statutory 'common carrier' requirement to accept whatever goods were offered to it, while road hauliers could 'cherry pick'. Railway companies were further undermined by the impact of the 1926 General Strike, when the availability of alternative bus and lorry service gave additional impetus to these competing modes of transport.

The first public bus service between Inverness and Dingwall was introduced in 1924, and by 1932 'the buses of seven different operators could be seen in Thurso'.[34] However, there were still no through services from Caithness to Inverness although, with changes at Helmsdale and Dornoch, the journey from Wick to the Highland Capital could be achieved in around eight hours.

Despite this background, the Far North Line saw few immediate impacts after the Grouping in terms of the general pattern of train services. The Highland railway system's post-1923 experience was far removed from the competitive quest by the LMS and LNER for high speeds and luxury accommodation on the West Coast and East Coast Main Lines respectively, which came to epitomise the inter-war period on the railways. The country served by the former Highland Railway had neither the volume of potential business nor the smooth route alignments to justify this type of enhancement and, of course, as this territory was the rail preserve of the LMS, the 'only' competition came from the road system.

Service cuts which been made during World War One were eventually reversed, and various, relatively modest, improvements introduced. The northbound *Further North Express* was reinstated in the summer of 1923, running only on Fridays. By summer 1933, and renamed the *John O'Groat*, it was running three days a week in both directions, and it ran daily the following summer. The Far North Line's only Sunday train, from Lairg to Inverness – the return working of a northbound newspaper train (which survived into the 1980s) – was reinstated in 1934. Trains connecting with Orkney steamers were named the *Orcadian* in 1936.

The quality of service had also changed, with refreshment cars introduced in the summer of 1923. The LMS had initially expanded operation of privately-owned Pullman dining cars in Scotland, but in 1934, on expiry of the contract, it bought them and ran them itself: 'They continued to be a feature of travel in Scotland for many years: some survived into the British Railways era, when their interiors brought a touch of fading opulence to travel on the Far North line.'[35]

The 1930s brought significant speed improvements on the Far North Line, with the fastest Inverness to Wick journey time just 4 hours 49 minutes in the August 1939 timetable. While Britain's most northerly railway was far from the cutting edge of railway developments, it was delivering steady improvement in services to the public, and was still playing a central role in the economies of Ross-shire, Sutherland and Caithness. However, growing road competition was having an impact:

> Between 1925 and 1934, passenger traffic originating on the Highland section had dropped by 40%, attributed to the decline in local industries due to the depression and to road competition. The situation so worried the LMS that in 1936 it investigated the impact of closing all lines north of Inverness. It found that receipts on the section were £253,000 but expenditure was £278,000. However, if the lines were closed, there would be a consequential loss of revenue on the rest of the system of £182,000, so there was no economic case for closure.[36]

Once more unto the breach

The Government took control of the rail system two days before the start of World War Two, once more through a Railway Executive Committee. This time, as recorded by Christian Wolmar *(ibid)*: 'The overall burden on the railways was far greater than in the First World War and again various outposts of the network became frantically busy.' However, the main focus was not now the north of Scotland but rather Norfolk, where no fewer than 150 bomber airfields were to be constructed.

Nevertheless, due to its large and sheltered waters and its distance from German airfields, Scapa Flow was again chosen as the main British naval base. Extensive repairs and enhancements of the World War One facilities were required, and the Far North Line regained its national importance, temporarily halting the decline of traffic experienced since the rise of road transport in the 1920s.

Footplatemen turn LMS loco No. 14406 on the turntable at Fortrose on 10 April 1946. Named Ben Slioch, this was one of the Highland Railway 'Small Ben' 4-4-0 passenger class and was built at its Lochgorm Works in Inverness in 1899. It was scrapped in 1947. Passenger services on the Black Isle branch from Muir of Ord survived until 1951 and freight until 1960. RM Casserley

Much less has been recorded of the World War Two role of the line than the earlier conflict, in which it played a bigger strategic role. However, significantly increased good traffic for the military had to be accommodated, as did through trains for naval personnel once again operated between Euston and Thurso. Admiralty requests to the LMS to provide catering on the leave trains between Perth and Thurso brought some of its Pullman cars back into use but, since no crews were available, it was arranged for them to be staffed by the Salvation Army.[37]

Classic junction scene at The Mound on 23 April 1952. 4-6-0 No. 45479 – one of the 'Black Five' class which were staple motive power on the Far North Line from the 1930s until the early 1960s – is about to pull away with the 8.25 am Wick-Inverness train. The branch from Dornoch trails in on the right. HC Casserley

A 27-page document entitled 'History of the LMS during the war (Inverness District)' came to the attention of Friends of the Far North Line in 2009.[38] This provides some fascinating snapshots of the railway's enhanced role over the six war years, particularly from 1 April 1940, when the area north and west of Inverness was declared a Protected Area, with strict controls on movement introduced. Government works on various aerodromes and port facilities greatly increased activity on the Highland lines, as did the large volume of stores and personnel for the fleet, coal supplies, timber despatch and the movement of mines for the Admiralty from Kyle to Easter Ross.

To alleviate congestion, new railway infrastructure was provided: not only additional sidings but also a new marshalling yard at Millburn, east of Inverness station, plus the associated connecting chord line known as 'the Burma Road', linking the yard (and the Perth line) directly to the Aberdeen line. New telecommunications installed at the end of 1942 permitted the Control Office in Inverness to talk direct to every station for the first time.

An appendix to the paper summarised passenger traffic and receipts at eight stations on the Far North Line. Three of these were un-named, one of which – in light of the massively increased throughput – is thought to have been Thurso, the railhead for Scapa Flow. The station concerned saw 8,231 passengers and £7,897 revenue in 1938, rising to 87,207 passengers and £239,271 revenue in 1940.

Coal tonnages on the line rose from 200,015 in the year ending 31 March 1939 to 330,810 in the year ending 31 March 1942. Annual volumes of timber despatched by rail from the Highland network centred on Inverness jumped from 16,938 tonnes in 1933 to 327,843 in 1942. New sidings were built at Beauly to handle trees felled by Canadian forces in the nearby glens, while at Invershin logs were brought to the Far North Line by a specially-constructed narrow-gauge railway. Among other goods facilities developed along the line was a War Department bakery at Muir of Ord, which in May 1943 sent out to the northern counties no fewer than 214 consignments by goods train and 377 by passenger train.

With military requirements taking precedence over civilian activities, the normal summer daily passenger service frequency between Inverness and Wick was cut from three to two, restaurant cars were suspended, and journey times were extended. Overall, however – thanks to the relatively greater resources of the LMS – the burden on the north of Scotland's railways was less severe than it had been on the smaller Highland Railway in World War One. On the staffing front: 'Women now worked in the signal boxes as well as in some of the same jobs they had done during World War One, as clerks, engine cleaners and porters'.[39]

Not all of the Highland system had a significant contribution to make to the war effort, the ill-fated Wick & Lybster Light Railway succumbing to complete closure (passengers and goods) in 1944. However, it would be another 16 years – and well into the new era of rail nationalisation – before any other routes or stations north of Inverness were closed completely.

Borrobol Platform was a request halt between Kildonan and Kinbrace, opened in 1878. It is seen here looking south, in April 1952, with its distinctive passenger-operated signals. Even this lonely spot had its own siding for engineering and freight purposes. HC Casserley

Nationalisation – but little immediate change

Britain's railways came out of the War in a similarly exhausted state to that which they had experienced in 1919. After the hostilities ended in 1945, rail recovery was generally slow. In the case of the Far North Line, the December 1947 timetable showed two trains daily from Inverness to Wick, with the fastest run of 6 hours 1 minute being 72 minutes slower than the immediate pre-War schedule.

However, the railways had again demonstrated the benefits of unified control and, following the landslide Labour victory in the 1945 General Election, it came as no surprise when the British rail system was fully nationalised. The new 'British Railways' (BR) was owned by the 'British Transport Commission' (BTC) and managed by the 'Railway Executive'. The radical change in ownership was effected on 1 January 1948, with a degree of devolved administrative control enshrined through the creation of six geographical regions, partly based on the territories of the old companies.

'Small Ben' 4-4-0 No. 54398 Ben Alder at Thurso shed on 23 April 1952. Built by Dübs & Co in Glasgow in 1898 for the Highland Railway, it was withdrawn from service in 1953 by British Railways, in anticipation of preservation. Sadly, after storage at a number of locations, it was scrapped in 1967. HC Casserley

Political pressures north of the Border ensured that Scotland, however, became a separate region – 'Scottish Region' – with its own Chief Regional Officer and supporting headquarters structure based in Glasgow. At the time of its creation the new region had a network of 3,625 route miles, of which some 480 were surviving ex-Highland lines. It was to be some time before any significant permanent changes in railway operations became apparent, but the new region was only a week old when its senior managers received a memo from the south 'on a subject which seemed to crystallise the concept of a unified British railway'.[40]

The new initiative was to trial locomotives from the various pre-nationalisation companies on routes where they had never previously been used. While this had no direct impact on the Far North Line – the only Scottish trials were on the Highland Main Line, where former LNER and Southern Railway locomotives were tested – it was a sign to railway staff in Inverness that change was in the air. Ironically, the conclusion of this particular trial was that the LMS 'Black 5' mixed-traffic locos, which since the 1930s had been the mainstay of the Highland system including the Far North Line, were on balance the best for the job.

The traditional solution applied to other aspects of railway operations. In the mid-1930s the LMS had introduced ex-Pullman dining cars, and in the early 1950s their deployment on the Far North Line:

> …represented the acme of luxury on wheels in the old pre-grouping days. Oval and bevelled plate-glass lights in the vestibule ends, movable chairs, the rich decoration scheme of inlaid veneer and the strong smell of gas emanating from the kitchen all stirred up memories of railway journeys of long ago.[41]

In 1951, peacetime railway goods traffic peaked across Britain, and the Conservatives were returned to power. The 1953 Transport Act abolished the Railway Executive, and membership of the BTC was increased, an additional member appointed being Lt-Colonel Donald Cameron of Lochiel, who might have been expected to have an insight into the challenges of railways in Highland areas.

Unsurprisingly, in view of its circuitous route to Inverness, the Fortrose to Muir of Ord branch could not meet that challenge in the post-war revival of road transport and had been closed to passenger traffic in October 1951. The summer 1951 season was the last in which this Black Isle branch featured as part of the 'Holiday Runabout Ticket' area focused on Inverness. These Runabout tickets offered a week's unlimited travel at package prices in traditional holiday districts where the density of the network provided a wide range of opportunities for day-trip explorations. They were an important aspect of BR's efforts to promote the tourist and leisure attractions of its still-extensive network in Scotland.

However, the late 1940s and early 1950s on the Far North Line were not entirely characterised by decline: the railway played an important role in the pioneering post-war hydro-electric power development programme fostered by the Labour Government, notably for the Strath Glass and Glen Affric schemes supplied with cement, machinery and transformers through Beauly station goods yard.[42]

The regional development idea

Transport, and its linkages with regional economic development as opposed to private profit, had long been a focus of public debate in the Highlands. However, in the 1950s this became a central focus of efforts to develop the region and overcome its longstanding problem of unemployment, poverty and population decline.

In 1953, Inverness Chamber of Commerce published its report on *The Highland Transport Problem*, which was approved by local authorities, including Caithness, Dingwall, Inverness and Sutherland. The 1953 report bemoaned the failure to respond to the 1950 'Cameron Report' by John Cameron QC, in particular the latter's conclusion that transport charges were 'an obstacle to the maintenance of the existing population and the industrial activity in the Highlands and Islands and to suitable economic and social progress in these areas'. Among the report's recommendations were that local officials of BR should be given authority to negotiate special rates, supported by the comment that:

> [The same officials] are always exceedingly anxious to help but are powerless to do so, as all rates are fixed from London by people who neither know nor care what happens in the North of Scotland. The remote control of disinterested civil servants is doing incalculable harm to life in the Highlands.

This underlined a widespread feeling that London decision-makers had little understanding of 'the Highland problem'. Nevertheless, the 1953 report was careful not to sound too much like special pleading from 'subsidy junkies':

> The Inverness Chamber of Commerce is most anxious to avoid a suggestion that the Highland area has any desire to live on the charity of more fortunately situated parts of the country, and their recommendations are based firmly on the belief that what they will cost will be repaid by the increase in traffic that will result.

Despite this plea for *enhancement* of the rail industry's role in regional development, in just a year's time the very *existence* of the Far North Line would begin to be questioned in behind-the-scenes analysis by rail and bus interests.

CHAPTER 6: CLOUDS ON THE RAILWAY HORIZON

By 1954, eight decades after its opening, the Far North Line was facing a growing threat from increasing household affluence and the resultant growth in car ownership, with the number of cars in use nationally more than doubling between 1933 and 1953. Despite the Highlands lagging economically behind other parts of Britain, the trend was ultimately inescapable in a consumer economy where American influences were greater than those from the European mainland.

Surprisingly, however, the bus service pattern north of Inverness established in the 1930s had little changed 20 years later: a half-hourly service ran to Dingwall, then hourly to Tain and about two-hourly thence to Dornoch and Helmsdale for much of the day. The train still had the advantage of speed over longer distances in 1955, with a modestly improved bus journey time of $7^{3/4}$ hours from Inverness to Wick comparing poorly with a fastest time of 6 hours 5 minutes on the (more comfortable) train, and just 5 hours 51 minutes on the summer-only afternoon train.[43]

Closer to Inverness, however, local bus services, with their greater frequency and flexibility, were clearly serving much more of the market than the railway, with its winter twice-daily through train service supplemented by just one 'short working' to Helmsdale and a couple of local services to Tain. But even over long distances the railway's dominance was being challenged. The 1952 introduction of a through summer coach service (with toilet) from Inverness to Scrabster via Wick and Thurso was to be the forerunner of the express bus service concept which underpinned BR's 1963 case for withdrawal of all passenger trains.

Fewer than 20 years after the LMS had assessed the case for complete closure, a joint examination of passenger services in the area was carried out in 1954 by the two key providers of public transport: British Railways and Scottish Omnibuses, both publicly owned. This initiative is examined in some detail by Fenwick, Sinclair and Ardern, but the key conclusion of the final report presented to senior management in early 1955 was that 'substantial curtailment of rail passenger facilities in the area is practicable' and even that 'a strong case could be made for withdrawal of all rail passenger services in the area'.

However, on the basis of a seemingly general acceptance that railway goods services would need to be maintained, the report recognised 'the attractions of a fast long distance rail service' and suggested that 23 intermediate stations (the majority of these between Inverness and Bonar Bridge) and the Dornoch branch (another four stations) should be closed, resulting in a net saving of £99,341 to BR and a profit of £3,680 to Highland Omnibuses. The report was shelved for three years.

The BR Modernisation Plan

In 1955, at least in public, the national emphasis would shift to evidently better prospects for rail. And the Far North Line had played an important part in the supply of materials for construction of the United Kingdom Atomic Energy Authority's (UKAEA) Dounreay nuclear complex, opened the same year. It would also be the last year in which BR made a profit, but it was the 'Modernisation Plan' which was then making the headlines across Britain. To give it its full title, the British Transport Commission's (BTC) *Modernisation and Re-Equipment of British Railways* was a 35-page 'blueprint' document, recommending a £1.24 billion investment programme over 15 years. The key areas for investment were to be:

- electrification of principal main lines

- large-scale dieselisation to replace steam locomotives

- new passenger and freight rolling stock

- re-signalling and track renewal

- closure of a small number of lines seen as duplicating other routes

- construction of 20 to 30 large mechanised freight marshalling yards

In practice, most of these types of improvement would bypass the Highlands, with its generally modest traffic flows and relative absence of duplicate routes. However, dieselisation was to have a direct and relatively quick impact. By the 1950s, the financial advantages of improved diesel technology over steam were clear. Steam was labour-intensive, requiring large numbers of men to fuel, water, clean, maintain and operate the locos. By contrast, diesels required significantly less time and labour to operate, with a much greater mileage range between refuelling.

The Highlands were further from major coal fields than almost any other part of Britain, and the opportunity to eliminate expensive haulage of locomotive coal to the Far North, plus the undoubted speed, operating cost and maintenance cost benefits of a switch to diesels, led to some of the earliest diesels to emerge from the Modernisation Plan beginning trials on the Far North Line in 1958. By 1962 the entire rail network based on Inverness had been dieselised.

The Modernisation Plan has been much criticised, generally for its failure to take on board the nature of growing road competition by not investing more selectively in the traffic and technologies of the future, and specifically for the production of a multiplicity of different untested diesel locomotive types (although this was in practice a consequence of the government being panicked – by mounting BR losses in the late 1950s – into swift and wholesale replacement of steam).

The former Highland Railway network escapes the latter criticism, however, since from the earliest days the staple motive power – based at the diesel maintenance and fuelling depot opened in 1960 at the former Lochgorm Works in Inverness – was the Birmingham Railway Carriage & Wagon Company 'Type 2' (later 'Class 26') diesel, later joined by the British Railways Type 2 (later Class 24), both of 1,160 horse power. These brought dramatic improvements in operational productivity and would prove to be the reliable mainstays of Far North (and other Highland) passenger and freight services until the early 1980s. The Type 2s did not finally disappear from the British railway network until the early 1990s, some 35 years after first entering service.

Even more dependable – but used only for freight traffic – were the English Electric Company Type 1 (later Class 20) diesels which would regularly be seen between Inverness and Invergordon. Remarkably, members of this class are still in operation for one of Britain's five rail freight hauliers – Direct Rail Services – in 2016.

Closure proposals go public

In early 1959, British Railways Scottish Region submitted to the BTC proposals for 'Re-organisation of main line services Inverness/Wick/Thurso'. These were an elaboration of proposals discussed internally in 1958, which in turn were a less draconian version of the original 1955 scheme discussed earlier. The 1958 BR document had proposed withdrawal of passenger train services from 24 stations, six of which were recommended for complete closure, 13 for withdrawal of passenger services only, and five to be reduced to the status of 'Unstaffed Public Sidings for full load traffic'.

The total estimated saving of £30,021 was modest. It was less than a third of the 1955 projected figure, and allowed for loss of receipts, after a cut of 14 staff and 78,573 train miles (the Tain locals and the Dornoch branch services). However, two additional cost-saving options were mooted: curtailment of hours of opening (through re-timing of freight trains, and subject to Post Office agreement) and elimination of 'block posts' (and the associated signal boxes) at eight locations between Inverness and Golspie – and were estimated to save a further £13,367. ('Block posts' are the signalled boundaries of the space interval maintained between trains on the same track in order to prevent collisions.)

The formal proposal for closures was finally articulated in a 9 May 1959 letter to the Transport Users Consultative Committee for Scotland (TUCCS) from Stanley Raymond, Chief Commercial Manager of BR Scottish Region. Raymond was a rising star of BR management and would replace Richard Beeching as Chairman of the BR Board in 1965.The TUCCS was a statutory body which considered objections to BR closure proposals for passenger (and, until 1962, freight) services, including assessing the adequacy of the proposed replacements.

The proposals were designed to reduce costs and concentrate faster end-to-end services on better-used stations and on those where there was no feasible bus alternative. It encompassed 24 passenger stations on 'the main line' and the Dornoch branch (the latter closing completely), and the withdrawal of service from the freight-only Fortrose branch, which had lost its passenger services in 1951. While closure of 20 of the 41 passenger stations along the 168 miles of the Far North Line would be drastic, there was at least one Scottish precedent in the 1956 axing of 26 intermediate stations over the 153 miles of the Glasgow/ Aberdeen main line.

The detailed saga of the closure proposals, their implementation and social consequences is admirably documented in *Lost Stations on the Far North Line*, but a number of key points can be made here.[44]

As was indicated by a table of average daily usage appended to Raymond's letter, a substantial proportion of the threatened 20 stations on the Far North Line were handling tiny numbers of passengers: none in the case of Bunchrew, Lentran and Loth, under 10 at Bower, Clunes, Edderton, Foulis, Halkirk and Watten, and under 20 at Conon Bridge and The Mound. The busiest station of the 20, Alness, saw 29 'outward' and 28 'inward' passengers daily, excluding 50 scholars who returned the short distance from Invergordon by train, having travelled outward by bus.

These levels of patronage could readily be accommodated by buses, although, with hindsight, Alness was probably one station which should have been reprieved. Beauly and Muir of Ord were also surprising closures in population terms, but even the combined frequency of Far North and Kyle line frequencies (seven trains a day in each direction) was poor competition for the half-hourly bus. Seen from today's perspective, the changing fortunes of these three stations makes for an interesting contrast, with rail enjoying a perceived physical 'permanency' – of bespoke tracks and stations – that bus services cannot emulate.

The closure proposal was considered by the TUCCS on 17 July 1959 in distant Edinburgh. It was perhaps not surprising, therefore, that the bulk of the deputation opposing closure were representatives of local authorities, the National Farmers Union and the Scottish Tourist Board, rather than individual passenger users of the line. Seen from a 21st century perspective, the presence of farming representatives may seem strange, but this was to be repeated, as we shall see, in the 1963-64 MacPuff campaign, reflecting the central role the railway still played in the regional economy, including the transport of livestock, grain, fertilisers, etc.

At least three speakers from the deputation drew attention to the mis-match of the closure proposal with the Government's ongoing review of transport in the Highlands. The latter was the 'Highland Transport Enquiry', created in June 1959 when Ministers, responding to growing concerns about transport and regional development, invited the Scottish Transport Council and the Advisory Panel on the Highlands & Islands:

> …to co-operate in a study of existing arterial transport services in the Highlands & Islands; the consequences of competition between sea and air, rail and road, and probable trends in the development of and the demands for, different means of transport; and the possible methods of securing adequate facilities in future – regard being paid to the need to avoid unnecessary duplication of unremunerative services.

The enquiry would not report until just a few weeks before the March 1963 'Reshaping Report'. However the STUCC's annual report did flag up the potential impact of the rail closure proposals on Highland development and depopulation. The main issue for its deliberation in the case of these closures was the adequacy for passengers of the proposed replacement services, in particular the bus – not just its frequency but also its quality compared to rail.

Ex-Caledonian Railway 4-4-0 No. 54491 on a mixed train at Thurso on 23 September 1959. Note the cattle wagons on the right. Stuart Sellar

A charming rural branch scene on 24 September 1959 at Dornoch. Ex-Great Western Railway (GWR) 0-6-0 pannier tank No. 1646 prepares to make up the 10.25 am mixed train departure for The Mound. Light axle weights were needed on the branch and, after the 1956-57 demise of two surviving ex-Highland Railway locos, two ex-GWR tanks were drafted in and provided the train service until its demise in 1960. Stuart Sellar

The Committee concluded that the BTC case was sound on economic grounds, and the consequent acceleration of the through rail service would be a benefit, but the alternative arrangements had to be adequate. Improved bus services were proposed, including three from Inverness to Wick (but taking over seven hours) and two as far as Helmsdale.

A deputation of objectors even secured a meeting – on 3 December 1959, just two months after the Conservatives had been returned to power in this Harold MacMillan era of 'you've never had it so good' – with Ernest Marples, the new Minister of Transport. The deputation apparently 'got nothing out of the meeting'[45], Marples having been advised by civil servants that, unlike the situation after the 1962 Transport Act, he had no powers to intervene and that to subsidise rail services on grounds of social need would be 'a major departure in policy'. The need for just such a policy would lie at the heart of the furore faced by Marples and Beeching three years later, and would then become enshrined in Government policy following the 1968 Transport Act.

A Scottish Development Department (SDD) memo was sent to the Scottish Office branch at Dover House in London in response to an 8 December Parliamentary Question from Hector Hughes, Labour MP for Aberdeen North. It noted that, on 4 December, the Scottish Board for Industry wrote to the Minister of Transport pointing out the difficulties involved in the transfer of passengers' luggage from bus to train at Inverness, and suggesting that the passenger closures at Beauly, Muir of Ord, Alness and Dornoch should be reconsidered.

No reprieve from the cuts was secured, but some additional bus services were promised, including a short-lived arrangement for buses to meet three trains from the south at Platforms 6 and 7 in Inverness station.

The last trains serving the doomed stations ran on Saturday 11 June 1960, with a large crowd marking the occasion at Dornoch. The new timetable began on 13 June, with the line north of Dingwall now served by just the two trains each way linking Inverness and Wick/Thurso, and one as far as Helmsdale, extended to the northern termini at the height of the season.

But there was a dramatic improvement in journey times for long-distance travellers, with one northbound train being cut by 37 minutes to 5 hours 29 minutes and the other by 42 minutes to 5 hours 22 minutes – and this was before the speed benefits of dieselisation had been realised. In some ways, the future of the Far North Line looked quite encouraging…

A temporary new lease of life

BR was anxious to promote the positive side of the changes it had at long last introduced on the Far North Line, more than five years after these had first been considered. One aspect of this promotion was a comprehensive multi-page leaflet titled 'Your railway services to and from Inverness' (an original of which is held in the Frank Spaven collection at the Highland Archive).

Although undated, it was clearly published in summer 1960 and lists no fewer than 37 remaining 'Station Masters' and 'Goods Agents'. 32 stations were still handling parcels and freight, and BR was offering local 'cartage' (road collection and delivery) services from Inverness, Wick, Thurso and six intermediate stations. In addition to the passenger timetable and details of key replacement buses, the leaflet also listed 'Principal Freight Train Transits from Inverness' on Mondays to Fridays, and advised a 4.30pm latest time of acceptance at Inverness for next morning arrivals at Dingwall, Invergordon and Tain, and next afternoon at Bonar Bridge and beyond. While it may be debated how many firms would actually be using rail for such short hauls even in 1960, here was a railway which was still performing multiple functions along its 168-mile length. The recent cuts must have seemed drastic to many observers, but they were as nothing compared to the shrinkage of the railway's role which would reach its nadir some 30 years later.

In September 1960, the Far North Line's place in the bigger rail and transport picture was articulated in detail by Iain Skewis of the Geography Department of Glasgow University – later to be Director of Industrial Development at the

Highlands & Islands Development Board – in his report on *Transport Resources of the Highlands and Islands of Scotland*. Describing the general pattern of the rail network, but one which specifically characterised the Far North Line, Skewis wrote that:

> Branch lines are not a prominent feature of Highland railways...It is a network of long straggling routes (in many cases following the only geographically possible route) which receive the traffic of the area from feeder road and sea services.

Skewis made some interesting Highland and Scotland-wide contrasts, noting that one mile of passenger route served twice the area in the Highlands, but only one fifth of the population, and that 'Each mile of Highland route has only 454 prospective travellers while the Scottish figure is over 2,000'. He pointed out that low population totals provide only limited traffic, whose revenues must cover charges on a considerable length of track mileage. Observing how very little acceleration had occurred on Highland routes over the previous 50 years, Skewis attributed this not just to single-line working, gradients and curvature:

> In this context the limited available traffic must be again mentioned. Little traffic means few trains daily. Few trains leave little scope for express services. On all but the Perth-Inverness line the normal winter trains stop at nearly every station. It was this aspect which was attacked on the North line in June.

This quest to improve speeds through elimination of minor stations received a very minor setback less than a year after the Far North closures. The TUCCS Annual Report for 1961 reported that an average of only one passenger per day had used the (thrice daily) buses put on to replace train calls at Rogart. Scottish Omnibuses had proposed to withdraw the service, and BR had agreed to re-open the station experimentally as a 'halt' for a limited number of passenger trains as from 6 March 1961.

This was a sensible decision, not least from the perspective of public spending. Rogart had remained a staffed crossing loop, so the cost of trains calling was modest compared to avoiding an annual loss of £1,500 to £2,000 on the new bus services. BR had made a mistake: the problem which had not been foreseen was that the replacement buses (running from Lairg through Rogart to Golspie) 'failed to cater properly for long distance travellers, the very traffic which the railway had previously handled'.[46]

In contrast to its initial fate in 1960, in 2016 Rogart is one of the 'busier' wayside stations on the line, still retaining a crossing loop. The station buildings are occupied by Frank Roach, Partnership Manager of HITRANS (the regional transport partnership) and his wife Kate who runs the 'Sleeperzzz' holiday accommodation in old railway coaches sited in the former station goods yard.

PART 2

Goods traffic still in evidence at Kinbrace as two passenger trains hauled by Type 2s cross on the surviving loop (thought to have been photographed in the early 1960s). By 1966, both the goods siding and the loop had gone. Dr DG Ewart, from the Alan Young collection

THE BEECHING ERA

CHAPTER 7: BEECHING ARRIVES ON THE SCENE

> Before the advent of severe road competition, a railway could make large profits on some part of the service and then cross-subsidise. But by 1960 the large profits had disappeared and the retention of loss-making services was driving the railway into further deficit.

So wrote retired senior railway manager RHN Hardy in *Beeching: Champion of the Railway?* (1989). BR's deficit in 1960 was £63.2m, the largest since losses were first recorded in 1956. In today's prices, this is around £1.3bn, or just one third of the cost to the taxpayer of supporting the privatised rail system. However, in 1960 the Government was alarmed, and in April of that year Transport Minister Ernest Marples created the Special Advisory Group (or 'Stedeford Committee', named after its chairman, the industrialist Sir Ivan Stedeford) to advise him on the appropriate size and structure of organisation to secure a profitable British railway system.

One member of the group was Dr Richard Beeching, Technical Director of the chemicals giant ICI. He came with an enviable reputation for thorough and clinical analyses of business problems. Beeching was appointed Chairman of the BTC in June 1961. The Special Advisory Group's deliberations led to the 1962 Transport Act and the associated abolition of the BTC, and Beeching then became the first Chairman of the new British Railways Board in January 1963. BR was charged with breaking even over a five-year cycle.

Beeching's work on reshaping the railway to achieve this target had in effect begun in late 1960. A week's comprehensive traffic surveys were undertaken nationwide by BR in April 1961, and the data which this generated provided much of the raw material on the different traffic types and methods of rail conveyance which underpinned the analysis by Beeching and his team leading up to the March 1963 publication of his famous (or infamous) 'Reshaping Report'.

While Beeching was working under the direction of the Ministry of Transport in London, any nationwide reshaping of the railway would have significant implications for the Scottish Office. The National Records of Scotland hold copious Scottish Office files of the time, and a number of these indicate that its initial position on rail closures, before the economic and political ramifications became clearer, was more amenable to cuts than would later be the case.

In response to a request from the Secretary of State for Scotland for 'an assessment of the desirable pattern for a Scottish railways system', a confidential memo on 28 March 1962 from Mr JB Fleming of the Scottish Development Department (part of the Scottish Office) summarised a meeting at St Andrew's House. This memo stated that a note to the Secretary of State should say – having consulted colleagues in the Scottish Home Department, and the Department of Agriculture & Fisheries for Scotland – that: 'The abandonment of all lines north and west of Inverness would be accepted but the [British] Transport Commission's wish to close the Perth-Inverness line would be opposed.' The same memo suggested acquiescing in the closure of all lines north and west of Aberdeen.

A fundamental lack of appreciation of the extent of likely opposition to closures was revealed in a throwaway comment in a 'Draft Joint Submission to [Scottish] Ministers' (undated and unattributed, but likely to have been written around the same time) titled 'Future of Scottish Railways': 'In the Borders as with the far north closures would probably be accepted after initial protests.' Fortunately for the Far North Line, and the swathe of other important routes which were being virtually conceded for closure before proper survey of their economic value, this kind of defeatist thinking had effectively disappeared from the Scottish Office 18 months later.

Frank Spaven stirs up the Scottish Office

The civil service attitude changed partly in response to a wide variety of commentaries on closures by my father, Frank Spaven, whose planning officer role at the Scottish Development Department (SDD) encompassed analysis of the regional development implications of the Reshaping Report. His first recorded rail memorandum, handwritten on 6 April 1962 to colleagues Messrs Jenkins and Sheldrake, commented:

> You may care to glance at the attached reports by the people who are usually regarded as Mr Marples' nominees to rubber stamp BTC proposals. Did you notice in yesterday's papers that the loss and misuse of <u>tarpaulins</u> in Scottish Region of BR is now costing them more than they will save from branch line closures?

This would not be the last time that Spaven – and others – would draw attention to alternative options for rail cost-saving, short of wholesale route closures. And by the time he had written this memorandum, BR – following the closure of 20 intermediate stations and the withdrawal of the Tain local service in June 1960 – had eliminated crossing loops at Conon and Foulis, with Culrain, Edderton and Evanton to follow in the next nine weeks, and The Mound in mid-1963.

Later that month, wearing a different hat, Frank Spaven participated in the inaugural meeting of a campaigning group, the Scottish Railway Development Association (SRDA), formed as an advance response to the emerging threat to Scotland's rail network. Indeed, he would continue to be an activist with the group (eventually renamed the Scottish Association for Public Transport (SAPT)) until his death in 2003. One wonders whether the Scottish Office knew of this civil servant's involvement in a campaign opposed to much of the Beeching Report's closure programme for Scotland?

The Minutes of the SRDA's first meeting, on 27 April 1962, record that four office-bearers and a committee of six (including Spaven) were appointed, chaired by the Reverend AO Barkway. The committee would soon be joined by student Tom Hart from Beith, who became Honorary Secretary and who in 2016 remains a leading light in SAPT and a well-regarded commentator on transport. Its membership was primarily in central Scotland, but strong support was given to the emerging campaign to oppose the threat to the Far North Line. A Scottish Office newspaper cuttings page (undated) in the National Records of Scotland carried a report from an unidentified newspaper (the typeface suggests the *Scottish Daily Express*), under the headline '"Tycoon force" plan for axed railways':

> A volunteer force of business men is to be set up throughout Scotland in a bid to save "doomed" railway lines from the Beeching axe. Their job: to use their personal influence on business friends to attract freight orders to the railways. The newly formed Scottish Railway Development Association hopes to recruit a working force of at least 200 such volunteers spread throughout every town in Scotland. They will augment the efforts of the National Union of Railwaymen and the Scottish Board for Industry to press home the hopeful new flexible policy of British Railways following the reprieve of the West Highland line.

It is striking that Beeching's name had entered public consciousness long before his ground-breaking report was published, and that the 'Beeching axe' phrase was already being used to describe, with suitable drama, the anticipated cuts. SRDA's bold (some might say naïve) initiative came to little, with few firms likely to redirect freight consignments to the railway unless the price and service were comparable to road haulage.

The reference to the West Highland line relates to the decision by papermaker Wiggins Teape to site a new pulp and paper mill adjacent to the railway at Corpach, on the Fort William-Mallaig extension, and the consequent removal of the otherwise anticipated threat to the railway. It was a mistake to interpret this as a 'new flexible policy', as BR were simply responding commercially to the planned demand for full trainloads of inward timber and outward paper products – just the method of rail conveyance and type of traffic which Beeching's hard-nosed analysis would identify as being well-suited to a modern profit-oriented railway.

Opposition from a Tory grandee

A higher level concern about the future of the rail system was voiced by Lord Polwarth (Chairman of the Scottish Council (Development and Industry) and a future Minister of State for Scotland in the early 1970s Conservative Government) in a House of Lords debate on the Transport Bill. The *Scotsman* of 9 May reported Polwarth's comment that:

> We have seen a large number of branches closed and stopping trains withdrawn. Financially each has been justified, and so far as we can yet judge none of them, I think, has struck a serious blow at the economy – though undoubtedly they have caused a lot of personal inconvenience. What does perturb us is the prospect that we may shortly be faced with a plan which promotes drastic rail cuts in Scotland and does not allow time for thought and adjustment…When the Beeching review is complete, take time to think and then to act. Otherwise you may strike a body-blow at the economy, and it will hurt most in those parts of the country which, like Scotland, are least able to stand it.

The latter comment could have been voiced specifically on the Highland circumstances, but a month later the same newspaper reported – under the headline 'Axe may spare Highland lines' – that the value of rail routes to Mallaig, Kyle, Oban and Wick to the tourist industry 'are likely to be enough to exclude them from Dr Beeching's forthcoming rail economies'. No source for the story was attributed, and it would prove to be unfounded in the case of both the Kyle and Wick lines.

The same story recorded that 230,000 tons of freight were carried annually on the Far North Line, plus 97,000 passengers booked at stations on the route ('but the number inwards to the line is about three times greater'). However, neither of these figures tallied with the more authoritative report of the Highland Transport Enquiry, which was by then reaching its draft stage.

Demonstrating that attitudes to closures within the Scottish Office were moving from hawkish to doveish – at least partly in response to the evidently softening view of the Secretary of State – on 24 May 1962, Frank Spaven drafted a long paper entitled 'Scottish Railways Submission to Secretary of State', which began:

> It is understood that the Secretary of State now wishes to counter-attack the Marples-Beeching position before the forthcoming Industry and Employment debate, so that he can be in a position to say that public transport services will continue to be available throughout Scotland. His brief might therefore be developed along the following lines, by way of amendment to the original draft.

Spaven then suggested that: 'The Beeching "economies" should be challenged under three heads'. The first of these was that: 'Closure of lines will not effect substantial economies, which are much more likely to be obtained by pressing on with the modernisation plan for re-equipment and more productive use of all the assets of the railway.' Here, Spaven was to allude in rather more detail to the almost comical comparison made in his first recorded rail memorandum: 'The *Scotsman* was able to report recently that the loss and misuse of tarpaulins is now costing the Scottish Region £250,000 a year, more than they will save from all the current batch of closures agreed or imminent.'

The second challenge to Beeching's claimed economies (and this would be a common refrain during the era of closures) was that: 'The lopping off of tributary lines and services will reduce traffic in the remaining trunk lines.' And indeed, in practice, in the absence of through bus-rail ticketing and physical integration of services, former rail passengers often chose to complete their whole journey by bus, or increasingly car. Spaven's third challenge was: 'The real public costs of providing other means of communication must be set against the internal rail deficit.' Interestingly, he here writes: 'This "cost-benefit equation" has been fully accepted by the U.S.A. as evidence in favour of retaining railway services.'

Emphasising that the rail system 'must be regarded as an integral part of the Scottish economy and geared to its expansion', Spaven then suggested that when specific closure proposals were to be made, four steps should be taken. First: the 'true internal financial position should be accounted for and published'. Second: 'every effort should be made to increase revenues and to allow the economies of dieselisation, etc., to take effect'. Third: a survey should be undertaken of 'the social and economic repercussions of closure and the cost of providing alternative services if any'. And finally:

> Either a positive plan should be drawn up for alternative means of communication, allowing the railways to run feeder bus and lorry services, or arrangements will be required to be made for a special subsidy to allow the railway services to continue (this is believed to be recommended by the Highland Transport Enquiry, as it is by the Norway Group of the Highland Panel).

(The Highland Panel, or in its full title, the Advisory Panel on the Highlands and Islands, was established by Attlee's post-war Labour Government in 1946.)

Spaven's paper concluded: 'Without this, none of the arbitrary and extensive closures of secondary and main lines which are being consistently rumoured for Scotland are acceptable.' He then added an afterthought – linked to his earlier reference to the rail system being integral to the Scottish economy – which related implicitly to the circumstances surrounding the Far North Line:

> Already the steam age has been abolished north of Perth and Aberdeen, many improved timings are imminent and traffic receipts, especially from passenger trains, have been maintained or increased on the majority of the routes, despite depopulation and increasing car ownership. Why is this advance not publicised and is it to be continued or not, at a time when the re-deployment of Scottish industry and population and the expansion of tourism call for it?

The Highland Transport Enquiry

Within the Frank Spaven collection at the Highland Archive is a June 1962 draft, hand-amended by Spaven, of the report of the Highland Transport Enquiry, which had been set up in 1959. The Enquiry was partly under the aegis of the Highland Panel, which he attended as a Scottish Development Department (SDD) representative. Its final report would not be published until February 1963.

Describing existing services on the Far North Line, the draft report noted that of around 170,000 tons per annum of freight, more than a third was coal, more than a third was 'general merchandise', while the balance included 'acutely seasonal' livestock traffic whose August peak coincided with 'the apex of the summer passenger traffic'. This created a heavily peaked demand for expensive locomotive resources which might have little other productive work for the rest of the year. Passenger traffic peaked more than twofold in the summer months, and the number of passengers on the Far North Line (booked at Highland stations) had declined from 137,259 in 1949 to 104,629 in 1960: a drop of 24% during a period of growing affluence.

Freight was also in decline, from 335,985 tons in 1949 to 191,831 tons in 1960: a drop of 43%. BR had commented on the draft to the effect that most of the Highland freight reduction consisted of coal, reflecting a wider market decline rather than road haulage competition, and also suggested that:

> If the aim of the report is to advocate the retention of the Highland lines this paragraph [about road competition and lack of rail-suited freight traffics] could rather stress the danger to the Highlands if left entirely dependent on road transport operators for their links with the rest of the country.

At the time, staff on the Far North Line must have felt they were still at the heart of the regional economy, handling goods as diverse as bitumen, grain, potatoes, scrap, timber and whisky, and no fewer than 458,000 parcels in 1959 (averaging 1,500 per day). Other intriguing statistical insights from 1959 within the report included the line's handling of 514,000 mailbags (1,600 per day) and 163,000 head of livestock in special trains from Thurso, Forsinard, Lairg and Dingwall. As Michael Williams wrote in *On the slow train again* (2012), reflecting on the days when 'the consignment of goods and chattels was the main function of the line' (and summarising a more detailed account by Fenwick, Sinclair and Ardern *(ibid)* in 2010):

> Back in 1963 John Chamney was a BR clerk tasked with analysing the flow of goods on the 6.40 a.m. train from Inverness, which at that time included parcels vans. He reckoned the revenue from parcels was about seven time that of passengers. In his manifest he found compressor parts from Camborne in Cornwall to Thurso, a crate from the Ministry of Defence at Devonport for Invergordon, a Bush Radio from Plymouth to Brora, a stool from Frome to Bonar Bridge, marine equipment from Henley-on-Thames to Wick, a Parker Knoll chair by mail order from High Wycombe to Dornoch, as well as two boxes of Swiss Rolls from Birmingham to Brora and two boxes of Tilley's crumpets from Cheltenham to Invergordon.

The draft Highland Transport Inquiry report's conclusions on railway finances and the future recognised that the whole of the Scottish railway system had been unprofitable since the end of World War One and that the Grouping into the LMS and LNER had been 'done in order that revenue from the traffic in the south might maintain the Scottish "peripheral" lines'.

Modernisation of the railway system was needed to improve its competitive capability against the challenge of road transport, 'but other forms of transport are being modernised too and the railways would have to go very far before they began to improve their relative position'. It was not known 'to what extent, if any of the Highland lines, though unprofitable in themselves, contribute on balance to the health of the trunk railway system', although BR was certain that they incurred 'a considerable loss'.

Clarity was awaited in the anticipated announcement of the results of the BTC studies led by Beeching, but in the meantime an internal SDD memo, on 29 June 1962, alluded to a discussion on the wider picture with Gordon Stewart, Assistant General Manager, British Railways (Scottish Region), who had indicated that: 'against the current British Railway *[sic]* losses of £136m., the Highlands only lose something of the order of £3m. and Scottish railways as a whole only lose somewhere between £11m. and £6m'. But this would not deter his ultimate boss...

First glimpses of the Beeching prescription

On 13 July, under the headline 'Beeching axe draws nearer', the *Scotsman* reported that a map of freight carryings on BR, issued by BTC the previous day as the initial outcome of Dr Beeching's traffic surveys, indicated that all railways north of Perth (except those linking Aberdeen with Edinburgh and Glasgow) were 'hopelessly uneconomic…This map is openly described by B.T.C. officials as a "softening-up" for the master hatchet plan which Dr Beeching will produce at the end of the year'.

In fact, neither the BTC's commentary nor the map itself implied such an unequivocal verdict. Unsurprisingly, given the nature of the region's economy and population density, all the Highland lines (except the Highland Main Line) were shown as falling into the lowest density category of freight traffic nationally, ie less than 5,000 tons per week. But the 3,000-4,000 tons weekly which the Far North Line was actually handling at the time would be a healthy volume, even in today's terms, provided that freight trains were only picking up the marginal costs of track and signalling attributable to their operation over and above passenger trains (the cost allocation rule which applies today).

In practice, in 1962, where a freight service still operated (and was expected to continue), the assumption was that it would bear the basic infrastructure costs necessary for that service to operate, with the passenger service only bearing the cost of additional track and signalling provision required over and above that level. This was to prove an assumption of grandiose but misguided proportions as the 1960s wore on and rail freight increasingly haemorrhaged away to road haulage – the *raison d'être* of many secondary and branch lines becoming overwhelmingly the passenger market. Beeching himself said that 'without freight the main railway network could not exist', but the situation since the 1970s has been that without *passenger* traffic, itself often heavily subsidised, most of the main railway network could not exist.

On 20 July 1962, under the headline 'Cartographic requiem', the *Scotsman* published the next BTC map, of passenger traffic densities. This showed that all the Highland lines north of Aviemore and Keith fell into the lowest density category of passenger traffic nationally, i.e. less than 5,000 passengers per week. The newspaper reported that: 'It would seem that more than a third of the network will be recommended for closure', while BTC's own press release commented that:

> [The freight and passenger maps] show how much of the railway is seriously under-employed. The freight map shows that 50% of BR is used for 95% of the freight traffic and the passenger study likewise reveals that 50% of it is used for 96% of the passenger travel.

Seemingly not spotted at the time was the fact that any analysis of usage of the national *road network* would probably show similar patterns. Beeching was to make this very point two years later, and to suggest that he should undertake a road system study to complement that which he had done for rail. This was not a suggestion which went down well with the 1964-66 Labour Government.

In any event, in mid-1962 it did not take the Highland media long to digest the implications of Beeching's maps. In what would prove to be one of his most restrained editorials on rail prospects during the entire 1962-64 closure saga, the redoubtable Editor of the *Inverness Courier*, Evan Barron – who had begun in that post in 1919 and would finally retire in 1965 – commented on 24 July:

> Mr Macmillan's Government has been given a new look *[after the major Cabinet reshuffle which came to be known as 'the night of the long knives'],* and a changed policy regarding railways will be expected of it – particularly recognition that the railway system in Britain exists to supply an essential public need and not merely to make a profit, and that sparsely-populated areas of the country like the Highlands stand in need of it just as much as people in the South.

Interestingly, a few months later, Harold Macmillan was privately to spell out not just such a general principle of policy but also a very specific reference to the Far North Line, which implied early political misgivings about some anticipated conclusions of Beeching's report. In his fascinating analysis of the bigger picture during the Beeching period, *Last Trains* (2013), Charles Loft writes:

> In September 1962, Macmillan set out the policy as he understood it in a letter to Marples:

> 'If the government decides that on social grounds a railway from Inverness to Wick is necessary then…Dr Beeching will quote a price…for keeping the line open…the government will pay this, it decides to do so, as a social service, but the management of the railway will not be accused of inefficiency or an increase in their deficit made a subject of attack on them on this account.'

The *Ross-shire Journal* gloomily concluded on 27 July: 'All the passenger railway services north of Aviemore are in the "doomed" category', and while there was some hope for tourist routes, 'the line from Inverness to Wick and Thurso is felt to be threatened.'

The line raises its game

On a more positive note, by August 1962 steam had been entirely eliminated from the network focused on Inverness, and the new Type 2 diesels were able to haul up to nine passenger coaches (320 tons), in contrast to the ex-LMS Black

5 steam locos which required double heading when the load exceeded 250 tons. The summer limited-stop *Orcadian* service, once daily between Inverness and Thurso (and Wick), took just 4 hours in both directions, an extraordinary improvement of more than 80 minutes compared to the same journey in 1960. This was just 14 minutes slower than the best journey time to Thurso today, and 18 minutes *faster* than today's best time to Wick.

Even the winter timetable commencing in September showed overall speed improvements as being as great as or greater than those achieved after the 20 station closures in 1960. The 6.40am from Inverness (a train with longer station dwell times to offload parcels and mail traffic) took 4 hours 57 minutes to Wick, and the 10.55am departure was scheduled to take 4 hours 45 minutes. Both of these trains (indeed all end-to-end passenger and freight trains) were hauled by the Type 2 diesels (later, Class 26 and Class 24) which established a special place in Highland railway history:

> As the class carved out a niche for itself in the far *[sic]* North later engines of the class had recesses in the cab for tablet apparatus. They put up good performances even in winter and small snow-ploughs could cope with drifts up to 4ft (1.2m). With a low axle weight and four-wheel bogies the 26s offered considerable flexibility.[47]

But the positive transformative impact of dieselisation – and its centralisation on Inverness, as a consequence of diesels being able to cover a much greater mileage than steam between refuelling and maintenance requirements – also had a downside in terms of local employment. Small engine sheds like Helmsdale and Wick were closed, and Thurso 'found itself with just a solitary examiner following the closure of carriage and locomotive sheds and the dispersal of electrical and mechanical and fitting staff'.[48]

By late 1962, Beeching's work was well advanced, and an undercurrent of worries about vulnerable routes continued in the media. On 14 December an unidentified newspaper cutting[49] reported that Colin Campbell, the Chairman of the Executive Committee of the North of Scotland Transport Conference, had received assurances in a recent meeting with Michael Noble, that 'in respect of railway closures, a categorical assurance had already been given that no railway line would be closed unless there were adequate alternative services for the transport of passengers and freight'.

Campbell, an Easter Ross farmer who would be a leading light in the 1963-64 MacPuff campaign, had told a press conference that: "As a result of my interview with the Scottish Secretary you can take it that the executive committee hail the assurance and reactions as a very major step forward in our future dealings with the transport problem.' Here was an early indication of the

Highland establishment, or old boys' network, moving to counter what was seen as an unacceptable potential threat to a wide range of interests across the North. And in just a few months, that would become a real threat.

The 1962 Transport Act had abolished the British Transport Commission and created the British Railways Board (BRB), which came into being on 1 January 1963, with Beeching as its first Chairman. On the same date, the Scottish Railways Board was established, with responsibility to oversee the commercial and operational management of British Railways (Scottish Region). The Minutes of its first meeting in January of that year spelt out that it did *not* have any responsibility for 'the determination of the future size, shape and nature of the national railway system' which was reserved for the BRB.

Nevertheless, it is remarkable how little reference the Minutes of the Scottish Board's monthly meetings through 1963 and 1964[50] make to the Beeching Report in general and closure proposals in particular. More frequent appearances were made by agenda items on 'ex-gratia payments to widows whose husbands are killed whilst on duty' and public namings of Type 5 'Deltic' locomotives which were now firmly established on express passenger duties along the East Coast Main Line. Another recurring reference was to

An 'Up' freight train approaching Bonar Bridge station from the north on 14 September 1962, headed by 'Birmingham' Type 2 No. D5335 (now preserved on the Caledonian Railway in Brechin). Note the surviving water column (minus hose) formerly used for steam locos, the automatic token exchange equipment on both sides of the line, and the small signal box controlling the immediate points and signals (the token instruments being held in the main station building, as was standard Far North Line practice).
Ben Brooksbank

efforts to solve the ongoing engineering problems of the troubled North British Locomotive Company Type 2 locomotives built in Glasgow: one of the worst of the 1955 Modernisation Plan classes, but which, fortunately for the Highlands, very rarely penetrated as far as Inverness and almost certainly never appeared on the Far North Line.

By early 1963, political pressure was growing for the creation of a Highland Transport Authority. With the Beeching Report also 'keenly' anticipated, a confidential memorandum on Highland transport was drafted for Ernest Marples on 13 March by the MoT General Division. The memo challenged the case for a Highland Transport Authority, since to announce this 'would make it more difficult, if not impossible, to take early decisions on railways in the Highlands'. The draft continued that:

> ...opposition to passenger closures will come from all quarters. But we must maintain our resolve to close the hopelessly uneconomic services. Services in the Highlands are a typical example...To weaken on Highland services would drive the thin end of a very broad wedge into our policy, with repercussions elsewhere...Delay on decisions on rail closures in the Highlands would delay general plans for rationalisation of services throughout Scotland. There would be an outcry if the Highlands were treated differently to other parts of Scotland which may be equally affected by closures...An announcement of special arrangements for the Highlands would cast doubt on the Government's declared policy on closures and might damage the railways plan as a whole.

The memo appears to have been drafted in response to a specific demand from Michael Noble, since the former states that: 'The Secretary of State recommends, as an immediate step, that Ministerial responsibility should be concentrated on him.' Marples was far from keen on the suggestion that Noble should have the final say on rail closure proposals in Scotland. His response was: 'I am not clear what he has in mind. We cannot change existing statutory responsibilities...unless we are to risk serious delay and repercussions, we have no practical alternative but to deal with the Railway proposals affecting the Highlands under existing statutory responsibilities.'

On 26 March 1963, the day before the Beeching Report was published, Frank Spaven sent a wide-ranging memo on 'Railways and Development' to his colleague Mr Stark. Perhaps indicating that BR's corporate position on Scotland's negative contribution to railway finances was now rather different from the view expressed by Gordon Stewart back in June 1962, Spaven commented: 'Whatever the British Railways Board have to say about their loses in Scotland, they should not be allowed to put it over that the Scottish Region is most in need of surgery.'

An early 1960s' view of a 'Birmingham' Type 2 departing from Georgemas Junction on the last leg of the journey from Inverness to Thurso, Britain's most northerly station. Frank Spaven

The memo made a number of suggestions and posed a variety of questions, including: 'What scope is there for further measures of economy in operating branch and secondary passenger lines rather than closing them completely?' Spaven then cited the unstaffing of small stations and the elimination of signal boxes and manned level crossings, measures which 'have already gone some way in the Highlands'.

He also alluded to one particular aspect of railway development potential where his familiarity with continental practice came into play. Assuming that some lines would survive in tourist areas, 'what are the prospects of extending services by Observation Car, "Vista-dome" or other open-view carriage designs which were known to be in demand by foreign travel agencies arranging visits to Scotland?'

However, these issues wisely raised by Spaven, and potentially central to the future of Highland railways, would occupy very much a back seat the following day.

CHAPTER 8: DR BEECHING PRESCRIBES – AND THE NORTH REVOLTS

The Reshaping of British Railways – 'the Beeching Report' – was published on 27 March 1963. Closure of 'unremunerative' lines had been gathering pace nationwide for several years and there was widespread expectation that Beeching would propose many service withdrawals. But the sheer scale of the proposals in his 148-page report came as a shock.

Passenger services were to be withdrawn from 5,000 route miles, and over 2,000 stations would be closed across Britain. The pessimists in the North had been proved right. Within the 35 pages, among the lists of routes and stations which were to lose their passenger services was the entire rail system north of Inverness.

But there was logic underpinning the closures element of the new strategy aimed at creating a profitable railway. The latter was in part to be achieved by bulk and container freight innovations and fast inter-city passenger trains to meet the challenge of road transport. The third chapter of the report – 'Analysis of the problem' – succinctly summed up the basic characteristics of railways and the circumstances which were likely to make them 'the best available form of transport':

> Railways are distinguished by the provision and maintenance of a specialised route system for their own exclusive use. This gives rise to high fixed costs. On the other hand, the benefits which can be derived from possession of this high cost route system are very great.

> Firstly, it permits the running of high capacity trains, which themselves have very low movement costs per unit carried. Secondly, it permits dense flows of traffic and, provided the flows are dense, the fixed costs per unit moved are also low. Thirdly it permits safe, reliable, scheduled movements at high speed.

> In a national system of transport we should, therefore, expect to find railways concentrating upon those parts of the traffic pattern which enable them to derive sufficient benefit from these three advantages to offset their unavoidable burden of high system cost. In other words, we should expect the provision of railways to be limited to routes over which it is possible to develop dense flows of traffic, of the kinds which lend themselves to movement in trainload quantities and which, in part at least, benefit from the speed and reliability which the railways are capable of achieving.

A dispassionate analysis at the time would have struggled to find any such circumstances on the Far North Line. From a purely commercial viewpoint, the railway was a 'dead duck', as was the Kyle line. While this was a strictly financial approach to the problem – ignoring environmental, regional development, road congestion and social impact issues – this was 'all' that Beeching had been asked to do by a Government alarmed by BR's mounting losses.

A beaming Dr Richard Beeching, Chairman of the British Railways Board, unveils his infamous report on 27 March 1963. There were few smiles in the Highlands, as the report confirmed that all 232 miles of railway north of Inverness were slated for closure.
Daily Herald Archive / National Media Museum / Science & Society Picture Library

The Reshaping Report did not hide its light under a bushel and, coming from a business background, Dr Beeching was perhaps naive in not foreseeing the political storm that such a transparent announcement of drastic surgery would cause. Part of that transparency was a fascinating portfolio of 13 detailed maps, with Map 3 of 'Passenger traffic station receipts' revealing that only four Scottish stations in the highest revenue category (£25,000 and over per annum) – Galashiels, Hawick, Stranraer and Thurso – were listed for closure.

As the map extract overleaf shows, however, the large majority of the Far North Line's stations – unsurprisingly, given population levels – fell into the lowest revenue category (less than £5,000 pa), with only Dingwall, Invergordon, Lairg and Wick in the medium category. Here was practical confirmation of the key point made by Iain Skewis in his 1960 report at Glasgow University: that low population totals provide only limited traffic, whose revenues must cover charges on a considerable length of track mileage.

There were some similarities in the freight picture. The extract of Map 4 of 'Distribution of freight traffic station tonnage' (opposite) again shows only Thurso in the highest category (25,000 tons and over pa), with most stations – unsurprisingly, given the low population and lack of industry – in the lowest category (less than 5,000 tons pa).

However, no fewer than 10 freight locations fell into the medium category, reflecting local concentrations of industry as well as some railheads serving wide hinterlands: at Beauly (freight depot and sawmill private siding), Muir of Ord, Dingwall, Invergordon, Tain, Glenmorangie Distillery, Lairg, Brora and Wick. The new Invergordon Distillery had only opened in July 1961 and therefore did not register in Beeching's April 1961 traffic survey, but by 1963 it would certainly have been in the highest tonnage category. Indeed, it was almost certainly the biggest freight traffic generator on the entire rail system north of Inverness.

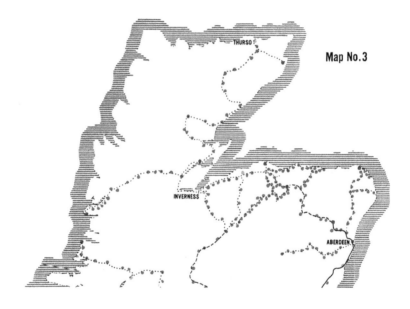

Map No.3

BRITISH RAILWAYS DISTRIBUTION OF PASSENGER TRAFFIC STATION RECEIPTS

Red • £0 to 5,000 per annum
Blue • £5,000 to 25,000 per annum
Green • £25,000 and over per annum
Stations in certain congested areas are omitted

An extract from Map 3 of the Beeching Report, 'British Railways Distribution of Passenger Traffic Station Receipts'. British Railways Board, 1963

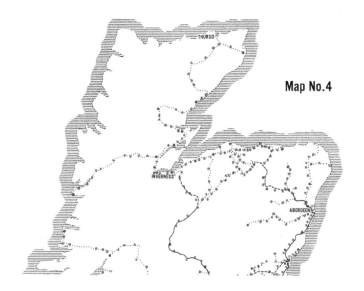

Map No.4

BRITISH RAILWAYS DISTRIBUTION OF
FREIGHT TRAFFIC STATION TONNAGE

Red ● 0 to 5,000 tons per annum
Blue ● 5,000 to 25,000 tons per annum
Green ● 25,000 tons and over per annum

Stations in certain congested areas are omitted

An extract from Map 4 of the Beeching Report, 'British Railways Distribution of Freight Traffic Station Tonnage'. British Railways Board, 1963

The most notorious of the maps was Map No. 9, 'Proposed withdrawal of passenger train services' (overleaf), which featured prominently on the front page of the *Scotsman* on 28 March under the headline: 'The lines that stay and the ones that may go'. The paper reported that 6,720 Scottish jobs were to be lost, and that the rail route network would be cut by 41% to 1,350 miles. Also, 435 of the existing 1,150 stations (of which 669 served passengers) would be closed.

The severity of what Beeching proposed was reflected in the *Scotsman's* coverage, occupying almost the entire front page plus pages six and seven. Little specific mention was made of the Far North Line, and rail passengers in the Highlands would have drawn little comfort from the news that 'The National Trust for Scotland is already taking an active interest in the possibilities of acquiring disused railway lines which run through areas of special beauty or interest.' And was it a mischievous sub-editor who inserted on the front page a holiday advert which exhorted readers to 'Make it French Railways. They have so much to offer.'?

Swift responses in the North

The 38 stations and 232 miles of the Far North and Kyle lines represented the largest rural route network to be threatened across Britain. In terms of likely hardship and strategic development impacts, there were even worse Scottish closure proposals, notably the double-track Waverley Route main line through the Borders, and both routes to Stranraer (from Ayr and Dumfries). However, that was no consolation to the Highlands, where over 300 miles of railway faced closure, including the original Highland Main Line from Aviemore through Grantown to Forres, and the Ballachulish branch. On 29 March 1963, in a foretaste of what was to be heard over the next 12 months, Evan Barron's editorial (of over 1,800 words) in the *Inverness Courier* thundered:

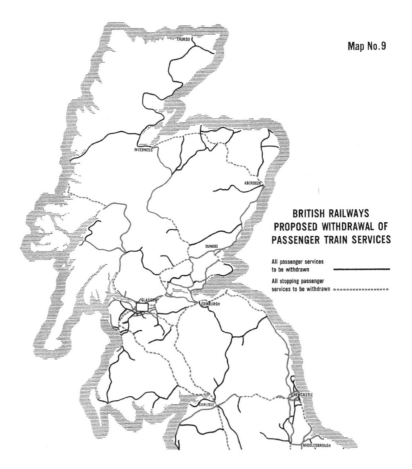

Map No.9

**BRITISH RAILWAYS
PROPOSED WITHDRAWAL OF
PASSENGER TRAIN SERVICES**

All passenger services
to be withdrawn   ————————

All stopping passenger
services to be withdrawn ═══════════════

An extract from Map 9 of the Beeching Report, 'British Railways Proposed Withdrawal of Passenger Train Services'. British Railways Board, 1963

Today this country is facing the greatest crisis it has ever had to face in peace… The political storm is only just beginning to rise, and it will, or certainly ought, to centre on the point that what is at stake is not merely the railway system of Great Britain but something vastly more important, namely the democratic way of governing this country.

Barron finished with a flourish which embraced not just the Inverness area, nor indeed just the Highlands, but rather the whole country – something which his long and trenchant editorials often did:

Dr Beeching's marvellous proposals, by envisaging the destruction of the existing communications of this country without any better compensation than vague promises that something helpful may be done in a few favoured places, are not only threatening the very existence of the Highlands, they are indeed rousing the whole of Scotland, and many parts of England and Wales, too, to defiance. It lies now with the people of Britain to see that short shrift is given to this latest piece of would-be government by executives, and we are glad to see that no time is being wasted in launching the campaign against proposals which can only be implemented with dire results for thousands of people in many parts of Britain, including the Highlands of Scotland.

That embryonic campaign was reported in the *Courier's* news columns under the strapline 'Mounting Indignation about Closure Plans', revealing that an early meeting of the Highland Transport Committee, representing local authorities and other bodies in the north and north-east of Scotland, was to be held to protest against the proposed closures 'in the strongest possible terms'.

The *Courier's* report showed that leading politicians from the region were (almost) unanimous in their opposition: Provost Alan Ross of Inverness said that 'the North had to fight every inch of the way'; Sir Francis Walker, convener of Inverness County Council, referred to the lines north of Inverness as 'vital arteries which should not be severed'; Brigadier Sir Keith Murray, convener of Caithness 'described the report as "disastrous" adding that during the winter the north often depended entirely on railway transport'; while Jack Macleod, MP for Ross & Cromarty, said that the cuts would be introduced 'only over my dead body'. But there was one dissenting voice:

Only Sir David Robertson, M.P. for Caithness and Sutherland, who has on many occasions advocated the closing of the Inverness-Wick/Thurso line and its conversion into a motor roadway for freight traffic and bus services, supported the plan.

The *Courier* reported that it had been the only Highland newspaper to send a member of staff to the BR press conference at the Central Hotel in Glasgow on the afternoon of 27 March. Cameron of Locheil, Chairman of the Scottish

Railways Board, and James Ness, Scottish Region General Manager, had faced 'a barrage of questions from a gathering of 50 journalists representing Scotland's principal newspapers'.

Locheil had been asked by the *Courier* reporter whether the decision to propose closure of the lines north of Inverness had taken into consideration the terms and recommendations of the Highland Transport Enquiry, jointly chaired by Lords Cameron and Kilbrandon (and which had finally been published the previous month). The paper reported that Locheil had replied that the Board was naturally interested in the report but he felt that in the main it had emphasised that there should be a good road system before there were closures.

Interestingly, it would appear that BR were publicly defending some closure proposals which privately they did not support. Charles Loft *(ibid)* wrote:

> The Regional Railway Boards created under the 1962 Act were subordinate to the BRB, which was directly responsible to Marples. The advantage of this approach (from the government's point of view) was exemplified by Beeching's ability to compel the Scottish region to put forward major closures such as Inverness-Wick-Thurso and Edinburgh-Hawick-Carlisle, which it would not have done on its own initiative (and which it privately invited the Scottish Secretary to direct it to retain in 1963).

Back in the Highlands, 29 March saw reactions to the Beeching threat from a variety of local newspapers. Under the headline 'SHOCKING', the editorial in the Dingwall-based *Ross-shire Journal* adopted similar near-apocalyptic language to the *Inverness Courier*:

> No other adjective is necessary to describe Dr Beeching's plans for the railways of the Highlands, especially the life-lines which run from Dingwall North and West, to Wick and Kyle of Lochalsh. The battle is only beginning and it is a fight that will have to be fought to the bitter end until a more realistic plan emerges for the two life-lines which most intimately concern us here in the North. There are various panels and commissions at the present moment working for the rehabilitation of the Highlands. The time has come for them to thunder forth with one voice to prevent the birth of an era that will make the very term rehabilitation an empty mockery.

That same day, the Wick-based *John O'Groat Journal* carried an editorial – which read more like a news item – in which it reported on a theme which had already become a recurring aspect of the closure threat, and which would prove to be a critical factor in the line's ultimate reprieve:

> The Scottish Secretary, Mr Michael Noble, said at a Press conference on Wednesday: "If the road system is not adequate the closure system will not be put into effect." Mr Ernest Marples, Minister of Transport, spoke in similar terms in the House of Commons: "No opposed closure may be carried out without

my consent. And I shall take into account all important factors, including social and defence considerations, the pattern of industrial development and possible effects on roads and road traffic".

The economic and social implications of the Beeching Report were a serious concern for a number of Government ministries, and the Minister of Transport was required to consult other departments and regional economic planning councils on the strategic impacts of closure proposals, as well as the Transport Users Consultative Committees (TUCCs) on personal hardship to travellers.

Since the 1962 Transport Act, the TUCCs no longer had any statutory right to comment on proposed freight withdrawals, but in the case of passenger closure proposals they could consider individual 'hardship' objections by rail users, then report their recommendations to the Minister of Transport. These could include enhanced replacement bus services or even a recommendation that the rail service should not be withdrawn. The Minister was not obliged to accept any recommendations, but could choose to make consent to closure subject to certain conditions, or indeed to reprieve the service partially or in its entirety. The Scottish Office – although it had no rail powers to complement its road powers – clearly took an early interest in the threat to the lines north of Inverness.

Being the area furthest away from a potentially shorn rail network, Caithness could be expected to voice the biggest concerns about closure. Provost Dunnett of Wick was reported by the *John O'Groat Journal* as being most disappointed from the general economic standpoint:

"The hopes we had for industrial development in the North will be dashed completely," he said. "It has destroyed any hopes of advancement. Instead of a reduced service we should be getting a better one, especially when the population of Caithness is increasing".

Within 18 months, Caithness would have the improved rail service which Provost Dunnett sought, but it would not feature the type of train he had suggested: 'Expressing a practical view – the Provost is a train driver himself – he said that instead of continuing to run long trains smaller diesel units should be used in the North, as was being done elsewhere.'

The introduction of Diesel Multiple Units (DMUs), with engines slung below the floors of their typically 2- or 3-car train length, had been among the first fruits of BR's 1955 Modernisation Plan. Generally, these improved journey times compared to steam haulage, created a (theoretically) cleaner travelling environment, and certainly reduced operating costs very significantly. They therefore held out the prospect of substantially improving the economics of those commuter and branch lines feeling the impact of growing road competition in an increasingly affluent era.

The first route to benefit – with the introduction of six-car 'Inter City' DMUs in 1957 – had been the main line from Edinburgh to Glasgow. BR had then successfully introduced, in 1960, two express DMU services daily from Inverness to Aberdeen, taking just 2½ hours for the 108-mile journey. But first-generation DMUs would never see regular service north of Inverness, due to the combination of steep gradients, inter-working of passenger and freight locomotive 'diagrams' (daily work programmes, which varied from day to day), worries about DMU performance in snow conditions, and presumably their limited parcels accommodation.

The locos working over the Far North Line were far from being a self-contained asset north of Inverness, and complex diagrams would often take them on passenger or freight duties as far as Aberdeen, Aberfeldy (a branch line which would disappear in 1965), Edinburgh (Waverley station and Leith Walk freight depot), Glasgow (Buchanan Street station and Sighthill freight depot) and Grangemouth.

By 2 April 1963, the *Inverness Courier* could report increasing opposition in advance of the planned conference of the Highland Transport Committee in Inverness the following week: 'The tide of indignation and protest against Dr Richard Beeching's Report…continues to rise rapidly and strongly.' Among the opposition was Allan Campbell McLean, a 'weel-kent' figure around Inverness and the prospective Labour candidate for the Inverness-shire constituency, whose scathing attack was quoted verbatim in the *Courier*:

> Was it really necessary to deprive I.C.I. of the services of Dr Beeching at a cost to the taxpayer of £24,000 per annum *[around £475,000 at current prices]*, to take the chairman of Batchelor Peas at a cost of £12,500 a year and various top executives from Unilevers, Shell International and Great Universal Stores, in order to conclude that if the operating costs of a particular line exceeded the revenue from that line, then that line was losing public money? I would have thought that any reasonably intelligent eleven-year-old would have arrived at the same conclusion without any great mental effort. But only an eleven-year-old would have gone on to advocate the wholesale closure of such lines without regard to the social consequences that would ensue. Of course, this is the logical outcome of the Tory Party's policy.

An amusing line, but hardly fair on Beeching (although the salary was eye-watering). One of the key purposes of his report was to identify in detail which services and types of traffic did not cover their costs, a basic management accounting exercise which had previously been neglected. Consideration of social and other non-financial consequences was an issue for Government, not BR, with its new duty to break even over a five-year period. But it was Beeching who took – and continues to take – most of the flak.

Government departments begin deliberations

On 2 April, civil servants met at St Andrew's House in Edinburgh to discuss the rail reshaping proposals. In attendance were representatives of five different ministries: the Scottish Development Department (five individuals, including Frank Spaven), Board of Trade, Ministry of Labour, Ministry of Power and Ministry of Public Building and Works.

Commentary on the Far North Line was brief, including a succinct summary that: 'The closure of this line would involve long and tedious bus journeys.' Perhaps confounding a wider impression that Frank Spaven was very much a 'dove' on closure, he had 'suggested that as a compromise Lairg might be retained as a railhead for the area'.

Although Beeching was taking much of the onslaught, the pressure on Government from the Highlands was also growing quickly. By 5 April the *Courier* could again report ministerial protestation that closures would not take place without adequate replacements being provided:

> ...some small crumb of comfort was offered in the House of Commons on Wednesday by the Secretary of State for Scotland, Mr Michael Noble, who said that millions of pounds would need to be spent on the roads in the Highlands if the Beeching proposals on rail closures were fully implemented... "This problem has been made clear by myself and the Minister of Transport – that adequate roads are a pre-condition of closing some of the lines," Mr Noble continued.

Other sources of opposition were quoted in the same day's *Courier*. The Convention of Royal Burghs, meeting in Edinburgh, had unanimously approved a motion that the provision of new roads was no substitute for the withdrawal of main-line railways 'and that their continuance was essential to the economic and social requirements of the Highland and other rural areas'.

Also in Edinburgh, an emergency meeting of the Northern Burghs' Association (formed only the previous month in Wick) had agreed that a strongly-worded memorandum against the proposed rail cuts should be sent to the Secretary of State and Minister of Transport, citing inadequate roads and bus services, and concluding that 'implementation of the Beeching plan "would mean the total execution of the possibility of attracting further industry to the area to combat the present unemployment situation"'.

5 April 1963 was a day of much rail commentary not just in the *Inverness Courier* but also in local newspapers across the North. The *Ross-shire Journal*, in its editorial, argued that 'a determined fight will be engaged in to stay the carrying out of this extremely callous surgery of our two principal

transport lifelines'. However, it also reported that: 'The Scottish Landowners Federation feel that the proposed rail closures, although frightening, could be a blessing in disguise to the rural areas of Scotland', since they would encourage road improvements and substantial employment in this sector. In evident contradiction of the National Farmers Union view reported that day in the *Courier* (supporting rail retention), the Federation had commented that: 'Rural industry has, in the great majority of cases, already opted for road freight services instead of rail.'

Meanwhile, the *John O'Groat Journal* was reporting that the closure of the railway had been 'the subject of some concern' at a meeting of Sutherland County Council in Bonar Bridge. Among the voices of opposition to closure had been the chairman of Sutherland Civil Defence Committee, who introduced an argument harking back to war-time experience when he 'said the North line must be preserved in the interests of the country's safety in an emergency'.

A (doubtless unintentional) comic note had also been brought to the debate by a Mr JP Whittet:

> There was a report that the British Transport Commission's hotel at Dornoch was to be sold, he said, but how could it pay when, at one time during the season, there had been only twenty-five guests and a staff of eighty-five?

In the *Inverness Courier* of 9 April, Evan Barron's editorial – 'The Highlands must fight' – set the scene for the well-publicised 11 April conference of the Highland Transport Committee in Inverness. Referring to an evident 18 April deadline for local authorities to send responses to the Beeching Report to the Ministry of Transport, the editorial warned that:

> ...delay of any kind would obviously be fatal to the Highlands' cause. Accordingly, the unfortunate impression which has been given too often in the recent past that the Highlands are half-hearted about these just complaints, or are even too timid to defend their interests in the teeth of Government or bureaucratic opposition, must be wiped out, and the Highlands must fight, and fight hard and wholeheartedly, with every intention of winning.

A significant number of Government departments were by now taking a close interest in the potential impact of rail closures. On 10 April, the Ministry of Labour's Scottish Headquarters wrote to its head office in London to advise that, in the case of the Far North Line, maintenance of the necessary labour force levels at the UKAEA complex at Dounreay was 'already difficult enough, and the withdrawal of this service would increase these difficulties'. Some 600 or so employees who had moved to the area did not have cars 'and they and their families rely on railway services when visiting their homes'.

The campaign takes shape

The Highland response to Beeching would prove to be nothing if not broadly-based. In his book *Highland Whistle Blower* (2001), Phil Durham, who as we shall see would be one of the key players in the MacPuff campaign against rail closures, recorded that:

> In the Highlands the fiery cross was hoisted high. The population north of the Great Glen temporarily abandoned such long-standing rivalries as Jacobite against Hanoverian, Presbyterian against Catholic, Laird against Crofter/Tenant, sheep against trees, or Stalker/Ghillie against Poacher to present a united front against a proposed rail-less wilderness planned from the south. Industries from the size of Dounreay Atomic Station or Invergordon Distillery down to local garages, potato growers, stockmen, sea fishermen, salmon netsmen and coal merchants all united in a howl of protest.

Reflecting that diversity of opposition, the keenly-awaited Inverness conference of the Highland Transport Committee on 11 April was attended – according to the next day's *Inverness Courier* – by some 80 delegates 'from Town, County, and District Councils and representatives of farming, hotel and other interests in an area embracing no fewer than 12 counties stretching from Perth to Orkney and Shetland and from Aberdeen to Argyll'. Colin Campbell of Invershin (chairman of the executive committee of the North of Scotland Transport Conference) presided over more than three hours of discussion, during which:

> Lord Lovat, the first speaker, said that they had to face up to a situation which was undoubtedly the gravest of its kind which had ever confronted the Highlands since the time of the Clearances. "It is as bad as that," he declared, "and whatever we decide to do, we must make it big and we must make it strong".

However, the conference did have some lighter moments, the *Courier* reporting that:

> Mr C.I.M. Gair, Easter Moniack, Kirkhill, representing Inverness Area National Farmers' Union, said they had a battle on their hands, and he was glad to see the Chief of the Clan Fraser *[Lord Lovat]*, as usual, in the forefront of the battle, and that, although over 200 years ago the Campbell clan had been in opposition to the Frasers, their representatives were on the platform together that day. (Laughter and applause). He was only sorry that the Chief of the Cameron Clan *[a reference to Lochiel, chairman of the Scottish Area Board of British Railways]* seemed to have defected. (Laughter).

Gair had told delegates that 56% of the traffic on the Perth-Inverness line came from north of Inverness. If the lines north of Inverness were cut, what chance, he had asked, would the Perth-Inverness section have of survival? "'We are being told to go to blazes," concluded Mr Gair, "and that is where the Government will be told to go at the next election if they approve of those proposals."' These were highly prescient words, and the spirit of what he had said would be taken fully on board by the Government over the ensuing 12 months. But the opportunities for humour on this otherwise serious occasion were not over, the *Courier* reporting that:

> Much amusement was caused at one part of the proceedings when the chairman said that he had got a suggested resolution from a non-car owner, proposing that representations be made to the Government that Mr Amos, the chairman of the Scottish Omnibuses Group, and Mr Ness, the general manager of the Scottish Railways *[sic]*, be given leave of absence to take a bus from Inverness to Caithness, with Mr Amos as the driver and Mr Ness as the conductor. The resolution proposed that if they survived the effort they could be taken back by rail to Inverness, given a civic reception, and presented with St Christopher medals. Needless to say, the resolution was not put to the meeting.

The conference unanimously passed a five-part resolution (which appeared to merge, or confuse, two previously separate organisations, i.e. the Highland Transport Committee and the North of Scotland Transport Conference), key elements of which were:

• opposition to the proposed withdrawal of train services in the North of Scotland, and support for the recommendation of the Highland Transport Enquiry that a Highland Transport Authority be created

• powers for that Authority to call for traffic and financial data, including that from local authorities and Government departments to determine 'what capital investment will be required before adequate road services can be provided as full alternatives to the rail services which exist at present'

• with respect to the proposed rail closures, the Government should take account of: 'the great distances involved; the lack of alternative services; the need for the encouragement of new and existing industries; the increasing tourist traffic; and the severity of the winters'

The *Courier's* editorial responded enthusiastically, arguing that everybody in the 12 counties represented at the conference would approve of the effort being made to impress upon the Government that the closures would be 'absolutely disastrous for the people who live, work and have their being *[sic]* in an area which, territorially, constitutes more than half of Scotland'. But Barron was worried about timescales:

> By all accounts Dr Beeching wants to see his plan brought into being in 18 months or two years – the age of miracles will certainly not be past if the good roads necessary for the "adequate" alternative services can be provided in the Highlands by then! –and next month the Government is to produce a

White Paper for Parliamentary approval outlining its policy. The Executive Committee of the North of Scotland Transport Conference will therefore have to move with speed if it expects to make any impression at all upon the Government. In that aim it can count upon the backing of everybody in the North of Scotland, apart perhaps from a few Tory die-hards who are so thirled to their narrow political loyalties that they are quite unconscious of the fact that they speak for nobody but themselves.

This was strong stuff, coming from an acknowledged Tory supporter. A further reminder of potential rebellion in the Conservative ranks was carried in the *Courier's* extensive coverage of the rail issue that day. The Scottish Unionist Members' Committee (the Scottish Unionist Party would only become the Scottish Conservative & Unionist Party in 1965) had met the Secretary of State for Scotland at Westminster, and the MPs 'were given the impression that Mr Noble was confident that he could put up a strong case for Scottish interests in any Government consideration of the Beeching plan'.

The *Courier* also reported that: 'The possibility of subsidising uneconomic lines which are a social and industrial necessity is believed to have been mentioned at the meeting.' It would not be until Labour's 1968 Transport Act that subsidising socially-necessary rail services would enter the statute book, but here was an early harbinger of cross-party support for the concept.

12 April 1963 also saw a thoughtful editorial in the *John O'Groat Journal* which, under the headline 'The End of the Line', began with the observation that: 'No community has a better right to protest at the threatened rail cuts than the people of Caithness. Wick is at the end of the Highland line, and Thurso, with its branch line, is the farthest north in Britain.' Unlike the entirely oppositionist stance of the *Inverness Courier*, the *Journal* commented:

> Dr Beeching's blueprint for the railways is based on hard economic facts and his report is accepted as a first-class one. After the initial shock of his proposals people are beginning to see how many of them are necessary if the railways are to be modernised and further huge losses prevented. Much of the criticism against the proposed cuts is obscured by sentiment and politics.

The editorial argued – perhaps naively, given the 168 miles of expensive rail infrastructure to be maintained – that freight trains would continue to operate even if passenger services were withdrawn, and that in any event, 'Much of the traffic already goes by road', thereby rejecting the argument that the passenger closure would impact on industrial development. Nevertheless, the writer concluded that: 'Local authorities and other bodies in the North are right to make the strongest representations they can for the retention of the rail services but it must be on realistic grounds.'

With the deadline fast approaching for local authorities to send responses to the Beeching Report to the Ministry of Transport, on 16 April the Convention of Royal Burghs completed its memorandum, which included the brief but memorable comment that: 'While it is difficult to fault the Beeching Report either in logic or in strict economics, there is more than these in the life of an individual or of a Country.' The Government's relatively narrow remit to Beeching left him exposed to this kind of critique, but the Government ultimately could not shake off its responsibility to consider the wider social and economic impacts of proposed closures.

The memo also made specific reference to the Far North Line (together with the Dumfries-Stranraer railway), commenting that the roads were 'not suitable to long distance bus traffic, where there are no through booking facilities and where there seems to be little co-ordination of Bus Services at present'.

On deadline day, 18 April, the Scottish Development Department (SDD) completed its observations on 'The Beeching Plan', following discussions with other Scottish Office Departments and BR Scottish Region. The memorandum had a markedly different tone to that which had been circulating amongst some elements of SDD a year earlier, and in the case of the Far North Line it commented:

> The closure of this passenger service should not be contemplated at least until decisions have been made on the recommendations of the Highland Transport Enquiry. Even then, before it can be acceptable, some road improvements and 'bus service increases will be essential.

And then, in a challenge to the conventional wisdom that such railways were expendable in the longer-term – and this sounds very much like a reflection of the thinking of Frank Spaven – the memo continues:

> It seems to be for consideration also whether in the case of the closure of long lengths of line serving considerable areas (e.g. Inverness-Wick) there should not be an appraisal of the relative costs of maintaining railway services and of providing adequate alternatives.

The Highland Panel intervenes

The Panel's 97th meeting was held in the Town House, Inverness, on Friday 19 April 1963, chaired by Lord Cameron, who had served on the Panel since its inception and had been Chairman since 1955. No fewer than 38 people were in attendance, including Frank Spaven as one of four SDD representatives.

The eighth item of a lengthy agenda concerned 'The Re-shaping of British Railways'. It was reported that the Transport Group of the Panel had discussed the Beeching Report, and were deeply concerned about the proposals in and implications of the report, 'particularly as to the adequacy of alternative facilities'. Reference was made to the fact that BR's surveys, on which the Beeching Report's conclusions were partly based, had taken place in April, 'a time of year when there were fewest passengers in the north'.

Foreshadowing a lengthy and ultimately pivotal querying of the closure proposals, the meeting minutes record that:

> The Chairman suggested and it was agreed that the Panel should express their firm opposition to any rail closures in the absence of adequate alternative arrangements. They welcomed the Government's assurance that no railway line in Scotland would be closed unless there was adequate alternative provision for passenger and freight transport. But they doubted whether adequate alternative facilities did exist at present, either in roads, amenities, equipment or co-ordination of services. The Panel also noted that the Beeching Report in its general statements and, in particular, those relating to rural areas, appeared to run counter to expressed Government policy in regard to Highland development.

The Highland case soon got a nationwide airing. The *Inverness Courier* reported on 26 April that a conference at Caxton Hall in London organised by the National Council on Inland Transport – and attended by 'between 300 and 400 delegates, among whom was Mr Charles Will, depute Town Clerk of Inverness, who had acted as clerk to the recent conferences on Highland transport' – had been 'violently opposed' to the Beeching proposals. A resolution from the District Councils' Association for Scotland was passed unanimously, stating *inter alia* that the Beeching proposals 'should not be accepted by Her Majesty's Government unless alternative services with adequate roads are provided'.

On 24 April, MPs of all parties had been lobbied at the House of Commons, and one of those present – Desmond Thompson, a member of Badenoch District Council and Inverness County Council – had told the *Courier*, as it reported two days later, that 'the delegation had gained the strong impression that if the Highlands "fought like hell" they would save the railway lines North of Inverness, even if, as expected, Parliament accepted the Report as a whole'.

The *Courier* also brought news of the Scottish Trades Union Congress at Dunoon, where Harold Wilson, Leader of the Labour Party, had stated that Beeching 'should have been asked to investigate all forms of transport so that an integrated system, with both road and rail taking their share of the traffic, could be planned'. He added that:

> ...the Government were on the one hand trying to encourage industry to go to the areas where employment was needed, and on the other hand were making it impossible for industry to do so by destroying the main transport facilities.

These were to prove to be breathtakingly cynical statements. By late 1964, Wilson was Prime Minister, and Beeching's suggestion that he should undertake a road system study, similar to that which he had done for rail, was quickly rejected, as Wilson did not want to upset road transport trade unions. This was one of the reasons for Beeching returning to ICI in 1965. In 1968 Wilson rubber-stamped the withdrawal of all rail services in the Central Borders, despite this being a designated development area with a planned 25,000 population increase. Fortunately for the Highlands, *realpolitik* was to work in the region's favour this time.

Rebellion in the House

Beeching was stirring up some unprecedented political positioning. The *Inverness Courier* of 3 May carried lengthy news of the debate on the Reshaping Report held in the House of Commons on 29 and 30 April, reporting that eight Government supporters – including Jack Macleod, MP for Ross and Cromarty – had abstained from voting in the division. Strangely, David Robertson, the Independent Unionist MP for Caithness and Sutherland – who had gone on record a number of times as backing conversion of the Far North Line into a road – had voted against the Government. More predictably, Michael Noble, the Secretary of State for Scotland – and MP for Argyll – had voted with the Government, as had Neil McLean, MP for Inverness, and Gordon Walker, MP for Moray and Nairn.

The Government motion welcoming the Beeching Report had been carried by 323 votes to 248. But, once more, Noble had been forced on the defensive, referring to the need for transport in the Highlands to be co-ordinated to avoid wasteful competition and to give an improved service. The *Courier* reported some strong hints that the Scottish Office was unconvinced by the case for closure north of Inverness:

> Mr Noble went on to say that he had been asked what alternative methods of transport he would consider adequate. "It is extremely difficult to define 'adequacy,' and I think I would be doing a dis-service to a great many people if I tried to do it," added Mr Noble. "I am quite clear in my own mind that a six or seven hours' bus journey over inferior roads is not the equivalent of a three or four hours' railway journey. I think it is too early yet to expect the Government to deploy a complete plan. We have still to have discussions with the omnibus groups. We have to look at the repercussions on other transport and roads. Obviously, in Scotland there are some special problems. The Inverness-Kyle road is totally inadequate at the moment to take modern buses.

> We have many miles of single-track roads and there is obviously a limit to the speed of building. There are problems also on the Inverness-Wick road, the A9.

I think that the position that we in Scotland and the North realise is that the Government have a duty to examine individual problems very closely indeed. But the aim must be, surely, to produce a realistic and positive improvement in our transport system.

The Church of Scotland had long taken an interest in the economic and social life of the country. On 10 May the *Inverness Courier* reported that a rail resolution put forward by The Rev. George Elliot of Ness Bank Church, Inverness – on behalf of the Inverness Presbytery's Church and Nation Committee – had been approved and would be sent to the Secretary of State for Scotland, among others. Over and above the familiar reasons for opposition voiced to date, the resolution cited a relatively unusual (but germane) objection: 'Railwaymen made redundant would find it difficult to find alternative employment in the Highlands, and if they went south in order to obtain work would be lost to the area, which is already suffering from depopulation.'

Continuing the flurry of news generated by reactions to the Beeching Report, the *Courier* of 10 May reported that the Inverness MP, Neil McLean, had issued a statement explaining why he had voted for the Government Motion on the Beeching Report. McLean, who had been criticised at Inverness Town Council's meeting on 6 May, had argued, not unreasonably, that:

…the Report is an essential preliminary to the reorganisation of our railway system which everyone knows is totally out-of-date, inadequate for present-day needs and expensive and wasteful. The present organisation and costs had to be broken down and analysed to see what was wrong. This the Beeching report has done.

As regards closures north of Inverness, to create an adequate alternative to the railways will be expensive and will take a long time; for at present the roads are inadequate even with the railways in operation, so that a great deal of money will have to be spent on improving our Highland roads. Perhaps the publication of the Beeching Report will mean that a great deal more money will be spent on roads and other communications in the Highlands than is being done at present.

BR argues its case behind closed doors

The adequacy or otherwise of alternative facilities was the main agenda item at the 29 May meeting of the Transport Group of the Highland Panel, held in the Station Hotel, Inverness, but this was preceded by a detailed explanation of the statutory procedure to be adopted for proposed closures, by Gordon Stewart, Assistant General Manager, British Railways (Scottish Region).

If no objections were lodged with the Transport Users Consultative Committee – following two separate advertisements of the intended closures in local newspapers and at the stations concerned – then BR would be free to effect the closure, within around 12 weeks of the first advertisement. While this was not recorded in the Minutes, there was, of course, no chance of there being no objections. In which case, the closure action would be suspended and a public hearing held by the TUCC, who would then report to the Minister of Transport on hardship and recommend measures, to alleviate it.

It would then be for the Minister, having first consulted the Secretary of State for Scotland, either to consent to closure (with or without conditions attached) or to refuse consent. Interestingly, the Minutes record that: 'Mr Stewart could not say at this stage when the Highland lines would be dealt with – possibly the closure of these lines would not be advertised until mid-1964.' However, as we shall soon see, the closure proposal was announced much earlier than this, almost certainly for party political reasons.

Mr J Amos, Chairman of Scottish Omnibuses, told the meeting that BR had supplied him with rail passenger figures for May and July and, having examined these figures, he did not think it would be difficult to provide replacement bus services. But he underlined the need for improved roads, with which he thought it would be possible for bus times to equal or better train times.

His forecast of faster journey times by bus would come true but not for some decades, culminating in 1991 with the opening of the Dornoch Firth Bridge, the third of three estuary crossings which would dramatically reduce the road distance from Inverness to Caithness. In 1963, he proposed:

> 4 services per day, using 36 ft. long single-deckers, experience of which had been gained on the Edinburgh/Glasgow-London service; in most cases passengers would be travelling in stages of 30-40 miles and as the call would be for speed, the service would be limited-stop, express or limited fare: comfort would be beyond question.

Travellers who had experienced the Scotland-London coach service in 1963 might have balked at Amos's latter description, and even today Inverness-Caithness coach services offer less comfort than the train, particularly on the unreconstructed sections of the A9 where tight schedules result in a sometimes bumpy and erratic ride. Amos was also confident that, with depots at intermediate points and an advance booking scheme, they could readily meet all demands, even at peak holiday periods. Having concluded his optimistic vision of a bus-based future, Amos and other transport operators withdrew from the meeting, and the Transport Group proceeded to discussion.

Mr RAH Allen of the Scottish Development Department (SDD) said that in the case of the road from Brora to Wick and Thurso (about 70 miles), his calculations showed that the road was so undercapacity that it could accommodate normal growth and any transferred rail traffic 'for the next 20-30 years or longer', but some improvements would be necessary for fast bus services.

His SDD colleague, Mr AN Sutherland, added that it was sometimes much less expensive to improve roads if the railways were closed because the rail-bed could be used (eg between Inverness and Dingwall) and that, in consequence, 'expensive improvements should wait until the closure of railways was decided'. I can guess the thoughts of the third SDD representative at the meeting – Frank Spaven, an advocate of rail development – but no comment was recorded in the Minutes.

Certainly it would have been very much his task to work on one of three fact-finding papers which the Group agreed should be prepared: in this case on 'the effect of rail closures on development', ie industry, agriculture and fisheries. The meeting also agreed that in order to carry out the Panel's remit 'they had to work on the assumption that both passenger and freight services would be withdrawn'.

The road upgrading implications

A Memorandum prepared by the County Councils of Caithness, Ross and Cromarty and Sutherland in response to the Beeching Report (undated, but thought to be from May/June 1963) revisited the familiar arguments against closure, plus the much greater safety of rail for both passenger and freight traffic. It argued that the Local Authorities 'cannot in any circumstances accept the blind application of the principles outlined in the Beeching Report to their area without due regards to the consequences of such action'.

But, as roads authorities, they were well placed to produce estimates of the cost of road upgrading to provide a practicable alternative to the Far North and Kyle lines, emphasising that 'necessary road improvements could not be carried out within a reasonable time'. How the Councils had determined so quickly which sections of road should be upgraded or diverted is unclear (although the explicit assumption was a 24-feet-wide carriageway throughout), but the sums were impressive: £3.1m in Caithness, £12.1m in Ross and Cromarty, and £3.5m in Sutherland. To these could be added the £1.4m estimated in an Inverness County Council memo dated 14 May, citing a then 39% traffic overload on the A9 between Inverness and Beauly, rising to 49% if the railways closed. The grand total of £20.1m is around £385m in today's values (and seems remarkably cheap for the mileage involved).

The Memo 'contended that modernisation of the present system mainly from the point of view of achieving economy should not be carried out without making every attempt to make the use of rail for passenger and freight more attractive to users' and then referred to five specific suggestions made by Caithness County Council for the Far North Line in a 9 May memo to Michael Noble – of which the first three had dramatic implications:

1. Closing 14 intermediate stations (including all nine between Helmsdale and Wick/Thurso), leaving just 10 open

2. Closing 11 crossing loops and associated signal boxes (including six between Helmsdale and Wick/Thurso), 'saving something like 18 signalmen and cutting journeying times considerably'

3. Closing booking offices at all stations north of Inverness except Dingwall, Wick and Thurso, with tickets issued on trains

4. Investigating fully the present staffing position 'in order to achieve all possible economies without necessarily interfering with the efficiency of the service'

5. A 'complete integration of road and rail passenger services', plus road freight services feeding into rail freight services.

These were remarkably far-sighted propositions, although not without some flaws. While closing all the stations between Helmsdale and Wick/Thurso would have worked wonders for through journey times, the experience of Rogart closing then re-opening in 1960-61 should have alerted the County Council to the difficulty and cost of providing a bus service up the single-track A897 road from Helmsdale to Forsinard. And providing any bus to isolated Altnabreac was a complete non-starter, due to its tiny population and lack of tarred road access.

Ten of the 11 crossing loops slated for closure did indeed disappear by late 1966, leaving only Forsinard between Helmsdale and Georgemas. Even allowing for post-1963 losses of freight traffic, this does support the view that there was over-provision of capacity at the time the memo was drawn up, and the level of knowledge demonstrated suggests that a railwayman was involved: possibly Provost Dunnett of Wick?

The de-staffing of all stations except Dingwall, Wick and Thurso (and Invergordon, Tain, Lairg and Brora until 1991/92) is exactly what happened in 1985, although it required the introduction of the innovative Radio Electronic Token Block system, replacing signalmen (who fulfilled a multiple function also issuing tickets, handling parcels etc) with central control from, initially, Dingwall, and eventually Inverness.

After two months of intensive campaigning and extensive press coverage following the publication of the Beeching Report on 27 March, there was something of a lull during the summer of 1963. The *Inverness Courier* of 14 June reported that the Secretary of State for Scotland had refused Inverness County Council's request for a meeting to discuss the rail closures. In his letter, Mr Noble had pointed out that as a Highland MP he was very well aware of the points the Council had raised, but he had sent a copy of their letter to the Minister of Transport. And on 21 June, the *John O'Groat Journal* reported that just 20 people had turned up at a public protest meeting in Wick the previous Saturday evening, despite it being addressed by WH Rathbone, national president of the NUR. The paper gave almost as many column inches to the Sutherland-Maclean wedding at Latheron:

> Given away by her father, the bride looked charming in a long, white dress of figured silk brocade and short veil (loaned by a friend). She carried a bouquet of pink roses and freesias. Her bridesmaid, Miss Elizabeth Stewart, Reisgill, looked delightful in a dress of pale blue figured satin with headdress to tone. Her bouquet of pink carnations made a pleasant combination.

> Life would go on, no matter what happened to the railway.

More official responses to Beeching

The Scottish Council, Development and Industry (SCDI) had been created in 1931 with a mission to 'examine and consider impartially the industrial, commercial and economic problems with which the country is faced' and to promote appropriate solutions. It had created the first industrial estate in Scotland (at Hillington) in 1938, and had been in the forefront of attracting overseas manufacturing investment to Scotland in the late 1940s.

In May 1962, SCDI'S Chairman, Lord Polwarth, had expressed concerns about the implications of the Beeching Report. And on 18 July 1963, SCDI formally submitted to the Secretary of State for Scotland a succinct three-page statement on 'The Beeching Report and Scotland'. This was a balanced commentary, beginning with a positive reaction:

> Many of the improvements proposed in the Beeching Report – for example the acceleration of freight services – are to be welcomed, and are of particular value to Scotland because of the importance of markets in the Midlands and South. Indeed if the Beeching Report is viewed solely as an analysis of the economics of the rail network considered as an isolated transport system, it serves its purpose well. It shows the changes which would produce an efficient rail service, towards which we all wish to move.

Having praised Beeching, SCDI then moved on to criticism of the failure, to date, to balance financial analysis with the bigger picture, not least economic and industrial development and employment in Scotland:

> In terms of the country's transport system, the Beeching Report is only half a report. To plan for large reductions in rail facilities without at the same time planning for large improvements in roads is unsound...To concur in the largescale withdrawal of rail services without even having specific undertakings, let alone the improvements themselves, would be irresponsible.

Interestingly, the SCDI statement observed that, 'Where the cost of making suitable road improvements appeared to be prohibitive, it might be more sensible to retain the rail service', but overall the implicit message was that once roads had been improved then the threatened rail services could be withdrawn – not the possibility that *both* might survive long-term:

> The Inverness-Thurso, Inverness-Kyle of Lochalsh and Edinburgh-Hawick-Carlisle lines should be retained until such time as provision is made for alternative roads in those areas capable of handling public and freight transport at speeds comparable with the railways. In the case of the important Edinburgh-Carlisle line such a time might well lie some time distant.

These services – and the threatened route from Dumfries to Stranraer – were described as 'the difficult lines' in an SDD memo of 23 July discussing the phasing of passenger closure proposals. And the same day, an SDD speaking brief for the Secretary of State, having alluded to problems with the Kyle road, commented: 'The road to Wick and Thurso also needs considerable improvement to measure up to the type of road transport which should replace the railway if it has to go.' The brief concluded that: 'Dr Beeching should be asked to defer action on these lines *[Far North, Kyle, Ayr-Stranraer, Dumfries-Stranraer and the Waverley Route]* so that these discussions can take place.'

A draft official paper amongst Scottish Office archive material – unattributed and undated, but almost certainly compiled in the second half of 1963 – sought, as suggested in an all-Scotland context by Frank Spaven in 1962, to quantify the wider benefits to be set against the allocated costs of the Far North Line. 'A Tentative Cost-Benefit Analysis of the Proposed Closure of the Inverness-Wick/Thurso Railway Line' attempted to test the validity (insofar as it related to social benefit in the study area) of Beeching's comment on page 56 of his report to the effect that:

> It might pay to run railways at a loss in order to prevent the incidence of an even greater cost which would arise elsewhere if the railways were closed. Such other costs may be deemed to arise from congestion, provision of parking space, injury and death, additional road building, or a number of causes *[most obviously the cost of replacement bus services, strangely omitted by Beeching]*.

'*It is not thought that any of the firm proposals put forward in this Report would be altered by the introduction of new factors for the purpose of judging overall social benefit.* Only in the case of suburban services around some of the larger cities is there clear likelihood that a purely commercial decision within the existing framework of judgement would conflict with a decision based upon total social benefit. Therefore, in those instances, no firm proposals have been made but attention has been drawn to the necessity for study and decision.' [*my italics*]

Beeching's sweeping dismissal of cost-benefit arguments in relation to the majority of threatened routes was breathtaking, not least because – in great contrast to the vast majority of his report – it does not appear to have been based on any evidence.

In any event, the cost-benefit calculation for the Far North Line estimated a net financial saving from closure of £15,000 per annum. Turning to quantification of non-railway costs arising from closure – including cost of replacement bus services, congestion, travel time, road casualties, railway unemployment, and 'loss of possible industrial development' – the paper suggested that total recurring costs (per annum, presumably) of £538,000 could be incurred, plus total non-recurring costs of £1,026,000.

It was noted that these figures excluded the 'multiplier effect', eg loss of local spending power, and the paper concluded that 'a strong case is presented for the maintenance of the railway'. Although the robustness of its assumptions and data sources cannot be verified, at the time it was almost certainly deployed as part of SDD's strong refutation of the Beeching line on 'social benefit' insofar as the railway to Caithness was concerned.

High-level lobbying

The North of Scotland Transport Conference secured a private meeting with the Secretary of State for Scotland in Edinburgh on 22 August, taking a delegation of 10, from Fraserburgh in the east, to Plockton in the west (Councillor Torquil Nicolson, who would also play a pivotal role in the 1972-74 campaign against closure of the Kyle line), and from Inverness in the south to Sutherland in the north. The note of the meeting records that the Conference Chairman, Colin Campbell, told the Secretary of State that they:

> ...represented a large body of opinion in the Highlands where the Beeching proposals had given rise to great anxiety. They had been most grateful for the public assurances given by the Secretary of State and the Prime Minister that rail closures would take place only if adequate alternative services were available. The Conference were, however, concerned as to the meaning to be

attributed to the word "adequate" and took the view that owing to their special weather and other conditions it would be very difficult to provide adequate alternatives to railways in the Highlands, and that dual carriage *[sic]* roads throughout the Highlands would be needed.

The Secretary of State had some words of comfort on the first concern, but brought realism to the road-building issue. On the question of adequacy of alternative services he suggested that the Conference need not be too apprehensive, as 'their views were not likely to be very far apart from his own. He did not, however, see any prospect of the provision throughout the Highlands of dual carriageways, the cost of which would be astronomical.'

The cost of road improvements was the subject of some detailed discussion, with the Conference delegation tabling estimates from the four northern counties totalling £13.4m. This was significantly less than the £20.1m in the earlier Memorandum produced by the counties, but was presumably in part explained by a revised assumption of 18 feet rather than 24 feet carriageway width. An important geographical elaboration of the roads argument was made:

> Cost was not the only factor limiting improvement of roads in the Highlands. As there were no alternative routes to which traffic could be diverted, there was a limit to the mileage which could be improved at the same time. The Conference felt that 15-20 years might be a reasonable estimate of the time required to complete the necessary improvements.

In practice, it was to be some 28 years before the large majority of the envisaged improvements were completed, essentially culminating with the opening of the A9 Dornoch Bridge in 1991. In 1963, the extent to which, if rail services were withdrawn, roads would then become overloaded and create a need for capacity improvements, was the subject of a paper submitted by SDD to the Highland Panel on 12 September.

It concluded that 'freight closures would generate about four times as much road traffic as passenger closures', but the survey found that 'the transfer of rail traffic to road represents an increase of 5% (one year's normal growth) or more on 420 miles of trunk and 119 miles of classified road', and consequently, 'the proposed rail closures would tend to aggravate conditions on the few routes where there is overloading already rather than to create new problems'.

The only stretches of the A9 between Inverness and Caithness where displaced rail traffic would produce an overload were from Inverness to Dingwall (42% overload) and from Dingwall to Evanton (25% overload). The report concluded that the priority to be given to the Inverness-Dingwall and Dingwall-Evanton road sections would depend on whether 'the rail bed were available' and this in turn would 'depend largely on what is decided about the future of the line for freight services'.

On the face of it, these cold statistics undermined some of the more emotional claims about road conditions made by rail campaigners, but the Highland Panel would have a much wider range of arguments to deploy.

A related issue was car ownership trends, and MoT statistics shown in an undated file from around this time, from the Scottish Development Group (comprising representatives of various ministries), provided some theoretical comfort for proponents of closure, quoting the following number of cars per 100 population:

Year	1957	1962
Caithness	10.22	16.20
Ross & Cromarty	6.90	10.97
Sutherland	10.49	15.10
Scotland	5.83	9.44

The economic impacts are explored

In July, in preparation for a paper on the impact of rail closures from the Department of Agriculture and Fisheries for Scotland (DAFS) to the Highland Panel, the Fishery Office in Wick had written to the Chief Inspector of Fisheries in Edinburgh, advising that BR was handling only 15% of fish traffic from the area (to markets such as Aberdeen, Birmingham, Inverness, London and Manchester) and that:

> The larger merchants…are none too keen on British Railways, they make out that the time factor is at fault and charges are too high. The smaller firms are quite satisfied and some of them talk in high praise of the service given. They are all, however, very much against rail closures as even the larger merchants like to feel that even if they have only a few boxes and cannot make a load they can always send them by rail (a van will be put on for an amount in excess of 15 cwts).

Here was a classic, lingering example of how under the traditional 'common carrier' requirement (only lifted by the 1962 Transport Act) BR had been obliged to accept any traffic presented to it, no matter how unsuited it may have been to rail economics. By contrast, road hauliers could 'cherry pick' what suited them. These were not sustainable traffics for a rail system charged with breaking even over a five-year period, and the transport by train of fish, with its perishability and peaks of demand, would cease in Britain by the late 1970s.

The DAFS preliminary study for the Highland Panel was submitted on 13 September 1963, seeking 'in the limited time available to obtain, by local enquiries, some picture of the present pattern of transport in the areas concerned and some estimates of the effects which train service withdrawals might have on the agricultural industry'.

The report in fact covered no fewer than 10 principal commodities (including barley, coal, fertilisers and milk), but its over-riding conclusions were that many goods then travelling by rail 'could possibly go as conveniently by road provided there were roads of sufficient standard' and 'measures would be needed to ensure that roads were kept open in winter'.

The verdicts on key agricultural commodities were not always favourable for rail, as illustrated in the case of Easter Ross potatoes (50% of which moved by rail): '...consignments sent by road are off-loaded at their destinations in markedly better condition than those sent by rail. Rail travel involves double handling at both ends of the journey.'

Ironically, the study also concluded that the part of the agricultural industry which appeared most likely to be affected by closures was that dealing in livestock, especially cattle: a highly-seasonal traffic which disappeared from the reprieved Far North Line in less than three years' time.

The report found that 'the cost of certain goods would be significantly higher were they delivered by road rather than by rail', but this could not take account of the selective pricing which BR would increasingly introduce to reflect more accurately the attributable costs of handling different types of traffic.

From today's perspective, the report's references to rail transport (by passenger train) of eggs from the Invergordon Egg Packing Station seem extraordinary:

On average over the summer season 30 to 100 dozen eggs daily are consigned from Invergordon, and all go by rail because, with trains daily, the eggs are at their destinations the following day...One could not expect road hauliers to quickly deliver small quantities of eggs from Invergordon to Scourie, Bettyhill, Gairloch and Kyle of Lochalsh, when eggs are probably the only commodity requiring transport from Invergordon to these places.

Given that three of these four destinations were not on the railway, and that road collection was also required at Invergordon, the idea that this could be an ongoing rail traffic was, at best, highly questionable. And the admission that the packing station 'last year made a profit of £39 on a turnover of £35,000' perhaps said it all.

Marples is shaken

At the Scottish Development Department on 11 September, Frank Spaven had submitted a note to the Transport Group of the Highland Panel, commenting, in relation to the Far North and Kyle lines, that:

> A general point…is that the railway provides the only fast, reliable link with the South for through bulk traffic in a region which is the most remote and isolated on the mainland of Britain and where its complete closure – perhaps even the present threat of closure – is, to put it at its lowest, likely to restrict the growth of industry and tourism. This is also the view of Board of Trade officers.

The latter comment caused some inter-departmental ructions, with CJA Whitehouse writing on 29 September to RA Fasken of the Department of Agriculture & Fisheries for Scotland to advise that he was 'rather surprised' by the statement', which 'certainly cannot be represented as the official view of the Department', since they did not have 'any evidence that complete closure would restrict the growth of industry and tourism'.

On 20 November 1963, Ernest Marples sent a short personal memo to Michael Noble, in response to the latter's concerns that six closure proposals (of which five were unidentified) should be quickly resolved. Marples indicated that, based on the figures available, five were straightforward:

> But you will see that Inverness-Wick/Thurso shows an apparent annual saving of only £6,000 on a turnover of about £200,000. I shall be pursuing this with Beeching, and there may be more behind the figures than meets the eye.

This unexpected bottom line was explored further in an SDD memo of 28 November commenting on financial information gathered for the TUCC:

> The Inverness-Inch *[sic]* picture that now emerges is one that we have rather expected; the contributory revenue in other parts of the system seems particularly likely to be significant when long lengths of passenger closure are under consideration. If this figure stands, the proposal to close seems ridiculous; *indeed it has shaken the Minister so much that he is probing it. (my italics)*

Despite all the effort, in the Highlands and beyond, which had since 27 March gone into official and unofficial opposition to the Beeching Report's closure proposals, there was little doubt amongst campaigners that they would in due course be confronted with the statutory process of specific closure proposals for individual routes, including the lines to Caithness and Kyle from Inverness.

The 'phony war' would end on 27 November 1963, but not before a remarkable organisation took shape in the small Ross-shire town of Invergordon.

CHAPTER 9: ENTER MACPUFF

According to Phil Durham, in *Highland Whistle Blower*:

It was only after a notice appeared in the press, that on 9th and 10th March 1964 in the Town House, Inverness the Scottish TUCC would hold its meeting to hear objections to the proposed abandonment of passenger services north and west of Inverness, that any concerted attempt to co-ordinate action to oppose such closures began. An informal meeting held in the Royal Hotel, Invergordon, since burnt down, agreed to form an association *[later to be branded 'MacPuff' by this new 'Vigilantes' group]* to that end. Most of those attending that meeting were farmers in Easter Ross. (*my italics*)

Durham's recollection was partly flawed (his health was failing while completing the book, and he died just two weeks after its publication). A broadly based opposition to closures, including local politicians and MPs, had formed across party lines throughout the summer of 1963, in part through the North of Scotland Transport Conference. The first informal meeting of the 'North of Scotland Vigilantes Association'[51] appears to have taken place at Invergordon Distillery office on 25 November 1963, Durham recording that:

Prominent at that meeting were two men: Mr William Munro, proprietor of the Royal Garage, main Rootes Group dealer for the North of Scotland and friend of Sir William Rootes, and Mr Frank Thomson, a charismatic bearded figure who had been active in developing at Invergordon the largest grain distillery in Europe.

Durham later elaborated on the background of this latter adventurer, who in due course would make Highland headlines.

Chairing both the Scottish Vigilantes Association and the Transport Conference of Scotland, Frank Thomson, a chartered accountant incomer from Aberdeen, had earlier persuaded Max Rayne of London Merchant Securities to put up the finance to take over the partly built grain distillery at Invergordon and complete it. With an annual capacity of ten million gallons of whisky, this became the largest grain distillery in Europe. Thomson had then formed a distillery pipe band which won the European Pipe Championship, taken over the ailing Ross County Football Club and then successfully tempted the mighty Glasgow Rangers team to travel north and play a friendly game on their Dingwall park, and was later to be elected Rector of Aberdeen University, no mean self publicity performance.

Reflecting on these times in 2015, Easter Ross farmer Reay Clarke – who, as the Chairman of the Easter Ross branch of the National Farmers Union, knew all the key MacPuff protagonists – described Frank Thomson as, 'tall, large as life, very personable, always well dressed – a great bloke for getting things done, but a chancer rather than a rogue'. It was a remarkable demonstration of the then importance of the railway to agriculture that a majority of the original Vigilantes group were farmers. However, public-spiritedness was also a key factor.

The surprisingly brief Minutes of the 25 November first formal meeting of the Vigilantes made no mention of the organisation's objectives, but recorded that 10 people were in attendance (including Phil Durham) and that Frank Thomson was appointed Chairman, William Munro Vice-Chairman, and Mr Fitz Herbert Wright Secretary and Treasurer. Durham *[ibid]* described the latter as 'an incomer to the area…an old Etonian, who travelled round in a vintage Rolls Royce and claimed, quite erroneously as it proved, to be on friendly terms with many of the old Etonians in the Government'.

Closure is formally proposed

Wednesday 27 November brought the long-awaited announcement, on posters at all stations from Inverness northwards, and over the next few days in adverts in the local newspapers, that:

> The British Railways Board hereby give notice, in accordance with Section 56 (7) of the Transport Act, 1962, that on and from 2nd MARCH 1964, they propose to discontinue all railway passenger train services between INVERNESS WICK and THURSO, and to withdraw all passenger services from 24 stations.

The advert advised that any user of the rail service 'and any body representing such users' could lodge an objection with the TUCCS in Glasgow within six weeks of 7 December 1963, i.e. not later than 20 January 1964.

If *any* objections were received by 20 January, then the closure process would be suspended, and BR would not be able to close the line on 2 March. Six months previously, Gordon Stewart, BR Scottish Region's Assistant General Manager, had speculated that the closures would not be advertised until the middle of 1964.

The reason for the notices going out much earlier are revealed in *Beeching: the inside track* (2012) by Robin Jones. This unique insight into what went on inside BRB Headquarters at 222 Marylebone Road, London, while the Reshaping Report closures were being planned and progressed, is in part based on a series of interviews with John Edser, then believed to be the last surviving member of Beeching's planning team. Under the section heading 'Get the big ones in first', Jones records:

Some of the closures in the Beeching report were political dynamite. If the report had been followed to the letter, there would have been no rail services north and west of Inverness, and Wales would have lost its Central Wales Line. There would have been a huge and immediate backlash from Scottish and Welsh politicians if such lines, though clearly big lossmakers, were closed.

Surely Beeching cannot be criticised here. He was asked to identity lossmaking lines, and his report duly did. It was up to the TUCCs to recommend keeping them open if there were grounds of hardship, and the minister to make that decision on social or economic grounds.

The ministry was clearly geared up to rejecting the political non-starts *[sic]* in the Beeching record *[sic]*.

John [Edser] recalls: "There was an extremely astute lady principal from the ministry, a Miss Fogarty, who was in charge of Wales and Scotland."

She said 'please get the regions to put these big closures in first, because they are almost a racing certainty to be refused, and therefore if we put refusals out quickly, people might think it was not going to be as horrible as they imagined under the original Beeching proposal.'

"That was political astuteness. We did so, and we got a lot of closure refusals."

The Vigilantes gear up

Back in the Highlands, under the headline 'Complete Extinction North of Inverness', the *Inverness Courier* reported on 29 November that: 'Throughout the Highlands there is widespread dismay, not to say consternation, about the drastic nature of the proposals', and that the Highland Transport Conference would be meeting the following week to decide its next course of action. And here we find the *Courier's* first report – and probably the only neutral one – about the organisation which would become known as MacPuff:

The group of Ross-shire business men, known as the Invergordon Vigilantes Association – of which Mr Frank Thomson, managing director of an Invergordon distillery, is chairman, and Mr Fitzherbert Wright, Dingwall, a former director of London and North-Eastern Railway is secretary – are also marshalling their forces to fight the closures.

Buried deep in another of Evan Barron's lengthy editorials was an interesting insight into the party political dimension of the controversial proposals:

In fact, if the new [Highland Transport] Board does not answer Highland requirements, the Government stands an even better chance than they already do – a chance, moreover, which will become a certainty should all the railway proposals be approved – of losing every Unionist seat in the Highlands, if not in the whole of Scotland.

Politics were also to the fore in that day's *Ross-shire Journal's* lengthy news report on the railways.

> A meeting of the Vigilante Association was held on Monday evening [the 25th], and afterwards Mr [Frank] Thomson said they were endeavouring to appoint an agent in every town and village beyond Inverness affected by the closures, in order to recruit members.
>
> When Mr Thomson informed the conference of the actions taken at Invergordon, he was cheered. He stated that his group were fed up listening to the politicians on both sides and in the middle, and thought now the time had come for them to take some positive action outside the political arena.

The minutes of the Vigilantes' next meeting on 29 November devoted to 'Chairman's remarks' would have done the Soviet Union's Politburo proceedings proud:

> The Chairman gave the meeting a very interesting talk and all members found themselves in full agreement with the plans he outlined. The meeting felt after listening to the Chairman that the Vigilantes would soon be speaking with the united voice of all Scotland north of the Firth of Forth.

A MacPuff campaign publicity poster, as designed in late 1963 by a Mr Shearer, an art teacher in Invergordon, for the North of Scotland Vigilantes' Association. Richard Ardern collection

The campaign spreads

On 3 December, the *Inverness Courier* reported a repetition of the by now familiar argument that, while the railways must be reprieved, by implication they could be closed once major road improvements had taken place.

The Unionist MP for Inverness, Neil McLean, had issued a statement in which he said: 'The British Transport Commission's *[sic, although the organisation no longer existed]* proposals, now published, stating their intention to close the Inverness-Kyle and Inverness-Wick lines should be resolutely opposed, for their closure now would be a most retrograde step for the Highlands'. His opinion was that there was an 'overwhelming special case' for keeping the railways 'open at this time and for a number of years to come, whatever may happen to some of the Branch lines in the south'.

Meantime, in his editorial column under the headline 'No time to lose', Evan Barron was exhorting readers on at least two fronts: first, to lodge written protests 'in vast quantities' to the TUCC by the 20 January deadline, and second, in the case of Government supporters, 'to refrain from voting for a Unionist candidate who is not pledged to the hilt to do his utmost, even to voting against the Government, to ensure that not a single one of these closures takes place'. And now we come to the first, of many, harsh words aimed at Frank Thomson's group:

> The Highlands may be slow to act, but when they gather themselves together to rise in righteous wrath over such an outrageous injustice as the removal of their rail services, their unique fighting qualities come to the fore, and they stop at nothing as they press on towards their goal. For that reason we are not enthusiastic about the title, "Vigilantes," which the group of opponents in the Invergordon area have called themselves, for it savours too much of melodrama and precautions against desperadoes, villains and hooligans rather than fitting a body girding itself to fight for its life and its lifeline against blind bureaucracy.

The Highland Panel had been taking a great deal of interest in the proposed closures and, although his letter cannot be traced, the Chairman, Lord Cameron, seemingly wrote to the Secretary of State for Scotland the day after the closure notices had been posted. Michael Noble's reply of 4 December sought to give a variety of assurances: first, on the suspension of closure proposals once objections to the TUCC had been lodged, and then:

> I do appreciate that the Highlanders are worried about the future of their railway lines, but it is now up to them in the first place, if they are users, to place their representations as regards hardship before the T.U.C.C. and then the hardship question will be properly thrashed out. In addition, local authorities and others affected can make representations to the Minister direct about matters outside the scope of the Consultative Committee. I can assure you that we are anxious that the Highlands, like the rest of the country, have the best practicable transport service.

These read like the words of a Minister acutely aware of a growing political storm and keen to find a way through it. And a new symbol of the fight against closures was about to enter the public consciousness, in the shape of 'MacPuff', as recorded in the Minutes of the 7 December Vigilantes meeting:

> Mr Thomson then welcomed Mr Shearer *[an art teacher from Invergordon, whose father was a train driver in Wick]*, the designer of "Macpuff" *[sic]* and said he would like the committee to give "Macpuff" a vote of confidence. It was generally felt that the symbol would appeal to the public, but there was a danger that we might be interpreted as being frivolous and irresponsible by some sections of the press, and in this connection it was agreed to keep in abeyance the "Macpuff Marching Song".

The words of the song do not appear to have survived, but Phil Durham *(ibid)* observes that the MacPuff logo was accepted 'not without some reservation'. The meeting also heard that no fewer than 10 public meetings had been organised for the remainder of the month, seven of them in towns served by the Far North Line, thus demonstrating that the Vigilantes could – unsurprisingly, as a group of businessmen – move much more quickly than their elected local authority counterparts.

One interested observer was Rae Montgomery who, following completion of his period of management training, was posted to the Northern Division office of BR Scottish Region in Inverness from September 1963 until February 1965. In early 2016, he recalled these heady times:

> I remember thinking that the Vigilantes were "over the top", with the MacPuff image appearing to trivialise their case, and I recall some derisory comments in the Traffic Manager's Office apropos the "Village Aunties"! I don't recall how Mr Herbert, the BR Divisional Manager, categorised Frank Thomson, but Eddie Thompson, the Commercial Manager, was hand-in-glove with Thomson, and made frequent visits in a chauffeur-driven BR car to Invergordon Distillery, which was of course a major customer of the railway.

Open – but one-sided – warfare

It is hard to summarise the range of attacks on the Vigilantes in the several thousand words of the *Inverness Courier* editorial of 6 December, but some flavour comes from his opening statements on the Inverness meeting of the Executive Committee of the 'Northern Transport Conference' held on 3 December:

> ...it achieved nothing but making the Highlands a laughing-stock in the eyes of the world, we are compelled [to deal with the meeting] in order to prevent the tomfoolery from doing irrevocable havoc to the Highlands' just cause and case.

Barron then went on to attack the Conference for:

> ...accepting a comic-cuts cartoon character, rejoicing under the wonderful name of "Macpuff" – in this day and age of the diesel, too, be it noted! – as the symbol on the banner under which the Highlands are to fight to save their railways.

He indicated that the name was greeted by the audience with 'an incredulous titter' rather than the 'enthusiasm' which a national daily had reported. Barron felt that the new name would reveal Highlanders 'as a set of half-baked nitwits' and reduce the campaign 'to the level of a children's bear-garden'. He then named as 'responsible for this unpardonable state of affairs', the Vigilantes, 'whose representatives at the Inverness meeting, were two *incomers'. (my italics)*

The editorial continued that these two – Thomson and Fitz Herbert Wright – had 'got away with... control of the meeting, and also of the administration of the conference', in the latter case because the meeting had agreed that, with common aims, the Vigilantes should absorb the secretariat of the conference.

As we shall see, this trenchant *Courier* criticism of the Vigilantes would not abate. It was to have no practical impact on the changed make-up of the ultimately successful campaign against closure. But what was driving Barron's antipathy? The prominence of two incomers to the Highlands, Thomson (from Aberdeen) – in particular – and Fitz Herbert Wright (from England), do seem to be part of the explanation for his vitriolic attacks on the new group.

The Scottish Office gathers evidence

Following the publication of the Beeching Report, the Scottish Development Group, comprising representatives of various ministries, had been evaluating the planning and regional development implications of the proposals. An SDD paper, dated '12/63', on 'The Dependence of Industries and Services on the Inverness-Thurso/Wick Railway' was accompanied by a compliments slip, addressed to a Mr Lorimer and a Mr McBain, and signed by Frank Spaven with the handwritten comment: 'Please let me know by return if you take exception to any of this!'

Spaven's paper indicated that, with help from County Development Officers in Caithness, Sutherland and Easter Ross, a sample of 31 industrial and service firms, mostly employing 20 to 100 workers, had been surveyed. Among the key points emerging were:

> Of 15 firms who mentioned parcels services, nearly all said they were entirely dependent on passenger trains for next-day deliveries of perishable goods in the South or receipt of urgently required spare parts etc., from the South.

Easter Ross farmer Phil Durham was one of the leading lights in the 1963-64 MacPuff campaign, and continued to promote the case for Highland rail service enhancement through to the late 1960s. Richard Durham collection

Half of the 25 firms using freight transport make some appreciable use of the railway. Nine of them are primarily or entirely rail users (over 60 per cent of their traffic) including the Atomic Energy Authority, Invergordon Distillery, Caithness Glass, Brora Woollen Mill, Woolworths and car deliveries to Mackay's Garage, Dingwall and Thurso.

Of 20 firms whose managers or staff interviewed were concerned with passenger services, about a quarter rely primarily on railway services, another quarter use it equally with other forms of transport and about a half use it when the roads are blocked to cars in winter or the plane (from Wick) is not operating or they reported a small proportion of users among summer visitors.

In the latter vein, among six hoteliers surveyed, the proportion of summer visitors arriving by train ranged from 'very few' to 'fully a third'. The final version of Spaven's paper – submitted to the Highland Panel on 29 January 1964 – included all the above analysis, and concluded (in slightly stronger terms than his original draft, following the consultation with colleagues) that:

It would appear that road transport agencies could only take over from the railway without serious damage to many existing businesses in the area if they had help from air and sea services and were properly organised and had improved roads, reliable in winter. Even then, an appreciable proportion of businesses would find it difficult or impossible to make an adjustment; the range of new types of industry and other developments would apparently be restricted; and other social costs would be incurred.

So here we have just the kind of dispassionate, evidence-based arguments which the Government needed to link with the powerful political case for reprieving the railway. It seems likely that this evidence would also have been fielded at the Highland Panel, to which Spaven was an SDD advisor. And that Government-appointed body would very soon make a dramatic intervention.

A major setback for the Government

The *Inverness Courier* of 10 December reported what would prove to be a pivotal development in the closure proposal saga:

> On Friday, after meeting at Inverness, the Highland Panel announced that if, in spite of certain assurances given, the lines north and west of Inverness were closed to passenger traffic as proposed by the British Railways Board, the Panel would resign.

At a press conference after the meeting, the Chairman, Lord Cameron, said the Panel felt that if the closures took place they would strike a grievous blow at the economy of the Highlands:

> "The Panel further felt", continued Lord Cameron, "that if in spite of these assurances the closures took place there would be little purpose in their continued existence, and they have so informed the Secretary of State. They did not consider that the policy of the Government, declared in White Papers of 1950 and 1959 could be effectively implemented; far less could any further development take place."

This must have had a major impact on the Government. An eminent judge and the advisory body which he chaired had given an uncompromising ultimatum. And the *Courier* that day reported a further blow, from a leading Unionist peer:

> The programme of rail closures for Scotland must be delayed, said Lord Polwarth, chairman of the Scottish Council (Development and Industry) last week: The Scottish Railway Board has announced a long list of proposed closures of stations and lines. If these take place when suggested, it will be a most serious situation. We are deeply concerned at this possibility…if the programme of closures takes place as proposed, it will mean that our case has been ignored, carefully considered and soundly based though it was. We cannot allow the projected Highland Transport Board to be faced with a fait accompli once it comes into operation. That is what will happen if some of the principal Highland lines are closed on March 2nd as proposed.

Polwarth went even further: 'While regretting the need to resort to such procedures, the Scottish Council has no alternative but to encourage individual objections', then supplying the TUCC address for objections on the grounds of hardship. This was way beyond SCDI's remit, but it must have sent an even more powerful message to Government. The *Courier's* editorial was in no doubt that the message was getting through:

> ...it is clear that the Government have become alarmed by the growing strength and force of the campaign which we ourselves, along with most of the local authorities and others in the North, have been waging ever since the first hints of what Dr Beeching and the Government were proposing leaked out.

In an unusually brief editorial on 13 December, Evan Barron emphasised the importance of an early delegation to the Prime Minister, ideally led by the Convener of Inverness County Council, Sir Francis Walker CBE, who, he reminded readers, was President of the Inverness Unionist Association. Barron suggested that:

> Surely he, if anyone, can capture the ear of the Prime Minister, the more so as in the general election next year the Government will lose practically every Scottish seat they hold at present unless they change their attitude and treatment of this country.

Here again is a reminder of just how embedded the Unionist (for which, read Conservative) Party then was in national and local politics in Scotland. And this was to be a key factor in the reprieve of the railway.

A reprieve in the offing

On 17 December, under the headline 'Highland Anger Rising', the *Inverness Courier* reported that:

> Throughout the North anger is mounting over the threatened closure of the railways. At the weekend Ross-shire Unionists called for the resignation of Mr Michael Noble, Secretary of State for Scotland, and Sir John Macleod, M.P. for Ross and Cromarty, announced that, if the closures took place, he would resign the Unionist whip and become an Independent Member.

A perfect storm was breaking over the Government. And on 20 December, the *Courier* reported, from the other side of the political spectrum, that Inverness Trades Council had sent a resolution to the TUCC opposing the closures, citing the argument that: 'Without these essential social services the people of this vast area concerned will have to endure siege conditions when winter blizzards make the roads impassable.' Elsewhere the paper reported that:

> Earlier in the week two Scottish newspapers reported that the Government intended to step in and prevent the closing of certain railway lines to passenger

traffic, including the Inverness-Thurso-Wick and the Inverness-Dingwall-Kyle of Lochalsh lines. No official confirmation has yet been forthcoming.

Behind the scenes, there was certainly evidence that the Scottish Office view was now almost diametrically opposed to the line which it had been taking 21 months earlier, with a 19 December memo from CJA Whitehouse noting that: 'Mr. Haddow *[a senior civil servant]* seemed confident that the Inverness/Wick line and the Dumfries/Stranraer line would be safeguarded on political grounds.' He would be proved right on the Highland route but – sadly for Galloway folk – mistaken on the future of the 'Port Road', which closed in 1965.

That day's *Courier* editorial returned to the fray, attacking what had now become the Scottish (as opposed to North of Scotland) Transport Conference, for:

> ...allowing itself to be stampeded into taking orders from the bumptious self-styled "Vigilantes," headed by two intruders into the Highlands, one the Aberdonian managing director of a new distillery at Invergordon *[an inadequate description of what was emerging as the biggest grain distillery in Europe]*, and the other a director of the long-defunct London and North-Eastern Railway Company.

On 20 December, the *John O'Groat Journal* reported that a public protest meeting in Wick, chaired by Provost Dunnett, had heard from him that 'the withdrawal of the passenger service was only the first phase; he believed the second would be the withdrawal of the freight service'. The meeting was also told that 60% of the materials going to Dounreay went by rail, and was reminded of the importance of the railway to the fish and livestock trades. The National Farmers Union representative, David B Miller, wisely suggested that if the railway was not paying its way, then the service should be streamlined and run on an efficient basis. As the Journal reported: 'Expensive luxury dining cars could be dispensed with north of Inverness and snack bars providing light meals could be substituted.'

Within the civil service, the political pressure was also building. An SDD internal memo of 20 December from W Baird to a Mr Russell indicated that the Secretary of State had asked Sir John Greig Dunbar, Chairman of the TUCC for Scotland, 'if administrative arrangements could be made to ensure that the most sensitive Scottish lines could be dealt with by the S.T.U.C.C. as quickly as possible. He had in mind particularly the Inverness-Wick, Inverness-Kyle and Stranraer-Ayr lines.' Sir John had said that he 'would certainly do all he could to achieve this'.

The *Courier* of 24 December reported that the meeting of the North of Scotland Transport Conference in Inverness on 20 December had been:

...held in private because there were divided views about the following proposal on the agenda:- "in view of the widespread public reaction in Scotland to further extensive rail closures proposed by British Railways, the North of Scotland Transport Conference should now be reconstituted as the Transport Conference of Scotland with its headquarters and secretariat, say, in Perth."

Reading these accounts more than 50 years later can be bewildering, particularly in the absence of any surviving witnesses to the events. Clearly, there was a variety of campaigning tensions at play, and some of the participants may well have had dual motivations for their involvement. But there was a bigger

Traditional practice not yet feeling the impact of Beeching: a barrow load of parcels and mail comes off a northbound train at Helmsdale in November 1963. Frank Spaven

picture within which the campaign was operating. The same day's *Courier* reported that the new Highland Transport Board at its first meeting – in Edinburgh, of all places – had 'agreed to give first priority to the question of rail closures'.

Reflecting a recurring theme about temporary reprieve of railways, the Board's Chairman, Mr RHW Bruce of Shetland (as far as you could get from a railway in the Highlands & Islands) had said that the Board considered it to be self-evident that no part of the British Isles could claim that they must for ever have a railway, regardless of how little it was used and of *road improvements to the district*.

The Vigilantes increase the pressure

It was not until its 27 December edition that the *Ross-shire Journal* reported that on 13 December a 'large and enthusiastic meeting against the proposed closure of the railways' had been held in Tain by the Vigilantes, 'who were part of the Northern Transport Conference'. The main speaker was the well-known local author, Eric Linklater:

> Those bureaucrats, who had ruled their lives had talked about alternative services. Passengers, who wanted to go from Inverness to Wick, were faced with a journey of over 10 hours by bus. Did they call that a reasonable substitute? He would like to see Mr Marples or Dr Beeching do the same journey by bus, and would gladly pay their fares for the pleasure of seeing them suffer.

Ten hours was a fiction (the latter, of course, being very much part of Linklater's working life), as even in the mid-1950s the bus journey (including several changes) took under eight hours. And the replacement express bus service cited by BR in its closure proposal involved journey times of less than six hours from Wick to Inverness. But this was fair game in a popular and populist campaign against what was seen symbolically as an attack on the entire Highland region. And the *Journal's* editorial that day took up this wider theme:

> Here in the Highlands much that is vexatious to life and living has yet to be swept away. The greatest danger at the moment is the proposed closing of railway lines North and West, the campaign of opposition to which gains momentum daily. M.P.'s *[sic]*, local authorities and the go-ahead Vigilantes, to name but a few, must be supported to the hilt in order to secure victory in 1964 for the retention of these lines. Defeat is unthinkable considering what is really at stake.

There was no comfort there for Evan Barron and his relentless criticism. At their 28 December meeting, of what was now the 'Scottish Vigilantes', Frank Thomson could report to the other 10 people in attendance that, at the recent Perth conference, 'support from all parts of the country had been forthcoming', while the 4 January meeting Minutes record that: 'Mr (Colin) Campbell reported that he hoped to have a meeting with the Prime Minister in January.' Clearly, the group was well-connected in Unionist circles, and benefited from the position of Prime Minister now being held by Borders landowner Sir Alec Douglas-Home, MP for Kinross and West Perthshire, who had taken over from Harold Macmillan in October 1963.

The previous day's *Inverness Courier* editorial had once again reminded those readers who were regular or casual users of the railways north of Inverness to make sure they submitted objections to the TUCC by the 20 January deadline. But, as well as this very practical suggestion, Evan Barron could not resist making another jibe against his current *bête noire*:

> We hope, too, that "Macpuff" and his sponsors, will not wreck the Highlands' chances by the way in which they are conducting their campaign, for ridiculing the people they profess to serve and lambasting those whom they hope to defeat is no way of winning a battle which, if the Highlands are to survive, must be won. Incidentally, it will amuse our readers to know that a supporter of the "Macpuff" buffoonery has had the temerity to accuse us of trying to split the Highlands by opposing it!

Perhaps at the time, in an era of limited alternative media sources, it did amuse some of the *Courier's* readers. However, seen from today's perspective, it is hard not to conclude that Barron was more of a divisive element in his unwillingness to accept that he had lost the argument about campaign tactics.

Many local folk – probably a majority of whom rarely, if ever, used the lines north of Inverness – would have been more interested in the contents of the traditional all-advertisement front page of the *Courier*. 'From Russia with Love', starring Sean Connery and Daniela Bianchi, was showing at the Playhouse Cinema, while more basic fare was available from Mario's on the Eastgate, where 'firm tomatoes' were 2/9 per lb and Golden Wonders 3/9 a stone, with an added bonus of 'Regal Stamps with All Purchases'. In the world of mass entertainment, the 'Record Rendezvous Top Ten' had the Beatles at No.1 with 'I want to hold your hand', and at No.6, my then particular favourite, 'Glad all over' by the Dave Clark Five.

The *Courier* had a long tradition of carrying only adverts on the front page. The first issue of *The Inverness Courier and General Advertiser for the Counties of Inverness, Ross, Moray, Nairn, Cromarty, Sutherland and Caithness* appeared on 4 December 1817. The *Courier* adopted its present-day publication pattern of Tuesday and Friday in 1885, with its running being taken over the same year by James Barron, who had been on the staff since 1865. His family were to remain involved in the newspaper until 1988.

In 1919 Evan Macleod Barron, the author of *The Scottish War of Independence*, became editor, and during his period in charge, the *Courier* printed the first report on the Loch Ness monster (in 1933).

It was not until 1965 that he was succeeded by his niece Eveline Barron, who, like her uncle, reveled in lengthy and trenchant editorials – and may indeed have been the author of some of those during the Beeching era, when she served as deputy editor. In 1988, she retired from the *Courier*, and ownership passed to Stewart Lindsay, who two years later sold the business to Scottish Provincial Press. It was not until 1989 that the *Courier* ceased to carry only adverts on its front page, one of the last Scottish newspapers to do so.

Back in the Beeching saga, on the final day of 1963, an SDD memo from WW Gauld to MV Stark submitted the draft for another memo, setting out grounds for opposing certain closures. This made a number of strong points on the Far North Line specifically:

> The present study by the Scottish Development Group may well highlight, as the most promising area for industrial development in the Highlands, the triangle Inverness-Dingwall-Invergordon (roughly the original Highland Development area scheduled in 1949).

The memo also mentioned Invergordon Distillery and 'a striking development of industrial activity in the Wick-Thurso area, following the establishment of the U.K.A.E.A. installation at Dounreay'. It concluded that 'it is thought that there may well be justification for retaining the [Inverness-] Wick-Thurso line in being indefinitely and the amount of through as opposed to intermediate traffic probably justifies retention of at least some passenger services.'

This seems to have been primarily a plea for retaining freight services but, as we shall see, BR intended to withdraw freight (over which there was no Ministerial control) if the passenger closure was approved. Nevertheless, the subsequent memo (the same day) from JE Stark to RDM Bell stated:

> The Scottish Development Group have been commissioned to examine the problems affecting the economies of the Highlands and the South of Scotland where special measures may be needed to promote industrial development. In this connection, the areas served by the Inverness/Wick line, the Edinburgh / Hawick / Carlisle line, and the lines serving Stranraer may well prove to be the most promising from the point of view of promoting economic growth and it seems essential that no decision to close these lines should be taken until the present studies have been completed and the importance of these services for the future of the areas has been assessed.

Direct access to the Prime Minister

By 3 January, the *John O'Groat Journal* could report that Sir David Robertson, MP for Caithness & Sutherland and who nine months earlier had been an acknowledged advocate of turning the Far North Line into a road, was now arguing that it should be reprieved in the interests of industrial development. Citing the Dounreay nuclear plant and Corpach pulp mill examples, Sir David, who had presumably observed which way the political wind was blowing, had said in the House of Commons debate on the TUCCs:

> If, by any chance, any Minister of Transport were so misguided as to attempt to use his powers over the head of the House of Commons, the House would be bound to take action. I cannot see any Government being returned who embarked on the large-scale closures which are threatened.

This forecast was now being widely articulated, and the link between railways and development was increasingly being emphasised. But the latter, for some people, could be controversial. On 7 January the *Inverness Courier* editorial had twin targets: the 'hunting, shooting and fishing' brigade, for resisting development, and a more familiar object of criticism, but now in a new context:

> These people want to preserve the Highlands, or at least their own particular nooks and crannies, as a paradise for themselves, but there are others, equally dangerous to the Highlands, who want to see them turned into an industrialists' paradise, and to exploit the resources of the Highlands for the benefit of big business. Of course, they try to hide it by talking high-mindedly about rehabilitating and reviving the Highlands, but a closer look at the grandiose [economic development] schemes for all Scotland which the Vigilantes, led from Invergordon, publicised yesterday, boil down to a bare-faced attempt to run Scotland, and particularly the Highlands, for their own benefit. And there are still some people in the Highlands, who ought to know better, supporting these outsiders in the mistaken belief that the Highlands cannot fail to benefit from their "help".

Meanwhile the Vigilantes were undoubtedly working hard on behalf of their supporters, with committee meetings held virtually every week. The 10 January Minutes recorded success in also mobilising the public, with some 80 people at a Helmsdale meeting that week, and reported that 'Tain and Fearn District Councils had agreed to resign if the closures took place'.

Exactly one week later, the *Courier* reported that the Prime Minister had agreed to meet a representative of the North of Scotland Transport Conference. It was announced at a press conference in Inverness that arrangements had been made for the chairman of the Conference, Colin Campbell (who was also a member of the Vigilantes), to meet the Premier on 27 January at Downing Street.

The official objections lodged

On 21 January, under the strapline 'Huge Number of Objectors', the *Courier* reported that the TUCC had been 'inundated' with objections to the Highland rail closures by the previous day's deadline. In fact, there had been 490 written objections, with the TUCC later advising that block objections had been treated as one. This was a good showing, since the daily total of passengers using the service in each direction was only 180-200 on Mondays to Fridays in winter, rising to around 350 in summer.

The National Records of Scotland contain a TUCC file on the proposed closure entitled 'Copy of the more important letters of objection'. Inevitably, many of these were from statutory bodies such as local authorities, with a particularly noteworthy example being Inverness County Council's seven-page letter of objection, supported by seven pages of appendices on snow blockages and road accidents.

During the winter of 1961-62, the A9 between Inverness and Beauly had been blocked for short periods on 46 separate days, with gritting required on 59 days. The following winter, gritting had been undertaken on 55 days.

There had been 90 accidents in 1962, and 69 in the first 11 months of 1963, leading the County Council to conclude that: 'The addition of express or limited stop buses and other vehicles to the traffic on the route would inevitably increase the hazards to all road users.'

Among the most explicit expressions of 'personal hardship', which would be the TUCC's key concern, was an objection from Mrs Joan MacKinnon of Beauly:

> I am the mother of three young children who though they have travelled all over Scotland by train without any discomfort, are incapable of travelling by 'bus for more than the shortest distance without either feeling or being sick.

> Since the closure of Beauly Railway Station in 1960, I have on many occasions been subjected to the strain of watching the children grow quieter and paler as the bus journey progresses and to the embarrassment of having one or more of them vomiting in public transport.

A decade before the reopening of two stations on the Far North Line (Alness and Muir of Ord) and more than three decades before the development of commuter services to Inverness began in the late 1990s, Mrs MacKinnon argued that expansion rather than contraction was needed, and that 'an augmented rail service should be run by suitable stock between Inverness and Tain, thus relieving the manifest strain on available resources already experienced by Highland Omnibuses Ltd'.

The diverse range of organisations which had objected to closure included: the Assynt Vigilantes' Committee (from Lochinver), the Duchess of Westminster's Lochmore Estate, Golspie Shopkeepers' Association, Highland Poultry Products, TM Hunter Sutherland Wool Mills of Brora, Invergordon Ratepayers' Association, The Moray Firth Salmon Fisheries Company, the National Farmers' Union Easter Ross Branch, the Scottish Farm Servants Section of the Transport & General Workers Union, Scottish Tourist Board, Scottish Women's Rural Institutes – Ross-shire Federation, Tain Laundry, and Viewfield Lodge Hotel of Culrain.

The objector facing the greatest isolation was undoubtedly the Lochdhu Hotel of Altnabreac, whose Manager Mr C Pern indicated that 'all Mail, daily papers and milk are brought daily [by train] to Altnabreac', elaborating that:

> There is no alternative service and it seems most unlikely that any could be planned. The County road ends 11½ miles from the station, access from this point being by private road which was certainly not built to take any regular heavy traffic.

> The Hotel itself was opened in 1960 and has been instrumental in providing work and bringing families back to the area. The school has been reopened. The Hotel [catering for up to 60 people at the height of the season] also plays its part for Scottish tourism providing shooting and fishing for guests from many countries.

At the opposite extreme was the UK Atomic Energy Authority complex at Dounreay, just 13 miles due north of Altnabreac, whence objections had been submitted by the local branches of the Institution of Professional Civil Servants, the Society of Technical Civil Servants and, crucially , the Head of Administration of the Dounreay Experimental Reactor Establishment, who wrote that, 'it is estimated that about 35% of southwards travel by Dounreay staff on business and leave is by rail and that this amounts to some 1,200 return journeys each year between Thurso and Inverness'.

The inadequacy of road and air alternatives was emphasised: 'Unless something is done to improve them the closure of the railway line to passenger traffic will in our view bring hardship to many of our staff and their families.'

Taken as a whole, the submission of 490 written objections – encouraged by local authorities, the Vigilantes and local newspapers like the *Inverness Courier* – provided powerful evidence that the proposed closure of the Far North Line was a cut too far. But the campaign had to press on.

London beckons

On 21 January 1964, in a subtle dig at the Vigilantes, the *Courier's* news report recorded that it had been announced that a Scottish delegation, comprising no fewer than 11 organisations, led by Lord Polwarth, would be meeting the Prime Minister on 27 January:

> There was no mention made [at the 17th January press conference in Inverness] of the big deputation from Scottish bodies, and the press representatives at the conference were left with the impression that only Mr Colin Campbell and the conference clerk were being invited to Downing Street.

The way in which the Vigilantes' purpose was metamorphosing – paralleling in some ways the shift in title in a matter of weeks from Invergordon Vigilantes, through North of Scotland Vigilantes, to Scottish Vigilantes – is illustrated by these extracts from the Minutes of the 'Sub-Committee Meeting' of 21 January:

> The present plan of operation of the North of Scotland Vigilantes Association has been put into three phases:-
>
> Phase 1. Stoppage of the closure procedure for the railways.
>
> Phase 2. All-over Transport Plan for Scotland.
>
> Phase 3. Objectives other than transport.
>
> [The Vigilantes] may help industry in Scotland, and serve any other Scottish national and industrial interest; and generally they may assist any other scheme or organisation which has the same or similar purposes in view. The Association may join forces and co-operate with any other body with similar purposes when it seems to be expedient to do so.

Fundraising for the fast-expanding activities of the Vigilantes was to prove a bone of contention with Phil Durham, and overall the set-up – in hindsight – does look like it was a recipe for confusion. Durham *(ibid)* would later write that:

> By Christmas the temporary office set-up was so inundated with letters that volunteer members had to help cope with the frenzy of interest...As well as farming the hill farm of Scotsburn where [Durham and his wife] lived and helping my father in law with his farm accounts and the wage payments of twenty employees, I had built up and run a co-operative egg and poultry packing station but was happy to turn over its day to day running and accept the new challenge as secretary of both the Scottish Vigilantes and the Transport Conference of Scotland.

More pressure on the PM

On 20 January, Colin Campbell signed, on behalf of the North of Scotland Transport Conference, a 15-page memorandum on rail closures, written by

Eric Linklater, to be sent to the Prime Minister. This covered generally familiar ground under the headings of social objections, economic objections and counter proposals, with detailed appendices on individual routes. And lest the PM should be in any doubt about the electoral implications, the Introduction commented that:

> Opposition…is uncoloured by political feeling. Many, indeed, who are active in opposition [to the closures] have always voted in the Conservative interest, and are now faced with the unpalatable fact that loyalty to their native country may have to supersede a life-long party allegiance.

Towards the end of this lengthy document, we find the first reference to Professor ER Hondelink, whom Phil Durham *(ibid)* would later describe as a 'Transport Consultant and Economist to the United Nations and the World Bank'. Hondelink had expressed concern about the Beeching Report and had offered to produce for the Transport Conference 'an alternative Scottish Transport Plan to co-ordinate road, rail, sea and air freight and passenger services'.

This was no modest task, and Hondelink would come to represent, for a time, almost mythic qualities of astute analysis and prescription in the eyes of the Vigilantes and other rail campaigners across the country. Some hint of why this might have been, comes towards the end of the memorandum, where it is noted that the Professor had concluded that only five levels of organisation were required to run Scotland's transport, compared to British Railways' 15.

How this memorandum would go down with the Prime Minister would not be known until at least the 27th of the month, but in the meantime British Railways were busy with rationalisation plans for the Far North Line, irrespective of the ultimate Ministerial decision. On 21 January, Gordon Stewart, General Manager of Scottish Region, wrote to the Secretary of the Highland Transport Board about the finances of Highland rail services, noting that while serving fewer stations along the line would reduce costs, 'the economies obtained would be small and bear little relation to the track and signalling costs which we would necessarily retain'.

Stewart then advised that BR were going ahead with a policy of concentration on fewer freight depots, with a programme of closures in hand – but various levels of freight facilities would be retained at no fewer than 14 stations.

His letter to the Highland Transport Board also included a table on the 'Net Financial Effect' of passenger service withdrawal, the detail of which was more comprehensive than that which would be given to the TUCC. The headline figure for the Far North Line – namely an annual financial benefit of only £6,590 from withdrawal of passenger services – was the same one which had 'shaken' Ernest Marples. However, the key lines of entry in the table – surprisingly not explained by Stewart in his letter – were the 'Balance of Track and Signalling Costs' at £235,250 (for freight) and the intention to withdraw freight services if the passenger service was withdrawn.

The Beeching Report and closure proposals focused on the direct track and signalling costs specifically attributable to a passenger service. Where a freight service still operated (and was expected to continue), the assumption was that it would bear the basic infrastructure costs necessary for that service to operate, with the passenger service only bearing the cost of additional track and signalling provision required over and above that level. However, in practice, the primary role of many secondary and branch lines would increasingly be to serve the *passenger* market.

Ernest Marples had been right to probe beyond the apparent saving of just £6,590. In corporate financial terms, the real prize for BR would be to save, in addition, the net sum of: (i) the balance of track and signalling costs of £235,250. plus (ii) freight movement and terminal costs, minus (iii) the freight revenue. This net sum is not identified in the statement, but presumably would have shown an overall saving, hence the reference to the intention to withdraw freight services.

In practice, it is very unlikely that BR would have been able to realise the full £235,250 saving on track and signalling, as a freight-only operation – with reduced infrastructure – would almost certainly have been retained as far as Invergordon Distillery (just 32 miles from Inverness), but the saving would still have been substantial. Of course, the wider public expenditure benefits of savings from service withdrawals always had to be weighed against the local social costs, Charles Loft *(ibid)* commenting:

> There can be no doubt that for many people the closure of their local railway represented a significant deterioration in their quality of life. The problem officials faced was how to balance the very real hardship caused by rail closures against the notional reduction in other forms of hardship that the savings from a closure produced. Every penny spent on a loss-making rail service was a penny not available to the health service, education, defence or for tax cuts which might generate greater benefits in the long run.

It was all highly political, and on 24 January the *Inverness Courier* was able to report further dissent in the ranks of the governing party. The paper had learned – presumably from a leak – that a key local body had agreed the previous month to send the following resolution to the Secretary of State for Scotland:

The Inverness-shire Unionist Association views with dismay the proposed withdrawal of railway passenger services in the Highlands, recently announced by British Railways, and calls on the Government for drastic modification of the proposals, as no adequate alternative transport can be provided, in many cases for some years owing to the restrictive width and condition of some of the roads and the wintry conditions which prevail in the Highlands. Furthermore, the closure of these lines would be contrary to the spirit of the Government's white paper – "Review of Highland Policy".

The campaign moves to the heart of the establishment

On 28 January, the *Courier* reported that the previous day's meeting of the Scottish deputation with the Prime Minister (and Michael Noble and Ernest Marples) had lasted 'almost two hours'.

A joint statement had been issued, and '[the Prime Minister] had assured the deputation that the implications for the future economic development of different regions of Scotland would be fully taken into account before decisions were taken.' Lord Polwarth, who had led the deputation, echoed that theme in his comment that:

> [The Prime Minister] "has, I think, given us a good degree of assurance that these implications will be examined much more carefully by Ministers than has previously been the case."…Lord Polwarth added that new industries would not go to places where no railway facilities existed, and he instanced the pulp mill at Fort William and the distillery at Invergordon as enterprises which would not have materialised if there had not been a railway.

In contrast to the impression given by Colin Campbell of the North of Scotland Transport Conference at its press conference on 17 January, there had been over 20 different bodies represented in the deputation, including the Convention of Royal Burghs, the Association of County Councils in Scotland, the Scottish Counties of Cities Association *[sic]*, the Council of Scottish Chambers of Commerce, the Scottish banks, the General Council of the Scottish Trades Union Congress, the National Farmers' Union of Scotland, the Scottish Tourist Board, the Scottish Board for Industry, the Scottish Council (Development and Industry), the Scottish Council of the Federation of British Industries – and the North of Scotland Transport Conference.

Before the meeting, the deputation had submitted a memorandum to the Prime Minister, suggesting that a period of about three years should elapse before closure decisions should be taken in all but a few minor cases. It also stated that they did not accept as valid the statement in the Beeching Report 'that it must be recognised that most of the lines to be closed have already been in existence for some 50 to 100 years, and their existence has not induced development so far'.

This was surely a rare example of Beeching being cavalier with the facts, as there was plenty of evidence that bigger regional centres (of which a not insignificant number were now threatened with rail closure) had grown substantially after the arrival of the railway.

In his editorial that day, Evan Barron was not convinced by the joint communique issued at the end of the Downing Street meeting, 'couched in the jargon so familiar to all newspaper reporters at the end of private talks, local and national'. No, the deputation had 'got what is commonly called "the brush off"', and instead Barron felt that:

> Highland Unionists, if they want to see the present Government returned, should lose no time in getting together and demanding an audience – if that is the right word! – with the Premier and Mr Michael Noble in order to tell them both that as associations supporting the Government they will not be able to guarantee the return of Unionist candidates in the Highlands, or for that matter throughout Scotland, if a Government decision on railway policy relieving Scotland of her present anxieties is not forthcoming immediately.

Yet both the Inverness-shire and Ross-shire Unionist Associations had already passed resolutions deploring the proposed closures, and there can be little doubt that various Tory grandees such as Lord Polwarth had already made the party political dangers (as well as the likely economic and social impacts) abundantly clear to the Conservative hierarchy. Charles Loft *(ibid)* writes:

> [In January 1964] the chairman of the party in Scotland, Sir John George, warned the Prime Minister that

> "feelings are red hot among the executive committees and Divisional Councils throughout Scotland …on the subject. No one believes that the [Inverness-Wick and Dumfries-Stranraer] lines will in fact be closed but all are distressed and dismayed that we are giving our opponents such a long run to flay us mercilessly."

In hindsight, the 27 January meeting at Downing Street – with its demonstrably wide cross-section of Scottish business, economic, political and social interests – must have been one of the pivotal moments of the entire campaign. Loft records: 'Pressure from Number 10 succeeded in squeezing a refusal of consent to the closures north of Inverness out of Marples as soon as was decent after the TUCC reports arrived.'

The next meeting of the Vigilantes, on 29 January (with an attendance of 16), got a detailed report of the London visit from Colin Campbell, who 'said that they had been surprised at the size of the Scottish Council's delegation'. It was reported that the Prime Minister had said that:

> ...he would prefer to use the existing machinery, but that both the Scottish Council and the North of Scotland Transport Conference would have access to the Secretary of State for Scotland on social and economic grounds for resisting closures. Mr. Noble would take the decisions with the Minister of Transport and would have just as big a say, and *the primary decision would usually be made on grounds other than personal hardship.* No firm assurances were given at the meeting but the delegation felt that the strong impression made on the Prime Minister was important. *(my italics)*

It seems remarkable that Douglas-Home had suggested that the one statutory ground for objection to rail closures – hardship – would not be the main consideration in the decisions made. But back at the Vigilantes meeting, Mr A MacFadyen noted that neither of the Vigilantes' objectives at the London meeting had been achieved. There had been no 'categorical assurances that the closures up here would be stopped and the T.U.C.C. hearings cancelled'. However, Mr L Cummings pointed out that 'what happened at the meeting was far more important than what the press reported'.

Back to the Highlands

In the *Ross-shire Journal*, of 31 January the editorial revealed that the MacPuff movement had effectively had two representatives at the Downing Street meeting: not just Colin Campbell (officially there as Chairman of the North of Scotland Transport Conference), but also Frank Thomson (as Chairman of the Transport Conference of Scotland), 'both of whom are leading lights in the now nationally-known Vigilantes'. The overlapping of roles must have been striking, but – taking a very different line from the *Inverness Courier* – the *Journal* was positive about the London meeting, since, whatever the ultimate outcome of the face-to-face encounter:

> ...at least the three Ministers most intimately concerned in the dilemma created by the Beeching plans for Highland railways, were left in no doubt whatsoever regarding the havoc such plans will create in the life and living of a large stretch of territory north and west of Dingwall.

Some caution was nevertheless advised, and the editorial returned to a theme which had become characteristic of the campaign, namely the implication that the railways could eventually be closed, but only once the roads had been upgraded:

> ...vigilance will have to be carefully maintained into future days until we have a definite and forthright assurance that the railways north and west of Dingwall

will not be closed until we have completely adequate alternative transport in these areas, a scheme which might well take a quarter of a century before reaching the "adequate" required compared with what we have today.

More resignations threatened

In December 1963, the Highland Panel had staked out its credentials as one of the key players in the campaign, with its threat to resign if the closures went ahead. Since then, the Panel had been busy compiling a substantial report on the closures which, as we shall see, would be submitted to the Scottish Secretary in early March.

Meantime, one of the key building blocks of their argument was recorded in the Minutes of the Panel's Transport Group's meeting on 4 February 1964: 'The Group agreed that the proposed [replacement bus] timings were both unrealistic and unsafe in relation to present road conditions', and 'it was unreasonable to expect passengers to go on a 6-hour bus journey without refreshments and the journey time would therefore require to be increased for a "break".' 15 buses would be required to cope with through rail passengers at peak summer periods, and this would be costly, as many would lie idle in non-peak periods: although, of course, the same was at least partly true of railway rolling stock.

Further mass resignation threats emerged in the 7 February news columns of the *Ross-shire Journal*: 'If the closure of the railway passenger services to the North and West take place, there is every likelihood that members of Invergordon Town Council will follow the lead of Dingwall Town Council and Tain, Fearn and Muir of Ord District Councils, and resign.' Provost Mackay had said that 'the Council had made it quite clear that the Council could not resign as such – it was up to each individual member', and he had 'declared adamantly that he was finished with work on both the Town and County Councils if the railways were closed'. On a more positive note, the Council adopted a motion to donate £20 to the Vigilantes Association.

The Downing Street meeting was still causing reverberations, and at the Vigilantes' meeting on 7 February Frank Thomson, who was a known Labour Party supporter, 'informed the meeting that he had held several meetings and conversations with Lord Polwarth', and, in reply to a possibly pointed question from Phil Durham, 'said that he had attended the meeting with the Prime Minister partly to represent Invergordon Distillers and speak on economic growth as a member of the Scottish Council delegation'. The blurring of organisational roles was intensifying but it does not appear to have been hindering an increasingly effective campaign.

And individual members of the Vigilantes were devoting much time to the campaigning effort, with the Minutes recording that: 'Messrs. [John] Forsyth, Richardson & Durham hoped to go to the T.U.C.C. Hearing to be held in Elgin at 2.30 p.m. on Tuesday 11 February and report what they had learned to our next meeting.' Phil Durham's son, Richard, recalled in 2016 being conscripted into the campaign at the age of 12, in a very practical way: 'I remember a very long afternoon at John Forsyth's Balintraid Farm [near Invergordon] when we had to do a mail-out from MacPuff to all 659 UK MPs. I think I licked every envelope!'

John Forsyth was to be a key objector to future industrial developments on prime agricultural land in the area. From the 1970s to the 1990s he was a leading light in local and regional rail campaigning with the Scottish Association for Public Transport, working alongside Frank Spaven.

The Minutes of the 7 February Vigilantes' meeting concluded, possibly illustrating Thomson's domineering style: 'Mr. Thomson asked if anyone disagreed with the action he had taken recently and was informed that all present supported his activities.'

Phil Durham and colleagues attended the Elgin TUCC hearing (dealing with the proposed closure of the branch railway to Lossiemouth and the coast line through Buckie) to observe procedure. This allowed Durham to draft an advice letter for distribution to objectors who approached the Vigilantes, 'making clear what was needed was a personal statement of the likely effect on their lives of the abandonment of passenger rail services, with particular reference to any hardship the proposed road alternative would cause them'.

The *Inverness Courier* of 11 February reported that the Branch Line Reinvigoration Society – officially delighting in the acronym SRUBLUK (The Society for the Reinvigoration of Unremunerative Branch Lines in the United Kingdom) – had produced a memorandum in advance of the TUCC for Scotland hearing in Inverness on 9 and 10 March. Among its suggestions for reducing financial losses on rail operations were:

> Bearing in mind that the service on this rail network is far from intensive, it is questioned whether even more passing loops could not be deleted and the need for staffing some of the remaining signal-boxes thereby eliminated by redrafting the time-table slightly so that the passing of trains was scheduled to take place at the minimum number of stations which could, perhaps, be as much as thirty miles apart. Acceleration of all schedules would ease the introduction of such a scheme besides attracting more passengers.

This was sensible stuff, and was much in line with what BR did after the Ministerial reprieve. Earlier implementation of such an approach (after the 1960 intermediate station closures, for example) had been discouraged by the danger of abortive capital expenditure on track lifting and re-signalling in the event of the threat to the entire line's existence being realised.

The memorandum had further radical ideas: 'Signal-boxes retained solely to operate level crossing gates could be closed and automatic barriers introduced in their place.' And echoing the recommendation of the paper prepared by the County Councils of Caithness, Ross and Cromarty and Sutherland in response to the Beeching Report in 1963, but with a caveat, the Society suggested: 'Withdrawal of all station staff except at Dingwall, Kyle of Lochalsh, Wick and Thurso, except where needed to handle parcels, freight or for signalling, etc, all tickets elsewhere to be issued on the trains.' However, in practice, almost all the staffed stations then, and for a further two decades, fell into the category of requiring staff for these other purposes.

Gearing up for the public hearing

On 14 February, the *Courier* reported that, in the House of Commons, Ernest Marples had rejected a Labour MP's suggestion that he should dismiss the chairman of the TUCC for Scotland, Sir John Greig Dunbar (a former Lord Provost of Edinburgh). And the Inverness Area Executive of the National Farmers' Union of Scotland had also called for Dunbar's resignation, having heard that he 'had suggested that "the Highland people were trying to take the mickey out of him and his committee by lodging mass objections to the closures of the lines north and west of Inverness."

The bewildering overlap of different campaign organisations and the fast-expanding objectives of the Vigilantes were demonstrated in the Minutes of their 14 February meeting by an almost surreal reference to another form of transport which had absolutely no connection with the fight against rail closures – not just north of Inverness, but anywhere – with Frank Thomson reporting that:

> In addition to the meeting with Lord Polwarth, a discussion was held with 'Scotjet', a body formed to with the main intention of co-ordinating all air transport in Scotland. They were told that we would accept a delegate as member of the Executive Committee of the Transport Conference *[an entirely different body]* but that we would not accept public debate of Edinburgh versus or Glasgow or Prestwick versus Abbotsinch. We accept the point that Prestwick is an international airport, the only one in Scotland, and that this Abbotsinch could never become.

The latter point would, of course, prove to be mistaken, but much more striking is the evidently soaring ambition of the Vigilantes (or, perhaps more accurately, of Frank Thomson), an ambition which would crumble and disappear within just a few years. However, at this stage, the Vigilantes' core purpose was still being single-mindedly pursued, with Phil Durham's 'advice letter' sent out to objectors on 14 February. Advice for local authorities included that:

> …if a general statement is made, it should be supported with <u>actual facts</u> i.e. the number of days roads were closed or dangerous, the cost of keeping roads open, the amount of snow clearing equipment available, the number of patients who had to be sent by train due to road conditions, the number of people in any community who will suffer hardship, etc.

The Vigilantes' meeting of 20 February heard from Frank Thomson that:

> As a result of the Prime Minister's recent statement *[it is unclear to which statement he was referring]*, the Chairman felt that Mr. Marples and Mr. *[sic]* Beeching had been dealt a tremendous blow and the North line was safe for a long period.

At the next Vigilantes meeting on 29 February most of the discussion focussed on the Kyle line, but there was an interesting insight into the lifestyle of the retiring secretary of the Vigilantes, who had been a Director of the London & North Eastern Railway some 16 years earlier:

> Mr. FitzHerbert Wright insisted that he did not want any payment for the expenses in which he was involved in setting up and running the office for over two months. After being pressed to accept some recognition, he agreed that he would greatly appreciate a MacPuff mascot for his Rolls Royce and the Meeting agreed to try and arrange this as soon as possible.

Frank Thomson apparently also had a Rolls Royce, so the establishment credentials were exemplary, at least visually. This would be no campaigning handicap when the object of protest and persuasion was a Conservative Government.

The Highland Panel repeats its ultimatum

Another member of the establishment was playing a key part in the broad front of opposition, as the *Inverness Courier* of 3 March reported, under the headline 'Lord Cameron's Plain Speaking on Rail Closures'.

The Highland Panel's Chairman had welcomed the Scottish Secretary to the Panel's meeting in Inverness on 28 February with news that, 'in a few days', Mr Noble would have their report on transport in the Highlands which, in Cameron's words, was 'packed with arguments of an extremely formidable character which weighed heavily against the proposals as put forward by the British Railways Board.' A lengthy press conference followed the private meeting, as reported in great detail by the *Courier*, including reference to both general and specific issues, such as:

"So far as the railways were concerned," Lord Cameron said, "the Secretary of State was very frank with us, and gave us as much help as he could, and we, in turn, were able to present him with the Panel's reasoned views against closure at this time..."

It was put to the Secretary of State, continued Lord Cameron, that there was no evidence available to indicate positive measures being taken, or having been taken, by the railway authorities to improve the efficiency and economy of the branch lines *[sic]* threatened with closure.

Lord Cameron had re-affirmed the Panel's decision to 'oppose resolutely' the closures, their reasons, in summary, being:

(1) In the light of the evidence available to them the Panel were convinced that adequate alternatives could not be provided

(2) The financial information available did not present a true picture of the alleged financial savings from the closures

(3) The closing of major Highland branch lines *[sic]* at this point, particularly those north and west of Inverness, would not only be a psychological blow, but, even more important, an active blow to the economy and would in large measure emasculate the active measures to which the Government was already committed.

The report covered the range of arguments already widely articulated by the Panel and other objectors, and once again implied that the railways could be closed once roads had been improved:

It is clear that if the Highland railways are closed, alternative passenger and freight transport will have in the main and for the foreseeable future to be provided by road. But however modern their vehicles, however efficient their arrangements, no road transport system operating over considerable distances in difficult country can hope to compete with the railways in terms of speed, safety and regularity of service unless the roads are equal in terms of width, alignment and standard of construction to the volume and weight of traffic they are required to carry. The Panel therefore consider that the essential prerequisite to adequate alternative services is the provision of adequate roads.

Noting road overloading of 42% on the A9 between Inverness and Beauly, the Panel argued that 'ideally, roads from Inverness to Wick, Thurso and Kyle should have a minimum width of 24 feet (compared to the then typical 16-20 feet)'. Snow and ice hazards were also highlighted, as was the inadequacy of the proposed replacement bus services. The Panel had inspected some of the buses which operated the existing alternative services, 'and they are not satisfied that these vehicles provide anything like the amenities now available to railway passengers'.

Highland Omnibuses had informed the Panel that in the event of closure they would provide new 'express' services, 'from Inverness to Wick in just over

5½ hours and Thurso in 6 hours 20 minutes', but nevertheless these proposed new services 'would take approximately 40 per cent longer to Wick and 60 per cent longer to Thurso than the present fastest trains'.

The appendix to the report recorded that on Mondays to Fridays in winter the trains carried 180-200 passengers daily in each direction, rising to 250-300 on Saturdays (there were no train services north of Lairg on Sundays). In summer, 350 travelled in each direction daily on Mondays to Fridays, rising to 600-650 on Saturdays. Spread across the two to four trains in each direction daily, these were fairly modest numbers which could have been handled by buses, albeit with a significantly longer journey time and much poorer levels of comfort.

Five years later, in contrast to the good fortune of Highlanders, Borderers would rue the loss of their railway which carried 9,300 passengers a week in winter and 12,900 in summer – around five times the patronage of the Far North Line. And folk in Hawick (larger than any town served by the Far North Line) would overnight find their former journey time to Edinburgh by train increased by 80% on the bus. Such was the rough justice of rail closures in the 1960s.

In their conclusions to the report, the Panel advanced a variety of well-rehearsed reasons why they would resign if the lines north and west of Inverness lost their passenger services, including a very pointed reference to the incongruity of closure in relation to the December 1963 appointment of the Highland Transport Board:

> In the Panel's view, it is absurd that at the start of their work the Transport Board should be faced with the removal of most of the Highland railway system; and they consider that if the Board is to fulfil its remit adequately, it must be given adequate time to review existing services including consultations with all the various transport operators concerned.

A critical week

The *Inverness Courier* on Friday 6 March reported that a 'huge crowd of objectors' was expected at the public hearings in the Town House on 9 and 10 March. To put this in a wider context, three days earlier, Ernest Marples had announced his decisions on 23 rail closure proposals in England, Scotland and Wales. There were just two refusals to closure consent, these being the Ayr-Kilmarnock line and the 'Central Wales Line'. The latter was one of the few proposed closures of a lengthy rural line (88 miles). It served a sparser intermediate population than the Far North Line, and just five years later it was to survive a second closure threat, escaping the axe due to its political good fortune of passing through three marginal parliamentary constituencies.

At his London press conference, Marples had been tackled by a large body of Scottish reporters who pointed out that the Chairman of the TUCC was evidently not going to listen to all the individuals protesting against the proposed closure of the Highland lines north and west of Inverness, and had limited the hearing of evidence of hardship to two days. Marples retorted that there were 165 duplicate letters of objection:

> "Every comma and full stop was the same. Had they been inspired or were they writing as individuals?" he asked. There were also duplicated forms and 568 signatures to a "Round Robin." Mr Marples said that more weight would be attached by the T.U.C.C. to letters that came from individuals and not from a central organisation. "If we let everybody who signed an identical letter come forward, we should have the most gigantic filibuster of times *[sic]*," he added.

The *Courier's* editorial could not resist this opportunity: 'We are glad to say that for once we are in complete agreement with Mr Ernest Marples', wrote Evan Barron, citing 'the MacPuffers or Vigilantes, whatever they may care to call themselves, who have arrogantly arrogated unto themselves the leadership of the campaign against the closures'.

Also on 6 March the *Ross-shire Journal* reported the widening horizons of Evan Barron's object of derision:

> A body of seven experts has been set up to study the whole transport problem of Scotland, Northern Ireland, and the Western and Northern islands, and an executive committee of the Scottish Vigilantes Association and the Transport Conference of Scotland has been formed.

> Mr Frank Thomson, Strathpeffer, chairman of both the Transport Conference of Scotland and the Scottish Vigilantes Association, said the expert sub-committee would have a very wide remit – "much wider than the one given to Dr Beeching" – and would study the whole transport field.

> They would begin work within a fortnight, possibly in Aberdeen, and it would be about six months before they could make any report. Their task would be to put forward a complete plan for Scotland's railways.

This news story gave no indication as to how such a major piece of work would be funded.

The public hearings

As the *Inverness Courier* reported on 10 March, the previous day of the hearing (lasting from 9.30am until 6.15pm) had concentrated on objections to the Kyle line closure, while the second day would 'hear evidence about the Railways board's proposal to withdraw the passenger services between Inverness, Wick and Thurso'. The stage was set for one of the key events in the fight to save the Far North Line, but not before Colin Campbell spoke in general terms on behalf of the North of Scotland Transport Conference and the Vigilantes:

> He said that he understood that the Chairman of the Committee did not look with approval on the attitude of the Vigilantes (in organising 165 objections in identical terms), but he wished, he said, to assure the chairman that they wanted to be helpful.

Challenged by the Chairman about his attitude to the possibility of some intermediate stations, rather than the whole line, being closed: 'Mr Campbell replied that near his own home there were three stations within three miles of each other – Bonar Bridge, Culrain and Invershin. "I am sure that to have only one station would not mean any hardship in the area", he declared.' 52 years later, all three stations are still open. From the mid-1960s to the mid-1980s, the half mile from Culrain to Invershin was the shortest journey which could be made in a buffet car anywhere on the British railway system, but the two-minute journey time was a challenge to purchasing anything, never mind consuming it!

Describing the events of 9 and 10 March in the 'impressive council chambers' of the Town House, Phil Durham *(ibid)* – who, after war-time sea service and two years of submarine command, had collapsed with polio, ending up in a wheel chair for life – also gave an admission:

> When the sitting adjourned for lunch, the chamber was cleared but, being up two flights of stairs from the pavement below, I was allowed to remain inside in my wheel chair; a mistake: the temptation was too great. Here was I alone in an empty room with the railway briefing papers lying open opposite me. From what I read it was clear they were well aware of the weakness of the argument that the alternative bus services were adequate.

The public version of BR's case for closure was in a brief 'Heads of Information' document, with lengthy appendices setting out, *inter alia*, the number of passengers using the rail services, the timetable of alternative bus services, and cost/time comparisons of typical rail and bus journeys. In addition to existing local bus services, Highland Omnibuses had made application to the Traffic Commissioners for five limited-stop journeys in each direction daily between Inverness, Wick and Thurso, taking 5 hours 27 minutes to Wick and 6 hours 20 minutes to Thurso.

There were no big surprises in the BR document, with total passenger numbers echoing the headline figures already deployed in the Highland Panel's report to Michael Noble a week earlier. But Appendix C – on numbers of passengers at individual stations 'on representative days' – revealed that in winter an average of just 54 passengers used the 10.55 Inverness-Wick/Thurso train on Mondays to Fridays. On these days of the week in winter, no train generated more than 94 passengers on average – just a couple of busloads.

Saturdays were generally much busier, however, with the 16.45 Inverness-Helmsdale service averaging 130 passengers. But only single figure numbers of passengers, on average, were joining or alighting trains at the overwhelming majority of intermediate stations in winter, and at six stations – Dunrobin, Salzcraggie, Kildonan, Borrobol, Forsinard and Hoy – *no* passengers used any of the Monday-Friday passenger trains on representative days.

Summer trains were significantly busier, even on Mondays to Fridays, but particularly on Saturdays when the 09.00 from Wick and Thurso averaged 366 passengers. These levels of rail traffic would have been a major problem for any replacement bus service, but the tinier stations on the line were still generating no traffic at all, with Dunrobin, Salzcraggie, Borrobol and Hoy, showing zero passengers on *any* day of the week. It would come as no surprise that in 1965 Ministerial consent to closure of these four stations was given.

Among relatively brief news coverage of the hearing in its 13 March edition, the *Courier* reported that a human touch had been brought to the proceedings by Mrs Joan Henderson of Wick, a qualified nurse and midwife, who had travelled with patients for 13 years and who 'said that she had no doubt that the best way of moving patients was by train':

> It was warmer, steadier and more comfortable. It was also quicker in winter and more reliable. Mrs Henderson said she was in an ambulance which once got stranded at Berriedale because of ice. There was a maternity case aboard and the baby was born in the vehicle. They were there for some hours. She was also in an accident to an ambulance at Berriedale, when the male patient fractured his ribs and she had to have four stitches in a head wound. The ambulance turned over because of the icy road conditions.

In his closing remarks, Gordon Stewart, Assistant General Manager of BR Scottish Region, had:

> …commented on evidence given by various objectors regarding the speed, reliability and comfort of rail services and the general convenience of rail transport. "I believe that if all the individuals and bodies used rail transport there would have been no need to propose the discontinuance of the services – and no need for the Inquiry", declared Mr Stewart.

This was not an unreasonable point, and other hearings into rail closures would feature embarrassing moments when objectors were asked what mode of transport they had used on the day: too often the answer was not the train. Referring to a February 1964 letter in the *Times*, Charles Loft *(ibid)* records: 'A certain amount of cynicism about claims of hardship was understandable; even in Wick a local claimed that "most of the people who are making all the fuss have not used the railways for years".'

Some may have felt that the railway was 'a good thing' for the region – and important for families without cars – while in their own cases it was comforting (but not much consolation for railway economics) to know that the railway 'was there' when the car was being repaired or snow was hampering the roads. Loft writes:

> Even when opposition was based on an arguably outdated attachment to the railway as a symbol of an area's continuing significance, this itself reflected a fear of being left behind while the rest of Britain was modernised…The withdrawal of a local facility, whether rail, hospital or post office, is almost always opposed.

Board of Trade backs reprieve

Meantime, on 10 March 1964, the Office for Scotland of the Board of Trade had privately submitted its final views on the Scottish rail closure programme. In a paper of seven pages plus Appendices, the Board assembled a much stronger position than that which it had evidently held in September of the previous year. It concluded that the risk of 'harm to regional development' arose from a limited number of longer-distance route closure proposals, namely: the Far North Line; the Kyle line; the network of lines in north east Scotland; the Dumfries-Stranraer line; the Ayr-Stranraer line; and the Waverley Route from Edinburgh to Carlisle.

The Board's main worry was that passenger withdrawal would lead to freight withdrawal, with a consequent impact on industrial development. It seemed reasonable to assume that a wider Government policy objective would be to secure a rate of development which would enable 'at least something like the present population to be sustained', and therefore:

> If this is so then it would seem unwise to close the passenger lines referred to with the inevitable threat of freight closures.

> It may be argued that most industries will use road transport in any event. This is so but if the railways are closed it will undoubtedly be read by most industrialists as a sign that H.M.G. is no longer seriously concerned with the prosperity of these areas and they will act accordingly.

> The time might come when the economy in these areas is stronger and when withdrawal of rail services would cause little damage. To withdraw them at a time when studies are being carried out as to the measures necessary to ensure a balanced economy in these areas would however seem likely to prejudice the success of any proposals which may emerge from these studies and moreover seems to prejudge the outcome of these studies.

The report recommended that all the routes noted above should be retained, with the caveat that it was 'not felt essential to maintain the whole network of lines in North East Scotland', but that Aberdeen-Fraserburgh and its Peterhead branch (and presumably the Aberdeen-Inverness main line) should be kept. Echoing the thinking of Frank Spaven and others in SDD, as well as the 'tentative' cost-benefit analysis of the Far North Line the previous year, the Board also commented on the wider picture both in terms of costs to the taxpayer and the role of the railways in attracting industrial development:

> It is not part of the responsibility of this office to balance the cost of road development against the savings from rail closures but it is arguable that the consequent expenditure on roads would far outweigh the savings on railways.

> It is noteworthy that the major developments which have taken place in the Highlands in recent years, e.g. the Invergordon Distillery, the Atomic Energy unit at Dounreay, the Pulp Mill at Fort William would certainly not have taken place had rail facilities not been available.

On the issue of rail's performance against the competition, the Appendices to the Board's report referred specifically to the finding of the 1963 Highland Transport Enquiry report that: 'It may indeed be significant that in recent years bus stage services show decreases in carrying while the railways appear to be holding their own.'

The TUCC reaches a decision

The politics of the Ministerial decision must now have been blindingly obvious to all concerned, but Ernest Marples would still need the TUCC's report to give him statutory 'cover' for a reprieve that would be driven as much by economic factors – and the wider political context – as by personal hardship issues. Signed off by Sir John Greig Dunbar and by the Secretary, James Reid, the TUCC report on the Far North Line proposal was sent to Marples on 20 March 1964. It is not a document which smacks of having had much time devoted to constructing a robust and convincing argument. Perhaps the Committee had been tipped off that the Minister was strongly minded to refuse consent to closure, so a perfunctory report, but with the right conclusion, would suffice?

Half the five-page report comprised a purely descriptive account of the line, its train services, the total number of passengers, and details of the proposed replacement bus services. Two pages then covered points from the hearing on 10 March when, in addition to four Queen's Counsel representing County Councils, District Councils, Town Councils and other associations, 'every individual objector, who desired to further his or her written objections, was given an opportunity to do so'.

Among the points which had been made to the Committee were a number relating to the inadequacy of replacement bus services (summed up in just five sentences) and the unsuitability of the roads over which these would run, particularly in terms of width, gradients and curvature (but covered in only seven sentences).

A single sentence on 'Industry' provided the underwhelming argument that: 'The withdrawal of the train service would hinder the efforts of the Local Authorities to attract *light industries* to the area.' (*my italics*) Yet, the key economic development argument which had been articulated for years was that the presence of the railway had been fundamental to attracting *heavy industry* in the shape of the Dounreay nuclear plant and the Invergordon Distillery, and the railway would in due course be crucial to the establishment of the Invergordon aluminium smelter.

Admittedly, there was a later reference to a representative from Dounreay stating 'that the Atomic Station would never have been provided at Dounreay had there not been a passenger train service', but the report's cursory analysis would not have convinced a sceptical reader.

There was no prioritisation of the different arguments against closure, with some crucial points being interspersed with unsupported and/or trivial points:

- It was contended that the Tourist trade, which has been increasing annually in the North, would be very seriously affected and that the Hoteliers, Boarding Housekeepers and Local Merchants would suffer financial hardship. (There was just this one sentence on what was surely a critical topic.)

- The Proprietor of the Northern Times stated he was dependent on the passenger train service for the distribution of his newspaper.

- The activities of the various S.W.R.I's in the area would be adversely affected.

The Committee's conclusions were contained in a single sentence. This incorporated a specific detail which demonstrated the lack of proportion in the report's approach:

The Committee, after considering the written and oral objections, were unanimously of the view that, even if the proposed additional facilities were provided, there would still be widespread hardship if the passenger train service was withdrawn, particularly in the isolated communities of Culrain and Altnabreac where no form of public transport would be available.

The tiny village of Culrain was only three miles by road from the main A9 road (and generated just four rail passengers per day on winter Mondays to Fridays), and Altnabreac was a handful of houses (and generated an average of one passenger per day). Yet these stations were being advanced as a key argument against closure. It was a classic example of how not to write a report, but Marples, and the opponents of closure, got the key phrase they needed: 'widespread hardship'.

Brave new world

The Highland Transport Board submitted its Interim Report on the proposed withdrawal of services to Caithness and Kyle to the Scottish Office on 3 April, adding further weight to the arguments against closure:

> The Board do not think that, even with radical improvements to the 125 miles of road to Wick, a 4-hour service is a practical proposition; nor do they think that a journey of over 5 hours could be reasonably regarded as an adequate alternative to the 4-hour rail service.

> The Board take the view that before closure of the railway line could be seriously contemplated all sections of road from Novar Toll to Wick and Thurso, some parts of which are only 16' wide, should be brought up to standard – this applies particularly to the Struie Hill road and the section of road between Helmsdale and Latheron; and that the road between Inverness and Novar Toll which is heavily trafficked should be reconstructed to the appropriate standard.

On the freight front, the report noted that total tonnage on the Far North line was approximately 225,000 tons, of which 31,000 tons were forwarded and 194,000 tons received. By far the most significant commodities were coal (60,000 tons) and grain and malt (62,000 tons), and two thirds of the tonnage received was concentrated between Inverness and Invergordon. It was also recorded that, in the event of passenger closure, BR's present preference was to close the entire line completely, to be serviced by road from a railhead in Inverness, 'but their investigations are apparently far from complete' – doubtless indicating deliberations over the possible retention of a 'long siding' from Inverness to Invergordon in order to retain the substantial traffic to and from the distillery.

The Highland newspapers were quiet on railway matters in the weeks leading up to the announcement of Marples' decision, and even the Vigilantes had a fairly lengthy gap before their next meeting, on 15 April. Frank Thomson boldly 'told [the other 15 members in attendance] that he expected a favourable announcement on the passenger service North and West of Inverness late this week or early next week.' We do not know his source, but it was certainly accurate. The Minutes continue: 'This would complete the first phase of our fight but we must waste no time in getting on with our next phase for forming a transport plan.'

Looking back in 2015, farmer Reay Clarke commented to me that the threat of rail closures had galvanised people in the region who had perhaps been too accustomed to acceptance of 'edicts' from outwith the Highlands. 'The rail campaign changed the atmosphere', he said, and, as well as the necessity of objecting to external threats, the idea of promoting positive development came to the fore. For the Vigilantes, however, this was to prove a step too far.

According to the Minutes of the 15 April 1964 meeting, there was further discussion about meetings with Professor Hondelink and his proposed transport study. So the scene was set for vastly greater expenditure than had been envisaged when the Vigilantes came together just five months earlier to fight the rail closures.

Victory for the Highlands

On 16 April 1964, in a written reply to a question asked by Neil McLean, the Unionist MP for Inverness-shire, Minister of Transport Ernest Marples wrote:

I have now considered the reports of the Scottish Transport Users Consultative Committee in consultation with the Secretary of State for Scotland. We have taken account of the advice he has received from the Highland Transport Board and the Advisory Panel on the Highlands and Islands and all of the representations made to us.

The ultimate annual savings the Railways Board expected to make from the *complete* closure of the Kyle line were about £120,000 and from the Wick line £240,000. On the other hand the transport problem in the Northern Highlands is of a special nature; the T.U.C.C. have reported that the closures would cause *extreme* and widespread hardship; and there is strong evidence that at present there are no adequate alternatives for long-distance travel on these lines, and there are not likely to be *for some years*. I have therefore decided that *in present circumstances* I must refuse my consent to the closures. *(my italics)*

This was a remarkable statement in two ways. First, and most obviously, it was a major victory for Highland campaigners. No other reprieve from closure in British railway history would involve a route anything like as long as the 168 miles of the Far North Line. But Marples' reference to 'complete closure' saving £240,000 annually (around £4.5m in today's money) indicates that the previously quoted annual 'loss' of just £6,590, attributable to passenger services only, was vastly outweighed by the net additional costs attributable to freight operation (in particular to the basic route infrastructure of track and structures), minus the freight revenue.

So, Marples had reprieved the passenger services despite effectively acknowledging that the overall picture was grim in terms of railway finances. Even allowing for economies which could and, as we shall see, would be made over the next couple of years, this was still a massive loss, which Marples was willing to endure in the wider political interest: not that it would do the Conservative Government any good in the General Election six months later.

In order to give himself political cover, Marples had even attributed to the TUCC a view that that 'the closures' (i.e. of both lines) would cause 'extreme' hardship – an adjective that was only used by the TUCC in its report on the Kyle line, but not that on the Far North Line, where the verdict was 'widespread' hardship.

The second striking point about Marples' statement is the strong hint that this would prove to be only a temporary reprieve – with references to the likelihood of there not being adequate alternatives 'for some years', that 'in present circumstances' he had to refuse consent to closure, and reference to the Highland Transport Board's 'study of the progress made with road improvements'.

Unsurprisingly, media reaction to the announcement was joyous. The *Inverness Courier's* editorial of 17 April thundered: 'The Highlands have won a great victory', and Evan Barron was not slow to take some of the credit, both implicitly and explicitly, as well as attacking a familiar target:

> Victory, of course, is due to the hard work over the past three or four years, ever since the first rumours of the proposed closures raised the alarm and roused those who had the interests and welfare of the Highlands at heart into immediate action.

> We ourselves are, of course, delighted that Mr Marples has listened to his Scottish advisers, and to reason, for we were one of the first in the fray, and we are sure that it was largely because so many objectors followed our advice, and submitted individual personal objections and evidence of hardship, which made a tremendous impression on the T.U.C.C., that in the end the day was comparatively easily won. Certainly no mass-produced objections could have had the same effect, and it is no thanks to the Macpuffing Vigilantes, who were responsible for such folly, that the Highlands have won the day, although they will no doubt be patting themselves on the back when they should be preserving a decent silence.

The news columns of the *Courier* recorded 'great satisfaction throughout the whole North', and was able to report local Unionist Party efforts to secure as much political capital as possible for the Government:

> Sir Francis W. Walker, Convener of Inverness County Council…[and]… president of the Inverness-shire Unionist Association, told the "Courier": "I am sure the Highlands and Islands will be delighted to hear that the Government have decided that the Inverness-Kyle and Inverness-Wick lines will not be closed, and it is particularly gratifying that the Government has

made this early announcement. The early consideration given to the proposed closures shows how keenly the Government is interested in the welfare of the Highlands and Islands".

Away from party politics, the *Courier* reported that James Cameron, Town Clerk of Inverness – who had acted as clerk to the North of Scotland Transport Conference, formed two years earlier at the instigation of the Town Council to oppose rail closures – had commented: 'There could have been no other decision. It was obvious that there would be hardship – in some cases extreme hardship – if the lines to Kyle, Wick and Thurso were not retained.'

William Dunnett, the Provost of Wick, focused on the economic benefits:

The announcement will bring great joy to the North. The uncertainty about the railways was having a bad effect on industrial development of the area. Now that all these fears have been removed we can go all out again to attract industrialists north.

Of course, the successful campaign had spanned both the Far North and Kyle lines. The story of the latter deserves a book in its own right, but it is only right to quote here the *Courier's* report of the reaction of a key campaigner from the West (who would also play a critical part in the second campaign, from 1972 to 1974, against Kyle line closure):

Mr Torquil Nicolson, Kyle, Ross and Cromarty County Councillor, who opposed the closure of the Inverness-Kyle line – "There could be no better news for the west. This line should never have been on the closure list. It has caused us a lot of worry. It will be a new lease of life to Skye as well as the mainland. We could not have survived the blow had our railway link been severed."

But not everyone welcomed the reprieves. As the *Courier* reported, Dr Beeching had issued the following statement in response to Marples' decision:

Commercially there is no case at all for continuing operations on these lines, and it is the Railways Board's responsibility to say so. It is the Minister's responsibility to decide whether the lines need to be kept open because of hardship or any other reason. The figure of £360,000 given by the Minister is a measure of the savings which would be made as a direct consequence of closing these lines, but the total losses on the traffic passing over them is substantially greater, and these losses, together with others resulting from similar decision *[sic]* on the continued operation of uneconomic lines will be shown separately in our accounts.

Beeching was presumably referring to the long-run costs of maintaining rail operations – including major works on structures in the medium to long term – as opposed to the day-to-day costs. This topic continued to be the subject of political debate about the cost of individual rail services, even after the introduction of a new railway accounting convention in 1968, as we shall see in Chapter 10.

But only half a decision

On 24 April, the *Courier* and other North newspapers carried the text of the official reprieve letter from the MoT to the BRB, which was also posted at stations throughout the Highlands. Much of this notice repeated key points made in Marples' Westminster statement eight days earlier, but any careful readers would have been astonished to see that, contrary to the overwhelming impression created by Marples' words, *he had only reprieved the stations at Wick and Thurso (and Kyle)*:

> [The Minister] has reached the conclusion that he would not be justified in agreeing to the closure of the through rail services between Inverness, Wick and Thurso at the present time... Accordingly, the Minister, in exercise of his powers under subsection (11) of section 56 of the Transport Act 1962 refuses to consent to the discontinuance of all railway passenger services between Inverness and Wick/Thurso and from Wick and Thurso stations.

The MoT's letter concluded by stating that a further communication would be sent to the BRB once the Minister had reached a decision on the proposed closure of the intermediate stations, then listed all 22 of them. The media do not seem have picked up on this stark fact, although there was some coverage of the phrase in Marples' statement to the effect that, 'I am still considering whether *certain* of the intermediate stations could be closed to passengers without causing hardship' *(my italics)* – but it is striking to reflect on how the decision to delay a verdict on *all* the intermediate stations might have exploded politically.

April 24 also saw a belated editorial in the *Ross-shire Journal* which celebrated the victory as 'ample proof that unified protest against injustice is the best answer, and that placing a reasoned and realistic case before the powers-that-be reaps its own reward'. Speculating on the prospects for 'a much more adequate system of alternative transport', the editorial concluded that: 'It will probably take another quarter of a century before the latter is constructed, if then.' The *Journal* had a firm view on one of the key developments of the campaign:

> While it would be invidious to single out any person or group for special praise in this matter, none doubts that the courageous decision of the Highland Panel to resign en bloc if closures were carried out gave the Scottish office and the Government very serious matter for concern. For this important and experienced body of men would not take such a grave decision lightly nor without being fully aware of the very serious situation West and North of Dingwall would find itself in if bereft of rail transport.

The editorial urged renewed promotion of rail services, both passenger and freight, and concluded with a warning to the public: 'For we must ensure that the calamitous axing which has just been averted does not again rear its head after a period of forgetfulness or lethargy.' This was a wise warning, for within eight years there would once again be an official threat to the Kyle line.

The news columns of the *Journal* also carried a quote from Marples' statement which was a reminder of the possibly temporary basis of the reprieve:

> The ultimate future of the lines themselves can later be considered in the light of the comprehensive review the Highland Transport Board have already started of transport in the area as a whole, of progress with road improvements and other developments in transport and industry in the next few years, and of the study the Scottish Development Group are making of the prospects for the region.

Frank Thomson, Chairman of the Scottish Vigilantes, had commented: 'The whole of the Highlands was behind this fight, and it is a perfect example of what can be achieved with unity and local initiative.' The newspaper reported that: 'Mr Thomson added that if it was the intention to streamline the two routes from Inverness to Kyle and Wick, and this entailed the shutdown of some of the stations, this would be acceptable.'

Colin Campbell, in his role as Chairman of the North of Scotland Transport Conference (rather than as a member of the Vigilantes) had welcomed this 'very good news indeed', but had also given a warning: 'We must not lose sight of the other battle ahead of us – the fight to keep freight services going. There is evidence of a deliberate rundown of freight services in the North.'

Such allegations could get confused with BR's efforts to tailor its business to those traffics to which it was most suited in an era of rapidly expanding road competition. Willie Thorpe, General Manager of BR Scottish Region, was quoted at some length by the *Journal*, on this topic amongst others, in a rather more emollient response to the reprieves than that of his boss, Dr Beeching. It also set the future of the two lines in the context of BR's wider strategic plans:

> We welcome a decision as to the future of these lines. It removes the shadow of redundancy from many railwaymen. It also removes uncertainty from the minds of many in the north of Scotland, anxious about their rail links with the rest of the country... On my part, I give an assurance that we shall spare no effort to make both the passenger and freight services on these lines as attractive as the future earnings prospects will allow. Development plans are already in hand.

> We need a steady flow of passengers and freight traffic on these lines throughout the year. At the T.U.C.C. hearings a great deal was said about the essential service the railways give the community in the winter. But foul weather friends are not enough.

We hope that now the uncertainties have been removed, we can count on increasing co-operation from such major industries in the north as agriculture and whisky distilling.

Far from deliberately letting Scotland's railways run down – as has been foolishly alleged – we have spent in the last nine years more than £70m. on developments.

Indeed we have in the North of Scotland eliminated steam traction and improved both journey times and the general standard of performance over the past few years.

We are very much looking to the future and these two lines now have an important place in our development plans.

This was an upbeat commentary on the prospects for the Far North and Kyle lines, and within a few months BR would be delivering its commitment both to improved services and reduced costs of operation, and demonstrating that the two were not mutually exclusive.

The Minutes of what was apparently the first meeting of the Vigilantes after the reprieve announcement, on 25 April, make no mention whatsoever of the success of the campaign against rail closures: the reason the organisation was set up in the first place. And strangely, Phil Durham *(ibid)*, who was also present at the meeting, omits any direct reference to Marples' decision in his book's narrative on the fate of the two railways, effectively jumping straight from the March hearings to the September establishment of, as we shall see, the Highland Railway Users' Council. Many of the Vigilantes' minds were already focused on aims much more ambitious than the saving of a rural railway.

A rare shot (from the 1950s) of Frank Thomson, the Aberdeen-born accountant and charismatic adventurer who was Managing Director of Invergordon Distillers and led the successful 1963-64 'MacPuff' campaign against rail closures. In 1967 he resigned from the Highlands & Islands Development Board due to a perceived conflict of interest with his ambitious plans for a petro-chemical plant on the Cromarty Firth. Thomson subsequently emigrated to the USA, and died in Australia in 1989. The Scotsman Publications Ltd.

Why was the Far North Line reprieved?

Between the publication of the Beeching Report in March 1963 and the General Election in October 1964, Ernest Marples consented to the closure of 127 services affecting 701 stations and closing 1,341 route miles in total. He refused consent to only 76 station closures.[52]

Cutting out the 232 route miles and 38 stations of the rail network north of Inverness would have made a significant contribution to the service withdrawal element of Beeching's plan to transform the finances of Britain's railways. So why were the Kyle and Far North lines reprieved?

Having explored in detail the pattern of public and behind-the-scenes deliberations, lobbying and campaigning activities over the period from Beeching's arrival at the British Transport Commission in 1961 to Marples' decision in April 1964, what can one conclude about the definitive reasons for the reprieve of by far the longest railway in Britain to be saved from closure?

The primary and secondary research for this book has revealed the importance of factors which have hitherto been hidden from public knowledge or not fully understood. And – as I found in my analysis of the Waverley Route closure – there was no single 'silver bullet' which determined the Government decision. The various determining factors can usefully be grouped under the headings of (i) the social case for reprieve, primarily expressed as 'hardship' (ii) the economic case, (iii) the political dynamics, and (iv) the conduct of the campaign.

The social case

The only statutory basis for objection to closures was on the grounds of personal hardship. Although other objections clearly played a major part in Marples' decision, the TUCC were presented with evidence which left little doubt that many existing rail users would experience significant hardship if forced to use replacement bus services. The planned express buses (much less comfortable than the trains) would have taken 40% longer from Inverness to Wick and 60% longer to Thurso than did the fastest trains.

While other threatened routes in Scotland which were ultimately axed, rather than reprieved, would face even longer relative increases in journey time, the sheer length of the proposed bus journeys to Caithness must have been a decisive factor. Five hours 37 minutes to Wick and six hours 20 minutes to Thurso would have been a pretty intolerable experience for most former rail travellers who did not have a car. Indeed, with hindsight, it seems surprising that the TUCC concluded only that there would be 'widespread' hardship, where in fact a more accurate forecast might have been 'widespread and in some cases extreme' hardship.

The fact that 490 individual objections were lodged with the TUCC gave powerful impetus to the social case, since this number compared very favourably with the average 180-200 passengers per day on Mondays to Fridays in winter, and even with the 350 in summer. The large number of objections was, of course, in part a reflection of the conduct of the campaign.

The economic case

The regional economic development case for reprieve was crucial. Local Authorities, the Scottish Office, the Board of Trade, the Highland Panel and the Scottish Council (Development and Industry), among others, had all drawn attention to the vital presence of the railway – and primarily, but not exclusively, its freight services – in the siting of the Atomic Energy Authority development at Dounreay (although cynics might say that distance from London was also a key locational factor), the new Invergordon Distillery and the coming pulp and paper mill on the not dissimilar West Highland Line.

It was widely anticipated – not without justification, at least for the line north of Invergordon – that the loss of passenger services would quickly lead to the withdrawal of freight. The attraction of industry to the Highlands was a key plank of Government policy as part of a wider policy to try to reverse the widespread decline of population across this most isolated region of the UK. To lose one of the key locational incentives would be seen as a perverse contradiction of that fundamental objective.

The railway was also playing a core role in freight transportation for a broad variety of businesses along the length of the Far North Line: not only the traditional staples of domestic and industrial coal and other bulk commodities, but also inbound and outbound traffic for whisky distillers, agricultural commodities, new cars and a wide range of other traffics. Royal Mail, parcels and newspapers by rail were also critical to regional economic activity and everyday life in the area.

In the early phase of the emerging threat to the railway, the Scottish Office view of the closure threat was far more equivocal than it would become by early 1964. At more than 50 years remove, and in the absence of most of the direct participants in these events, it is hard to identify the relative importance of the role of particular individuals. However, archive papers do point to the key part played by Frank Spaven in informing positive attitudes to the railway, not only in the Scottish Office but also at the Highland Panel and perhaps also the Board of Trade. There appears to be enough evidence to support the view of his 2003 obituarist, Gordon Casely, that he was 'instrumental in saving the bulk of the Highland rail network'. But, as we have seen, the regional economic development argument was just one of a range of factors at work in influencing Ernest Marples' decision.

The political dynamics

Political dynamics were fundamental to the reprieve.

1964 saw the tail-end of a tired Conservative Government, which had been in power since 1951 and was now increasingly seen as out of touch with the times. The Beeching Report had created a nationwide furore since early 1963, so the background 'mood music' exacerbated opposition to the closures north and west of Inverness, and the MoT was obviously keen to get the big closure proposals, and crucially their refusal, out of the way quickly in order to dilute overall opposition to the Beeching plan.

The sheer scale of what was proposed north and west of Inverness – closing 232 miles of railway and leaving a vast tract of already isolated country with no trains – guaranteed opposition across the political spectrum. There had been a large Conservative vote in Scotland throughout the 1950s, and the Unionist Party was very much the political establishment across local government in the Highlands. Also, the three MPs who represented the constituencies through which the Far North Line passed were Unionists. It is clear that grassroots Unionist Party opposition to the closures, because of the social and economic impact and the political backlash it would create, was increasingly obvious to the party hierarchy both in Scotland and London.

Part of the political dynamic surrounding the proposed closures was not *party* political: the opposition of both the Government-appointed Highland Panel and Highland Transport Board undoubtedly had a powerful impact on the climate of public and political opinion. And the Panel's threat to resign, led by its Chairman, and pillar of the establishment, Lord Cameron, must have shaken the Government.

The conduct of the campaign

The campaign ranged across local, regional, Scottish and UK platforms, and was clearly crucial to the ultimate Ministerial decision.

As viewed by railway historians and rail campaigners in recent decades, what was actually a broadly-based opposition to closure – encompassing a range of connected, loosely-tied and independent elements – has tended to be encapsulated by its association with the powerful MacPuff image. I was therefore surprised in the course of my research to find that the Vigilantes were formed only days before BR announced its closure proposals in November 1963. Yet the threat of closure had been firmly in sight since well before the publication of the Beeching Report in March of that year.

In a way, the forthright Evan Barron of the *Inverness Courier* was right to bemoan the belated arrival of this outspoken group and its charismatic leader. A wide range of statutory and other bodies across the Highlands and beyond had been voicing opposition to the closures before and after the Beeching Report. There is no reason to doubt, had the Vigilantes not been created, that there would still have been an impressive lobby which would have continued to make itself clearly heard in the corridors of power after the line closure proposals were posted.

Frank Thomson and his group did bring a new dimension to the campaign, but it is hard to believe that this tipped the Ministerial balance against closure. By December 1963, the Unionist Party was already in open revolt: from the grassroots, through MPs, to grandees such as the influential Lord Polwarth of the SCDI. And the Highland Panel had threatened to resign. Taken together with what was, in any case, a poor social and economic case for closure, it must have been obvious to the Conservative Government long before the TUCC hearing in March that there could be only one decision.

And so, Britain's longest rural railway was saved.

CHAPTER 10: A NEW LEASE OF LIFE

Having taken the dramatic reprieve of the Far North and Kyle lines very much in its stride, the Scottish Vigilantes Association continued to meet frequently until January 1965.

Thereafter, meetings were sporadic, and in October 1965 the organisation was to be wound up, having abandoned its grand (some might say grandiose) transport and development aims for the Highlands and Scotland. Ill-will over the financial fall-out and disillusionment over the blurring of personal advancement with public-spirited objectives were both to linger on for several more years, as we shall see.

Meanwhile, however, the Vigilantes spent much of their meeting on 2 May 1964 discussing the reverberations of their being party to public claims that BR had been running down the lines north of Inverness, through the policy of concentration on fewer freight depots, which had been announced earlier in the year. Frank Thomson had suggested that 'perhaps we had blundered in coming out with our information on run-down publicly', and 'Mr. Wright said that he had formed the opinion that we had lost unanimity for our destructive activities and that we ought to do our best to let British Railways know that we were concentrating on our future plan and wanted their co-operation in getting it accepted.'

One person's 'run-down' can of course be another person's 'efficiency measures'. Writing in the 8 May edition of the *John O'Groat Journal*, George Mackie, Prospective Liberal Candidate for Caithness and Sutherland, suggested that 'we need an entirely new management set-up for the railways in the Highlands', since 'it also appears to me inevitable that the line will sooner or later be closed unless there is a startling difference in the general efficiency and vigour of management.' Mackie would not have to wait very long for his wishes to be realised.

BR now had to re-group in the light of Marples' decision, and a fascinating insight into behind-the-scenes thinking is contained in an SDD memo produced by RDM Bell on 20 May, including the following key sections:

> After a diversion to Renfrew last night I had a long gossip with Mr. Thorpe, General Manager of the Scottish Region, on the bus over to Edinburgh. It might be worthwhile to record some of the points we discussed although it would be inappropriate to take any action on them.
>
> I have little doubt that the Scottish Region never expected authority to close the Highland lines and this confirms my view that the Ministry of Transport are more vicious in the assault on Scottish railways than British Railways themselves.

I asked Mr. Thorpe about reports we had seen which seemed to imply that he had undertaken to discuss railway matters with the unofficial MacPuff groups *[sic]*. He denied this and said that his intention was to keep his discussions to the official bodies like ourselves, the Scottish Council, the Highland Panel and Highland Transport Board, etc. Probably what had been misrepresented was a meeting which he had with Mr. Frank Thomson and a number of business and agricultural people in Inverness. He had no objection to such meetings where he could invite those present to look seriously at their own ability to make more use of the railways; it was meetings with unofficial groups with no traffic to offer the railways which he wished to avoid. He told me that Mr. Thomson has now signed on the dotted line for railway transport in and out of Invergordon distillery. The period of the agreement is 10 years.

Thorpe's hard-line rejection of input from railway development advocates and other friends of the railway, would in due course give way to a devolved management structure which was open to new ideas and constructive criticism from what we can now describe as 'key stakeholders'.

An early example of informed thinking by an 'outsider' came in the shape of a 20-page May 1964 report on the Far North Line by naval engineer (and SRDA member) George Davidson, originally from Caithness, who had a strong personal interest in railway development.[53] A number of his suggested passenger service improvements were to be taken on board by BR in their winter 1963-64 timetable. But many of his recommendations would either be seen as too radical and/or were to prove to be 'before their time'.

Among Davidson's suggestions for the next 15 years, as well as faster journey times and improved connections at Inverness (which BR would implement in September 1964), were:

- a Glasgow-Thurso overnight sleeper service

- containerisation of southbound fish and returning perishable food traffics

- a potential siding from Thurso to Dounreay

- palletisation of mail and parcels traffic, switched from passenger to freight trains to reduce delays to the former, and concentrated at fewer railheads

- introduction of more powerful Type 3 locomotives, plus consideration for 'fitting rheostatic braking equipment to reduce tyre wear, increase brake block life and permit higher downhill average speeds' (Type 3s, aka Class 37s, would eventually be introduced in 1982)

- welded rail joints, concrete sleepers and deep ballast – 'to create a stable track requiring the minimum of attention though costing slightly more to install' (another change in practice which would increasingly be implemented)

- consideration of a reduction in the 31 block sections and associated crossing loops, which seemed to be 'very large' for the number of trains handled (BR were to begin this process within months)

Much of Davidson's thinking – and his longer-term suggestions, such as automated train control systems, lighter vehicles giving lower movement costs, and computer control of rolling stock distribution – was visionary stuff. Many were to fall foul of the wider malaise to which he referred in his conclusions:

> The British railway system as a whole has suffered from under-investment for some 50 years and is now technically inferior to many foreign systems. This is the main reason for the present operating loss and inadequate performance.

Back in the day-to-day world of railway campaigning, an early hint of the Vigilantes' mounting financial problems came at their 23 May meeting, when 'Mr. Butler informed the meeting that the Chief Inspector of Taxes had refused the tax rebate on Mr. Thomson's Deed of Covenant and that our Edinburgh lawyers were now fighting this.' Emerging internal discord, as well as external concerns, were to the fore at the next meeting on 6 June, the Minutes recording, *inter alia*, that:

Water column and water tower stand defiantly at lonely Altnabreac in the summer of 1971, a decade after the end of steam. The station still had an engineers' siding, but the crossing loop had been lifted five years earlier. The entire water tower survives to this day. David Spaven

Mr. Thomson informed members that he had twice met Mr. Thorpe, who was not prepared to have anything to do with the North of Scotland Transport Conference or the Vigilantes, but was prepared to have an unofficial meeting with one or two big users.

Mr. Campbell suggested that Mr. Thomson was in danger of going off at a tangent and that there was already a feeling that negotiations were taking place unknown to members.

Mr. Thomson said that he had advantages as a big user, denied often to other Vigilantes and that he only got the treatment he did because he was Chairman of the Vigilantes. He could combine the advantage of being a big user and being able to wield a big stick.

The pitfalls of being involved in issue advocacy in two different capacities were to come back to haunt Frank Thomson, culminating in his March 1967 resignation from the Highlands & Islands Development Board (HIDB) over a perceived conflict of interest between his membership of the Board and his personal stake in proposed Cromarty Firth industrial developments which the Board was helping to promote.

This affair – notorious in the Highlands at the time – was, ironically, triggered by a leak to an MP from then HIDB employee, Phil Durham, formerly a Vigilantes colleague of Thomson, as told in his *Highland Whistle Blower* (1997). Durham's disillusionment with Thomson was first prompted within the Vigilantes, before exploding on to a much bigger stage at the HIDB.

A better service and lower costs

Overdue economies of operation on the Far North Line were largely delayed until after the Minister's decision, but even the line's reprieve could not soften all the cuts which would inevitably follow. On 1 June 1964, Willie Thorpe of BR responded to a letter from the Unionist candidate for Caithness & Sutherland, Patrick Maitland, who had raised concerns about cost-cutting measures on the Far North Line. Thorpe replied that, with a view to running the line 'in the most economic manner possible':

> …we have been examining the working of the various schedules and by making adjustments to them which will enable the Inverness and Wick men to change over at Brora, it has been found practicable to close the motive power depot at Helmsdale. This will mean that probably 8 drivers and 6 firemen at Helmsdale will become redundant although it may be necessary to make 1 or 2 additional appointments at Wick.

This economy was to go hand in hand with a major passenger service improvement which eliminated Helmsdale as a service terminus. On the freight side, illustrating the fundamental mis-match between some surviving railway activities and modern rail economics, Thorpe continued:

> Insofar as Forsinard is concerned it is the intention to close the freight facilities at the station, the alternative facilities being at Helmsdale. To give you some idea of the freight traffic being dealt with at Forsinard, I think I should indicate that for a complete year there were only 3 tons of sundries and 10 waggons of livestock forwarded and 20 tons of sundries, 11 tons of goods and 1 wagon of coal received.

On 1 July BR confounded allegations of run-down and demonstrated their commitment to operating the Far North Line as attractively and efficiently as possible for passengers, with an announcement of major timetable improvements to be introduced with the start of the winter timetable on 7 September. Instead of two trains daily from Inverness to Wick and Thurso, with a third only as far as Helmsdale, the latter would be extended to Caithness throughout the year. End-to-end journey times, which had been as long as 5 hours 6 minutes the previous winter, were cut to a maximum of 4½ hours, and the fastest train (previously taking 4 hours 45 minutes) would involve a timing of just 4 hours 10 minutes on the 5pm service from Inverness.

A further benefit of the new timetable was the opportunity to travel all the way from Wick or Thurso to London in a single day, with a journey time of 16 hours. The 6am departure was to connect with the 10.30am train from Inverness to Edinburgh Waverley, where its 3.50pm arrival would (just) connect with the 4pm *Talisman* service taking only six hours to London Kings Cross.

Marples' second reprieve

On 31 July, more than three months after the MoT's little-noticed announcement that the fate of *all* the intermediate stations had yet to be decided, the Scottish Office issued an MoT press notice which advised that Ernest Marples 'announced today his decision on the proposal to close to passenger services the intermediate stations' on the lines north and west of Inverness.

Consent was given to closure of Invershin, Dunrobin, Salzcraggie, Borrobol, Forsinard and Hoy, 'subject to the provision of a bus service on Saturdays from Forsinard and Helmsdale'. The Highland Transport Board had some influence here, an appendix to its 1967 report indicating that it had recommended closure of all of these other than Dunrobin (plus Kildonan), but with caveats:

> The Board recommended that Forsinard should be retained as a request halt because, in their view, it would have been less expensive for British Rail to stop the train than to bear the cost of an unremunerative bus service. In the event British Rail have not yet closed Forsinard or Kildonan, because they

have been unable to comply with the Minister of Transport's requirements for the provision of alternative bus services; and Invershin has been retained as a request halt following the withdrawal of the bus services which were to have provided the alternative transport services. The Board also recommended that Dunrobin should be retained as a private halt [with the Duke of Sutherland presumably paying for maintenance] and trains now stop there at the beginning and end of school terms.

This was an important reminder that there was more to the economics of rail closures than simply a narrow consideration of railway finances.

With a faster passenger service now in place in a bid to boost the line's revenue, BR turned its attention to the, arguably long-overdue, consideration of bigger cost-cutting measures. In fairness, the prevailing convention of the era – that major changes to a threatened line's service or infrastructure were not made until a Ministerial reprieve decision had been announced – had inhibited management action.

Details of the planned operating economies emerged in one of the very few mentions of the Far North Line in the Scottish Railways Board's Minutes of meetings held in 1963 and 1964.[54] At the meeting held on 7 October 1964 in Glasgow, reference was made to a memo submitted by the AGM (Finance), 'outlining proposals designed to reduce annual costs for track work from about £200,000 to about £110,000 on the Inverness / Wick / Thurso line'. Frustratingly, there is no further detail, but the 'about £200,000' figure appears to relate to the basic infrastructure costs of £235,250 (evidently allocated to freight) in BR's letter of 21 January to the Highland Transport Board.

This was a very significant saving, primarily realised through the removal of crossing loops no longer needed to support the prevailing traffic levels. As we have seen, Ernest Marples had referred to a £240,000 annual saving from complete closure. Taking the £235,250 figure for freight track and signalling costs with the quoted passenger-only loss of £6,590, it can be concluded that freight services on the Far North Line must have been just about breaking even, against allocated terminal and movement costs, at the time of the reprieve. So, in the context of the Ministerial passenger reprieve and the projected £90,000 cut in annual track costs, it made sense for BR to maintain general freight operations, as indeed it did for another two decades.

Although the Board Minutes noted 'that it was desired to make a start with the cost-cutting project at the beginning of 1965', the first crossing loop to be eliminated since mid-1963, at Scotscalder, was taken out of service only six weeks later, in November 1964. This was followed by Beauly and Kildary in 1965, Altnabreac, Fearn, Golspie, Kildonan, Kinbrace and Watten (plus singling of the six miles of double-track from Clachnaharry to Clunes) in 1966, and finally Alness in early 1967. Thereafter, only one further loop would be lost – at Lentran (mid-way along the previously double-track section) in 1988.

Further tribulations for the Vigilantes

Despite the Vigilantes having employed consultants Martech, at a fee of £1,500, to undertake a study of Highland economic opportunities, the Minutes of the 21 July Vigilantes meeting discussed the possibility of the group now abandoning their 'third phase' and withdrawing into the transport field only. The 7 September 1964 meeting Minutes demonstrate that internal discord was growing.

Following reference to the fact that 'Invergordon Distillers had instructed Mr. Michael Taylor [of Martech] to make a further study of the production of Urea from CO2, a grain distillery by product', the meeting heard that:

> Mr. Butler was anxious that people would say that this [Martech] report [on Highland economic opportunities[55]] had been produced for a few individuals' private ends. Mr. Thomson believed that this criticism was likely to be made in any event and he did not think this should deter action.

Phil Durham *(ibid)* recorded that Vigilante members had been 'assured by Thomson that it was a safe assumption that the distillery would meet a considerable proportion of the cost of the Martech Report, once again alleviating their, as it later proved, justifiable anxiety over its financing'. Finances had to be juggled, and 'juggler' would perhaps have been an apt description of the Vigilantes' leader. Durham wrote:

> While Frank Thomson did deposit sufficient funds to maintain the rented office in Invergordon and the modest salaries of myself and my most intelligent and experienced American part-time secretary, there was no money to pay for the Martech report, all available funds being used to meet the cost of producing the Hondelink plan for an integrated transport system, a draft of which had been passed to Eric Linklater to edit.

At their 19 September meeting, the Vigilantes were advised that they had 'paid directly over £650 for the Hondelink Report so far and it now looked as if this Report would not now be ready until 1966.' Exactly a month later, more worries were expressed about finance, with outstanding debts of roughly £400 (around £7,000 in today's prices), and:

> Mr. Linklater stated that he was in the middle of a study of the draft Hondelink Report and of a part of it which had been rewritten by the Secretary. His preliminary examination did not fill him with much hope that it could be

published without drastic rewriting and clarification but he would spend more time on this as soon as possible.

On the broader rail development issue, as recorded by Phil Durham (*ibid*), 'British Rail agreed, once the Inverness lines had been spared, to set up a Highland liaison body with users'. The Highland Railway Users' Council (HRUC) held its inaugural meeting in Inverness on 28 September, with Phil Durham and Colin Campbell among those in attendance. The purpose of the organisation was agreed as:

To facilitate the interchange of information and ideas with the object of assisting British Railways in providing appropriate services. To encourage the customer to user these services. To improve the net revenue of the division.

It was also agreed that there would be a joint chairmanship, comprising James Dunlop the County Clerk of Ross & Cromarty and the new Divisional Manager of BR's Northern Division, Bernard Allison, based in Inverness. (Coincidentally, when Allison (in 1967) moved back south, his house in Inverness was bought by my father and mother. The former lived there until his death in 2003 and the latter until her move to Edinburgh in 2010.)

Allison indicated at the September 1964 meeting that the new Highland body would be 'the first of its kind in Britain'. Ex-BR manager Rae Montgomery recollected in 2016 that after the new Divisional Manager had become established in Inverness, local BR staff would refer to their 'Allison Wonderland'.

The next HRUC meeting, on 30 November, heard that Bernard Allison had been formally appointed as Manager of the newly designated 'Highland Lines', with Eddie Thompson as his Commercial Manager. The new division, which hoped to start operation on 1 January 1965, was to cover all the rail territory north from Stanley Junction (north of Perth) and Inveramsay (between Insch and Inverurie). The meeting was advised that a new reduced fares structure was now in operation on the Far North Line, including a day fare of 45/- between Wick/Thurso and Inverness, allowing seven hours in either Wick, Thurso or Inverness.

A Mr Matthews from the UK Atomic Energy Authority commented that only 25-30% of traffic from 'the Forth to the Trent' moved by rail to Dounreay. He thought that something like 75% of road traffic could come by rail 'if the conditions were right'. 90% of traffic *from* Dounreay already moved by rail.

By this time, the General Election had been held – on 15 October – with the Conservative Government replaced by Labour. Despite the relatively swift reprieve of the Far North and Kyle lines, the Unionist (or Conservative) Party was rewarded with loss to the Liberals of all three local parliamentary constituencies: Inverness, Ross and Cromarty, and Caithness and Sutherland. There were deeper political pressures at work than the Beeching Report and the fate of the railway north of Inverness, after what the Labour Party characterised as '13 wasted years' of Conservative Government. In practice, it was the 1964-66 and 1966-70 Labour Governments which would implement the vast bulk of the Beeching-inspired cuts, despite Labour's claimed hostility to closures while in opposition.

The seeds of the collapse of the Vigilantes and Frank Thomson's ultimate fall from grace continued to be sown. Phil Durham *(ibid)* and the Treasurer of the Vigilantes had been 'voicing anxieties about finance', and in Durham's words:

> Then, at a committee meeting in November 1964, Thomson in the Chair reported the formation by himself and Colin Campbell of the Polyscot group of companies which he emphasised were private and quite separate from any Vigilante activities which might follow from the publication of 'Highland Opportunity' [the Martech report]. Polyscot Group, an association of existing companies, had formed a bank and an insurance company and their first development was to produce Polycast plastic in Campbell's home farm steading.

As the (2 November) meeting Minutes confirm, 'Mr. Thomson invited anyone interested to join Polyscot'. According to Phil Durham:

> He suggested its prospectus to the public would look for £3 million...They looked for the participation of several large companies of 250 to 1,000 employees. While sounding most impressive, such large sums of money and expectations lay well beyond the experience of the ordinary farmers and businessmen serving on the Vigilante committee, such developers' kite flying, adding an extra nought or two for effect, being totally new to them.

The same meeting discussed changing the organisation's name, with a Mr Paterson suggesting that 'Mr. MacPuff had served his turn and must now be dropped'. The beginning of the end came the following Spring, as described by Phil Durham:

> When in March 1965 the Vigilantes held their first annual general meeting, our Chairman at the last moment sent his regrets, due to Invergordon Distillers being about to float in a few days as a public company...Eric Linklater was persuaded to chair the AGM, which accepted that the Labour Government's proposed formation of a Highland Development Board should in no way be allowed to delay the developments signposted by Martech Consultants. The well-attended meeting offered its support to our continuing transport and economic activities. Without any specific activity or firm financial proposals, such support was meaningless and a further six months elapsed before Thomson managed to find time to attend a meeting.

The Highland Railway Users' Council (HRUC) meeting in Inverness on 12 April 1965 heard that the Highland lines had been completely dieselised since April 1962, with locomotives now averaging 1,600 miles per week compared to 1,000 miles three years earlier. The Minutes record that Mr [Syd] Atkinson of BR had reported that Highland Lines locomotive availability (for service) stood at 86-87% and, if this was any higher, maintenance would suffer. Looked at from today's perspective, here was a group of lines, including the Far North Line, which was clearly enjoying the benefits of modernisation, streamlining of services and effective local management.

One of the consequences of streamlining, in the absence of funds for investment, was reported at the next HRUC meeting on 7 June 1965 when Bernard Allison of BR advised that, in light of disappointing traffic levels, the only future regular movement of livestock by rail would be between Inverness, Dingwall and Kyle, and even that only on a six-month experimental basis.

More positively, the first Sunday excursion train from Inverness to Wick had made 'a reasonable start' by carrying 153 passengers (there were no scheduled Sunday train services north of Lairg). Later that year, on 25 October, in Inverness, the HRUC meeting heard that, as part of a major shake-up of management/supervisory staffing across Scotland, over 60 Stationmasters on Highland Lines would be replaced by 11 Area Managers, reporting to Inverness. Key aspects of the old railway were gradually disappearing in the bid to survive against road competition.

Although its influential report would not be published until 1967, by late 1965 the Highland Transport Board had covered a lot of ground, and on 29 November submitted its 'Review of Progress', in confidence, to St Andrew's House[56]. It was stated that, in view of the growth of industry in the Thurso area and in the light of a 5½ hour bus journey versus one of '3½ hours' by train (the fastest train actually took 4 hours 10 minutes), 'closure of this railway is unlikely in the foreseeable future'. The surprising 'tentative conclusions' which then followed were that:

> The long-term future of rail services in the Highlands is also [like bus services] limited. *The Highlands are not railway country* and there seems to be little prospect of large regular flows of freight traffic which would justify their retention indefinitely. Long-distance passenger traffic is likely to be carried increasingly by air, while medium-distance and local traffic will in future rely more and more on the bus and private car. *(my italics)*

In the margin beside this paragraph, Durham hand-wrote on his copy, 'UGH!'

The Board's eventual report was to produce a much more favourable verdict on rail, including the Far North Line, and in part this would reflect the views of the new Highlands & Islands Development Board (HIDB) created by the incoming Labour Government. The HIDB began its work on 1 November 1965 (eventually taking over the functions of the Highland Transport Board), and the notes of an early meeting between the two organisations (on 9 December, with Professor Robert Grieve of HIDB in the Chair) record that:

> The Development Board noted that in paragraph 16 of their Review of Progress the Transport Board stated that the Highlands are not railway country but weather conditions indicated that this was not so. The Development Board would have difficulty in attracting industry to the Highlands if businessmen found there was no rail transport and they had to rely on roads which may be blocked.

The end of the Vigilantes

The final two meetings of the Scottish Vigilantes Association were held in the Royal Hotel, Invergordon, on 28 September and 7 October 1965. The Minutes of the former record that:

> [Mr. Thomson] feared that our two reports, Martech and Hondelink, had not had the full impact that we had hoped for but that our initiative had been successful in making the voice of the Highlands heard and had had a considerable effect on the Scottish Council and on the Secretary of State and his servants [sic] in St. Andrew's House.

> The Martech report was authorised and out of the Vigilantes contact with Martech came useful investigations for Invergordon Distillery. They got in touch with the Product Planning Branch of Martech, in particular with Jonathan Jenkins [whom Phil Durham later described as 'a sunken-eyed boffin'], and these revealed two revolutionary chemical processes. When Mr. Thomson set out to grasp this unique chemical opportunity many attempts were made to have the plant sited elsewhere, particularly in Newfoundland. Very influential oil and chemical interests tried to oppose it. But the complex is going to be built in Invergordon…The complex would employ directly 2,700 which meant that with their families 11 or 12 thousand people must be housed and, with the necessary services and other population dependent on the development, housing for 30,000 people would be needed within 10 years.

> Advance notice of the development was leaked out by those opposing the complex but it has already been lobbied and accepted by both the Government and the Opposition.

> Mr. Thomson emphasised that he had no need to start this tremendous operation but he believed that it would solve the Highland problem once and for all, not in small pieces but in one major operation. (my italics)

This charismatic and dominating leader then 'invited each person present to comment on the venture', and there followed virtual unanimity of endorsement, typified by the thoughts of one of the founder members:

> Mr. Fitzherbert Wright believed that the Highlands and in fact all Scotland should and would be grateful to Mr. Thomson whose Invergordon distillery had been the basis from which these far reaching plans had grown. This represented one bite at the cherry of Highland development instead of a lot of small concerns. He believed that for proper development a bit of a dictator would be needed to combine all the vested interests involved.

He had perhaps already found that dictator, but a couple of reservations were nevertheless expressed, including this from Phil Durham:

> Mr. Durham joined the welcome for the proposed complex but expressed anxiety what benefit it would bring to Stornoway, the Islands and the West where development looked to depend on land reclamation and the ideas propounded in "Highland Opportunity". We had promised the establishment of a development trust to develop these opportunities and now appeared to be abandoning this. Mr. Thomson agreed that Stornoway and this area was a problem but suggested the complex could bring benefits and that *the new growth would badly need a recreation area with suitable motels and such developments.' (my italics)*

'There's snow on the Ben' is a traditional Invernessian weather commentary. Here, the distant Ben Wyvis is coated in early snow as Type 2 (aka Class 26) No. D5344 edges across the Caledonian Canal swing bridge on a crisp autumn afternoon in 1966. Frank Spaven

A balanced and comprehensive development plan for the Highlands this was not, and, as Phil Durham later wrote, the Minutes of the two final meetings of the Vigilantes demonstrated 'how, in the hope of its Chairman's dream becoming reality, its members continued to exist in a cloud of euphoria'. The stage was now set for the end of the affair.

At the start of the 7 October meeting, Thomson suggested that 'now might be a good time to put the Scottish Vigilantes in mothballs, particularly if we are all prepared to leave the problems we have considered to the new Highland Development Board.' Returning to the perennial finance question, Phil Durham pointed out that:

> ...had we been repaid the £2,000 debt of the Transport Conference, and had Invergordon Distillers made the contribution promised on 7 September 1964, we should be able to meet all our debts. Members had expressed disquiet at the financial situation at every meeting held over the past year and the time had come to deal with it before discussing anything else.

In response, 'Mr. Thomson said it was only reasonable to suppose that finance would be forthcoming from either Invergordon Distillers or Invergordon Chemicals to clear our debts'. Later in the meeting, to decide the future of the Vigilantes and the Transport Conference, Thomson suggested 'that those who had made loans should write them off and that Martech should write off the cost of their report in view of the profit they would make on work for the complex'. In response, 'Mr. Durham pointed out that, even were all these debts to be written off, £800 would be needed to close the office and repay the overdraft. At that Mr. Thomson said he would sign a guarantee form.'

This brought an ignominious and confused end to an organisation whose roots lay – by later standards – in the relatively straightforward task of contributing to the campaign against Highland rail closures. As Phil Durham *(ibid)* subsequently wrote:

> Thus, without any agreement on debt cancellation, the association drew to an inconclusive close. Just eighteen months would elapse to disprove the bold statement that finance was no problem and prove that many of Thomson's statements would stretch even the vivid imagination of Walter Mitty.

Thomson's major chemical complex at Invergordon never materialised and, following his resignation from the HIDB in 1967, he left Scotland to become the Vice President of Holiday Inns of America, based in Memphis. He later moved to Sydney, Australia, where he died in 1989. His ashes were brought back to Invergordon for burial.

More settled times for the railway

Following its founding in September 1964, the Highland Railway Users' Council continued to meet regularly through 1965 and 1966. At its 10 October 1966 meeting in the Station Hotel, Inverness, BR had five members in attendance , and welcomed a further 17 people, including Phil Durham (now a junior part-time employee of the HIDB), Colin Campbell, another ex-Vigilante, and Provost Dunnett of Wick, who had played a leading part in the protests against the 1963 closure proposal.

Bernard Allison, as the Manager of Highland Lines, drew attention to the ongoing rationalisation of operations, including singling of double track, destaffing of level crossings, introduction of tokenless block (eliminating hand-exchange of physical tokens for single-line working between Perth and Inverness), collection and issue of tickets on trains, and introduction of the Area Manager scheme. The Minutes noted that the implementation of these measures 'would mean that we were operating the railways in the north of Scotland as economically as possible with the present level of traffic, but there is still a trading gap that could only be reduced by bringing more traffic to rail'.

Sadly, 1967 was to prove to be the last summer season during which a former Southern Railway *Devon Belle* observation car was attached to the tail-end of the mid-morning Inverness-Kyle of Lochalsh train. This car had originally been part of a short-lived post-war Pullman train, and was one of four cars (two of which had been built for the LNER's pre-war streamlined *Coronation* express) progressively introduced by BR between 1956 and 1961 on Scotland's key tourist routes: from Glasgow to Fort William, Mallaig and Oban, and from Inverness to Kyle.

All four were withdrawn in autumn 1967, with BR reported as claiming, according to the *Railway Magazine* of March 1968, that 'the existing coaches were life-expired and receipts from them could not justify the cost of building new ones'. Given that all four were still either in revenue-earning service on heritage railways in England or undergoing further restoration work some 49 years later, this was an outrageous claim, and represented the worst of post-Beeching management negativity towards surviving rural routes.

More disappointment for some of those who had been involved in the 1963-64 campaign against closure was expressed in private correspondence between Phil Durham and the Treasurer of the Vigilantes, Peter Butler, on 2 May 1967:

> With the record of broken promises, half truths, and authorisation of payments without consultation of the Committee, all I can hope for is that Frank Thomson may pay the legal fees which he had promised to pay.

Durham conceded that despite the financial experience:

...at least we have served the area well in our transport activities. On the financial side it looks as if there are quite a few who will not accept the evidence of their experiences but are willing to be influenced by smooth talk and ever more unfulfilled promises. For long I was among them.

I fear the drawing up of the accounts appears to me an academic exercise. Please cancel any balance that you have entered due to me; I have already received far more than I expected when our Association folded up.

By this stage, to put it mildly, there was no love lost between Durham and Frank Thomson, who had finally resigned from the HIDB following Durham's leak of papers which pointed towards a conflict of interest. Durham had then been sacked by the HIDB.

On 17 May the *Highland Transport Services* report of the Highland Transport Board was finally published. The first pages of the report revealed mixed messages about the future of the railways, citing 'the rapid increase in the number of private cars and the development of other road traffic in the area', yet offering hope for the Far North Line in its comment that 'the Inverness-Wick/Thurso line can usefully serve industrially developed areas on the Moray Firth and in Caithness'. The subsequent paragraph on the specifics of the Far North Line was less equivocal:

This line is still operating at a considerable loss. Passenger numbers and freight tonnage carried in the years 1964 and 1965, were less, although not appreciably so, than the traffics carried in 1963. Nevertheless, all the reasons given by the Board in their report of 3rd April, 1964...for keeping the line open are still relevant. The H.I.D.B. have indicated that they think there will be considerable growth in the Moray Firth area north of Inverness, and it has been decided to set up the prototype fast reactor at Dounreay. Furthermore, British Rail have made economies in running costs. These factors suggest that the line may become more viable in the future and the Board recommend that it should remain in operation.

The breakdown of freight tonnage in the report showed some decline from 1963 (221,744 tons) to 1964 (205,811 tons), but then some recovery to 1965 (216,191 tons). The commodities which increased their throughput each year were 'agriculture' (presumably including maize to Invergordon Distillery, as well as fertilisers, seed potatoes, etc), which was the largest single commodity group, with 110,614 tons in 1965; and 'food and drink', which included whisky from the various distilleries served by the line.

The number of parcels handled dropped from 409,865 in 1963 to 397,625 in 1965. Passenger traffic – like freight – showed a drop from 1963 (62,454) to 1964 (57,388), then partially recovering in 1965 (59,070). Overall, the pattern of business, combined with the significant economies being made by BR, must have given reasonable grounds for optimism about the Far North Line's future.

The report also contained a map summarising rail freight facilities across the Highlands, indicating that the full range of traffic types (coal, full wagon loads and sundries) was dealt with at the following stations north of Inverness: Dingwall, Invergordon, Tain, Bonar Bridge, Lairg, Brora, Georgemas, Wick and Thurso. Stations only dealing with coal and full wagon loads were Muir of Ord, Alness, Fearn, Golspie and Helmsdale. Remarkably, despite the relentless growth of road haulage over improved roads, this pattern of service was to remain broadly in place until the demise of conventional wagonload traffic over the Far North Line in 1984.

In addition to referencing classic railway traffics, the report highlighted the potential to extend rail containerisation in fast, fixed-formation trains, far beyond Beeching's vision of the Highlands being served by road from an Aberdeen railhead:

> The Board have noted the significant increase which has recently taken place in the volume of freight carried by rail as a result of the introduction of the freightliner container service on the main trunk routes between England and Scotland. A service of this kind requires considerable capital investment in terminals and rolling-stock, and the Board recognise that the volume of freight traffic on most routes in the Highlands may not be large enough to justify substantial investment at present. In view of the evident advantages in cost and speed however, the Board recommend that British Rail should be invited to make a detailed study of the possibility of extending the freightliner system to Inverness.

In November 1967, HIDB Board Members attended a 'liner train demonstration' in Inverness but, in practice, BR's Freightliner division and its various successor companies[57] would never establish a terminal in Inverness, although during the 1980s both Freightliner and international containers were to appear briefly on the Far North Line. And in 1985 the road-rail logistics company John G Russell was to base a mobile container crane for handling domestic coal supplies at Inverness, to be followed in 1999 by the pioneering development, also in Inverness, of handling Safeway supermarket supplies from the south.

The 1968 Transport Act: clarity at a price

Labour's 1968 Transport Act, implemented during the course of 1969, was ground-breaking on a number of fronts.

The Scottish Transport Group was formed, combining the state-owned Scottish Bus Group and Caledonian Steam Packet Company shipping company. The Act also established the principle of Passenger Transport Authorities and Executives (PTAs and PTEs) to co-ordinate and operate public transport in large conurbations. The Greater Glasgow PTA and PTE were to be established in 1973, in due course becoming Strathclyde PTA and PTE, which would become renowned for the large number of passenger station and line re-openings it promoted from the 1970s through to the first decade of the 21st century.

From a Highland railway perspective, the key change was that the Act provided final recognition that British Rail's financial target, set in 1962, was untenable. As Christian Wolmar *(ibid)* says, Minister of Transport, Barbara Castle:

> ...relieved the railways of the impossible target set by Marples of breaking even or making a profit. She recognised, for the first time, that the railways needed financial support from the government, creating a distinction between commercial services which should pay for themselves and 'social' ones which needed subsidy.

Section 39 of the Act introduced the first Government subsidies for railways which were 'unremunerative' (loss making) but deemed socially necessary. Grants could be paid where three conditions were met: (i) the line was unremunerative, (ii) it was desirable for social or economic reasons for the passenger services to continue. and (iii) it was financially unreasonable to expect British Rail to provide those services without a grant.

Modern Railways magazine in March 1969 reported the announcement by the Minister of Transport of the levels of grant aid for 222 unremunerative passenger services. Eighty-nine of these were for two or three year terms. The balance of 133 included a grant of £595,000 to maintain services between Inverness, Wick and Thurso for a period of one year. The latter was not an indication that there were doubts about the line's survival, but more a case of bedding in an entirely new method of costing, and paying for, loss-making lines.

This method of costing proved highly controversial, with rail campaigners bemused by the typically large jump in subsidy compared to the losses quoted at closure proposal hearings in the years following the Beeching Report. In the case of the Far North Line, the comparison was inevitably with Ernest Marples' 1964 reference to the 'ultimate annual savings' from complete closure of the line as £240,000. Even allowing for inflation it was a big jump to a figure of nearly £600,000.

The grants were calculated by the 'Cooper Brothers' formula (named after the firm of accountants involved), and identified the deficit which would be required to be met in continuing a passenger service in the long run. These included an allowance for the interest liability of the British Railways Board and provision for the replacement of assets at current costs. In contrast, the data presented to the TUCC was based on the 'Carrington' formula for short-term savings, ie the net financial effect of withdrawing the passenger service, with amortisation and depreciation charges based on historic costs, and interest excluded. As a 1968 BR memo in relation to the Waverley Route was accurately to comment: 'The use of these different methods undoubtedly causes confusion to the layman'.

While the last of the post-reprieve programme of rationalisation of the Far North Line track infrastructure had been completed in early 1967 with the elimination of the Alness crossing loop, of much more significance for perceptions of the railway in the Highlands generally was BR's decision in 1968, implemented in early 1969, to abolish the Highland Lines Division. This removed the management tier between Scottish Region HQ in Glasgow and the new network of Area Managers which had been introduced since 1965.

Arguably, there was corporate logic in this move, probably hastened by the wider economic picture, which always had an impact on BR finances. Chris Harvie – already a rail campaigner in the mid-1960s and later an office-bearer of SRDA – commented to me: 'The Labour government was deep in financial mire after devaluation in November 1967', and as Terry Gourvish notes[58], 'there is no doubt at all that the government was responsible for constraining the level of investment resources available to the railways after 1960'. He shows that aggregate disinvestment in 1963-73 was such as to cancel out the net investment of 1948-62, with the worst year being 1967, when the disinvestment amounted to £55 million in 1948 prices.

By the last 'working timetable' of the 1960s, despite ever-expanding competition from road haulage, freight was still playing an important role on the Far North Line. In winter 1969-70, a daily (Monday to Friday) wagonload train from Wick to Inverness (with traffic fed in from Thurso at Georgemas Junction) called at a number of intermediate freight depots, such as Helmsdale, Brora, Tain and Invergordon, balanced by a return working which it crossed – and where Wick and Inverness train crews swapped trains – at Rogart loop.

A daily return working from Inverness to Lairg (including oil tanks for the latter's railhead, serving the fishing fleets at distant Kinlochbervie) and a daily multi-traffic train to Invergordon Distillery (also shunting intermediate locations such as the Lentran bitumen railhead and general freight depots at

Muir of Ord, Dingwall, Alness and Invergordon), were supplemented by an 'as required' company trainload of oil from Bowling on the Clyde to Invergordon distillery and a twice-weekly train of barley from Doncaster to Muir of Ord (for the whisky industry). This was a freight railway which was still at the heart of the regional economy, and it was to assume an even more important role with the opening of the Invergordon aluminium smelter in 1971.

By late 1969, the HIDB had taken over the role of the Highland Transport Board and, as Eddie Thompson of BR explained to Phil Durham in his letter of 28 November, 'the terms of office of the former Highland Railway Users' Council expired in September 1968'. It had thereafter been held in abeyance pending discussion of the proposal to create a 'Transport Users' Sub-Committee Group' of the Transport Operators Group of the HIDB. Rail supporters such as Durham could have been excused for feeling that this was a poor substitute for the direct contact with BR which the HRUC had provided.

However, on a more positive note, HIDB 'Special Report No. 1' by its Wick-Thurso Working Party concluded, possibly with industrial growth in mind, that the Far North Line 'would continue to provide the best and surest means of passenger transport', and suggested that, 'notwithstanding the fact that the Government have already scheduled the line for improvement, a guarantee should be sought that the rail route would be retained and developed'.

As 'Beeching's decade' ended – the last of his Scottish cuts was implemented in 1969, when the Waverley Route closed – rail campaigners' focus switched to much-needed improvements to the rail network in a very competitive transport environment. In his foreword to the Scottish Railway Development Association's *Scottish Railways in the 1970s* booklet, issued in October 1969, the SRDA President, Sir James Farquharson, set out the core arguments for change:

> The Scottish Railway Development Association consists of individuals and corporate bodies interested in railways playing, within a well-conceived transport system, the part for which they are technically and economically fitted. The reasons why this desirable situation has not been achieved in Scotland are complex and varied. Transport infrastructure is provided and services owned and operated by a wide assortment of public and private organisations. No coherent transport policy has evolved over the years and investment in the various modes of transport has, quite wrongly, been made on entirely different criteria. The fiscal policies of Government have not been designed to secure the optimum distribution of traffic. The working conditions and remuneration of staff in the different transport fields have varied widely for no reason. A powerful road lobby has ensured high investment in roads but there is no comparable influence at work for railways.

In order to foster such an influence, the SRDA's priorities for development included a reduction in average journey time between Inverness and Thurso from 4¾ hours – it had deteriorated from the maximum of 4½ hours following the 1964 speed-up – to 2¾ to 3½ hours. In part, this would be achieved through the construction of a new direct route from Tain to Golspie (which would become known as the Dornoch Bridge link), with a possible surviving branch from Golspie to Lairg. Freight was not forgotten, with a recommendation that a Freightliner container terminal be established in the Moray Firth area, supplemented by 'simple terminals' in the Dornoch Firth and Thurso areas.

Lots of liveries: a train from Kyle on the Rose Street curve passes a service arriving in Inverness from Perth. This Spring 1968 shot captures a period of changing liveries, from British Railways' maroon to British Rail's blue and grey (for hauled coaches), and – for Diesel Multiple Units – from green to blue. Frank Spaven

Reflections on Beeching

On 23 January 2003, nearly 40 years after Beeching had delivered his seminal report, Frank Spaven recorded his reflections on those momentous times, from which fortunately the Far North Line had escaped unscathed – in no small part due to Spaven's own endeavours behind the scenes. These are the words he typed on a single sheet of A4, just five days before his death at the age of 85, under the heading 'Looking back from 2003 on Beeching's "The Re-shaping of British Railways" 1963':

Points for.

1. It was a badly needed, thorough investigation and plan on how to make the railways pay. That was the remit given to the British Railways Board by Government, who were responsible for most of the omissions and flaws noted below.

2. There were positive advances in it or related to it, notably on diesel services, signalling and freight, including "Liner Trains" of containers on trunk routes between main road-rail terminals.

3. Some secondary main lines and station closures were reprieved, notably in the "special case" of the Highlands, following strong local and central agencies' opposition.

4. The local passenger services on some short rural lines have been as well or better provided for by those bus services which have been continued and linked with main railway stations, often with the help of Local Authorities.

Points against.

1. These drastic proposals were worked out in private from 1960/61 by MOT and BRB without consultation with users or public agencies; and then referred to the TUCC for passenger services, whose sole criterion was any objections from users on "hardship" that couldn't be relieved by existing or potential bus services.

2. No account was taken of the social, economic and environmental benefits of the railway to the communities or regions served.

3. There was no parallel assessment of road transport costs, direct and indirect, and no overall, co-ordinated transport plan for regions.

4. There were wide discrepancies between the BRB figures of losses and far lower independent assessments; and no account was taken of, for example, contributory revenue of lines feeding traffic into main lines.

5. The report shied off electrification.

6. A procedure which completely closed the Waverley Route, the only line serving a population of 70,000, far more than any other region affected in Britain, was disgracefully incompetent.

7. One reason for (6) was that the Scottish Office and the Scottish Secretary had no final say in it, only the MOT, despite behind-the-scenes disagreements (nor have they to this day on many railways decisions).

This succinct review of a very specific driving force behind a tumultuous period for railways throughout Britain helps us to draw a line under a decade of highs and lows for the Far North Line. The 1970s would be altogether different, bringing a commercially-driven local freight boom which underlined the importance of Ernest Marples' politically-driven 1964 decision to reprieve Britain's longest rural railway, against Dr Beeching's wishes.

Based on a working life in and around the rail industry, I conclude that much of the Beeching Report's broader analysis was actually correct, *within the narrowly-conceived financial framework set by Government*. In a world of intense road competition, the industry needed to concentrate more on what it was best at, and to focus investment where it would make the best return.

However, Dr Beeching had at least one blind spot: the failure to consider properly how costs could be reduced by destaffing smaller stations and introducing a wide range of other economy measures, short of complete closure. Fortunately, the Far North Line escaped the latter fate, unlike other equally or more deserving cases across Scotland: notably Aberdeen-Ballater, Aberdeen-Fraserburgh, Dumfries-Stranraer, Dunblane-Callander, Edinburgh-Galashiels-Hawick and Gleneagles-Crieff. But the core problem of the Far North Line which Beeching raised in 1963-64 – the large gap between costs and revenues – remains just as valid an issue more than five decades later.

The wider economic, social, and arguably psychological, trends which led to the threat to the Far North Line and hundreds of other railways across the country have to be acknowledged. Christian Wolmar *(ibid)* reflects that both Conservative and Labour administrations at Westminster through the 1950s and 1960s were strongly influenced by 'the feeling within government that cheap fuel for motoring was a permanent fixture and therefore the demand for travel by railway would inevitably fall over time'. Charles Loft *(ibid)* concludes his masterly analysis of the Beeching era with these words:

> As Kenneth Glover put it, to predict and provide a response to road traffic growth "has become politically incorrect, but at the time it seemed democratic", because it gave people what they showed they wanted. That downland car park, that train puffing slowly and peacefully through green meadows no more, the lane that is now a road, the houses that have numbers instead of names, that cloud of diesel dirt that hangs over every city, those melting ice caps – that was not Beeching and Marples, it was us; we did it. We liked trains, but we used buses and then we bought cars. Why? For the same reason we built railway lines across the hitherto unsullied estates of the aristocracy. We do not want to spend our lives within five miles of the village we were born in. We want to move, we want convenience, we want speed. We want new things. We want to get where we're going. It is almost as if we can't help it.

Three generations of the photographer's family watch the mid-day train for Inverness slow to a halt at Lairg in the summer of 1969 behind Type 2 (aka Class 26) No. D5344. Note the milk churns at the end of the low platform, which was subsequently removed from the front of the station building and re-created further north where full height could be accommodated without awkward changes of level. Frank Spaven

PART 3

On 24 October 1972, the photographer captured the 4.10pm Class 24-hauled freight departure to Inverness from a signal gantry at Invergordon. Noting that it was shorter than usual, he recorded within the train consist: four wagons of aluminium blocks for Falkirk, four hoppers of alumina for Fort William via Cadder Yard, and two 'Speedfreight' container wagons plus two tanks of whisky for Glasgow. Frank Spaven.

AFTER BEECHING

CHAPTER 11: THE FREIGHT BOOM

Despite the final Beeching cut in Scotland having been implemented a year earlier, the new decade began inauspiciously from a Highland railway perspective when, on 5 January 1970, all passenger services were withdrawn between Perth (Hilton Junction) and Cowdenbeath, forcing Inverness-Edinburgh trains to make a lengthy detour via Stirling.

As late as 1967 this direct route from Perth, through Kinross and over the Forth Bridge, to Edinburgh was classified as a 'route for development'. But when BR applied for grant aid in 1968, the Ministry of Transport's response was that re-routing trains via Stirling would give better value for the taxpayer. A key part of the rationale, however, was that closing the railway through the narrow defile of Glenfarg would simplify the construction and cost of the Scottish Office's planned new M90 motorway.

So, a 48-mile rail journey became one of 69½ miles, thereby increasing journey times and operating costs. It is hard to avoid the conclusion that this was one of the worst railway policy decisions perpetrated in Scotland in the latter half of the 20th century. The newly uncompetitive position of Edinburgh-Perth (and Inverness) train services was only partially alleviated when BR began re-routing some trains via the previously freight-only (and still just single-track) Ladybank-Perth route in 1975, a journey of 57 miles. By that time the Edinburgh-Perth road journey had become one of only 43 miles, over motorway and dual-carriageway.

By 1970, BR in the North of Scotland was well on its way to completing a phased withdrawal from directly serving individual malt whisky distilleries. The volumes of regular traffic at any one distillery – inward grain / malt / barley / coal and outward spirit and co-products – were simply too small for rail, with its high fixed costs, to compete profitably against the flexibility of the lorry. The most swingeing cut had come in November 1968 when a clutch of private sidings and BR freight depots were lost with the closure of the by-then freight-only Speyside Line between Aviemore and Aberlour, with BR re-focusing its efforts on upgraded railheads at Dufftown, Elgin, Keith and the Burghead maltings.

The same policy was applied to the Far North Line, with the Canal Junction to Muirtown Basin branch in Inverness (serving Glen Albyn and Glen Mhor distilleries) closing in early 1970. The private siding to Glenmorangie Distillery was also taken out of use that year.

But BR were certainly not withdrawing unilaterally from the whisky business. In the mid-1960s a new rail-served silo was developed at Muir of Ord, receiving twice-weekly trainloads of east of England barley from Doncaster for the nearby maltings. And Invergordon Distillery would continue to be a source of rail freight traffic into the 1980s. Like a number of other grain distilleries (in Central Scotland) it generated substantially larger flows of inbound and outbound freight traffic than did a typical malt distillery, and therefore had a good fit, at least initially, with the modern freight railway.

Until the 1982 displacement of Class 26s by Class 37s (the Class 24s having left Inverness in 1975), the only other locos seen regularly north of Muir of Ord were the 1,000 horse power Class 20s, hauling oil trains from Bowling (on the Clyde) to Invergordon Distillery. Here, one of the class accelerates a southbound empty tank train out of Invergordon loop in the summer of 1973. David Spaven

Virtually the whole portfolio of what rail could offer the whisky industry in the summer of 1974 is seen here at Invergordon goods yard: a (grubby) hopper wagon which had brought grain to the nearby distillery sidings and would return south with waste product used for animal feed; an equally tarnished early-generation 'Speedfreight' container for casks of whisky; and, in the distance, a spotless 'Cutty Sark' tank container for bulk spirit. David Spaven

The smelter and North Sea oil

The most dramatic change in the peace-time fortunes of the Far North Line resulted from two key developments in the early 1970s: the initial realisation of the HIDB's vision of heavy industry development along the Cromarty Firth and the exploitation of North Sea oil.

In *The Moray Firth: A Plan for Growth in a sub-region of the Scottish Highlands* (1968), the Jack Holmes Planning Group had set out for HIDB a strategy for substantial population growth and development between Inverness and Invergordon. Much of this was linked to the unique combination of deep water, flat land and trunk road and rail services in and around Invergordon, which had played a big part in the World War One effort.

Frank Thomson's plan for a petro-chemical plant had come to nought, but HIDB promotion and Government assistance persuaded the British Aluminium

The driver of a Class 26-hauled non-stop freight from the north exchanges single-line tokens at speed with Magnus Campbell, the Invergordon signalman, in the summer of 1973. David Spaven

Company (BAC) to site a new smelter north east of Invergordon, with direct rail connection and a two-kilometre conveyor belt from a new deep water jetty where Jamaican alumina was offloaded.

There had been a long tradition of aluminium smelting in the Highlands, beginning in 1896 at Foyers on the eastern shore of Loch Ness, then developing on a much larger scale in Kinlochleven and Fort William. According to Dr Andrew Perchard, in *Aluminiumville* (2012), 'on the eve of the First World War, Foyers and Kinlochleven accounted for 12% of the global production of aluminium'. The common factor for the three smelters was cheap hydro-power, allowing profitable production despite huge electricity demand, but, tragically for Invergordon, its power source was to be the nuclear station at distant Hunterston on the Clyde.

According to Reay Clarke, the Prime Minister, Harold Wilson, had announced the plan for a hydro-powered Invergordon smelter (and other smelters in Anglesey and Northumberland) without first consulting the North of Scotland Hydro-Electric Board, which had to advise him that it simply didn't have the capacity to guarantee constant electricity supply to the smelter. The Dounreay nuclear plant – part of the then vision of nuclear being 'too cheap to meter' – became Plan B for the smelter, with a new power line constructed from Caithness.

When it, in turn, proved unable to guarantee supply, Plan C was Hunterston, nearly 200 miles distant, adding transmission losses to already high costs and thereby contributing significantly to the smelter's demise in 1981. Nevertheless, over its 10-year life the smelter was to have an enormous impact on the Far North Line, as I witnessed working for BR at Invergordon and Tain in the summers of 1973 and 1974.

Construction of the smelter began in 1968, and the first aluminium was produced in 1971. By the time it reached full production in 1973, the smelter could supply 100,000 tonnes of aluminium annually, with around three-quarters of the product (ingots of aluminium) moving south by rail for finishing at other BAC sites. Remarkably, BR also moved alumina from Invergordon to Fort William for the two Lochaber smelters, a rail distance (via Glasgow and the West Highland Line) of over 330 miles, compared to the direct road journey of less than 100 miles via the Great Glen.

Traditional practice at Lairg in 1979, after the departure of the lunch-time train arrival from Inverness, with the Sutherland passenger and mail bus for points north and west straddling both tracks to ease loading of parcels and postal traffic. Frank Spaven

The number of daily freight trains over the Inverness-Invergordon section grew from three to five, typically with four of these serving the various depots and private sidings in the Invergordon area. Following the advent of North Sea oil production, MK Shand in 1972 opened a pipe-coating plant north of Invergordon. The plant had two separate private siding connections, with the inbound steel pipes and cement and the outbound concrete-coated finished product all being transported by rail. BR acquitted itself well in gearing up for this traffic development, with a quarter of a mile of track laid by its civil engineers in one week: 'Only three weeks after a site meeting to investigate the possibility of building the siding the first section of 450 tons of North Sea pipe line left by train.'[59] This was a speed of delivery which is inconceivable in today's privatised and risk-averse railway.

The rear end of an Invergordon-Inverness trip freight – with aluminium slabs prominent – seen from the Invergordon station footbridge in May 1973. Frank Spaven

Also in 1972, Highland Fabricators opened their oil platform construction yard at Nigg, near the mouth of the Cromarty Firth, and this too generated rail traffic: inbound steel piles offloaded from rail to road at the quiet country station of Fearn, which hitherto had been more familiar with the entirely different business of loading seed potatoes to rail. Around this time, the Graham Wood steel stockholding yard at Evanton also secured its own private siding, avoiding the on-cost of delivering steel by road from BR's nearest 'general merchandise' depot at Invergordon.

Invergordon Distillery was no longer generating the same amount of rail traffic as it had in the mid-1960s, with road haulage taking an increasing share – but the large distillery complex retained two separate private siding connections on the east and west sides of the Far North Line. As well as regular trainloads of oil from Bowling, wagonloads of whisky were typically sent to Glasgow's High Street freight depot: casks in BR 'Speedfreight' (pre-Freightliner) road-rail box containers and bulk spirit in privately-owned tank containers. Whisky co-products included waste turned into pellets for animal feed, and these were sent south by rail in bulk hopper wagons.

Rail campaigning takes off again

While Frank Spaven had been a founder member of the Scottish Railway Development Association in 1962, and an active campaigner ever since – initially in Edinburgh, then from 1966 in Inverness – his employment with the HIDB from 1966 to 1978 circumscribed the extent to which he could front the campaigning activities of SRDA in the Highlands.

Fortunately for SRDA, by 1970 it had attracted the attention of Adrian Varwell, who had moved to Invergordon in 1969 as an Aberdeen University Research Fellow charged with undertaking a study of the social impact of the aluminium smelter. Varwell took up the (voluntary) post of Highland Area Secretary, and was to have a major impact on rail campaigning in the north.

The August 1971 'Newsletter and Development Report' of the SRDA was jointly edited by Alex Aitken of Edinburgh and me, by then a student in the Scottish capital. News from the Highlands included a downbeat verdict on the Far North Line, commenting that: 'A speeding up of the existing abysmally slow timing (45 minutes more than in 1964) is essentially a hoped for advantage if present patronage is to be retained, much less increased.' The 45-minute contrast referred to 1964's summer-only *Orcadian* service, but BR's pocket timetable for the Highlands for May 1971 to April 1972 showed that all trains were a minimum of 15 minutes slower, the fastest at 4 hours 37 minutes compared to 4 hours 10 minutes in winter 1964.

The main cause of deceleration was the conversion of the Far North Line's many level crossings from manned to 'open' crossings (i.e. without barriers): with resultant Government requirements for trains to slow severely (to 10 or 20mph) or even come to a complete halt before proceeding. This was another example of the lack of a level playing field between road and rail, and one which has continued to dog the efficiency of the Far North Line to the present day.

On a more prosaic note, BR's 'Passenger Train Marshalling' circular for May 1971 to April 1972 noted that on the first train of the day from Inverness to Wick, the 'RMB' passenger coach incorporating a Miniature Buffet Car had '16 Fluid Dining Seats'. This prompted rail campaigner Richard Ardern to comment in 2016: 'Shurely not at 6.15 in the morning!' But, joking aside, in those years before the 1976 relaxation of the strict 11.00-14.00 and 17.00-22.00 bar opening hours in Scotland, train buffet cars had no such restrictions on alcohol sales and consumption: a small but useful 'unique selling point' for 'droothier' passengers.

An article I wrote in SRDA's November 1971 Newsletter and Development Report drew attention to the economic impact of the railway in Inverness, with echoes of its Highland Railway days: 'With some 600 of a staff, including

26 038 awaits departure from Brora with a southbound train on 25 August 1979, while a northbound service is due at the platform adjacent to the now B-listed station building.
Alan Young

Low winter sun highlights a cargo ship at Inverness Harbour in early 1973, while in the background a Class 26 slows its train from the north across the Ness Viaduct as it approaches its destination. David Spaven

100 drivers and second men (the legacy of firemen from steam days), BR is the biggest industrial employer in the Highland Capital (pop. 32,000).' As a foretaste of an important campaigning report which would be published in 1972, the Highland Area Secretary of SRDA wrote that:

> Year by year the rail service on the Far North line seems to deteriorate further. With the fast road over the Black Isle now more of a likelihood for the 1970s, the time is ripe for a forum of ideas, simple or radical, for the rationalisation and maximum low-cost improvement of service from Inverness to Caithness before the shadow of closure proposal falls any nearer. Send your proposals to Adrian Varwell.

Local concerns about a closure threat were well judged, Charles Loft *(ibid)* recording that:

> By early 1971 the Department [of the Environment] had a list of 110 lines failing to cover even their short-term marginal costs. Fearing that another Beeching-style list would unite opposition, [John] Peyton [the Minister of Transport] and his officials decided to announce only the seventy to eighty cases needed to hold the grant at a consistent level and to do so in batches of twelve, a few months apart. Even this proved impossible as the Scottish Secretary refused point blank to accept closure of the Wick line, proposing commuter services as alternatives.

Token exchange at Georgemas Junction on 13 August 1975, as the Wick portion of the Inverness-bound train draws into the island platform. The Thurso portion will be shunted on to the rear of the train. Alan Young

By February 1972, SRDA was proposing to change its name to the Scottish Association for Public Transport (SAPT), but railways remained very much the focus. In that month's Newsletter and Development Report, Adrian Varwell penned a fascinating comparison of 'Two Northern Railways', commenting, *inter alia*, that:

> The Wick/Thurso line has been described before as the Trans-Siberian Railway of Britain – a rather harsh and unnecessary comparison, perhaps, and one which can hardly attract passengers. Probably a more valid comparison is with the Nordland Railway of Norway. This 453 mile line from Trondheim to Bodo was completed in 1960 as part of a general government policy to improve communications in the north of Norway.

Noting the similar sparsity of population – Bodo with 6,344 inhabitants, compared to Wick with 7,480 and Thurso with 8,037) – Varwell commented on the presence of restaurant and sleeping cars on the Nordland, with much better connections for the south at Trondheim than Far North passengers experienced at Inverness. Varwell concluded: 'The Norwegian railway also shows more enterprise: not only is it a newly-built line, but the philosophy behind it is interesting', with a sharp downward scaling of railway freight rates according to distance, and large flows of fresh fish.

The daily Far North freight – hauled by a Class 24 – looks a little cramped as it shunts 'sundries' traffic at Brora goods shed in the summer of 1973. At that time, Brora station offered a full range of rail services: for passengers, parcels, mail, newspapers, and wagonload and sundries (less-than-wagonload) freight. David Spaven

The Far North Line had particular prominence in the May 1972 SRDA newsletter, with Adrian Varwell's challenging article on 'The Great Northern By-Pass', sub-titled 'Were the right stations closed?'

Varwell wrote:

Many a traveller on the train from Inverness to Wick or Thurso might be forgiven for thinking that the train stops at all the small places and rushes through all the big ones. Just to see how true this was we did a quick check on the populations of the settlements contiguous to the railway stations, both closed and open…[This] suggests that the last round of station closures was based on the wrong set of priorities.

The analysis showed that of the 12 most populous settlements along the line, four – Alness (population c.3,500), Beauly (1,386), Conon Bridge (1,111) and Muir of Ord (739) – had lost their train services in the 1960 cuts. By contrast, the seven least populous settlements had all retained their stations: from Kinbrace with 42 residents to Georgemas with four.

Varwell's article was to prove to be an early stirring of various campaigns for re-opening, which were ultimately to culminate in all four of the biggest bypassed settlements re-securing a train service: Alness (1973), Muir of Ord

A timeless scene at Tain goods yard in the summer of 1974, with the original Highland Railway wooden goods shed, and – just visible on the right – a 'NE Div' (North East Division) engineers' accommodation coach. Frank Spaven

(1976), Beauly (2002) and Conon Bridge (2013).The extent of use of these four stations today, as explored in Chapter 13, provides a useful yardstick to measure the validity of the SAPT's 1972 claim.

Elsewhere in the newsletter, I reviewed the ground-breaking 'Blueprint for Survival' document produced by *The Ecologist* magazine. Noting its support for the environmental credentials of rail, I then elaborated on six areas of advantage: land utilisation; resource, waste and pollution; congestion; casualties; physical damage; and the lowering of the quality of life. My conclusion, that, 'The road user just does not pay for the costs he imposes on the

Seen from Tain's B-listed station building, southbound empty oil tanks, headed by a Class 26, wait in the loop for 'the road' to Invergordon, in the summer of 1974. Frank Spaven

community; if he had to it is more than likely that the motor car and lorry would be used only when really necessary', could equally be drawn today, demonstrating that 44 years have brought little change in the underlying mismanagement of transport policy.

A new threat to the railway

An item in the May 1972 SRDA newsletter provided another pointer to the future of road v rail competition, in the Far North specifically:

In a written reply to the M.P. for Caithness and Sunderland *[sic]*, the Secretary of State for Scotland *[Gordon Campbell]* said: "I have myself for some years past been aware of arguments in favour of such a scheme (a road crossing of the Dornoch Firth). I have already promoted the bridging of the Beauly and Cromarty Firths, and these schemes have been warmly welcomed. For the present design, engineering and money resources must be concentrated on improvements to the A9 road between Perth and Invergordon, but the necessary studies will be put in hand as soon as I am able to envisage a place for a Dornoch Firth bridge in the roads programme."

If envisaged development in the far North take place might it not be well to make this bridge suitable for a railway as well?

The concept of the 'Three Firths Crossings' had originally been raised in 1969 by Easter Ross farmer, Reay Clarke. As he told me in 2015, he had been asked to speak 'in a controversial manner' at a conference in Inverness Royal Academy (where I was a pupil at the time) on the future of the Highlands.

The Jack Holmes report for the HIDB had backed the concept of a new dual-carriageway A9 from Inverness to Invergordon, linking the intermediate towns via the heads of the Beauly and Cromarty Firths, which Professor Robert Grieve, Chairman of the HIDB, had described as 'a string of pearls'. But Reay Clarke was not convinced.

Before the Inverness conference, Clarke sat down with his old friend, John Smith, a lecturer in geography at Aberdeen University, and redrew on a map their preferred line of the A9 for the future, with the three crossings. The local *Scotsman* correspondent attended the conference and, on hearing Clarke's proposal, immediately invited him to write an article on the road plan for the paper. This attracted the attention of Patrick Hunter Gordon, the influential head of the AI Welders company in Inverness, who enthusiastically promoted the concept to local authorities, MPs and the Scottish Office. Frank Spaven subsequently recorded that:

...the pamphlet "The Crossing of the Three Firths" was issued in 1969 by Reay Clarke, Pat Hunter Gordon and John S. Smith. It makes no references at all to rail crossings, though it postulates that by 1980 there would be a Freightliner manager at Inverness looking for the shortest road transits into his depot![60]

In parallel with this public promotion, the road plan also benefitted from some classic *realpolitik*. Through a mutual friend of Clarke's, the map reached Gordon Campbell, then the Conservative Party's Shadow Secretary of State for Scotland, who was impressed and soon swung into action. Fielding a phone call from Willie Ross, Labour's Secretary of State for Scotland – who was trying to get another measure through the House of Commons – Campbell offered a *quid pro quo*: the Tories wouldn't oppose Ross's measure if he agreed to drop the 'string of pearls' route.

The deal was done, and three months later, in June 1970, the Conservatives returned to Government, and one of Campbell's first actions as Secretary of State was to commission an engineering survey of the proposed new A9 route. Clarke's route proved to be £10m cheaper than the alternatives, so the die was cast.

The practical completion of the Three Firths Crossings – the Cromarty Bridge (1979), Kessock Bridge (1982), and Dornoch Firth Bridge (1991) – were to undermine severely the competitive position of a railway which was already highly circuitous compared to the road alternative. And the SRDA's 1972 mention of a possible rail bridge across the Dornoch Firth, in part to counteract the damaging impact of the upgraded A9, was eventually to lead 13 years later to its becoming a Highland *cause célèbre*.

A blueprint for the Far North Line

In October 1972, the Scottish Association for Public Transport (SAPT), as the SRDA had now become known, published an 18-page 'Study Paper 1' on *The Far North Line: a plan for the future*. Produced by Frank Spaven and Adrian Varwell, it incorporated a prominent caveat to the effect that its suggestions and proposals were 'a basis for discussion, and do not represent a statement of the Association or its Highland Group' – a sensible precaution, as some of these were relatively controversial. The purpose of the document was set out as 'to demonstrate that the Far North Line has a continuing value for the area it serves, especially in view of industrial developments in Easter Ross and Caithness and of the growing connection between the Orkney Islands and Caithness'. The Paper noted that the line was receiving an annual subsidy of £444,000 (a significant reduction from the first grant of £595,000 announced in 1969, and presumably reflecting ongoing economies in operation).

Jocky Ross, the Tain P-way Inspector, checks the track gauge at Fearn station in the summer of 1974. David Spaven

It cautioned that:

Definitions of social service change, either due to changes in Government attitudes or due to the relative levels of social facilities. Thus grant-aid for any railway is always on a short-term basis, and is never given for more than three years ahead.

The future of the Far North Line is therefore by no means secure. The social service provided by the railway to Northern Scotland may be deemed to have expired in a few years time if the region's roads are up to a given standard, or if car ownership rises to a given percentage of the population…Only deliberate political decisions which permit railways to play a full and fair part in the life of the nation can, in the long run, enable the Far North Line to remain open.

Poor connections with buses (other than at Lairg], other trains (at Inverness) and ferries were cited, a particularly bad example of the latter being the arrival of the ferry at Scrabster at 11.30, just two minutes after the train had left Thurso for Inverness, forcing passengers to wait six hours for the next train at 17.23.

Having concluded that Thurso was the prime Caithness target (compared to Wick, having a much larger catchment area and less geographical disadvantage in rail v road distances), the SAPT paper suggested that there were four possible futures, and that 'public opinion must decide which is best':

1. Retain the line as at present and develop and improve the service

2. Retain the line, building a 'Dornoch cut-off' and a new chord at Halkirk (avoiding reversal at Georgemas en route to Thurso)

3. Truncate the line at Helmsdale, or Brora, or Lairg, or Tain

4. Close the line to passenger traffic completely and retain it for freight traffic as far as Tain or some other point

The Group's recommended short-term programme comprised, in summary:

- secure assurances on the longer term future of the line, and mobilise public support

- re-organise bus services to co-ordinate with rail and eliminate wasteful competition

- develop the line as a major route to Orkney, with special interchange facilities between Thurso and Scrabster (and the possibility of building a branch line was mooted)

- close certain stations north of Helmsdale and re-open others in the Cromarty Firth area (Beauly, Muir of Ord, Conon Bridge, Evanton and Alness)

- reduce the overall journey time to the 1964 best time of four hours, by palletisation of parcels, and installation of fully automated level crossings, eliminating speed restrictions (notably at Bunchrew, Delny, Nigg, Kirkton, Brora, Kinbrace, Halkirk, Watten and Hoy)

- augment the service between Inverness and Tain, 'to be implemented as soon as possible, but certainly initiated not later than May 1974'

Looking to the longer-term, the Group's strategic programme had three key elements:

- construction of a direct route from Tain to Golspie, with an intermediate station at Dornoch

- closure of the longer route via Lairg, provided connecting buses were provided and the track bed was reserved

- routing of all trains to Thurso via a Halkirk / Georgemas chord, 'with the institution of a subsidiary Thurso-Wick service upon the reorganisation of local bus routes'

Viewed from today, we can see that only a few of the SAPT paper's visionary objectives in 1972 have been even partially realised: assurances on the long-term future of the line (through the post-privatisation franchise process); most of the proposed new stations (but only achieved over a 41-year period); services augmented between Inverness and Tain (and beyond), but only after a wait of more than 30 years, and with an irregular interval timetable; and routing of all trains via Thurso (but without the Halkirk chord).

The appendices to the SAPT paper included a table setting out 'best times' by train from Inverness over historical, and hoped-for future (in italics), time-frames. It is salutary to review key extracts from this in conjunction with additional columns showing 2016 best times for train and bus:

Table: Best times by train from Inverness (1910-2016)

	1910	1939	1964	1972	1974?	1985?	2016 (train)	2016 (bus)
Tain	1'25"	1'9"	1'1"	1'10"	1'1"	45"	1'10"	45"
Brora	2'54"	2'47"	2'10"	2'33"	2'10"	1'15"	2'19"	1'29"
Thurso	4'45"	4'49"	4'	4'37"	4'	2'35"	* 3'46"	2'54"
Wick	4'50"	4'49"	4'	4'39"	4'	** 3'5"	** 4'18"	2'54"

* the fastest Inverness-Thurso time in the line's history was 3'23" between 2000 and 2005
** via Thurso

The SAPT Newsletter and Development Report of November 1972 reported that over 50 people from across the North, including local authority representatives, attended a subsequent conference in Wick organised by SAPT. The latter's Chair, Tom Hart, pointed out that bridges which shortened road journeys without carrying new sections of railway so as to shorten rail routes too would 'kill the railway', but such projects were not necessarily dictated by economies as the A9 would show a loss if interest were charged on the capital for its improvement.

Hart felt that rail's advantage for longer journeys could be enhanced by concentrating buses on feeder services, and improved connections at Inverness might increase direct receipts by 10-20%. He suggested that as much as £350,000 of the £444,000 social grant might be attributable to the line north of Tain, for which quoted receipts were £55,000 (excluding contributory revenue to the rest of the network).

At the conclusion of the conference, the new Highland Area Secretary of SAPT, David Martin (having taken over from Adrian Varwell, who had resigned following his appointment to a community development post with Ross and Cromarty County Council), 'said that two years ago everything in connection with the Kyle line looked impossible. The change in its prospects showed how sustained effort was well worth while.'

Only five months later, such effort was – in a small but symbolic way – to start turning the tide away from passenger service contraction to expansion on the Far North Line. Following a campaign initiated by Adrian Varwell and Alness Community Association, Alness station re-opened to passenger services on Monday 7 May 1973. The Department of the Environment granted BR permission to re-open the station, on the basis that its 1960 population of little over 1,000 had more than doubled, and was expected to rise to 16,000 as a result of continuing industrial expansion in the area. Three trains a day in each direction was far from being a regular-interval commuter service. But it was a start.

Life on the railway

In the spring of 1973, I heard from Adrian Varwell that the BR Area Manager's office at Invergordon was on the lookout for temporary summer staff. I jumped at the opportunity to work on the railway, which had been a big interest since becoming a 10-year-old train spotter in Edinburgh in 1962. Through the summers of 1973 and 1974, I lodged from Mondays to Fridays with Varwell and his wife Margaret in their terraced home in Invergordon, just two minutes' walk from the station.

When I reported for BR duty at the Area Manager's busy office in June 1973, among the first new colleagues I met were the two Invergordon signalmen, Magnus Campbell and Iain MacDonald. MacDonald – aka 'the Blackbird',

The Class 24-hauled mid-morning train from Inverness marks the official re-opening of Alness station, on Monday 7 May 1973, by breaking through a modest ribbon, held on the left by the author. Frank Spaven

reflecting his hair colour – had begun his railway career in 1952 at nearby Delny, where he was born and brought up.

As in many traditional labour-intensive industries, the railway had lots of distinctive characters, and MacDonald witnessed and participated in his fair share of amusing (and sobering) incidents in a 50-year career, which concluded at Inverness in 2002. He had wanted to become a motor mechanic, but with no garage in the vicinity – and after what he describes as 'coercion' by his family – joined the railway as a junior porter, straight from school. Looking back more than 60 years in 2015, MacDonald reflected:

> Life was fine at Delny, but a bit quiet for a young guy of 15. I pottered about, doing bits of gardening and cutting firewood for the stationmaster, cleaning out the henhouse and jobs like that – which you don't normally do at bigger stations!

After three and a half years at Delny, MacDonald did his National Service, but on returning to civilian life he found that his job at the Ross-shire village station had been filled, so he had to report to BR management at Inverness to find another post (which he was guaranteed). MacDonald was offered jobs at Struan, Strome Ferry or Achnasheen, 'none of which I fancied', so he decided to look for a job outside the railway in Easter Ross. But there were none:

> So I went back humbled and said I'd had a think about it, and yes, I was willing to come back to the railway service. And the response was: "Oh, we don't have Struan now, and we don't have Strome Ferry. The only place we can offer you is Achnasheen *(which of course was infinitely more isolated than Delny)*." That did learn me.

After just three weeks' training at Achnasheen, MacDonald was a passed-out signalman, although he would spend only 11 months at this lonely crossing place on the Kyle line, where the settlement comprised little more than the station and adjacent hotel. Promotion to a Class 2 relief signalman post at the metropolis of Inverness was a mixed blessing. One of the first signal boxes he learnt was Rose Street, controlling the tracks to Platforms 5, 6 and 7, the 'Rose Street curve' lines avoiding the terminus station, and a level crossing:

> You needed to watch your back when working in Inverness; there was always somebody willing to report you. On one occasion at Rose Street, I was sitting reading a book, and for some reason I had to stand up, still holding the book. Somebody spotted the book and reported that I'd been reading rather than working. I think I told management that it had been the Rule Book!

MacDonald also worked Clachnaharry box on the outskirts of Inverness, which controlled the swing bridge over the Caledonian Canal. Today it is the only remaining signal box north of Inverness. The swing bridge was originally worked manually, by the signalman and one of the canal staff but, once the locks were mechanised, the signalmen had to send into Inverness for BR support when a boat was expected. On one windy day, as MacDonald recollected, that support was careless, and allowed the mechanism to get out of control:

> The winding wheels were going like the propeller of an aeroplane and he couldn't get near. So when the bridge reached its stop point, the gearing didn't stop – and there were cogs and lumps of iron flying in all directions. And that was the end of the winding mechanism.

In another incident, at Lentran, the first crossing loop north of Inverness, MacDonald was about to exchange the single-line tokens with a southbound freight train. A northbound passenger train was already sitting in the loop and, just as the freight arrived, and as MacDonald was holding the hoop up to do the exchange:

> …the passenger train driver or secondman switched his headlights on, as if to say "hello" to the freight. The freight driver got dazzled, couldn't see the hoop, missed it, then slammed on the brakes. It was big long train, and the rebound *[from the slack of the wagons' chain couplings]* almost pushed the train back through the catch points. Luckily it didn't de-rail, so I ran up to the driver and gave him the hoop.

> The guard thought I was to blame, by throwing the signal against the freight, which I hadn't done of course. He was soon passing Clachnaharry and giving a "character reference" to the signalman there, who was a close friend of mine and duly told me all about it. So I phoned into Millburn Yard and told them I wanted to speak to the guard as soon as he got in, so that I could give *him* a character reference.

> Lentran had no shops, nowhere you could get a newspaper, so it was a bit humdrum really. Anyway, the next day the train's going through, and he's hanging out of the guard's van, throwing newspapers to me. "Apologies, apologies, Iain, a hundred apologies to you." So that was that.

MacDonald had a lucky escape at the next box up the line, Clunes, where the single track from Beauly became double track eastwards towards Clachnaharry (until it was singled in 1966). Such locations, and crossing loops, were generally equipped until the late 1960s with Manson Automatic Token Exchange equipment, which avoided the need for the potentially hazardous hand exchange of tokens between signalmen and drivers/secondmen of non-stopping trains. Short horizontal metal arms (at different heights for receiving and delivering tokens) extended from a recess in the locomotive cab, allowing the exchange of tokens with equivalent arms on short platform structures by the lineside.

Forsinard's well-tended gardens complement the original station building (now an RSPB visitor centre). Seen here on 13 August 1975 from a southbound passenger service, with an engineer's machine in the northbound loop. Alan Young

On this particular occasion, due to an exchange mishap at Beauly, a southbound train had the token stuck on its receiving arm, and the train driver at the last minute blew his horn in the appropriate way to indicate to the Clunes signalman (MacDonald) that hand exchange was needed. But the warning came too late for him, standing on the lineside platform:

> The loco and platform arms were at the same height, so the two smashed together, ripping up the platform I was standing on, including the posts and the rodding, and I was catapulted backwards, fortunately not forward towards the train. A hairy moment, but I wasn't injured – I had nine lives.

After a total of ten years as a relief signalman at Inverness – covering a vast territory from Georgemas in the north to Dunkeld in the south, and from Kyle in the west to Forres in the east (including the original Highland Main Line over Dava Moor) – MacDonald shifted job to become a relief signalman at Kyle in 1967. During six years in the area, 'a lot of time was spent at Strathcarron, where there was a very attractive clerkess, who I married'.

In 1973, with the Kyle line under renewed threat of closure, MacDonald moved to Invergordon, where BR was desperately short of staff due to the competing wage attractions of the aluminium smelter. There he joined forces with the sole other signalman, Magnus Campbell. They would work together at Invergordon for no fewer than 12 years, both then shifting to Dingwall when, as we shall see, the Radio Electronic Token Block system was introduced.

Two outsiders sample the world of the railway

As a Railman in 1973 (and in 1974 a Senior Railman, a higher rate paid to try to attract staff in light of the smelter competition for labour) I found that the duties were varied. But, in the early weeks at Invergordon in 1973, spending the whole day shift up at the smelter – securing aluminium ingots in open rail wagons with wooden balks – was not the most stimulating of activities.

Portering work involved loading and offloading parcels from passenger trains, with occasional forays to the goods yard and good shed to help with the handling of 'sundries' traffic. Invergordon was one of the success stories of the BR freight empire, aided by the energetic Area Manager, John Gough. On an official visit by the BRB Chairman, Richard Marsh, I recollect watching the two of them conversing on the station platform, the lofty Marsh towering over the diminutive Gough. I was still smarting from Marsh's 1968 decision, as Minister of Transport, to close the Waverley Route through the Borders – but didn't have the bottle to chastise him, given the gulf of grades between us.

Hauled by a Class 24, a northbound freight hammers through Fearn in the summer of 1974. Senior Railman Mark Nolan's caravan home nestles at the side of the now B-listed station building. David Spaven

The distillery sidings were still busy, and I shudder to recollect climbing into the bowels of a closed hopper wagon, to help spread the load of animal feed pellets being gravity-fed from an overhead pipe. Asphyxiation in industrial accidents in such circumstances was not uncommon in those days, and the working environment of the railway then was much less safe than it is today.

As recorded in BR's 'Sectional Appendix' issued in 1983, a very traditional arrangement which I observed in 1973 was still required to work trains over the Invergordon Harbour branch, including the coal sidings:

> Trains worked over this branch must travel as slowly as possible to exchange points and locomotives must not pass the notice board. Men carrying red flags must stop the road traffic at the level crossing before allowing the trains to pass over the crossing.

Meantime, Willie Black and Malcolm Munro, the signalmen at Tain (one on each of two shifts), were finding their multi-purpose duties – not just signalling, but also issuing tickets and handling parcels – an increasing handful, so I was re-allocated to duties there. This involved catching the first train of the day, the 07.14 from Invergordon, on which there was always the prospect of a cup of tea from the 'mini-buffet' attendant, Alec Elliott, who had just joined the railway.

Alec came from a railway family. Indeed, when I worked on the railway in Inverness from 1974 to 1975, there were four Elliotts employed by BR: Alec, his two brothers, and his father, who would regale the wide-eyed youths around him with eye-witness tales of Red Army ruthlessness in World War Two. Alec Elliott would in due course shift to working on griddle and restaurant cars on the Highland Main Line, and then to the *Clansman* and *Highland Chieftain* trains from Inverness to London. A familiar face over those 40-plus years, he eventually retired in 2014 from the then still state-owned East Coast train operating company.

The Glenmorangie Distillery, just up the line from Tain had lost its own private siding in 1970, but wagons full of sacks of malt from the south were occasionally shunted into the goods yard at Tain. On one happy occasion (in every sense of the word), I was deployed on the task of off-loading sacks on to the ubiquitous 'NCL' (National Carriers)[61] lorry and accompanying the driver on the delivery. The sacks were emptied at Glenmorangie, and we were then quietly ushered into the bowels of the distillery, where an official-looking chap unlocked a tall cupboard, poured two large glasses of whisky, handed them over, and invited the two railway staff to enjoy their dram. The 'dramming' for distillery visitors was a long-standing tradition, which is now unthinkable, but I did get back to the station in one piece.

Another incident at Tain involving 'the drink' occurred one day when – having despatched the northbound passenger train at 12.11, and knowing there were no trains due until the returning Lairg freight just after 14.00 – the relief signalman and I decided to walk into town for 'a pint'. The station was duly locked up, and striding up the hill to the Railway Hotel we were mildly intrigued to pass two official-looking gents in smart suits: not the sort of person we often saw near the station.

Thinking nothing more of it, a couple of pints were sunk (in railway time), and the two pleasantly refreshed railwaymen strolled back down to the station, to find the two gents kicking their heels in the waiting hall. Could we help them? Yes indeed, we could: they were auditors from BR Scottish Region HQ in Glasgow, and could they check the books? While I opened up the ticket office and kept them talking, the signalman dashed into the mess room and stuffed his mouth full of Pan Drops, before returning with a brave face to take the unexpected visitors through all the details. Fortunately for the two aberrant railwaymen, there were no repercussions.

A further vivid recollection is of the Caithness-based 'permanent way' team which travelled around the Far North Line in their own accommodation coach, the Norse inflection of their accents – 'toon haal' rather than 'town hall' – reminding me of my summer 1972 experience as a student worker in a Shetland fish factory.

Perhaps the strangest day I experienced across the two summers was in 1974, when I was asked to cover for Mark Nolan, the Senior Railman who normally staffed, on a single shift, the quiet country station at Fearn. Climbing down from the early train on to Fearn's low platform, I unlocked the ticket office and found himself in a world rather different from the average railway accommodation. There was a large 'sound system', a mattress and a guitar. Recovering from my surprise, I spent an untaxing shift – not a ticket was sold – listening to music, weeding the platform and photographing passing freight trains. The background to this unexpected railway environment comes from Nolan's entertaining blog, 'A Railman Remembers'[62]:

> It was 1973 and I was fresh out of school, floating around the Highlands with two A levels, five university rejections and absolutely no idea what I was going to do. I was dossing with some remarkably tolerant friends, playing with a local dance band and enjoying the novelty (which still hasn't quite worn off) of not having to attend school or stress over exams.

> After a few months someone told me I was supposed to register for a national insurance number. This was news to me, and I wondered why no-one had ever mentioned it before. So I duly presented myself at what was still known as the Employment Exchange, before it was brutally renamed 'Job Centre'.

"Apparently I need a national insurance number." The clerk was young, keen and helpful. "Do you want to sign on for unemployment benefit?" he said. "Not particularly" I replied. "Do you want a job then?" "No, not really." "Well, you're supposed to do one or the other…" Then he made an inspired choice. "How would you like to work for the railways?" My response was involuntary; "Gosh I'd never thought of that, I love trains!"

Half an hour later I was in the Area Manager's office at Invergordon station having my first job interview. It was authority versus feckless youth and we took an instant dislike to each other. The vacancy involved working alone at Fearn Station, selling tickets and dealing with parcels. The hours were 7am till 3pm but I could use the 7.15 train to get to Fearn. "I suppose I could manage that" I muttered.

I could tell he really didn't want to give me the job. If it hadn't been for the labour shortage I'd never have got through the door. "How do I know you'll even turn up?" he said as he shoved the keys across the desk. "Who else are you going to get?" I replied as I picked them up.

Nolan, like me (travelling to Tain), would regularly catch the early train to Fearn from Dingwall or Invergordon (before establishing a caravan home on the platform at Fearn) and soon struck up an acquaintance with the aforementioned Alec Elliott:

> Alec, the buffet car attendant on those services, was a similar age to me, friendly, cheerful and as delighted with his job as I was with mine. And bless him, every time he came through Fearn he left a cup of tea for me on the platform, much to the shaking of the guard's head and anyone else who saw it.

I had to come up with some sort of response. I worked out that one thing Alec couldn't do in the buffet car was fry bacon. This led to feverish preparation and a miracle of timing. By pre-heating the frying pan, lining everything up and listening for the train whistle at Nigg Station crossing, I was able to hit Alec with a hot bacon and egg toasted sandwich just as the train arrived. This signalled the end of the Fearn master chef catering competition, but the morning tea continued to be a much appreciated perk until the end of my time at Fearn.

Nolan soon put his guitar to wider use in a local band, having been persuaded to join by the Fearn postie, Jimmy, who had been playing in jazz bands for 30 years.

> We called ourselves 'Summer Set', and with Jimmy's charm and our relaxed sound, we were quickly booked up every Thursday, Friday and Saturday. A pair of secondhand Wem PA speakers got ordered from London, which arrived a week later on the midday train. We played places like the Aluminium Smelter club and the Invergordon Social Club, as well as the many neighbouring British Legions. Then the Jackdaw Hotel in Barbaraville topped and tailed the

weekends with a residency every Wednesday and Sunday. It was crazy, we were playing five nights a week, and I was earning far more with the band than the railway. For a couple of mad months I couldn't get away to take advantage of my free train travel, and I had to fight for a weekend off.

Naturally, with my new found wealth, I did what any sensible nineteen year old would do; I bought an Amstrad stereo amp with speakers, and a Garrard SP25 Mk III record deck. These were proudly set up in the ticket office. Although it wasn't a particularly expensive stereo, it's doubtful if there has ever been a better sound system, or more music played, in any operating British railway station. While I was bopping round the ticket office, the autumn with its potato traffic was looming ever closer. But for the time being it didn't matter. Fearn was now officially the Music Station.

My life on the railway was conventional by comparison but, nevertheless, overtime work took me on some memorable Sunday trips to distant spots, working on the 'P-way'. At the time, track maintenance workers were the only railway staff to be paid double-time – and travelling time – on Sundays, so a stupendous windfall beckoned for a non-tax-paying student. The drawback was that this was the hardest physical work of my life.

Whether it was at Beauly (shovelling ballast for a new stretch of continuously welded track), Slochd Summit (the same) or on the climb from Rogart to Lairg (recovering broken metal chairs and wooden sleepers after a freight train derailment), as a 21-year-old from a world of reading and writing I found that I sometimes struggled with hard physical labour compared with men three times my age.

Transport to track maintenance locations could be by van or train, but the train was always the means of getting back for the weekend to my parents' home in Inverness, after completing the Friday shift. If the 15.22 passenger train from Invergordon was missed, there was always the 'pipe train': the return working from MK Shand to Inverness of cement-coated pipes en route for offloading at Maud on the Fraserburgh branch line. Train drivers were happy for railwaymen to have a free ride in the back cab of either of the two locos (it was a big train), and would bring it to a brief halt on the Rose Street Curve at Inverness, handy for my walk along Platforms 5, 6 or 7 to the centre of town – or, occasionally, to 'Platform 8', as the nearby British Railways Staff Association club was known in the local vernacular.

Train drivers often went by nicknames. In Inverness there were, for example, 'the Bandit', 'the Cowboy' and 'the Crow', at least two of whom had earned the monikers through their driving style. One of the signalman at Tain, Malcolm Munro, was known – for some never-explained reason – as 'the Duck'. Iain

MacDonald recollected in 2016 that there was also 'the Hen' at Tain, and, earlier in his career, 'we had a Budgie when I was at Achnasheen, some couldn't tell us apart, so we had a Blackbird and a Budgie working at the same station'.

The drivers were regarded as a cut above everyone else in the 'conciliation grades', but they could still be patient souls when dealing with those not honoured with footplate status. On one happily remembered occasion, I was relaxing in the Varwells' home in Invergordon on a Friday afternoon, when there came a loud knock at the door. It was signalman Magnus Campbell, and could I get a move on, as the pipe train was waiting for me?

The Far North Line centenary

By 1974, a further three minutes had been added to the lengthy passenger train journey time to Wick and Thurso, but SAPT, buoyed by the re-opening of Alness, was determined to accentuate the positive in this centenary year of the Far North Line. The campaigning group joined together with the Wick Society, with assistance from BR, to organise a special train from Inverness to Wick, and return, on Sunday 28 July.

Keeping a lot of lorries off the road: a trainload of cement-coated pipes from the MK Shand plant waits to head south, as the first northbound passenger train of the day pulls into Invergordon in the summer of 1974. David Spaven

There was something of a disappointing turn-out for the 6-coach double-headed train, but the participants enjoyed glorious weather, as well as three unusual journey features, over and above being able to reach Caithness by train on a Sunday. The train called at the closed Dunrobin station, giving passengers time to visit the castle and grounds, and at Helmsdale a brief ceremony on the platform formally marked the line's centenary.

A trainload of pipes bound for the cement-coating plant at Invergordon heads north from Inverness in 1978. The harbour branch and coal yard are to the right, with Ben Wyvis in the far distance. David Spaven

Even more of a departure from normal, and inconceivable today, was a brief halt at the 708-feet high County March Summit, where dignitaries clambered down from the train for a 'photo opportunity' in front of the summit name board. At Wick, students of history could view a special collection of railway exhibits in the Assembly Rooms or join a coach tour to John O'Groats or an organised visit to the Caithness Glass factory. As well as entertaining the day's passengers, SAPT was seeking to highlight ways in which rail-based tourist and leisure opportunities could be developed.

Later that summer, anticipating the creation of new Regional Councils the following year, BR published a 30-page briefing on 'Rail services in the Highland Region', noting that the imminent re-organisation of local government would provide an opportunity to co-operate fully with the new authorities, in order to improve the public transport systems for both passenger and freight traffic.

Taking a quick break from the 100th anniversary special train at County March Summit on 28 July 1974, the official party includes the BR Area Manager Thurso (far right), David Cobbett, BR Scottish Region General Manager (third right), Lord Thurso (centre, in kilt), and David Martin, SAPT Highland Area Secretary (second left). David Spaven

A further context for this BR briefing was the 1974 abolition of the Government's service-by-service grant-aid system, replaced by a nationwide 'Public Service Obligation' (PSO) payment to BR, with no route breakdowns of subsidy. Arguably, this has kept any closure ideas well away from the Far North Line, a former senior railway manager commenting to me in 2016: 'The PSO simply got difficult things off the table, and played a big – effectively passive – role in maintaining a steady state.' However, as we shall see, there would also be other nationwide factors at work which made railway closures increasingly unattractive from a political perspective.

The BR briefing identified the six area managers covering the Highlands, four of whom shared management of the Far North Line: at Inverness, Dingwall, Invergordon and Thurso. Intriguingly, reference was made to the possibility of capital investment to improve journey times and 'to the operation of additional services to Invergordon and as far north as Lairg'. However, it was to be a further eight years before services were accelerated (with the introduction of more powerful Class 37 locos) and 24 years until commuter trains were permanently introduced at the southern end of the line.

On plans for road-rail co-ordination, the briefing optimistically noted that: 'Plans which are in hand for siting a new 'bus terminal in an area adjacent to Inverness station, facilitating transfer between the trunk rail services and distributory 'bus routes, are welcomed.' Forty-two years later, Inverness bus station remains in the same location, and a shopping mall sits adjacent to the railway station.

An appendix showed that 'representative' passenger numbers per week at Far North Line stations were extremely modest in winter, ranging from 10 at Invershin, through 467 at Thurso and 402 at Invergordon, to 949 at Dingwall (which enjoyed double the train frequency). Patronage was better in summer, but not much more so, ranging from 21 at Scotscalder to 2,069 at Dingwall. With journey times still deteriorating, and roads improving, there were fears for the future of a railway which was carrying not much more than bus loads of passengers.

Under 'Future Developments' (which did not mention the Far North Line), the BR briefing referred to the capability of the Highland Main Line (HML) 'to relieve traffic on the A9 road':

> The maximum effectiveness of the route could only be achieved, however, by constructing a double line railway over the greater part of the distance from Perth to Inverness, installing modern signalling and electrification and providing locomotives of higher power and performance. The cost of such an ambitious programme, although less than the development of the A9, would be quite beyond the scale of investment at present available to British Rail, Scottish Region, but would warrant capital being made available specifically for this purpose.

Surprisingly, observation cars have never regularly graced the Far North Line. Here, in a Spring 1979 view of Achnasheen, the finer points of the Kyle line's history are no doubt being explained by Inspector Jack Rennie, who for many years was the familiar face welcoming summer visitors to that line's observation car. This car was one of a number which served the Kyle line intermittently after the 1967 withdrawal of 'Coronation' and 'Devon Belle' cars from all the Highland routes they had served. Frank Spaven

Forty-two years later, the Highland Main Line is still two-thirds single track, with predominantly traditional electro-mechanical signalling, and diesel-operated. Meanwhile, work is progressing on the Scottish Government's £3bn dualling of the A9 (which was completely rebuilt in the 1970s and 80s) but, at the time of writing, even the *specification* for work on the substantive phase of the piecemeal upgrade of the HML, capped at £600m, had still not been agreed.

On freight in 1974, BR could report that the total handled by rail in the region (including the West Highland Line to Fort William) 'will be nearly 1,000,000 tonnes'. Noting that capital grants for freight facilities were now available under Section 8 of the Railways Act 1974 – which still survive in Scotland in 2016, as 'Freight Facilities Grants' – the briefing went on to indicate that further private sidings 'meriting consideration' were at Alness (Taywood Seltrust), Ardersier (J Ray McDermott) and Nigg (Highland Fabricators).

In this mid-1970s view at Inverness, a Class 26 propels a train from the north into Platform 3 or 4, while a Class 47 prepares to depart from Platform 1 with the Clansman service to London via the West Coast Main Line. The two sidings on the left were used for Motorail car traffic, and later – temporarily – for coal container handling. David Spaven

All were North Sea oil-related, but none was ever constructed. Fourteen freight stations were identified on the Far North Line, as well as seven private sidings at the following four locations:

- Alness (Dalmore Distillery, but this was by then out-of-use)

- Evanton (Graham Wood, steel stockholders)

- Invergordon (British Aluminium, Invergordon Distillery, McGruther & Marshall coal merchants on the Harbour Branch, and MK Shand)

- Lairg (Shell Mex / BP).

Rail freight figured significantly in the following year's 'Highlands & Islands Transport Review' produced by the HIDB. On 14 August 1975, Frank Spaven drafted a revised version of its 'Summary of Priorities'. Two of the seven priorities related to the Far North Line, namely 'increased operating capacity on the Perth-Inverness-Invergordon railway' and 'improved container or specialised railheads at Thurso and Fort William'. The draft report as a whole was signed off for a Board meeting that day by Spaven and his colleagues Stan Pickett and Roy Pedersen, including a commentary on changed trends:

Whereas until recently [rail] facilities have tended to be curtailed because of declining traffic, traffic is now increasing on a number of lines as a result of the demands of oil-related enterprises and other economic activity and emphasis is being placed on seeking ways of enabling these lines to handle the increased number of trains.

Another station re-opens

1976 witnessed the second station re-opening in the space of four years on the Far North Line. Writing in the letters page of the *Highland News* on 30 September, the SAPT Highland Area Secretary, David Martin, however, wanted to put the record straight:

Next Monday, 4 October 1976, will see the positive, but long overdue step of re-opening Muir of Ord Railway Station to passengers. How did this come about? From the British Rail Press handout it would appear that they and the Highland Region were the only parties involved. I should like to put it on record it is my belief that it was the sustained pressure supported by facts from two small voluntary bodies, the Muir of Ord Community Association and the Scottish Association for Public Transport (SAPT) which caused the gigantic British Rail and Highland Region to consider the matter.

Bemoaning the three years it had taken, since a local household survey, to get the rail service reinstated – the trains were passing through anyway, and both platforms were fully intact – Martin felt compelled to comment on the inadequacies of the new train service, with the first train service not reaching Inverness until after 10 am, and the last train back departing Inverness at 17.45:

Those who go shopping and visiting within 50 miles of Muir of Ord will be pleased when the station opens. Those who want to go further or commute will not be so delighted…What is clearly required is for there to be an earlier morning train and a later evening train, as of course there used to be, and which would act between Tain and Inverness as – (a) a commuter train from the Moray Firth area and (b) as a feeder service to the Inter City routes.

Martin, and Muir of Ord, would have to wait another three decades for this relatively modest vision to be realised.

On the freight front, statistics later compiled by Frank Spaven[63] demonstrated a big contrast between the southern and northern sections of the Far North Line. In 1965, the line had generated a total of 216,000 tonnes of forwarded and received freight. In 1976, on the back of the aluminium smelter and North Sea oil developments, this had jumped to 303,000 tonnes, but only 41,000 tonnes was generated north of Lairg. Excluding coal traffic along the line (around 80,000 tonnes), some 185,000 tonnes of freight were generated by the various depots and private sidings at Invergordon alone, two thirds of it forwarded traffic, but just 5,840 tonnes came from the distillery (reflecting the impact of road competition), whose rail traffic was now dwarfed by MK Shand (40,261 tonnes of outgoing cement-coated pipes) and British Aluminium (75,280 tonnes of ingots and alumina). Few observers could then have imagined that, compared to the 303,000 tonnes total on the Far North Line in 1976, just 10 years later it was to decline to only 52,000 tonnes of traffic – and by the early 1990s it would be almost zero.

The Far North Line makes global headlines

Snow has always been a threat to Far North Line operations, particularly in the moors around the 'Fairy Hillocks' between Forsinard and Altnabreac. This returned with a vengeance on 28 January 1978. Former BBC reporter, Bill Hamilton, in his autobiography, *Man on the spot: a broadcaster's story* (2010), recounts the events.

> In these days of sophisticated signalling and an array of mobile phones, it is unthinkable that a main-line train could simply *'disappear'*. Yet, thirty years ago, as blizzards raged across the Scottish Highlands, anxious and overworked railway controllers were forced to admit they had no idea what had happened to the Great North Express *[sic]* or of the fate of its 70 passengers.

> Frantic phone calls to station staff, signalmen and the emergency services produced no answers. The Inverness to Wick train was lost in the snow and no-one could establish precisely where it was.

> At 17.15 that evening a diesel-hauled train with its six coaches left Inverness on the Great North *[sic]* railway heading for Georgemas Junction where the train was scheduled to divide… the front half turning eastwards to Wick, the end coaches proceeding to Britain's most northerly station at Thurso. As it proceeded northwards, falling snow and gale force winds meant at times speed had to be reduced to a crawl, with swaying tree branches and even a loose telegraph pole striking the side of the carriages.

> British Rail, heeding warnings that things would take a turn for the worse, decided it was wise to double-head the train and ordered driver Stewart Munro and second man Jimmy Forbes to take the Thurso branch engine as far south as Helmsdale in Sutherland to meet up with the Inverness train. By the time they had reached the rendezvous point, conditions were deteriorating fast.

> The double-headed train pulled out of Helmsdale shortly after 21.30… At the controls of the locomotive, Stewart Munro found himself battling at once against the ever-worsening conditions. Driving snow rendered the windscreen wipers and headlight useless. Now and then he could pick out a landmark, but most of the time he could see nothing and frequently he would feel a jolt as the nose-plough hit a drift.

> As the train continued into the teeth of a gale, some of the passengers likened the journey to being on a frightening carnival ride. At times, the noise reached

almost intolerable levels, the carriages were continually being buffeted about with luggage tumbling out of the racks.

The train finally reached Forsinard a full 90 minutes late but the locomotive crew knew the worst still lay ahead. Between Forsinard and Altnabreac the rails reach an elevation of 708 feet *[at the County March Summit]*… Suddenly, there was a horrendous crash and the train came to a juddering halt. Five of the six coaches were derailed and the wheels of the third coach had been running on the sleepers for over a mile when the coupling between the second and third carriages sheared, together with the air-brake pipes. The two parts of the train finished over 150 yards apart.

Although alarmed, all the passengers, including several children and two hospital patients recovering from major surgery were unhurt. Guard Martin Marke did what he could to calm them and the crew of the two locomotives managed to get a foothold in the snow and erect a ladder to get everyone safely out of the derailed coaches and transferred to the front carriage, the only one to have stayed on the track.

Crammed they may have been but the combined warmth by so many packed into one coach would prove a real blessing during the ordeal ahead.

Eventually, the train was on its way again, but not for long. About two miles further north, a massive drift brought it to a complete standstill. Looking out the windows, the passengers could see nothing…There was nothing for it but to bed the passengers down for the night. The one consolation was that the heating was working and they had plenty of fuel.

Dentist Chris Andrews had a half bottle of whisky in his pocket *[there was no buffet car on the train]* but with at least a dozen crammed into his compartment was embarrassed by the thought that there wouldn't be enough wee drams to go round. To his amazement, he found there were no takers. All his fellow passengers were teetotallers!

The fate of the train and its passengers was unknown to anyone beyond the scene. BR decided to send a relief loco from Wick out from Georgemas towards Forsinard under emergency operational arrangements, and as Hamilton recorded:

The crew of the relief loco were instructed to proceed with extreme caution with the headlight on and the whistle sounding continuously…Moving very slowly, the diesel loco disappeared into the white gloom, the sound of its whistle soon devoured by the howling wind.

Elsewhere across the Highlands there was widespread chaos, with many motorists stranded and temperatures expected to drop further. There seemed to be no firm plan to reach the stranded train by rescue service helicopter, but the presumably-marooned passengers had not been forgotten, as Hamilton recounted:

At the BBC studios in Aberdeen, News Editor Arthur Binnie and I were hastily thumbing through our contacts list. Could there be just one helicopter somewhere in the country that had been overlooked by the rescue organisers? There was, and of all places, it was sitting on the tarmac at Aberdeen. The only problem was getting it airborne would cost the BBC licence payers a great deal of money.

The helicopter pilot offered to drop the price from £1,200 to £1,000 an hour. With the go-ahead from BBC London, and hearing that ITN were on the way in a chartered helicopter, Hamilton was soon in the air, having suggested to Highland Police that they should have emergency supplies ready at Wick airport, en route to the white-out:

> Battling against gale-force winds and heavy snow, it took two hours to reach Caithness *[a distance of less than 100 miles as the crow flies]*. On the tarmac, the police and volunteers were waiting. Food supplies, refreshments and blankets were all boxed and ready for an airdrop if we could successfully pinpoint the stranded train.

> As we took off again the helicopter crew were confident and determined. With one set of eyes constantly trained on the instrument panel, the other trying to find anything that resembled a railway line, this was certainly an adrenalin-pumping experience of the highest order. Within a matter of minutes, the navigator spotted what he thought was the booking hall of Georgemas Junction. If he was right, it would be a case of following the tops of the telegraph poles, jutting barely a foot above the snow line, and the hunt for the stricken train would be over.

> He WAS right. As flying conditions took a decided turn for the better, we spotted the relief locomotive, which had set off from the north, hopelessly stuck in the drifts.

> Then, a few miles further south, through the cockpit window, there it was – the 'lost train' – the outline of the two locos and sole remaining coach barely visible through the drifting snow which in places was now ten feet high.

> The relief and sheer excitement of the moment is hard to describe. Some of the 70 passengers were so elated that they temporarily forgot the world blanketed in white outside the carriage door. Down into the snow they jumped, falling over like a pack of cards in the noiseless drift, believing rescue was now at hand.

> In fact, all we had planned to do was give them the necessities to ease the hunger, fear and discomfort of a second night in the train. Not for a second had we contemplated that we might be able to land.

But after the supplies were dropped, as Hamilton recounted, the helicopter captain thought he could see some harder ground nearby:

> We all held our breath as the helicopter was lowered to blow away the loose lying snow. Now everything would depend on a further descent to discover if there was any significant updraught of snow which could suck into the engine intakes, endangering the aircraft and everyone aboard.

A thumbs-up indicated the captain was happy. With darkness descending, snow still falling and the wind still gusting at over 60 miles an hour, we finally set down. On the ground exhaustion gave way to ecstasy. The great escape was now under way. All we had to do was let the camera roll – the snowbound passengers and a myriad of stories about life aboard the 'lost' train were heading straight towards us.

The majority of women and children was helicoptered to Wick airport, where refuelling was required anyway for the return flight to Aberdeen. Hamilton and his cameraman were left beside the train, giving them half an hour to interview those left behind, including the train crew:

Soon the survivors' accounts began to flow. Most recalled the sheer courage and constancy of the train crew. One engine had been kept running to provide some warmth but during the early hours of Sunday morning the water to heat the boiler had run out. The temperature dropped dramatically and the passengers had to huddle even closer together to allow their body heat to build a human cushion against the bitter cold. As conditions worsened, one of the locomen had volunteered to dig through the snow to try to connect the pipes from the carriage to the other engine. This could only be done by tying a rope round his legs and hauling him back up from the huge mound of snow.

In the meantime, the crew of the relief locomotive which had itself become derailed one and a half miles to the north, trudged through the drifts with two tins of soup and a pint of milk. This was all mixed together, heated at the engine exhaust, and offered in tiny amounts to the passengers via an unsavoury looking tin with jagged edges.

Hamilton and the helicopter in due course got back safely to Aberdeen, and their extraordinary filmed story provided a four-minute lead for the UK National News that evening. Meantime, the remaining passengers were ferried three at a time in an RAF rescue helicopter to the nearest house with a road (at Scotscalder), but their plight was not yet over. They were dismayed to find that the phone was out of action and the road blocked, and so had to trudge more than two miles along the snow-covered railway line to Halkirk, the nearest village. As Hamilton recorded, the abiding memory of one passenger was

…being taken into a railwayman's home and the alluring smell from a huge pot of home-made soup bubbling away on the stove. The taste to frozen, hungry folk was out of this world. He eventually arrived in Wick at seven o'clock that night and was amazed to find that there wasn't a drop of snow in the town.

News of the lost train was soon flashing around the world. In distant New Zealand, my parents – on a once-in-a-lifetime holiday to see old friends – found that Altnabreac was on the front page of the local newspaper. The Far North Line had made global headlines for the first, and probably last, time.

Not just a passenger station: a multiplicity of shapes and sizes of parcels (and mail) is offloaded from the train at Thurso in the summer of 1979, most of them into two 'BRUTEs'. BRUTEs (British Rail Universal Trolley Equipment) were used from 1964 until the nationwide demise of the 'Red Star' parcels service in 1999. Red Star ceased on the Far North Line in 1991. David Spaven

A decade of change ends

By 1978, most trains were a few minutes faster than they had been in 1974, but the biggest improvement – nine minutes faster on the 17.15 from Inverness – gave the line a best journey time of 4 hours 31 minutes, a far cry from the 4 hours of 1964's *Orcadian*. One train in each direction still had no buffet car, including the 17.15 service which came to grief in January, but that aspect of the timetable was soon rectified and, in any event, after the lost train incident all services carried emergency rations.

The severe weather spell in early 1978 was to sow the seeds of an eventual transformation of the line's signalling. More than 40 miles of signal telegraph pole route – linking the traditional electric token instruments at each 'block post' (signal box) – were brought down by snow. The simplest and quickest way of restoring the links between the instruments was found to be by radio, with manual exchange of the tokens continuing as before. This improvised arrangement would prove to be the forerunner of the dramatic signalling changes wrought in 1985 by the Radio Electronic Token Block system, as described in the next chapter.

On the competing road network, in April 1979, the first of the three firths' crossings was completed, with the opening of the £5m Cromarty Bridge across the Cromarty Firth, linking the A9 south of Evanton to the Black Isle near Culbokie. It was not to become part of the A9 until the 1982 completion of the Kessock Bridge by Inverness, but the writing was on the wall in terms of road v rail competition.

In late 1979, SAPT was pressing the case for radical action on the Far North Line in its 'Scottish Transport – a New Era' proposals:

> In view of the advanced stages of planning for the Dornoch Firth Bridge, it is particularly important that provision should be made for the inclusion of a railway on this bridge. With other improvements, this would reduce rail journey times from Caithness to Inverness from 4½ hours to around 3 hours.

Of course, at that time, the railway's key function was as a mover of freight, particularly on the southern half of the route. But the next decade would bring an unexpected – and drastic – contraction of that role.

A Class 40 eases the regular Muir of Ord-Doncaster empty barley train across the Caledonian Canal at Clachnaharry in the early 1970s. The balancing northbound loaded working (for the Distillers Company) was one of the first dedicated company trainloads (as opposed to mixed freights) in the Highlands when introduced in the mid- 1960s. David Spaven

CHAPTER 12: A TALE OF TWO BRIDGES

By the start of the 1980s, there had long been interest from the Highlands & Islands Development Board (HIDB), local government and rail campaigners in the prospects for siting a Freightliner container terminal in Inverness and perhaps also in Caithness.

Studies involving Freightliner, the HIDB and others in the 1960s and 1970s found that the Highlands did not generate enough realistic traffic potential – in competition with road haulage over rapidly improving roads – to justify both the capital and operating cost of such a terminal. However, a two-stage consultancy study for Highland Regional Council in 1979-80 suggested that a limited service from Glasgow to an Inverness 'mini-terminal' could be feasible, although this in practice did not materialise. Just seven years later, due to shortage of funding for reinvestment in its rail wagon fleet, Freightliner closed its Aberdeen, Dundee and Edinburgh terminals, leaving only Coatbridge and Glasgow open in Scotland.

A Class 26 with independent snow plough eases past Welsh's Bridge signal box in Inverness on 6th January 1982. In the background, at the west end of Millburn Yard, is the 'Blue Circle' cement silo which still receives regular supplies by rail today. Built in 1889, Welsh's Bridge box (together with Millburn, Loco Shed, Station Frame and Rose Street) was closed following the 1987 Inverness resignalling scheme. Frank Spaven

The 1979-80 study extended to the potential for 'conventional' wagons (as opposed to those carrying intermodal containers designed for easy transfer between the rail, road and sea modes), as part of the nationwide Speedlink network of reliable, overnight wagonload services which had been progressively introduced between major centres since 1972. These air-braked services replaced traditional vacuum-braked wagonload trains.

Two private siding locations on the Far North Line merited specific mention and the ongoing need for 'an aggressive marketing policy'. In the case of the smelter, rail had a two-thirds share of outgoing traffic within the United Kingdom, but a major road haulier (Smiths of Maddiston) was 'obtaining traffic on routes that are rail connected at both ends, and should logically be rail traffic'. At Invergordon Distillery, the dark grain by-product (for animal feed markets) generated 25,000 tonnes per annum on a regular basis and was 'a particular example of a location ideally suited for rail freight that has gradually made a transition to road. We recommend that further effort be made by British Rail to regain the lost business.'

At the distillery, 90,000 tonnes of corn/barley annually was arriving by sea at Invergordon, while the 20,000 tonnes of fuel which had formerly arrived by the trainload from Bowling was now being roaded from Inverness Harbour. Of 53,000 tonnes of outbound spirit annually to Central Scotland – for maturation, blending, bottling etc – just 5,000 tonnes was moving by rail. At MK Shand, 20,000 tonnes of steel was arriving by sea, but cement was still being delivered in a weekly trainload of 500 tonnes payload.

Of the smelter's total production of 106,000 tonnes (including 25,000 tonnes export, by sea), 56,000 tonnes was moving by rail, and 25,000 tonnes by road. British Aluminium's traffic in fact represented no less than 27% of the entire rail freight volume of 417,252 tonnes on the Highland rail network focused on Inverness, and a mighty 84% of the outgoing traffic. This was to prove an unhealthy over-dependence.

The smelter shuts

The British Aluminium Company (which dated back to 1894, and had pioneered aluminium smelting in the Highlands) was taken over in 1981 by the giant Canadian company, Alcan. The Invergordon smelter was then closed the same year, with the loss of more than 700 jobs. According to David Ross, writing in the 17 August 2012 edition of the *Herald*, it was not wider health or environmental concerns about the aluminium industry which 'did for Invergordon':

It was the government's determination that Scotland's first Advanced Gas Cooled Nuclear reactor (AGR) at Hunterston would be able to provide Invergordon with enough electricity at a competitive price. Delays to the AGR programme, unsustainably high prices for electricity in the interim and a slump in aluminium prices spelled the end 30 years ago.

BA's directors had failed to sign a proper contract with government, remarkably – and tellingly – relying on a gentleman's agreement.

Dr Perchard [author of *Aluminiumville* (2012)] says the closeness of BA to the government appears to have blinkered the company, and that its story may provide a valuable insight for businesses today.

The effect on the Far North Line was dramatic. According to statistics later collated by Frank Spaven, where the various depots and sidings in Invergordon had generated no fewer than 185,000 tonnes in 1976, by 1986/87 this had fallen to only 21,100 tonnes. Forwarded traffic from Invergordon, which had totaled 121,756 tonnes in 1976 (from the distillery, MK Shand and the smelter), shrank to a miserable 2,306 tonnes – from the distillery only – in 1986/87.

With renewed worries about the peripheral Highland routes, following the loss of the smelter (and the earlier closure of the Corpach pulp mill in 1980, albeit with the paper mill remaining), in 1981 the HIDB and BR Scottish Region commissioned the 'Highland Rail Study' from consultants Transmark. As Frank Spaven would write in his future MSc thesis:

It assessed the financial, economic and community role of the north and west Highland networks, on the basis of traffic data, sample surveys of existing and potential users, and various options and forecasts, and found that both networks were viable in the widest sense. The costs of closing the networks would be greater than the costs of retention…It was, in the event, over-optimistic about freight usage and it did not deal with the still outstanding question of appropriate local management of these lines, but it was a valuable and encouraging appraisal with strong recommendations to its sponsors, which they gave a joint, public commitment to follow up, on how to reduce costs and increased revenues.

A 1983 briefing by BR for Highland Regional Council focused on potential new traffics to help fill the massive gap left by the smelter, expressing the hope that 'the development of Wick/Thurso container traffic will proceed beyond the experimental stage' and highlighting the need for the Council to reserve development land adjacent to rail and to support potential 'Section 8' grant applications (to the Department of Transport) which could include 'container transfer at Inverness and Wick'.

The Wick/Thurso potential was realised, albeit briefly, through the resurrection of an old Highland railway tradition: the mixed train. Beginning in

March 1984, the concept was tried again when the 13.55 Aberdeen-Inverness and 17.40 Inverness-Wick services were made into mixed passenger and Freightliner trains (with balancing workings in the return direction)[64]. The service was operated for Sutherland Transport Ltd but, as was sometimes the case with switching traffic to rail, industrial relations problems arising from underutilisation of the firm's established lorry drivers led to the demise of the service in 1985. The fixed cost of operating a road-rail crane at Wick, for modest volumes of freight, may also have been a factor.

The 1983 BR briefing also reminded readers of other aspects of its business which were still very much present on the Far North Line: Rail Express Services (RES) operating throughout the region, conveying Royal Mail letters and parcels, newspapers, and general parcels by Red Star and Night Star premium services between local stations and places nationwide. It commented: 'The Postal and Newspaper arrangements are long established and RES confidently expect to maintain their role as trunk-haul contractors for the foreseeable future.'

No fewer than three Royal Mail vans wait for the train from Inverness at Helmsdale in this 1983 view. Some five years later, all postal traffic was lost from the Far North Line. Frank Spaven

This confidence was to prove mis-placed: within eight years all this traffic was to be lost. This was due to air and road competition and the introduction of new 'Sprinter' trains which precluded the possibility of passengers, parcels and freight being hauled together in a single train. It was a potentially serious loss for rural routes like the Far North Line where aggregation of flows was needed to create the critical mass for efficient rail movement. However, an item of good news on the passenger front directly concerned the Far North Line:

> A policy of line speed improvement is being vigorously pursued and this has been demonstrated in a reduction of some 45 minutes over the last three years between Thurso and Inverness. The latest stage in this (an overall saving of some 10" [minutes]) comes from modernisation of 6 level crossings which enable trains to pass over the crossings at higher speeds.

Much of the journey time improvement had resulted rather from the replacement in 1982 of the original late 1950s' vintage Type 2 diesels (later Class 24/26) of 1,160 horse power with Type 3 (Class 37) locos of 1,750 horse power, built in the 1960s. Average overall timings of four hours 44 minutes in 1980 were reduced to 4 hours 21 minutes in 1982, with further reductions to 4 hours 11 minutes in 1983-84 and 4 hours 2 minutes in 1985/86. The Class 37s were to represent the apotheosis of diesel locomotive traction on the Far North Line until their replacement by 'Sprinter' diesel units in 1990.

For a short period in the mid-1980s a through container wagon from Aberdeen Freightliner Terminal was attached to passenger trains between Aberdeen, Inverness and Thurso. Here, the container wagon forms part of the 12.35 mixed-train departing Platform 3 at Inverness for Aberdeen on 19 September 1984, hauled by a Class 47. Frank Spaven

A speed-up was badly needed on the railway, as 1982 had seen the completion of the Kessock Bridge and the A9 across the Black Isle, leaving a rail distance of 31 miles from Inverness to Invergordon comparing poorly with 24 miles of largely new road – and further adding to the railway's long-standing circuitous disadvantages compared to the A9 further north. But even worse was to come when the Dornoch Firth Bridge was completed in 1991.

The year 1983 also saw the completion of a Technical Memorandum by British Rail Research on 'The movement of coal to the North of Scotland'. This had been prompted not only by ongoing market decline, and declining rail market share v road haulage, but also by the fact that most coal was being moved in old flat-bottomed vacuum-braked wagons (with a maximum payload of 16 tonnes) to unmechanised low-throughput station yards, where wagons were manually discharged.

The study involved a variety of rationalised networks served by hopper bottom-discharge wagons or containers (of 15 feet or 20 feet length) – the most extensive of which included just two railheads on the Far North Line, at Ardgay (projected throughput 8,900 tonnes pa) and Thurso (10,700 tonnes pa). The favoured method was containers, due, *inter alia*, to lower costs, avoidance of degradation and also the fact that: 'It would be relatively easy to operate mixed trains north of Inverness with this system, given BR Board approval for this type of operation.'

The report suggested that mixed train working north of Inverness would contribute £71,450 annually to passenger revenues. But, in practice, the ultimate solution north of the Central Belt, provided by air-braked freight trains, included coal railheads at only Dundee, Aberdeen, Keith and Inverness. Aberdeen and Inverness were serviced by containers (of 30 feet length) and Dundee and Keith by hopper wagons.

The (brief) Serpell threat

A new threat to the future of many, if not all, of the remaining Highland railways, including the Far North Line, came in 1983. As recorded in *Holding the Line* (2012) by Richard Faulkner and Chris Austin:

> In 1980, Peter Parker [Chairman of the British Railways Board] had sufficient confidence to ask the Government to set up a major review of the board's objectives, in the hope it would help create a fresh financial framework and allow the railway to escape from the "crumbling edge of quality" as he called it.

The review, commissioned by Government in mid-1982, and chaired by

Sir David Serpell, a former Department of Transport Permanent Secretary, in practice did not deliver a plan for modernisation. Rather, it set out a number of network options based on different, mostly reduced, levels of financial support. At the time, the network comprised just over 10,000 route miles, down from the 11,000 route miles envisaged in the 1967 'basic rail network' set out by the Labour Government. Six network options were examined by Serpell, five of them based on a reduced network (in terms of routes and/or stations): in all five of these, there was no future for the railways north of Inverness.

Fortunately, the Serpell prescriptions – with much flawed analysis, and railway *expansion* never seriously evaluated – were soon discredited, not least through a judicious leak from the BRB to the media in early 1983. The overwhelmingly adverse reaction from politicians, the press and the public ensured that none of Serpell's options was implemented. BR did quietly pursue the potential for bus substitution on selected routes for a few years – and infrastructure rationalisation schemes continued to be implemented to cut costs, in a number of cases creating long-term capacity problems on the network. But the long search for a mythical 'profitable core' was abandoned, and passenger growth through the mid and late 1980s ensured that by 1990 the emphasis had switched to extension of the network of routes and stations rather than retrenchment, for the first time in many generations.

The end of through freight

Just over a year after the BR Research report on the future of coal traffic north of the Central Belt, the loss of Far North Line freight traffic resulting from smelter closure was compounded by the cessation of all domestic coal traffic to 10 freight depots along the length of the route. By 1983, the final full year of coal traffic on the Far North Line, this commodity, which had generated 60,000 tonnes of traffic for the railway in 1963, accounted for just 11,829 tonnes. Even the busiest coal depot, at Thurso, received just 2,491 tonnes, while the quietest, at Muir of Ord, handled only 317 tonnes. This was not a sustainable future for the freight railway.

The traditional wagonload train to Caithness could not survive the loss of baseload coal business. What had latterly become a twice-weekly freight service from Inverness to Wick and Thurso (with wagons staged intermediately at Brora, and worked north the following day) was – following further loss of traffic due to the miners' strike – withdrawn in 1984. General freight services also ceased at Muir of Ord, Dingwall, Alness, Ardgay (as Bonar Bridge had been renamed in 1977), Golspie, Brora, Helmsdale, Georgemas, Wick and Thurso.

Surviving traffic to private sidings was thereafter conveyed, in the case of Muir of Ord, by a daily Speedlink service for distillery barley from eastern England, while a daily Speedlink train to Invergordon (extended twice-weekly to Lairg) handled pipes to British Pipe Coaters (formerly MK Shand) at Invergordon and oil to the Lairg railhead.

One of the few positive freight developments at that time came briefly in the summer of 1984, when a short-lived national dock strike – in sympathy with the miners – resulted in a Deep Sea container feeder ship being loaded at Invergordon with export traffic which normally would have been routed via specialist container ports such as Liverpool and Greenock.

Freightliner, the market leader for overland movement of containers, operated a number of special trains from the south to Invergordon freight depot, whence the company's own HGVs shuttled the containers to Invergordon Pier (built for the aluminium smelter) for onward shipment to the USA via a hub port on the European mainland.

Following the rationalisation in 1984 of BR's coal distribution network, the remaining railway coal business in the Highlands was concentrated on just two railheads in Inverness, one of which was already established adjacent to Millburn Yard for gravity discharge of hopper wagons (with a 25-tonne payload). After the miners' strike, a temporary new terminal for coal in containers (of 30 feet length and 30-tonne payload) was created in the goods yard adjacent to the passenger station, replaced in 1988 by a bespoke facility on the truncated harbour branch. I had responsibility for rail traffic through these railheads in my 1985-90 role as BR's Marketing & Contracts Manager, Speedlink Coal (Scotland).

The retention of the stub of the harbour branch resulted from the agreement of ScotRail's General Manager, Chris Green, to my request that the line as far as the traditional coal yard part-way down the branch, should not be severed – as originally planned – by the Inverness rationalisation and resignalling scheme, implemented in 1987. Green had arrived from the south at BR Scottish Region in 1980, and after becoming General Manager in 1984 he soon shook up the rail industry north of the Border, with the memorable new brand name (ScotRail), entrepreneurial marketing and a fierce response to the challenge of the newly deregulated bus industry.

In 1986 he would return south to blaze a trail with Network South East, leaving behind an industry with a much enhanced belief in itself, but not before he had played a central part in the Far North Line's controversial Dornoch Bridge saga.

The signalling economics are transformed

While BR had implemented substantial economies, notably elimination of surplus crossing loops, over the three years following the 1964 reprieve, plus the later nationwide end to the practice of the driver having a 'second man' (driver's assistant) in the cab, by the early-1980s the economics of the Far North Line were looking increasingly precarious. The competitive advantage of the A9 had increased further, with the completion of two of the three firth crossings by 1982, and rail freight traffic was in steep decline.

Meantime, a service of just three passenger trains and one freight train running the 168-mile length of the line daily required signalmen on two shifts at no fewer than 13 block posts (12 crossing loops, plus Clachnaharry to control the Caledonian Canal swing bridge). At most loops, the instruments were housed in the station building, with the levers controlling points and signals sited at signal boxes at each end of the loop. This was a highly labour-intensive operation for a line carrying modest, and declining, traffic flows.

BR research engineers turned their attention to the scope for greater automation of signalling, not only on the Far North Line but also on other peripheral Highland routes and the likes of the Cambrian Lines in mid-Wales. The system would have to be cost-effective, ie less expensive than the 'Integrated Electronic Control Centres' controlling busy main-line operations, but with more flexibility than, for example, the 'No Signalman Token Remote' system later introduced on the lightly-trafficked Central Wales Line, which involves drivers leaving their trains to operate electric token instruments in cabins on station platforms.

The Far North Line's improvised hybrid system, which had been created in 1978, provided the basis for the development of the new Radio Electronic Token Block (RETB) system which it was hoped to introduce on a trial basis on the Kyle line in 1984, with the control equipment initially located in Dingwall.

Radio allowed the interlocking of single line token instruments, with these instruments effectively moved from staffed signal boxes to the control centre and the cabs of trains. In the new system, on arrival at a 'token exchange point', the driver reports his/her position to the signaller by radio and requests the electronic token for the next block section. If the signaller is in a position to do so, he/she issues the electronic token for the section ahead.

Simultaneously, the driver has to operate a button on an apparatus in the cab to receive the token. The token is then transmitted to the train by radio, being displayed electronically in the cab. The 'Solid State Interlocking' controlling the system prevents the issue of any token permitting conflicting movements.

'Self normalising' points at the end of each loop are operated by the passage of the train, at a maximum speed of 15mph, and sidings are controlled by mechanical points released by a physical 'Annetts Key' which is interlocked with the token system.

The formal inauguration of RETB was undertaken by the Chairman of the BRB, Sir Robert Reid, and ScotRail's Chris Green on 6 July 1984 in Dingwall, with folk singer and BBC presenter Jimmy Macgregor naming an RETB-fitted Class 37 locomotive 'Radio Highland'. The Highland Archive holds a copy of Reid's speech notes (all in upper case), revealing an interesting insight into the technique and delivery prompts used by a major public figure, such as:

> The main problem in operating a railway through a thinly populated area is one of <u>simple</u> <u>economics</u>. // Income does not and cannot cover the operating <u>cost</u>. // And so we must find every means possible of <u>reducing</u> that cost / while at the same time <u>improving</u> our <u>income</u>.

Referring to the BRB's aims of eliminating waste, increasing productivity and improving facilities and services in order to increase revenue, Reid's notes then state: 'Radio train despatch is <u>typical</u> of the <u>innovative</u> <u>investment</u> that helps us <u>meet</u> these objectives.' Chris Green's speech notes took up a similar theme about this 'all-British invention':

> The Kyle line is typical of so many rural routes in Britain where the operating costs are two or three times the revenue. The secret of getting these routes off the danger list must centre around a radical cost reduction which does not affect the train service to the customer.

Green's reference to 'the danger list' was timely. And in mid-1985 – as worries about the Far North Line's future in the absence of a Dornoch Firth rail bridge were being widely articulated – RETB was extended to the railway from Dingwall to Caithness. A major reduction in operating costs was achieved virtually overnight, through closure of all signal boxes north of Dingwall.

A perhaps unpredicted benefit of RETB was the greater ease with which railway engineers could take 'possession' of the track for maintenance and renewal works. Jim Summers, ScotRail's Regional Operations Manager from 1986 to 1991, recollected in 2016 that Mike Chorley, the Area Civil Engineer controlling the Highland lines used to say he did a year's work in nine months. Furthermore, it was now economic to accept charter trains at weekends – a particular benefit for the Kyle line, but also potentially useful for the railway to Caithness.

However, the new system was to constitute an increasing time penalty for train journeys, with the relatively lengthy procedures between drivers and the Dingwall signalman often lasting longer than the required station stop for passengers.

Coincidentally, the two signallers permanently staffing the new RETB signalling centre at Dingwall were Magnus Campbell and Iain MacDonald, the Invergordon signalmen whom I had met on my first days on the railway in 1973. In view of the density of traffic between Dingwall and Inverness, carrying both Far North and Kyle trains, the conventional Electric Token Block system was initially maintained over this section, with signalmen at Muir of Ord, Lentran and Clachnaharry.

1985 also saw three important station developments on the Far North line, all in the month of June. Passenger facilities at the two northern termini were upgraded, without detriment to the character of the original station buildings: Wick, built of flagstone, and Thurso of sandstone. And 20 years after its Beeching era closure, Dunrobin station – still privately owned by the Duke of Sutherland – was ceremonially re-opened as 'Dunrobin Castle', with daily train services calling throughout the summer season.

The Dornoch Bridge saga

From the late 1960s onwards, rail campaigners had been raising the possibility of substantially improving the connectivity of the Far North Line by constructing a bridge across the Dornoch Firth.

Added impetus for a rail cut-off came, indirectly, from the 'Three Firths Crossings' road campaign launched in 1969, and then, more pressingly, from the completion of the new A9 route across the Black Isle in 1982. And in 1984, the Scottish Development Department (SDD) announced that it planned to continue its £300m rebuild of the A9 between Perth and Wick with an £11m road bridge over the Dornoch Firth.

Frank Spaven later traced the start of the transition of the Dornoch Firth Rail Crossing (DFRC) concept, from campaigning aspiration to official project, to two events in 1984/85:

- the local Business Group under BR's Inverness Area Manager, Bill Wood, pressed publicly for the rail crossing, in view of the impending road bridge, for which the Scottish Office had just published a revised Traffic Regulation Order

- SAPT urged the same in a meeting with Chris Green, 'though his own staff advisers were still against it (mainly, apparently, in view of minimal impact on huge losses on Far North Line.)'[65]

According to the Railway Development Society (RDS) in its 'The Dornoch

Bridge Saga' paper, circulated in 1986: 'As early as November 1984 ScotRail approached the SDD with the suggestion that a rail element be included in the road bridge project.' That same month in 1984, probably before the ScotRail initiative, SAPT circulated its paper on 'The Dornoch Bridge and the future of the Far North railway'. SAPT had a straightforward message:

> Amidst the general welcome given to the Scottish Office's allocation of funds for a Dornoch Firth Bridge at Meikle Ferry, there has been virtually no discussion of the implications for the future of the Far North Line of a road-only bridge.

> The purpose of this paper is to stress the urgency for open discussion of these implications and to highlight the case for a professional study of the costs and benefits of incorporating a rail link on the bridge as a means of safeguarding the Far North Line from the very real threat of complete closure within a few years of the opening of a road-only Dornoch Bridge.

> Politically, it is also important that rail investment north from Inverness should be seen to be evaluated on the same basis as road investment. Both south and north of Inverness, the A9 has been – and is being – improved through massive expenditure. This is being done for development reasons rather than for any urgent traffic need to improve road capacity.

> With such thinking being applied to road investment, it is vital that rail investment should be seen to be considered no less favourably. Investment in a direct rail link from Tain to Golspie is therefore something which must be considered now. Such a link would give substantial operating savings and would allow rail to offer journey times of below 3 hours between Inverness and Wick/Thurso.

> Without the direct rail link, coach travel times on a modernised A9 would be substantially below those offered by rail and in this situation, it is unlikely that the other benefits of rail – e.g. safety and reliability in winter, extra capacity for summer peak travel and specialist freight facilities – would be sufficient to secure the continued operation of the Far North Line on its existing route.

The RDS paper set the scene for its analysis of the saga with a dramatic statement:

> With the prospect of losing over 50% of its passengers British Rail have also sought the opportunity to bridge the Dornoch Firth. Unfortunately its attempts have floundered on artificial barriers and mis-information. The provision of a rail bridge would enable the railway to offer similar journey times and to compete more effectively with road, but the set-back to BR's plans could well precipitate the closure of the Far North Line with catastrophic results for the Highland communities.

Of course, we now know in hindsight that the former did not happen, and the latter scenario was debatable even then, given the fast-reducing role of the railway compared to its undoubted regional importance in 1963-64. However, the missed opportunity for a Dornoch Rail Bridge is certainly a scandalous story, which reflects badly on the management of transport policy in Scotland.

The RDS paper recorded the sequence of key events in 1984-86, beginning with ScotRail's November 1984 expression of interest in the project. Talks on 17 January 1985 between BR, Highland Regional Council and the HIDB found that some £8.2m of the £12.7m costs of the rail bridge could be found from these bodies and the EEC.

At the subsequent press conference in Inverness, Chris Green, ScotRail's General Manager, warned 'that if the major opportunity of the rail bridge was missed, the hour's difference between road and rail times could prove catastrophic to the line's future'. The RDS summary of the story continued:

> In record time ScotRail then obtained an independent feasibility study for a Dornoch rail bridge which also showed that the Far North Line stood to lose 25% of its business by competition from the new road in 1990 which could result in closure of the 168 mile line. The study found that a new rail bridge would reduce track mileage and save £375,000 pa in track, signal and operating costs. Thus the line's £1m annual loss would be reduced and the Government contribution of £4.5m for the bridge repaid in 12 years.

Bill Wood, BR's Inverness Area Manager (right), shares a joke with John Bruce, Traction Inspector, prior to a Spring 1985 inspection saloon trip to Helmsdale. Unusually, this was hauled by a Class 27 loco (27 052), these being rare visitors to Inverness at a time when they were most associated with the West Highland Lines radiating from Glasgow. Frank Spaven

In March 1985, the front page of the ScotRail Staff Bulletin had a forthright message from General Manager, Chris Green:

Full marks to Bill Woods *[sic; it was actually Bill Wood, the Inverness Area Manager]* and his Inverness Business Group on their swift response to the decision by Government to build a road bridge over the Dornoch Firth.

The implications for our Inverness/Wick/Thurso Line of substantially reduced journey times are obvious *[the bus one hour faster than the train to Thurso, one hour 35 minutes faster to Wick]*.

The Inverness Business Group had been a significant and successful development of management devolution, involving locally-based managers nurturing local contacts, being ever alert for traffic potential, and working together to meet it with operational innovation – an arrangement which, sadly, does not exist in today's centralised and divided railway.

Green continued his March 1985 message to staff by advising that ScotRail had quickly 'got the Scottish Office to agree to consider a road rail option' and had then commissioned a detailed technical study, while also setting up an internal project team to assess how ScotRail's business would be affected by three options: (i) taking no action, (ii) building a joint road/rail bridge and 15 miles of new railway and closing the Lairg Loop, and (iii) as in (ii), but retaining some or all of the Lairg Loop.

Green concluded that: 'The urgent priority now is to discuss the options with the local and central Government organisations who could provide the necessary financial support for a project which could attract 50% funding from the EEC.' The RDS paper recorded that, at an 18 March meeting of Highland Regional Council, he suggested that contributions to the £11.2m capital cost of the rail bridge might be as follows:

European Economic Community	£5.6m	(50%)
Scottish Development Department	£2.2m	(19%)
Highland Regional Council (HRC)	£1.0m	(9%)
HIDB	£0.5m	(5%)
British Railways Board	£1.9m	(17%)
Total	£11.2m	

BR in due course received pledges of support from HRC, the HIDB and the Scottish Council for Development & Industry. In November, the Minister for Public Transport, David Mitchell, advised that his Department 'had told British Rail that proposals for a joint venture would be considered favourably'. But the story now gets increasingly murky. According to the RDS paper, under the heading 'THE TIDE TURNS':

> The Government's deadline for submission of proposals for a rail bridge element to the Dornoch Firth crossing had been set for 1 June 1986. But in Parliament on 17 June 1986 Mr David Mitchell told Mr Maclennan [the MP for Caithness & Sutherland] "British Rail have not submitted a detailed submission for a grant under Sec 56 of the 1968 Transport Act for a rail bridge."

The RDS paper then quoted from a 24 June 1986 adjournment debate in the House of Commons[66]. Robert Maclennan MP cited the 'modest sum indeed' being sought from the Scottish Office, and contrasted earlier favourable noises about the rail bridge made by the Government with an announcement the previous week:

> Imagine my astonishment when a Department of Transport Minister announced last week that British Rail could not show that sufficient additional funding would be available from other sources. The funding from other sources that was missing was the £4.5 million from the Scottish Office. I exploded in rage and anger at the thought that there had been some deception. I do not know where the deception was and I make no charges against the Minister, who did not answer my question and simply said that he had nothing to add to what he had already said.

Ancram gave a lengthy response, within which some of the following statements arguably added confusion rather than satisfying his claimed wish 'to set the record straight':

> I should like to begin by establishing categorically three crucial facts. The first is that, when ScotRail initially approached my Department in November 1984 with the suggestion that a rail element be included in the road bridge project, it was given a positive response and the offer of technical assistance.

> It was made clear to ScotRail then, and again throughout the following year, that the assistance was being offered on two conditions. The first was that ScotRail should not delay the road bridge project, which the hon. Gentleman supports, and the second was that ScotRail would meet its own share of the costs...In other words, ScotRail was aware right from the start that in working up its proposals it should not expect any special Government funding for the project...The second point which I should like to establish clearly is that neither I nor my Department was ever approached formally by ScotRail with a request for special funding to be made available from Government...at no stage was ScotRail given any indication that special funding from the Scottish Office would be available...Nevertheless, I did not in the course of consideration of this issue rule out any possibilities of special funding. If a detailed case had been made to me, I would have considered it on its merits.

> The third area in which clarification is necessary is that concerning possible European funding. Here, too, we were not prepared to consider recommending

European regional development fund grant until we had a detailed application in our hands and could see whether or not it was plausible. It would have been quite wrong of us to have prejudged an issue without all the facts being available. But to obtain the facts we needed an application from ScotRail. We never received it...ScotRail's repeated public statements that 50 per cent. funding of the proposed Dornoch rail crossing would be provided by the European Community were, to say the least, premature.

So why then did ScotRail never make a formal application for funding, either by my Department or by the European Community? ...The purpose of the investment would have been to secure a revenue of some £120,000 a year— that is 20 per cent. of the present passenger custom which ScotRail estimates will be lost if the road bridge proceeds without the rail bridge. I emphasise that these figures are not mine — they are ScotRail's. It is self-evident from them that the investment could not have been justified on any sensible criterion. That is surely why no application for funding was made...I hope that misrepresentations and misinformation similar to those that were put out about the project during last week will now cease.

For all its contradictions, and perhaps an underlying suggestion that there was an element of 'Catch 22' involved, Ancram's response was a major blow to the rail project's prospects. The RDS paper continued the story: 'At a ceremony in Inverness on 17 July Mr Jim Cornell, who had succeeded Mr Green, said "ScotRail has not abandoned hope of building the Dornoch Firth rail bridge"' – implying that the prospect of a joint rail/road bridge (cheaper than two separate bridges) was now ended, but a rail-only bridge might still be feasible. The story then continued:

> In a letter to RDS dated 29 July the BRB Chairman Sir Robert Reid said "There is no question of our being constrained by procedural difficulties or by a Catch 22 situation. What I cannot do is commit my Board to spend £12.7m to safeguard revenue of £120,000 that might be lost *[he did not mention the £375,000 operating / maintenance cost which would be saved on a shortened route]*. For the time being we shall continue with our application for statutory powers to construct a railway between Tain and Golspie in the hope that funding is available." At a meeting with Mr Maclennan in London on 30 July Sir Robert said "The Government's unwillingness to help finance a rail crossing of the Dornoch Firth has not altered BR's assessment of the desirability of a rail shortcut to the north".

Eight months later, the saga was still not over. On 31 March 1986, under the headline 'BR seeks £4.5m for Dornoch link', the *Scotsman* reported support for the Dornoch plan from Jim Cornell:

> Decision time on a rail link along with the road bridge proposal runs out in June and ScotRail's general manager, Mr Jim Cornell, is preparing a submission to the Scottish Secretary which he says will clearly demonstrate that the future of the line north of Inverness must be in serious doubt if rail can no longer compete with road in journey times between Wick and Inverness.

Cornell, with his career railway engineering background, had been closely involved in investigating the feasibility of the link over the previous 18 months as Deputy General Manager. The *Scotsman's* reporter, Alex Main, had secured some unequivocal comments:

> "Without special financial help from Government there is simply no way that British Rail can justify a case to the Department of Transport for a rail crossing," Mr Cornell told *The Scotsman* at the weekend. "It does not take much imagination to realise the strain that would be put on the future of the line if a rail link is not included in the crossing of the firth.

The newspaper quoted a memorable comment from the previous General Manager as well as further clarifications of Cornell's stance:

> Mr Green is already on record as saying: "The person who does not throw his money into the hat will be the person who closes the railway north of Inverness." And in a frank interview during his first public visit to Inverness as general manager, Mr Cornell confirmed: "It is now-make-your-mind-up time. By June we have to say if we wish to proceed with the rail link, but we cannot do it without Scottish Office help.

> "We are in a catch-22 situation," Mr Cornell said. "If the road bridge goes ahead without a similar rail link we stand to lose from 22 to 25 per cent of our existing traffic.

> "The ratio of expenditure to revenue on this route is already three to one, probably the highest of any route in the BR network...we can only compete [with the improved A9] if the Government is prepared to treat this as a special case and release extra funds."

Anticipating one objection from the Scottish Office, 'Mr Cornell said a precedent was set in the 1970s when the Government came up with £1.5 million to help restore double-line track between Blair Atholl and Dalwhinnie [on the Highland Main Line].'

Highland Regional Council were not prepared to let the project drop, and in October 1986 commissioned Mackay Consultants to produce a report on 'The social and economic case for the Dornoch Firth rail bridge'. Due to the urgency of the decision-making process, the consultants had just three weeks to compile their report, which unsurprisingly 'had to rely heavily on existing information'.

In its November report, Mackay noted that ScotRail's financial appraisal of the project concluded that the benefits to ScotRail did not justify the investment, with a 'Net Present Value' (NPV) of minus £7.6m, calculated over 25 years. However, the wider benefits (journey time savings, increased tourism and 'other economic benefits') were valued at £5.6m – still leaving a deficit, but excluding other social benefits which were 'very difficult or impossible to value'. Career railwayman and former senior manager with ScotRail, David Prescott, commented in 2016: 'That's a very short time span over which to evaluate a big piece of infrastructure: we use 60 years now. It would probably pass on a STAG *[Scottish Transport Appraisal Guidance]* appraisal these days.'

The Mackay report argued that if it was accepted that (a) the line would close without a Dornoch Bridge, and (b) the existing service generated economic and social benefits, over and above ScotRail revenues, equivalent to an NPV 'of at least £6.1 million', then, 'the net social NPV is clearly positive (approximately +£4.1 million). This means that the rail bridge is a worthwhile investment from society's viewpoint.' The report's Executive Summary concluded:

> Even if the closure argument is not accepted, the inclusion of the other measurable benefits reduces the negative financial NPV from -£7.6 million to -£2.0 million. Against the latter figure must be set those social and economic factors which cannot be quantified. It is a matter of judgement as to whether or not these are sufficiently important to justify the investment, but clearly a strong social and economic case can be made for the Dornoch Firth rail bridge.

The Dornoch Bridge leak: and I come under suspicion

I had no idea in late 1986 that, following a leak of confidential BR papers to the *Glasgow Herald* in early 1987, I would come under direct suspicion of being the culprit. The *Herald* did not mince its words in its 11 February editorial, under the heading 'Rail bridge facts', which is reproduced in full here:

> Much duplicity surrounding the Dornoch Rail Bridge was exposed yesterday, and much hypocrisy, too. After months of hiding behind British Rail, the Scottish Office has been exposed as the villain of the piece. Those who followed the saga had long suspected as much, despite repeated denial of involvement from Scottish Office Ministers, most notably Mr Michael Ancram. The simple, brutal truth is that the Scottish Office lied when it said ScotRail was free to make application for assistance with the provision of a rail crossing over the Dornoch Firth. All along the Scottish Office has said that in the absence of any such application there was nothing it could do. Even when the EEC offered to pay half of the cost, the Scottish Office stood aloof and sanctimoniously declared that it was a matter for ScotRail; in the absence of any ScotRail application there was no responsibility to be laid before the Government. This is now exposed as humbug. According to documents made available to this newspaper the staff of ScotRail were put under pressure by the Scottish Office to withhold an application which would in normal circumstances have been made automatically.

> The fact that the truth emerged on the very day that Mr Rifkind formally announced that the rail bridge was a non-starter should not necessarily be an end to this sequence of events. Indeed it should spur supporters of the project

to further effort. So much embarrassment will be felt in high places that with an election in the offing a new happy ending could yet be written into the script.

It is now patently evident, as this newspaper argued many months ago, that the Scottish Office's real motive was parsimony and its aversion to its public spending. The social and economic needs of a remote area for whom a rail link is indispensable came a poor second. If the Government had supported ScotRail and welcomed the EEC's contribution it would have been embarrassed into stumping up its own share. ScotRail, for its part, should have had the guts to put up a public fight against mealy-mouthed politicians.

While agreeing with the overall sentiment, with hindsight one might conclude instead that the Scottish Office's real motive was not so much parsimony *per se*, but rather an institutional bias towards road rather than rail spending, demonstrated by the lavish expenditure on the A9 between Perth and Thurso through the 1970s, 1980s and 1990s. The road lobby has been a powerful advocate for investment in this mode of transport since at least the 1950s.

In any event, a few days after the *Herald* furore, I returned from a business trip to London to find that my stapler had disappeared from my office in ScotRail House in Glasgow. Freight colleagues knew nothing about it, but I subsequently heard that there had been a mass 'seizure' of staplers from the passenger department, in a bid to track down the leaker. My stapler was certainly visually distinctive: it bore a sticker exhorting 'Free Mandela – Jail Thatcher!'

I made unsuccessful enquiries of the Personnel Department, and then on 23 February proceeded to the ninth floor of ScotRail House, where Senior Management was based. Without warning I found myself facing a 'kangaroo court' of three Senior Managers – Vivian Chadwick, Vic Gilchrist and Hugh Watson. Among staff at ScotRail House, Chadwick, the Deputy General Manager, was renowned for several 'cutting edge' proposals, like banning biscuits at meetings in order to save money, and proposing a non-stop lift from the ground to the ninth floors so that senior management could save time (and doubtless also avoid mixing with the lower orders).

Having – naively – not refused to be interviewed without trade union representation, I was then quizzed at length on all kinds of aspects of my personal, political and professional life. This included membership of outside organisations, family connections at Inverness, media contacts, attitudes to the Dornoch Bridge and the recent leak, and, bizarrely, querying the consistency of my work in coal transport with my membership of the Green Party. The interview concluded, inconclusively, after around three quarters of an hour, with Chadwick commenting: 'Well I think we would like to leave that for the moment. Almost certainly we will want to talk to you again but I am not quite sure when and obviously we will give you a shout as soon as we are ready to do so.' I heard nothing more from the kangaroo court, but I certainly found that I now had even greater sympathy for the leaker, whoever he or she was.

The Dornoch Bridge saga, which probably deserves a book in its own right, was far from over at this stage but, as regards the wider *realpolitik*, it will perhaps suffice here to quote Frank Spaven from his future MSc thesis. Noting that the 1984/5 rail proposal by ScotRail had 'the support of all the local authorities, the H.I.D.B., M.Ps, transport users, voluntary bodies and, in one document, the Scottish Office', Spaven then summarised the turning of the tide, as follows:

However, by 1986/7 the B.R.B. and the Scottish Office, if not ScotRail, had back-tracked and would not proceed with the project on the grounds that:

- it would not meet the required commercial rate of return for B.R. investments;

- it would make little difference to the high operating cost and low revenue of the line especially if the line to Lairg was kept as a branch, to retain the only freight traffic;

- ScotRail was committed to the future of the line, as indicated by the installation of R.E.T.B. signalling and by the programme for Sprinters which would reduce journey times;

- the Scottish Office was not prepared (despite a precedent...*[with track doubling on the Highland Main Line in the mid-1970s]*) to fill the final gap in funding of £3-4M itself or to apply to the E.R.D.F. (to which it had earlier made a provisional case).

The Scottish Office (S.D.D.) has, however, committed itself to spending £100M on further improvements to the parallel A9 from the Cromarty Firth to Caithness so this peculiar episode at least reflects the priorities in central government thinking.

The Dornoch Firth rail bridge was never built, while construction of the road-only bridge commenced in 1989 and it was opened to traffic in 1991, at a cost of £13.5m. The entire A9 'Three Firths Crossing,' as originally envisaged by Reay Clarke back in 1969, was then complete. The railway did survive, but at an even more severe competitive disadvantage than previously. It left the Far North Line searching for a robust and cost-effective role, as forewarned in SAPT's Winter 1986/87 newsletter:

Caithness-Inverness coaches are already faster than the rail service and will be even more so once a road bridge is open. Is it sensible to retain a long and lightly used railway under such circumstances?

Infrastructure retrenchment

The basic track infrastructure of the Far North Line remained largely unmodified, even with the introduction of RETB north of Dingwall in 1985, but what would ultimately prove to be a very significant reduction in capacity was implemented in 1988, following the continuing losses of freight traffic.

By that year, BR was firmly organised along 'sector' lines, with individually identified businesses within the corporate whole – such as Inter-City, 'Provincial' (non-Inter-City passenger services outwith South East England) and Freight – allocated costs and revenues attributable to their own activities. Of the two crossing loops breaking up the 18½ single-track miles between Inverness and Dingwall – Lentran (6 miles) and Muir of Ord (13 miles) – only Muir of Ord was deemed necessary by Provincial to support its then limited frequency of daily train services (three in each direction to/from Kyle, and three in each direction to/from Wick / Thurso).

Industrial change, as well as road competition, had seen rail freight contract further in the middle and latter part of the decade. Rail movement of barley to the Muir of Ord maltings ceased in 1987, and the British Pipe Coaters yard – which had employed almost 700 people at the peak of its activity – was mothballed for two years in the late 1980s, following a slump in the offshore oil industry.

Last day at Lentran: on 9 January 1988, Signalman Gordon Kennedy exchanges single-line tokens with the driver of a northbound passenger train. The crossing loop – six miles west of Inverness – was closed as an economy measure later that day, and is now sorely missed, leaving a 13-mile single-track section between Inverness and Muir of Ord. Frank Spaven

The remaining single daily freight north of Inverness (to Invergordon / Lairg) did not need to use the Lentran crossing facility. Indeed, no trains of any description were latterly timetabled to cross there, and therefore neither of the sectors operating over the line – Freight or Provincial – was willing to bear the ongoing operating and maintenance costs. After several years' experience of RETB working north and west of Dingwall, BR was keen to extend the cost-cutting benefits to the Dingwall-Inverness section, bringing the control equipment into the same building as the new Inverness Signalling Centre which had replaced five manual boxes in the town in 1987, at a cost of £3m.

Despite objections from experienced railwaymen such as Iain MacDonald, the absence of a strategic perspective – which might have foreseen the growth of local commuter services from 1998 onwards (as well as summer demand for tourist charter trains) – led to the Lentran loop being taken out of service after the last train on Saturday 9 January 1988, some six months before RETB working was introduced. The closure of the loop would prove to be a crucial loss from the early years of the 21st century onwards.

From mid-1988, the entire rail network north of Inverness was controlled from one RETB signalling centre, but with the mechanical box retained at Clachnaharry to operate the canal swing bridge. However, eight stations remained staffed: Dingwall, Brora (but only until 1992), Thurso, Wick, and Kyle for passenger ticket sales, and Invergordon, Tain and Lairg for shared ticket sales and Red Star parcels duties (but only until 1991). Once again, the RETB control centre would be operated by the former Invergordon signalmen, Magnus Campbell and Iain MacDonald. They would continue to work together in Inverness until Campbell's retirement in 1995, MacDonald then retiring on reaching 50 years of railway service in 2002.

Unexpected freight – and new passenger trains

The miners' strike had given a major boost to imported domestic coal (notably from Poland), which further reduced BR's coal business. But in 1986 this market played an unexpected, if brief, role in the life of the Far North Line.

I negotiated a BR contract for rail haulage of imported coal from Invergordon to Mossend, and a total of 13,350 tonnes moved south on Speedlink services that spring. Southbound movement of coal was not unique. In the past, the Brora coal mine (closed in 1974) had sent some of its output by rail, but there must have been a few 'double takes' from unforewarned observers, when they spotted heaped coal in hopper wagons heading in the 'Up' direction (railway parlance for towards Edinburgh, on internal Scottish routes), as opposed to the usual northbound direction of coal traffic.

A unique working, which ended after BR's loss of major nationwide newspaper contracts in 1987, was the Sundays-only 08.05 newspaper train from Inverness to Lairg, the final leg of the 20.32 Saturdays-only train from London Euston. This had been introduced in the 1930s, and latterly conveyed through vans from Euston, Manchester, Glasgow and Perth, with road distribution from Ardgay (where the train had a booked 13-minute stop to offload papers) and Lairg across the vast territory to the north and north-west.

Readily apparent from the cab of 37 418, hauling the Inverness-Lairg freight on 25 February 1986, are the heavy rock works required to take the Far North Line up the 1 in 72 gradient from Invershin to Lairg. Frank Spaven

Passenger coaches were attached at Inverness, but until the early 1970s these were only advertised for public use on the return 11.20 working from Lairg. In the summer of 1982, this service had been extended through to Wick and Thurso, and a balancing working departed the Caithness stations at 11.10.

While the Class 37-hauled passenger trains had brought significantly faster journey times on the Far North Line in 1982, by the mid-1980s BR nationally was turning its attention to the replacement of the life-expired first-generation diesel multiple units (DMUs) and, as a by-product, seeking to reduce the heavy operating and maintenance costs of locomotive-hauled trains on lightly-trafficked routes like the 'North Highland' (a collective description of the Far North and Kyle lines) and West Highland lines.

The early DMUs (mostly 1950s' designs) had been ruled out for operation on the Far North Line, due to concerns about climbing steep gradients, performance in snow conditions and presumably their relatively limited parcels accommodation, plus the wider factor of operational efficiency of inter-working passenger and freight locomotive diagrams.

But now rural freight was in steep decline and a new generation of more powerful DMUs (with operating costs half that of loco-hauled trains, and imposing less wear and tear on the track) could be procured for robust working over all kinds of routes. The Government agreed to a major new-build programme for commuter, regional and rural services throughout Britain (and

37 418 shunts Lairg oil depot on 25 February 1986, prior to attaching timber wagons (and coal) for the return leg to Inverness. Frank Spaven

inter-city services within Scotland), but with just two DMU coaches replacing the previous three. However, the vehicles were longer than their predecessors and had only minimal space allocated to parcels traffic.

It was planned to operate the Far North and Kyle lines with the Class 156 (dubbed 'Super Sprinter'), starting in May 1989, and BR was keen to begin promotion as soon as possible. The March 1988 issue of *Railnews* reported that: 'A sneak preview of the new class 156 Super Sprinter blossomed into a triumphal tour as Scottish VIPs, media and members of the public applauded the new train on its first trip north of the border.' This unit made history on Scottish soil by running the class's first ever revenue-earning timetable service, on the 11.35 Inverness-Wick/Thurso on 26 January, *Railnews* commenting that: 'Provincial chiefs reckon the sight of the new train has effectively banished any lingering doubts about BR's intentions to remain in business on the Far North line.'

A BR publicity brochure from 1988 indicated that journey times from Inverness to Wick / Thurso would be reduced to 3½ hours, and that 'the Super Sprinter's flexibility may allow us to improve frequency on some routes and to look at a Wick/Thurso service'. There was inevitably a certain amount of hype in the description of the train: 'The elegant trains seat 160, with plenty of room for luggage. Inside you'll find passenger comfort second to none. Throughout the train, windows are tinted and double glazed – easy on the eyes and ears!'

Having been attached at Invergordon on the northbound leg – for ease of shunting – nine HEA hopper wagons of imported coal sit at Lairg on 25 February 1986, awaiting the southbound journey to Inverness, en route to Mossend. These wagons were part of a 13,350 tonne-contract secured for BR by the photographer's son. Frank Spaven

There could be no such optimism in the declining day-to-day world of regular rail freight, but there were occasional grounds for hope. One of the most unusual workings I trialled in my role as BR's Marketing & Contracts Manager for coal in Scotland was movement of peat from Scotscalder to England.

The North of Scotland Hydro Electric Board in conjunction with John Brown Engineering had opened in 1959 an experimental two-megawatt peat-fired gas turbine on a 60-acre site (with its own internal rail system) near Scotscalder, but commercial viability could not be achieved and the power station closed in 1962.[67] However, large quantities of peat had been dug out and stockpiled, and in the mid-1980s a local company identified potential horticultural markets south of the Border. BR operated trial trains in December 1987 (to Immingham) and August 1988 (to Leicester), back-working empty containers which had brought coal to Inverness from England. On Saturday 20 August, the *Press & Journal* reported, under the headline 'Ghost train of the North':

> A long train of heavily-laden wagons thundering through the still Highland night stirred thoughts of nuclear waste on the move from Dounreay, with armed guards and dimmed lights.

> But it was nothing more sinister than a load of 300 tons of Caithness peat being transported at night over quiet tracks on the way to a horticultural company in Leicester, 600 miles away.

> A ScotRail official said yesterday: "The train should have reached Inverness by midnight, but there was some loco trouble *[the loco actually broke down and had to be replaced by the Thurso branch engine]* and it was slowed down a little."

> That is why light sleepers heard it at 2.30a.m., with its long load of 20 wagons, in Highland hamlets where the last train passes by at 10 p.m. and the first does not run until 6 a.m. on the far North line *[sic]*.

Following the successful trials, with both trains loaded directly from the lineside – the first during the night, and the second in daylight on a Sunday – we developed plans for a weekly train from Scotscalder, making marginal use of otherwise idle locomotives for Sunday loading, and back-loading otherwise empty coal containers from Inverness. Integral to the success of unusual workings such as these was a 'can do' attitude among BR staff and managers, epitomised by the ScotRail Manager at Inverness, Ronnie Munro: a classic railwayman who would get things done, provided you didn't ask too many questions about how he did it...

While we were evaluating the peat trials, another unlikely coal flow was taking shape on the Far North Line. As a result of previous miners' strikes (and probably a wish to strengthen their negotiating position with Scottish Coal,

Early on Sunday 14 August 1988, a Class 37 heads north from Inverness with 20 x 30-feet length containers for lineside loading of peat at Scotscalder. Frank Spaven

Peat loaders hard at work at Scotscalder on Sunday 14 August 1988, with the train headed by the Thurso branch engine, which had come to the assistance of its failed sister (behind). On completion of loading, the train ran forward to Georgemas for the locos to run round the wagons before commencing the southwards journey to Leicester. David Richard-Jones

with whom they had major coal supply agreements) the then South of Scotland Electricity Board (SSEB) was concerned about coal supplies to its two coal burning power stations at Cockenzie and Longannet. A decision was taken in 1988 to purchase shiploads of imported coal and ideally to transport the coal by rail to their power stations. A bold move was then made to import 50,000 tonnes through Invergordon, using the deep water jetty which had been built for the aluminium smelter and remained in good condition.

My BR management colleague, John Holwell, agreed a rate for rail haulage to Longannet power station, with the coal moved by lorries from the pier to the smelter site, for stockpiling and loading to rail. The contract was undertaken in late autumn 1988, with tranches of wagons 'tripped' from Invergordon to Inverness, and then consolidated into 36-wagon trains, headed by pairs of Class 37 locomotives for the stiff climb over the Highland Main Line. The movement was a success but the rail haulage rate, reflecting the much longer distance travelled than on most port or coal mine to power station hauls, precluded any repetition of the traffic.

Meanwhile, I had been finalising plans for a contracted weekly peat train from Scotscalder. On a site visit to Leicester on Tuesday 7 February, I identified a suitable location for regular offloading of containers – but returning to Glasgow later the same day, I discovered that Joseph Mitchell's 1862 viaduct carrying the Far North Line over the Ness had collapsed that morning!

The collapse of the Ness Viaduct

The Ness is a very short river, just six miles in length, and it is the only outlet to the sea from Loch Ness. The catchment area of this stretch of water is no less than 700 square miles and from time to time very heavy rainfall feeds the loch from many hundreds of tributaries. During such occasions any weaknesses in bridge structures are sought out by surging waters as they make their way to the sea.

When Joseph Mitchell designed his Ness Viaduct he was well aware of the occasional fierceness of the conditions on the river, and he built accordingly. However, as recorded in a ScotRail commemorative booklet, *The Ness Viaduct* (1990), in early February 1989:

> ...[there was] a period of unprecedented rainfall in the catchment area of Loch Ness...[which] rose 1.88 metres to its highest ever level since records began. The meteorological experts reckoned that the rainfall at the time was as much as 300% of the long term average...These were conditions that Mitchell... could not have foreseen.

On the morning of the Tuesday [7February] all three structures [over the Ness, Beauly and Conon Rivers] were being continuously studied for faults. Apart from the height of the water nothing untoward was reported. The Ness Viaduct was examined twice between 05 00 and 07 00 and nothing could be seen amiss.

However, at 08 30, a member of the public reported to Inverness station that part of the bridge over the River Ness had been washed away. Pier number three along with arch spans three and four had disappeared completely leaving a 55 metre gap over which stretched an unsupported section of continuous welded track. About nine hours later pier number two along with span number two were swept away by the torrent and three hours later the same fate befell pier number four and span number five. By 21 00 hours on the same day there was a gap of 110 metres in Mitchell's beautiful masonry viaduct.

According to ScotRail's then Regional Operations Manager, Jim Summers, looking back in early 2016, the signalling cable was still intact across the gap, so that the signals in both direction were actually showing 'clear' (green). But, of course, the line had been immediately barred to traffic, with the next train – the 06.00 from Wick, due in Inverness at 10.10 – terminated at Dingwall. As Summers recalled with some pride, and amusement: 'The folk arrived on time in Inverness on the replacement buses!' The last train to pass over the old viaduct – a freight to Lairg, less than an hour before the collapse – was now marooned north of the Ness, as were four passenger trains.

A remarkable coincidence was to contribute to this unprecedented drama for the railway *not* turning into a disaster. As John Ellis, BR Scottish Region's General Manager from 1987 to 1990, wrote in *Far North Express* in April 2014:

On 6th February, 1989 I travelled to Inverness for a meeting with Highland Regional Council the following day. There had been a huge amount of rain in the north and I was told that the River Ness was in full spate. In the evening I went down to the river and it was lapping the embankments and running at a fearsome rate. The Ness has the steepest fall of any river in the country, and it was certainly evident.

The following morning I was having breakfast in the hotel (porridge and kippers of course!) when an ashen-faced Ronnie Munro, the Station Manager, came in to tell us that the railway bridge had been washed away. When I went down to look, the rails were suspended above the raging river, with no sign of the bridge spans.

There was obviously great concern locally that the bridge would not be replaced. I had a hectic morning of telephone calls with British Railways Board Headquarters and many others, and was able to get a verbal agreement that the bridge would be replaced. I therefore arranged a press conference that afternoon to make this announcement. This was to ensure that there were no second thoughts at Board HQ, in the Other Provincial Services business sector, or in the Department of Transport!

High tide on 11 February 1989, just hours after the Ness Viaduct had begun to collapse. Frank Spaven

A few hours later on 11 February 1989, it is low tide at the Ness Viaduct, but most of the railway bridge has now collapsed into the river. Frank Spaven

In Spring 1989, as part of a major logistical programme to bring new trains to the still-severed Far North Line, a low-loader departs from Inverness freight depot for a specially adapted siding at Invergordon, carrying a single coach of a Class 156 'Super Sprinter' unit. Frank Spaven

Ellis announced that the new bridge and restored rail link would be available for traffic by May 1990. Jim Summers considers that 'a degree of sheer good luck' conspired to provide circumstances which allowed the railway to be saved for a second time, 35 years after the reprieve from the Beeching axe.

As Councillor John M Young, Transport Convenor of Highland Council (and a Caithness Councillor), recollected in BR's 1990 commemorative booklet: 'We feared that this would spell the end of Railways North and West of Inverness. If ScotRail (or the Government) had been looking for an excuse to close these lines, then here surely was such an excuse.'

It took over a year to rebuild the bridge, but an emergency road-rail operation was quickly established, with passengers and Red Star parcels shuttled by bus between Inverness and Dingwall stations. There was another pressing issue, as recorded in BR's commemorative booklet:

> However, a looming difficulty, was the programmed introduction of the Class 156 Super Sprinters in the May of 1989. A great deal of emotional capital was tied up in the Super Sprinters – they were seen as a vote of confidence in the North lines and an indication of ScotRail's long-term commitment in the area.

A decision was quickly made that the new trains would be introduced on time, and a massive stock movement operation began on 28 March, with five new 2-car trains moved by low-loader lorry from a specially-adapted siding at Inverness freight depot to another at Invergordon (this was said to be the

Major engineering works on the new Ness Viaduct near completion on 12 February 1990. Frank Spaven

first time that railway rolling stock in Britain had routinely been moved by road). The low-loaders then brought back the diesel locos and freight wagons not required for continuing services on the north side. A temporary train maintenance depot was created on spare railway ground at Muir of Ord by the transfer of a 32-metre long shed from Barassie in Ayrshire.

Despite the difficulties of a railway without an umbilical cord, ScotRail maintained a service with high punctuality, and transported over to the Kyle line the high-quality tourist train coaches (known as the 'raspberry ripple' set), to maintain faith with the operators of long-distance charter trains from the south.

A new bridge was soon being designed, and the financial disciplines (or narrow-minded approach, depending on your perspective) created by 'sectorisation', led to BR's Provincial sector insisting that they would not underwrite a bridge any heavier-duty than that required to carry the light-weight Super Sprinters. This fell into the category of narrow-minded.

According to Jim Summers, some sensible engineers involved in the design process then concluded that this would be a short-sighted approach to the future of the railway, and quietly designed a bridge which could accommodate the previous 'Route Availability 10' (RA10) designation between Inverness and Invergordon, allowing the heaviest (25.5-tonne axleload) freight wagons to use the new bridge and the first 33 miles of the Far North Line.

The previous Ness Viaduct had been a listed structure, but the urgency of re-creating the rail link meant that a simple steel girder design was chosen for the new bridge, resting on the old stone abutments and two new concrete piers in the river. In *British Railway Bridges & Viaducts* (1994), Martin Smith, describes the new structure as 'a functional but decidedly unlovely three-span girder bridge which, cosmetically and aesthetically, was as far removed from Mitchell's original viaduct as was possible', but this is surely an over-critical view of a modern bridge with robust, clean lines.

Construction began in August 1989, and, despite further floods almost as bad as those early that year, the bridge was completed in 40 weeks, ready for the May 1990 timetable as promised by John Ellis. Built at a cost of £3.4m, and extending 128 metres, the new structure required 320 tonnes of steel piles, 270 tonnes of steel beams and 750 cubic metres of concrete. It was a solid declaration of faith in the future of the Far North and Kyle lines.

Frank Spaven benchmarks highland railways

Following a long civil service career – in which, *inter alia*, he had been a valuable advocate of railways as a civilised form of transport with important economic, social and environmental benefits – Frank Spaven retired from the HIDB in 1978, at the age of 61. Keen to pursue his interest in railways and regional development, in the mid-1980s he began field work on a thesis for the degree of Master of Science at the University of Aberdeen. The thesis – 'The role of rail transport in the development of highland regions in Scotland, Norway, Sweden and New Zealand' – was presented (and the MSc degree awarded) in 1989.

Spaven's analysis, based on BR's passenger counts, indicated that – in contrast to the heavy concentration of West Highland Line passengers at Fort William – 'less than one third of those on the Far North line were using stations at the Caithness end and nearly a half the southern end up to Tain (though the latter may now be less since the opening of the Kessock Bridge in 1982/83 has given shorter road journeys to Inverness).'

Spaven also tackled the impact of 'sectorisation' on the prospects for Highland rail development:

A Provincial Sector Manager for both Highland and West Highland passenger services is based at Inverness *[but was due to be moved to Edinburgh in Autumn 1989]*. He is the only senior railwayman in the region and there are no management or marketing staff of the Freight, Parcels or Inter City sectors. In

1988 the office of the Highland Area Manager at Inverness, who had chaired a co-ordinating Business Group and a Customer Care Panel, was closed, leaving a ScotRail Manager (Highland) primarily for traffic operations and withdrawing remaining functions to a new North Area Manager at Perth, who also covers the territory of former Area Managers at Aberdeen and Dundee. These streamlining changes are intended to devolve some authority from Scottish Regional H.Q. to the new, larger Areas, as well as to save costs. It is difficult to see what they can do to strengthen the railway's contact with present and potential [passenger and freight] customers in the North and North east of Scotland.

In 2016, looking back on this period, Jim Summers, formerly ScotRail Regional Operations Manager, commented:

The Area Business Management group, chaired by the Highland Area Manager, consisted of the most senior local chiefs of the various disciplines involved in running the railway: operations, commercial, engineering, brought together to apply combined wisdom to a common end. Hitherto, they had reported exclusively up and down their departmental trees to HQ in Glasgow. Now they reported also to the group.

The concept had its greatest successes in Inverness, which became a blueprint for elsewhere. The Area Business Management team was given its head and that produced results like Sunday excursion trains to Dunrobin Castle and an observation car to Kyle. They had their own budgets and learned to work together. Today the structures and mechanisms do not exist to allow and facilitate such focused management.

Spaven then reviewed current circumstances against those he had assessed in his 1964 SDD paper for the Highland Panel on 'The Dependence of Industries and Services on the Inverness-Thurso/Wick Railway'. Whereas in 1964 half of 25 firms (six of them named) using freight transport made some appreciable use of the railway, Spaven estimated that by 1989: 'Of the 6 firms named, only Invergordon Distillery still uses the railway regularly, but on a reduced level (grain now comes in by sea); and A.E.A. (and possibly others) from time to time.' It was also noted that: 'The speed and reliability of the parcels service is still highly valued by many firms, through fewer will now be entirely dependent on it.' He quoted, and then reviewed, his 1964 conclusion:

'It would appear that road transport agencies could only take over from the railway without serious damage to many existing businesses in the area if they had help from air and sea services and were properly organised and had improved roads, reliable in winter. Even then, an appreciable proportion of businesses would find it difficult or impossible to make an adjustment; the range of new types of industry and other developments would apparently be restricted; and other social costs would be incurred.' *[1964]*

The proposition in the first sentence has virtually come to pass for many firms, but the last sentence is still valid. It would be more difficult to make a case on

The rarely-photographed Frank Spaven stands in front of a Swedish-built NOHAB Di3 at the Andalsnes branch terminus on the west coast of Norway in the summer of 1995. The visit was part-holiday, part up-date on the findings of his 1989 MSc thesis on 'The role of rail transport in the development of highland regions in Scotland, Norway, Sweden and New Zealand'. David Spaven

need for the railway today in terms of many firms' dependence on it. There is at least a case on merit for some of the region's firms deserving to share in the benefits of having a railway which a more affluent society ought to be able to afford and for the privilege of which they are willing to pay. *[1989]*

The latter observation was noticeably less bullish than 1964's endorsement. And the range of benefits offered to businesses by the Far North Line would shrink further – following the introduction of Super Sprinters lacking suitable parcels accommodation – with the nationwide decline, and then, in 1991, the end of the residual Red Star parcels service on the Far North Line.

Within the conclusions of his thesis, Spaven commented that: 'The highlands *[sic]* are difficult country for railways but they have proved their worth as secondary main lines.' In a later (1991) reflection – in the context of the prospects for re-opening a railway to the Borders – he commented on the latter region having 'the resources potential for "tourists and timber", which my researches in Norway, Sweden and New Zealand have shown to be a winning traffic combination for Highland-type lines.'[68]

And that could prove to be a crucial business mix in securing the long-term future of the Far North Line in the 21st century.

A traditional railway scene which survived until the early 1980s. Taking a break from his job as a TOPS (Total Operations Processing System) wagon number-taker in the winter of 1974-75, the photographer captured this shot of a tranquil Inverness coal yard, looking south towards the passenger station. The 16-tonne vacuum-braked mineral wagons seen here were in due course replaced by air-braked coal container wagons, handled at this site from the late 1980s until the mid-1990s. After coal traffic ceased, the location was used for rail to road transfer of the pioneering Safeway supermarket traffic from Central Scotland. David Spaven

CHAPTER 13: RENEWED HOPE

A special train to mark the 100th anniversary of the completion of the Dingwall-Kyle line is hauled across the new Ness Viaduct by ex-BR Standard Class 4 loco No. 75014 on 6 October 1997. Frank Spaven

An era of renewed hope for the Far North Line began on Monday 9 May 1990, when the Secretary of State for Scotland, Malcolm Rifkind MP, flagged off the 11.45 train from Inverness to Wick and Thurso, the first public service to cross the Ness since February 1989.

The once-threatened railway now had a modern signalling system, new trains and a new bridge to underpin its future. A related point made to me in 2016 by Jim Summers was that it was a conscious ScotRail policy to boost Inverness as an operational centre (with benefits for employment etc), motivated by social responsibility. Maintenance work was moved to the Highland capital, a new carriage cleaning/maintenance shed constructed, and the station refurbished. These significant developments, and the work of BR's local Area Business Group, complemented the investment in resignalling and the new Sprinter stock: 'It added up to a really tangible commitment to, and act of faith in, the Highlands, for which the sometimes maligned British Rail deserves due credit.'

Train services were also substantially speeded up with the introduction of the Class 156 units, reducing the journey time from Inverness to the Caithness termini by typically 30 to 32 minutes, although the southbound speed-up was less pronounced. The best timing to Thurso was 3 hours 41 minutes and to Wick, 3 hours 40 minutes: the fastest since the Far North Line had opened in 1874.

There were still only three trains a day in each direction over the entire length of the line, supplemented by a 'short working' from Inverness to Tain at 15.30 (and return), which had been introduced on a trial basis and was extended through to Wick in summer. The off-peak service was not a long-term success, and was withdrawn in 1995 on the orders of the Franchising Director in the run-up to privatisation. Yet this was just three years before the start of commuter service developments which have continued to the present day.

Following the collapse of the Ness Viaduct in early 1989, freight traffic on the Far North Line had ceased for the first time in its long history. Latterly, the core traffic for the daily Invergordon / Lairg train had been oil tanks from Grangemouth to Lairg. This traffic did not resume when the railway re-opened in May 1990, and it would be another 12 years before Grangemouth-Lairg oil traffic returned to rail.

An early intimation of a future sustained freight flow (which would commence in the mid-1990s and is still in operation today) was a temporary rail contract for movement of steel pipes for the offshore oil industry from Hartlepool to Georgemas in 1991. Barley traffic from eastern England to the Muir of Ord silo (for the nearby maltings) resumed in due course, but by 1994 had fallen foul of the process of smoothing the path towards rail privatisation, when even individual trainload flows were discarded if they did not meet a target eight per cent notional return on capital. Reflecting on the circumstances in the *Scotsman* of 20 March 1997, the paper's Transport Correspondent, Allan McLean, wrote:

> British Rail abandoned much freight traffic because it had to meet public sector financial targets which took no account of the long term and were restricted to each financial year. But the private operators can take on business that will make only a marginal profit until operations develop over several years.

The freight development hiatus on the Far North Line coincided with the completion of the road-only Dornoch Firth Bridge in 1991, exposing the railway to even stronger competition. This prompted renewed concern about the line, with Highland Regional Council publishing in 1992 a six-page colour briefing on the future of the Highland rail network, in light of the anticipated privatisation of the national network by the Conservative Government, which had been returned to power that year. However, BR in Scotland remained bullish, with the briefing reporting the comments of Cyril Bleasdale, Director of ScotRail, on the lines north of Inverness:

> On the Far North Line, he saw little sign of traffic being lost due to the opening of the Dornoch Road Bridge, and in the month the bridge opened there had been record takings. Further, ScotRail were about to spend £750,000 in upgrading the radio signalling system on the Kyle and North lines.

Retrenchment was still in the air, with Invergordon, Tain and Lairg being de-staffed when Red Star parcels pulled out in 1991, and Brora lost its staff in 1992.

The line wins useful friends

Recent events, including the passage of the 1993 Railways Act, did nothing to assuage the worries of rail supporters, including school teacher Frank Roach who with his family had moved from Bristol to live in the station building in Rogart in 1993.

In early 1994 Frank Roach posted a short letter in the *Inverness Courier* in which he suggested that if the Far North Line were to survive, a support group needed to be formed, in much the same way as the Friends of the Settle & Carlisle Line had done, and would anyone who was interested please telephone him? The outcome was that, a few weeks later, a meeting was convened at Rogart Station to discuss the best way forward. As recalled by the first Treasurer of the Friends of the Far North Line (FoFNL), Ian Jamieson, writing in FoFNL's May 2010 newsletter: 'About seven or eight of us managed to cram into Frank's sitting room, and various ideas were tossed to and fro for a couple of hours.' Next, a committee was formed, comprising Jamieson (from Inverness), John Melling (Inverness), Harry Miller (Tain), John Moore (Fortrose), Frank Roach and Frank Spaven (Inverness). Jamieson commented:

> It was apparent to me, even at this early stage, that Frank, although quietly spoken, had tremendous drive and enthusiasm and was clearly undaunted by the task that lay ahead of us, and it was no surprise therefore, that he made an early approach to The Rt. Hon Robert MacLennan MP *[MP for Caithness and Sutherland]* and invited him to become the first President of FoFNL.

FoFNL's first newsletter was published in September 1994, with others following in quick succession in December 1994 and March 1995 – establishing a regular pattern of well-written and informative newsletters, later under the title *Far North Express*, which continues to the present day.

The Highland Area Group of SAPT and the recently-formed Dornoch Firth Action Group (not to be confused with the Dornoch Rail Link Action

Group [DORLAG] launched in 2006) decided it was time to review the current situation and future role of the railway to Caithness. 'A Future for the Far North Line', drafted by Frank Spaven and I, was distributed to interested parties, including the media, in April 1994. Over its 13 pages the briefing paper sought to assess the value of the railway and how it might play a more useful role, concluding that:

> Despite loss of traffic in recent decades, the Far North Line is still functioning in a useful but minor local role. It has considerable potential, through revived freight and increased passenger traffic, to bring more benefits to developers, visitors and residents in the North. However, these will only be realised if new but feasible policies, practices and projects are put in place, such as has been happening in other countries. Privatisation appears to be irrelevant or dangerous to these real needs of the railway and its region; however, there are a few promising possibilities which should be exploited, and modifications and guarantees should be sought to ensure that the worst features of privatisation are avoided.

The first freight on the Far North Line after the opening of the new Ness Viaduct was a short contract for movement of steel pipes for the offshore oil industry from Hartlepool to Georgemas. Hauled by 37 423, this left Inverness at 06.30 on Sunday 1 September 1991, and is seen here at Muir of Ord. In the left background is the rail-connected barley silo for the nearby maltings, while in the right background is the temporary train maintenance shed surviving from the period when the line was physically isolated from the national network. Frank Spaven

While highlighting the lineside population of 35,000 from Inverness to Tain and parking restrictions in Inverness, the paper did not specifically advocate the development of local commuter services (which in due course would prove to be one of the enduring modern service improvements on the line), focusing instead on freight (particularly timber) and tourism potential. Its regional recommendations included:

- key public, private and voluntary sector stakeholders 'should form a local partnership' to promote the use and development of the line.

- A Highland Railway Company to operate all basic services on at least the Far North and Kyle lines should be formed as a long-tenure sub-franchise of the new ScotRail passenger company and as a new local operator of freight and parcels services. It or the partnership…should have staff at several stations selected as focal points for local community enterprises, using redundant station buildings.

- Railtrack should assess the Dornoch Firth Rail Crossing while [European Union] Objective One grants are still available for it, and, with the Scottish Office and the EU, should see this as an integral part of the measures outlined here, and the one most likely to convince potential users that the line does have a future.

The first two recommendations reflected, in part, inspiration from the work of Huddersfield-based rail advocate and consultant, Paul Salveson, whose *New Futures for Rural Rail: an Agenda for Action* (1993) had stimulated interest in the concepts of both micro-franchises or sub-franchises geared to regional needs, and 'community rail partnerships' which were to be created throughout England and Wales in the late 1990s and first decades of the 21st century.

1994 also saw the publication, under the auspices of Highlands & Islands Enterprise (HIE), of *The Highland Railway Survey* undertaken by the Nairn-based railway author and publisher, David St John Thomas, with the support of 13 freelance survey staff. This 47-page booklet was commissioned by HIE 'to consider the possible effects of privatisation on each of the Highland lines, state the main purpose each line fulfills, and generally explore what problems and potential can be foreseen'.

Based on a survey of over 6,000 passengers on the North and West Highland lines in August 1993, the report was nevertheless far from comprehensive. In a November 1994 commentary for SAPT, Frank Spaven noted the gaps:

It says relatively little about their role for residents and nothing about the future for freight and these aspects should be looked into further…the lesson from the past in the Highlands and the present in other countries is that a railway with the inherently sparse traffic potential of such a region must have a lively freight (and parcels and mail) business as well as passenger (tourist and some local), an integrated, cost-sharing, local management and operation of both (and a 'level playing field' with road hauliers and coach companies) and good links with national and wider networks.

St John Thomas had however much to say about tourist potential, Spaven praising his suggestions for promoting this market, particularly 'by train/bus/ ferry round trips – but who is going to arrange them? ScotRail's Area Managers used to do it!' On the Far North Line specifically, the report noted that it had the largest percentage both of residents and overseas visitors of all the lines studied, the proportion of visitors from elsewhere in the UK being the lowest 'and English visitors being especially rare':

Some trains are veritable mini-United Nations in their loads, overseas visitors often predominating or even accounting for four fifths of passengers on certain sections, especially in the far north. Whether from Australia, North America or

Early morning mist lingers as the Hartlepool-Georgemas pipe train heads away from Beauly on 1 September 1991. Frank Spaven

Eastern Europe, the passengers were delighted with the scenery and the service. The sparsity of English visitors is no doubt explained by the popular 'southern' image of all the best scenery being on the West Coast…Yet if this was Scotland's only scenic route it would bristle with activity and hardly anyone using it for the first time failed to be surprised by its grand mixture of coastal and inland scenery.

This was a valuable insight, which is just as relevant in 2016. On other Far North Line specifics in the report, SAPT particularly welcomed the suggestion of 'the re-design of Sprinters with a better outlook and the 158 railcars even more so; and why not at least one "vistadome" observation car?' A failure to address some key aspects of the line's circumstances was however noted:

The much greater local population of this line in terms of lineside population should be recognised. It amounts to 64,000 (not including the hinterland and Orkney), compared to 2,000-17,000 in the other four *[the Kyle, Mallaig, Fort William and Oban lines]*.

The Friends spread their wings

Less than 18 months after SAPT had talked up the prospects of freight on the Far North Line, the vision turned into reality, but the context requires explanation.

As the rail system moved towards privatisation, following the 1993 Railways Act, the Government had ordered the reorganisation of BR's Trainload Freight business into three geographically-based shadow companies, which it thought would ease the path towards sale and facilitate on-track competition.

The company covering Scotland – Transrail – was established in 1994 with a large operating area extending from the West Coast Main Line axis to Wales and the west of England. The nationwide Speedlink wagonload network had disappeared in 1991, but in 1995 innovative BR management in Transrail took the dramatic step of reintroducing a limited network of long-haul wagonload services under the brand name 'Enterprise'.

One of the fruits of this wider initiative was the first general freight train to run through to Caithness for 11 years, and the first freight of any description on the Far North Line since the viaduct collapsed in 1989. Waved away from Inverness on 29 September 1995 by Robert Maclennan MP, this train conveyed 230 tonnes of domestic coal, and 100 tonnes of steel for use in the manufacture of chest freezers by Norfrost of Castletown, which at the time employed 300 people producing 10,000 freezers per week.

This initial flow developed into a regular weekly Enterprise service in 1996. The same year, what had been in late 1995 a trial trainload movement of large steel pipes from Hartlepool to Georgemas – for fabrication at the nearby Rockwater yard – became a regular (initially twice-weekly) service. As David Richard-Jones, Economic Development Manager (Caithness) for Highland Council, commented in a presentation to the Scottish Rail Freight Conference in Inverness in April 1997:

> The rail haulage component of the journey from steel mill to site has reduced 420 miles of escorted road haulage to a journey of less than 12 road miles. Each train carries the equivalent of eleven lorry loads of pipes and this saves the equivalent of nearly 9000 lorry road miles per train load!

The weekly Enterprise service was soon carrying a somewhat exotic mix of (mostly heavy, rail-suited) traffics, including Sutherland marble via the Channel Tunnel to Italy, Caithness flagstone paving to Kyle (for Skye) and Stranraer (for Belfast), and timber from Wick, Thurso, Georgemas and Lairg to various board, paper and saw mills. Unfortunately, for market and road competition reasons, too few of these loads ever became regular movements.

In October 1995, Friends of the Far North Line (FoFNL) held their first conference, in Inverness, designed to highlight the potential of the Far North Line and to acquaint individuals and groups with FoFNL and its stated aims. Speakers included Robert MacLennan MP, John Holwell, Market Manager Scotland for Transrail, who had been a key catalyst for the development of freight services, Paul Salveson (advocate of micro-franchises and community rail partnerships) and Donald MacPherson, ScotRail's Area Manager (based at Perth), who afterwards wrote: 'The quality and variety of the speakers was excellent and it was extremely encouraging to see all the major bodies committed to working together to improve railway services in the Highlands.'

As recorded by John Allison[69], a number of encouraging 'commitments' were made at the 1995 conference. ScotRail proposed to introduce, in the next summer's timetable, a commuter train leaving Tain at approximately 07.30 and arriving in Inverness at around 08.30 using an existing two-car Class 156 unit between turns. It would then, for the first time for many years, be possible to commute to Inverness by train in the rapidly expanding travel to work area to the north.

ScotRail would also attempt to achieve a three-hour journey time from Wick to Inverness by a programme of running line improvements and a careful inspection of speed limits on the line. Highlands & Islands Enterprise (the replacement for the Highlands & Islands Development Board) immediately committed themselves to 50% of the cost of an estimated £25,000 engineering survey of the line.

Dr Ken MacTaggart of Highlands & Islands Enterprise offered to hold a meeting of interested parties to attempt to establish a line 'partnership' and to see what steps could be taken to integrate the transport network, perhaps by the establishment of a Passenger Transport Authority as suggested by Brian Wilson (Labour MP and Shadow Spokesman on Transport) to examine the development and promotion of all the railways in the Highlands, and to look closely at appointing a Railways Development Officer.

Writing in 2010, FoFNL's first Treasurer, Ian Jamieson, commented:

In retrospect, the conference must be seen as pivotal, both for FoFNL, and for the Far North Line itself... In conclusion, the question must be asked: 'Would FoFNL have been formed if someone had not had the foresight to encourage its establishment sixteen years ago?' Well, yes. Probably someone else would have come up with the idea somewhere along the line [excuse the metaphor], but, make no mistake about it, FoFNL is where it is today thanks to the flair, the vision, and the commitment of one man – Frank Roach.

Preserved ex-LMS class 8F 2-8-0 No. 48151 heads away from Helmsdale after taking on water on the Inverness-Thurso section of the Railway Touring Company's 'Great Britain' tour on 12 April 2007. This was only the second time the line had seen steam on it since the end of BR steam nationwide in 1968. Ben Collier

Rail improvement opportunities

In October 1995, HIE published a report it had commissioned from consultants Pieda and MDS Transmodal on 'The Economic and Social Impact of the Rail Network in the Highlands'. This concluded that the whole network generated, directly and indirectly, some 829 jobs and income of £12.4m – of which 77 jobs and £1.1m income related to the Far North Line. 60% of the 63,000 annual passengers using the Far North Line were 'locals', compared to just 25% on the tourism-dominated Kyle line.

The report highlighted recent deterioration in the passenger service in the run-up to privatisation, with the previous pattern of four trains a day in summer reduced to three, and trains to Wick being routed via Thurso (instead of splitting the train in two at Georgemas Junction). This enabled the train crew depot at Thurso to be shut and reduced the number of diesel units required to operate the service, but ensured that Wick retained its passenger trains despite having half as many customers as Thurso.

Among the HIE report's recommendations was consideration of a 'joint initiative on the part of local authorities, ScotRail, HIE and the Scottish Tourist Board involving the appointment of a rail development officer'. The consultants identified a longer-term, post-privatisation, opportunity for micro-franchising:

> Entirely new approaches could be adopted to the presentation of the rail product. It is vital to recognise that much of the Highland rail network is already a 'tourist' railway. It would perhaps be better to manage it as such, and not to operate it as a poor relation of the 'proper' railways operated to the south. That need not mean that local needs are not addressed.

The Far North and Kyle lines were mooted as the basis for a micro-franchise, 'separately managed within an overall franchise for Scottish services', and within which 'staff could be deployed on a different and more flexible basis, in order to maximise tourist revenue and volumes.' The report then suggested an even more dramatic break from traditional structures:

> In addition, the considerable local interest and enthusiasm in the railways could be marshalled within the railway enterprise, to provide voluntary labour and add to the revenue generating activities. There is clear evidence from 'tourist' railways in England and Wales that it is possible to exploit a tourist market in this way, create permanent jobs and help to develop the local tourist industry.

Rail industry recognition that there was a need to improve passenger and freight services on the Far North Line lay behind the June 1996 appointment by Railtrack of consultants Scott Wilson Kirkpatrick to undertake a desk-top feasibility study of route speed / loading improvements on the Far North Line. (Following the 1993 Railways Act, the new company, Railtrack, had taken control of Britain's rail infrastructure in 1994, and was floated on the Stock Exchange in May 1996.)

The introduction to the study report, published in August 1996, noted that 'any improvements will need to be attractive from an economic viewpoint, on what will still be a lightly used line, although there are particular circumstances which may allow funding from a variety of sources related to economic development in the area.'

The report's principal conclusions were that, 'without great expense a 9 minute reduction in journey time would appear possible', and that there was potential 'for a further 17 minutes at increased costs', a test train run having confirmed their feasibility. On the freight front, 'it would also appear possible to accommodate the desired increase in freight axle loads from RA5 (18.75 tonnes) to RA8 (22.5 tonnes) with work to a number of structures.' Among the key recommendations were:

- examination of the impact of increasing speeds through crossing loops from 15mph to 25mph
- survey and design of a west to north chord at Georgemas, eliminating reversal there and slightly shortening the distance to be travelled (with the physical works estimated to cost 'a six figure sum')
- assessment of the scope for conversion of open level crossings (with train speed restrictions) to 'automatic half barrier' operation (without train speed restrictions), with physical works estimated to cost a 'six figure sum' per crossing
- assessment of the scope to telephone-link, or close completely, some of 'the plethora of user worked crossings'

More freight – and a new rail partnership

The revival of rail freight north of Inverness, carried on a weekly train, grew to such an extent that, by May 1997, Paul Shannon could write in RAIL magazine:

The most remarkable freight renaissance in Scotland has been the return of freight traffic to the Far North line...The staple traffic on the line since the service started in September 1995 has been fridges and freezers manufactured by Norfrost, destined for Leyland business park in Lancashire. The economics of the operation have been enhanced by back-loading the wagons with various other goods, including steel plate for Norfrost.

Other traffic that has been conveyed to and from the Far North line on a regular basis includes timber from Lairg to Plean, agricultural lime from Thrislington to Fearn and containerised aviation fuel from Purfleet [in Essex] to Georgemas Junction [a journey of over 700 miles].

Movement of timber is an area into which EWS [English Welsh & Scottish Railway, the private company which had acquired five of BR's six freight companies in 1995] is hopeful of making great inroads, and it has strong support from Forest Enterprise, the Government body which co-ordinates all forestry activity. There have also been a large number of occasional or one-off movements.

Not a viable trainload: 66 103 nears Lentran on the daily Caithness-Inverness freight on 21 July 2004, hauling just two empty Safeway containers and a van (probably loaded with freezers from the Castletown factory of Norfrost, subsequently closed). Ewan Crawford

In 1998, following pressure from Friends of the Far North Line (and its equivalents on the Kyle and West Highland lines), in 1998 the Highland Rail Network Development Partnership (HRP) was set up by Highland Council, Argyll & Bute Council, HIE, Railtrack, ScotRail, freight operating companies and the rail user groups. Initially it employed two Rail Development Officers for the separate networks in the North and West Highlands, with the former covered by Frank Roach (who gave up his teaching job at Dingwall Academy, and resigned as Secretary of FoFNL). In due course, Roach's 'empire' encompassed all the Highland lines and the Inverness-Aberdeen line as far east as Keith.

An early benefit of the new partnership fronted by Roach was the instigation in 1998 of a commuter service from Dingwall to Inverness, departing daily at 08.00. This was the first new service to be introduced during the ScotRail franchise, which had begun in 1997 and was to be operated by National Express until 2004, to be followed by First Group until 2015. ScotRail was the last BR train operator to be privatised, in March 1997, just months before the General Election which brought Labour to power.

The financial risk of the new service was underwritten by HRP, so ScotRail were protected and there was no immediate impact on the franchise. As ex-ScotRail manager David Prescott recollected in 2016: 'The unit was spare until around 10.00, so there were only train crew and mileage costs to be borne. The break-even load was about 80 passengers.'

The Dingwall train was the first step in a sustained process of commuter service development over the next 15 years, comprising new stations and in particular more frequent services (in due course marketed under the somewhat contrived 'Invernet' branding). Arguably, this was to prove to be the most significant change in the fortunes of the Far North Line to date wrought by Roach's rail leadership for the partnership and its eventual 'HITRANS' (regional transport partnership) replacement.

The year 2000 saw a significant passenger service development. The Class 156 diesel units which had operated the Far North Line since 1989 were replaced by Class 158 'Express Diesel' units which had been redeployed from inter-city services, following introduction of new Class 170 units on the latter. The 158s were far from the cutting edge of rail travel, with a relatively cramped interior, and were prone to engine faults and air conditioning failure. But they were higher-powered (reducing the through journey time by an average of 18 minutes), had two toilets per two-car unit (as opposed to one on the 156s), cut out the draughts from opening windows to which the 156s were susceptible, and represented in a modest way some upgrading of travel standards.

English Welsh & Scottish Railway (EWS) No. 66 111 propels the 08.07 (Fridays only) Inverness-Lairg oil train into the Lairg depot on 31 August 2007. John Furnevel

The short period from 2000 until a general deceleration in 2005 saw the high-point of speed on the Far North Line in its entire operational history from 1874 to 2016, with a fastest Thurso-Inverness journey time of 3 hours 21 minutes, and 3 hours 23 minutes northbound.

An early morning commuter train from Tain to Inverness had been proposed pre-privatisation – with Highland Council offering funding of £30,000 pa towards its costs – but this extension of the Dingwall service only fell into place in 2000, with funding from what was now generally referred to as the 'Highland Rail Partnership'.

The year 2000 brought mixed news on the freight front. In 1999 the supermarket company, Safeway, had pioneered the rail movement of supermarket supplies with its daily Mossend-Inverness train, and the following year the concept was extended northwards to Caithness. Facilitated by a Freight Facilities Grant (FFG) of £897,000, the daily train from Inverness carried bespoke Safeway containers for delivery – from an enhanced rail facility at Georgemas Junction – to stores in Thurso, Wick and Kirkwall. The grant from the Scottish Executive was made on the basis of rail removing some 567,000 lorry miles from the roads every year.

The FFG scheme – which still functions in Scotland, but not in England – is a valuable (and explicit) acknowledgement by Scottish Government of the environmental benefits of rail freight, and also helps to reduce the heavy wear and tear imposed on trunk road surfaces by 44-tonne lorries. But the FFG budget has always been extremely modest by comparison with investment in the trunk road network.

Despite the Safeway FFG award in 2000, EWS shareholder pressure for commercial returns led to a first rationalisation of the Enterprise network that year, notable in Scotland for withdrawal of wagonload services from 12 of the 18 timber terminals established over the previous eight years (including all of those on the Far North Line). The fragmented flows of timber – particularly to those board, paper and saw mills which were not directly rail-connected (the majority) – did not lend themselves to competitive pricing or service quality.

The loss of timber on the Far North Line abstracted volume from the train service just when its frequency had been increased from weekly to daily to meet Safeway requirements. And the regular sight of the Inverness-Georgemas train with only two or three containers hauled by a £2m Class 66 loco presaged the demise within five years of this innovative enterprise by EWS.

However, the long hauls between Caithness and markets/supply areas did in principle offer rail a key strength to compete with road haulage, and EWS intensified efforts to build a critical mass of volume to cover the cost of the daily 295-mile round trip from Millburn Yard in Inverness to Georgemas. In 2001, Thurso Building Supplies was awarded a £289,000 Freight Facilities Grant for rail movement of building materials from the south, on the basis that the grant would allow 356,000 lorry trips annually to be removed from the roads. In practice, there was only some modest movement of traffic between 2002 and 2004, and, most unusually, the Scottish Executive had to 'claw back' part of the grant award from the recipient.

While most of the focus of attention in those years was on short-to-medium term enhancements to passenger and freight services, the dream of a truly transformative Dornoch Bridge still remained alive for some. One of the most indefatigable campaigners for improved rail services has been the Reverend Alistair Roy, who served as a Church of Scotland Minister in Wick for over 50 years. Active in community politics, he long championed the Far North Line, seeking faster and more convenient passenger rail services, and he actively supported the Dornoch campaign.

But support for a rail cut-off was far from restricted to local campaigners. Perhaps the most tenacious advocate of a substantial speed-up on the Far North

Line – and indeed for rail improvements across Scotland – has been Bearsden-based Ken Sutherland, often in his voluntary capacity as Research Officer for RailFuture Scotland.

It is fair to say that Sutherland is not rail management's favourite campaigner, but since the early 1970s he has assiduously argued, in newspaper columns and the wider media, for a bigger role for rail in Scotland. In the case of the Dornoch Bridge, he has been pursuing the campaign for more than thirty years – and still he does not give up. Ever alert for conspiracy, in 2016 he drew my attention to a strange episode in 1999-2000 which has never been fully explained. In early 1999, the draft version of the Highland Council Structure Plan stated:

> A considerable shortening of the journey time for rail passengers between Caithness/South East Sutherland and Inverness could be achieved by construction of a direct link between Tain and Golspie, crossing the Dornoch Firth.

The Highland Structure Plan Written Statement in late 1999 then *removed* the word 'considerable', supposedly at the behest of one very influential Councillor. Sutherland described this 'as a way of trying to psychologically "diminish" the value of a Dornoch Rail link': given that journey time savings of 27-45 minutes were projected, it is hard to disagree with him that 'considerable' was a highly appropriate adjective.

An Examination in Public was held into the Written Statement version of the Structure Plan, and objections were made against the removal of the key word. The Reporter sustained the case that the word 'considerable' or 'significant' was appropriate to apply to the magnitude of time saving, and concluded that it was perverse to seek its removal.

Highland Council nevertheless appealed against the Reporter's Recommendations and continued to argue for removal of the word, but the appeal was rejected as incoherent by the Scottish Executive Minister for the Environment, Planning and Transport (Sarah Boyack), and the word 'considerable' was restored to Highland Council's Structure Plan document in 2000. As Sutherland commented to me in 2016: 'You really couldn't make it up!'

A heritage corridor

A Highland Council register compiled in 2002 showed no fewer than 21 'listed' railway stations and structures along the Far North Line. The one Grade A listed structure was the Shin (or Oykel) Viaduct carrying the railway across the Kyle of Sutherland between Culrain and Invershin. It consists of a 280-feet lattice girder span and five approach arches built of stone, each with a 30-feet span. Of the other 20 listed structures, all – bar the C listed Fearn Railway Cottages – were Grade B listed, comprising:

- station buildings and related structures at Ardgay, Brora, Dingwall, Dunrobin, Fearn, Golspie, Helmsdale, Kildary (subsequently demolished as part of the A9 upgrade), Tain, Thurso and Wick

- bridges at Alness, Brora, Clachnaharry (plus the signal box), Conon Bridge, Golspie and Kildary

- a warehouse at Dingwall and a farm at Golspie (the connection with the railway is unknown)

Collectively, these structures form part of a corridor of distinctive architectural, geographical and historical interest, which should be better promoted as part of a bigger role for the railway in the life of the Far North of Scotland.

Preserved ex-LMS 4-6-0 loco No. 44871 hauls the 'Cathedrals Explorer' charter train (which had originated in London) over the A-listed Oykel (or Shin) Viaduct, between Culrain and Invershin, on 12 May 2014. Dave Collier

Originally a private station serving the Duke of Sutherland's nearby castle, Dunrobin station was reconstructed to this Arts & Crafts design in 1902 – and is now open to the public throughout the summer season, as a request halt. Seen here on 27 August 2007.
John Furnevel

The line also offers a unique diversity of scenery over its 168 miles, as described in Chapter 2, and various unusual attractions, as listed in Appendix 1, such as Dunrobin Castle, the Royal Society for the Protection of Birds (RSPB) centre in Forsinard station building (and controversial nearby star-gazing tower), the tastefully refurbished Helmsdale station, and the railway-themed accommodation at Rogart, to name only a few.

To date, whether in public or private ownership, the rail operators have all failed to develop sufficiently imaginative marketing of this remarkable railway. Increasingly centralised railway management, and too often a 'one size fits all' approach to Scotland's rural routes, do not lend themselves to making the most of the Far North Line.

More passenger breakthroughs

In 2001, following research and lobbying by Frank Roach for the Highland Rail Partnership, Sunday train services, which had previously been summer-only, became an all-year feature of the timetable. And the afternoon train from Caithness to Inverness became the busiest southbound train of the week, demonstrating the value of the 'visiting friends and relatives' market for a train service which was slower than both the car and coach competition, but offered enhanced quality of service benefits compared to the coach.

One of the most symbolic breakthroughs in the passenger market came with the re-opening of Beauly station in 2002. This had been one of the more contentious of the 1960 station closures and with an enhanced train service of seven trains a day to Inverness passing through the station site (including morning and evening peak hour services), Roach saw the opportunity to promote a re-opening which would also have wider repercussions for rail enhancement.

On 23 November 2003, the guard of an Inverness-Wick train is about to close the single designated door opened at Beauly's 15-metre platform – Britain's smallest station. The original station building is to the left of the rear coach of the train. John Furnevel

However, the original station building (including the former private waiting room for Lord Lovat) and its adjacent platform had long been in private ownership. The big challenge facing Frank Roach was the likely capital cost: while new stations on single lines had typically cost between £50,000 and £100,000 during the peak period of station re-openings by BR in the 1980s, costs had mushroomed following privatisation and the creation of Railtrack. A figure of £380,000 for a conventional new station at Beauly would not stack up financially against a projected patronage of 28 passengers per day.

Ever the lateral thinker, Roach successfully pursued the idea of a short (15 metre) platform, for which just a single door on the train would be opened by the conductor. The Strategic Rail Authority – set up by the 1997 Labour Government to oversee rail development – agreed to part-fund the £247,000 capital cost of this initially 'experimental' station, with contributions also from Inverness & Nairn Enterprise, Highland Council and the Highland Rail Partnership.

After delays while Her Majesty's Railway Inspectorate debated the safety of the single-door and short-platform option (despite this being a trifling risk compared to the hazards of the competing A9 road), the station opened to a fanfare of publicity in April 2002, and patronage went from strength to strength. The precedent created at Beauly was a welcome rejoinder to the extremes of Health & Safety requirements increasingly being imposed on the privatised railway. The industry has been a self-contained and easy target for the 'tick box' culture. Yet if the levels of safety required were applied to its more ubiquitous (and more dangerous) competitor, the entire road system would be shut down overnight.

Also in 2002, regular oil traffic returned to Lairg, as part of a £10m FFG award to BP Oil UK Ltd for upgrading the facilities at the Grangemouth refinery and five distribution railheads across Scotland. The train ran – and continues to run – as an up to once-weekly service. It is one of the most remarkable rural rail freight operations in Britain, its survival owing much to the length of haul involved (200 miles) from the rail-connected refinery and the lack of back-loading opportunities for road hauliers.

Meanwhile, the loss of regular timber traffic from railheads in Caithness and Sutherland in 2000 did not stop efforts to develop the timber-by-rail business. The Highland Rail Partnership homed in on the Flow Country around Kinbrace, where single-track sub-standard roads placed a significant constraint on getting harvested timber to market on 44-tonne lorries. However, the absence of suitable long rail sidings in the area (and the cost of installing them) meant that the daily Safeway train to Caithness and return could not be utilised, so a more innovative approach was required.

Learning from the pioneering 'lineside loading' work of BR on the West Highland Line in the 1980s, (loading timber on to wagons on the 'main line' without the expense of providing sidings), a £100,000 project was developed by the Highland Rail Partnership, Highland Council and the Forestry Commission – with contributions from the European Regional Development Fund, James Jones Ltd (saw millers) and the rail industry – to construct a 250-metre-long loading pad adjacent to the Far North Line, just south of Kinbrace. Timber brought in by road over a number of days was stockpiled on site and, once the weekly train of 21 wagons arrived in the evening, after the end of passenger services, it was then loaded for the night transit to Inverness (conveying some 500 tonnes of timber).

The first train ran in August 2002, then developed into a pattern of running five nights a week every third week between April and September, with timber distributed by road from the Inverness railhead to various local users. While lineside loading minimised capital expenditure, it involved very high operating costs, partly through catering for the complexity of night-time working (and the associated intense peak of loading activity, and double-handling of the timber), and also through the cost of detaining a £2m locomotive on site for several hours while the train was loaded.

Over the following three years, 50,000 tonnes of timber were taken by rail from Kinbrace to Inverness by EWS for onward road distribution, primarily to the large Norbord board mill at Dalcross, just east of Inverness. The mill had its own private siding when opened in 1985, but this was built over at a time of plant expansion (and regional rail freight contraction) in the 1990s.

The economics of the daily Enterprise service to Caithness looked to be on the verge of further improvement when the Scottish Government awarded a £642,000 Freight Facilities Grant to Norfrost in 2004 for increased rail movement of fridge freezers to the south. But in 2005 external market changes (to which rail is always vulnerable) led to the abrupt end of the daily train to Caithness, with rail becoming a casualty of the takeover of Safeway by Morrison and the subsequent enforced sale of its Caithness stores to the Co-op, which had different supply chain arrangements.

Without the (admittedly small) Safeway baseload, the rail economics could not be made to work. In any event, the nationwide Enterprise wagonload network (which could accommodate disparate part-trains of traffic to different parts of the country) was steadily shrinking in the face of unprofitable operation. Once more, the Far North Line lost its mixed freight service, although the full trainloads of pipes, with their much superior economics, continued to operate from Hartlepool to Georgemas.

Ed Burkhardt, the Managing Director of EWS, had been committed to expanding rail's market share. However, he had rashly indicated that one of his aims – using cost-control and marketing lessons learned in the USA from the big rail hauliers and flexible 'short line' operations – was to redevelop rail freight to the extent that his trains could eventually serve every branch line in Britain. The Americans had partly mis-read the British market, with its generally much shorter hauls than in the USA and a highly flexible and cost-effective road haulage sector. Also, strong trade union representation among train drivers – plus unforeseen competition for labour between the private rail companies – led to wages being driven up significantly, although to some extent balanced by greater staff flexibility.

2005 also saw the end of the Kinbrace-Inverness trainload timber flows. The complexity, cost and risk associated with securing a reliable rail service, for relatively modest volumes of around 15,000 tonnes a year, proved to be too high for the Flow Country's timber markets to bear.

A Class 37 on snow clearance duties rests at Rogart in the winter of 2005-06. This class of loco has been associated with the Far North Line since 1982, latterly on engineering and nuclear traffic duties for Carlisle-based Direct Rail Services. Frank Roach

However, the same year also saw investigation of the scope for innovative rail kit to overcome some of the barriers encountered catering for relatively modest and/or short-term timber flows. Scottish Enterprise commissioned my Deltix Transport Consulting business, and IBI Group, to analyse the potential timber transport applications of the 'Non-Intrusive Crossover System' (NICS) for new freight sidings.[70]

In terms of ease of access to the rail network, NICS could be characterised as a compromise between, on the one hand, the low operating cost, high flexibility and high capital cost of conventional rail siding connection and, on the other hand, the high operating cost, very limited flexibility and very low capital cost of lineside loading (as practised at Kinbrace).

The Deltix / IBI report identified 21 potential NICS timber sites across Scotland, including two on the Far North Line – at Kinbrace and Dunrobin Glen – plus a further two on the Kyle line. Securing Network Rail's approval for use on the national network, even on a trial basis, was, however, to prove elusive, although renewed interest was to come with 2015-16 studies of the scope for rail movement of much-increased volumes of timber from the Flow Country.

'Invernet' takes off

The expansion of the Inverness area commuter service took a major step forward in 2005, with much of the development focused on the Far North Line, the business case being based on earlier service improvements yielding a 49% increase in passengers.

Two additional services were introduced from Inverness to Invergordon and return, and two to Tain and return. What had originally been the first commuter service of the day from Dingwall, and later Tain, was also extended to start back from Lairg. The 'Invernet' package was partly locally-funded, but also supported by the Scottish Executive's Public Transport Fund – costing £1.5m annually in total – but in due course would be subsumed in the overall ScotRail franchise funded by the Executive.

Unfortunately, 2005 also saw a major deterioration in journey times along the Far North Line, with a particularly severe impact on end-to-end travellers. RETB operational rules required drivers to pass through loop entrances and exits at 15mph, but this limit was routinely ignored. The introduction of the Train Protection and Warning System (TPWS) had the effect of rigidly enforcing the speed limit, with drivers having to approach stations more slowly to avoid TPWS applying emergency braking.

TPWS automatically activates brakes on a train that has passed a signal at danger or is over-speeding. It is not designed to stop trains at or before a signal that is at danger: rather, it aims to stop the train before the point at which a collision with another train could occur. Punctuality dropped significantly after TPWS was introduced and, in order to accommodate the extra time needed to avoid emergency braking (by running more slowly through the loop points and then over the length of the loops), decelerations of 21-27 minutes between Inverness and Wick/Thurso were incorporated in the timetable.

Consultants Scott Wilson Railways were commissioned by Highlands and Islands Enterprise in 2005 to undertake the substantial *Room for Growth* study of the Highland rail network, to complement Network Rail's first *Route Utilisation Study* covering the rest of the country. This was set against the background of the devolution of further rail powers to the Scottish Executive. The aim of the study was to identify the main constraints on the capacity of the network's infrastructure which were limiting potential development opportunities. The study was also required to identify, on the basis of growth predictions and aspirations, the work that was required to remove the constraints and, in so doing, provide an estimate of the associated costs.

This 151-page report was published in 2006 and provided a wealth of information on the capacity and capability of the Far North Line, among which key points were:

- an average speed of just 39mph was achieved between Inverness and Thurso (compared, for example, to 54-59mph between Inverness and Perth)

- there were two key pinch points on the route, based on a theoretical capacity of two trains per hour between Inverness and Muir of Ord, and one train per hour between Helmsdale and Georgemas

- 67% of route capacity was utilised between Helmsdale and Georgemas, but just 17% between the latter and Wick/Thurso

The second part of the report evaluated various aspirations for development identified during the stakeholder consultation. Insofar as the Far North Line was concerned, the key short to medium term conclusions were that (i) four train services a day in each direction between Inverness and Wick/Thurso could be accommodated within the existing fleet based at Inverness, but additional train crew would be required at Wick, and (ii) creating a new station at Conon Bridge (at the former station site) would be feasible, at an estimated cost of £0.25m (15 metre length) or £0.35m (2-car train length). Four major longer-term aspirations were considered in some detail: (i) reduce journey times by improving line speeds; (ii) increase capacity on the route; (iii) create a chord line at Georgemas; and (iv) install a direct line via Dornoch.

On the key issue of line speeds, the report concisely summarised the line's biggest problem: 'The present tortuous route of the railway combined with low average speeds makes the train uncompetitive when compared to road-based journeys.'

It noted that the main constraint to reducing journey time was the 15mph speed limit imposed through train-operated points at the crossing loops controlled by the RETB signalling system introduced in the 1980s, compounded by the subsequent introduction of the Train Protection and Warning System (TPWS), resulting in trains travelling through loops being restricted to 15mph from one end to the other. With relaxation of standards, a possible time saving of just five minutes over the entire route was postulated, a modest recovery from the 21-27 minute time penalty imposed in 2005.

Destaffing of level crossings in the 1960s and associated speed restrictions imposed on trains (primarily to protect motorists) had imposed a heavy time penalty on the railway. No fewer than 48 level crossings are scattered along the 67 route miles north of Helmsdale, for example, of which 41 are private user-operated crossings, typically linking pieces of land in one ownership which were separated when the railway was built.

A variety of other types of level crossing is deployed on the line today, with different train speed limits reflecting different levels of road and rail usage at different locations: two crossings are 'open' (ie non-automatic, with no gates or barriers, and no flashing road traffic signals); some are 'AOCL+B' (automatic, with short barriers and flashing signals); while one (at Nigg) is a full Automatic Half Barrier (AHB) arrangement.

The Scott Wilson report evaluated the time-saving impact of upgrading eight key crossings, and concluded that 6.5 minutes could be saved at a capital cost of £3.6m. It also quoted a 1986 report which identified a maximum theoretical potential time saving (uncosted) of 18.5 minutes through 'recanting' works – adjusting the height difference (to counteract centrifugal forces) between the two rails – on the 158 curves along the route.

The report highlighted capacity constraints on the line, commenting that: 'Whilst there is a perception that the Far North Line is lightly used and therefore has plenty of spare capacity the reality is that south of Dingwall particularly the line is at capacity.' It noted that the hardware for the RETB signalling processes was obsolete, and suggested consideration of extending the Inverness colour-light signalling regime north to Dingwall to increase signalling capacity. Also mooted to tackle the main capacity constraint south of Dingwall – the 13-mile single-track section between Inverness and Muir of Ord – were two development options:

- reinstating the double line from Clachnaharry to Clunes (singled in 1966), at a cost of £15m

- reinstating the loop at Lentran (created as part of the singling scheme in 1966, and taken out in 1988), at a cost of £7m.

The idea of a chord line at Georgemas had been proposed as far back as 1972 by the Scottish Association for Public Transport. Scott Wilson evaluated the scope to construct such a west to north chord, and concluded that a 'shot estimate' (excluding signalling) was £4m, providing a three-minute time saving.

Finally, Scott Wilson re-evaluated the scope for a direct line via Dornoch, noting that the Dornoch Firth Road Crossing 'now acts as a physical constraint to the rail route'. Estimated costs for a new route from Tain to Golspie were £73m (+/- 50%, and excluding signalling costs), yielding an impressive time saving of 37 minutes, bringing the Inverness-Thurso journey time down to three hours.

Class A1 4-6-2 No. 60163 Tornado heads north from Dingwall on the 'Seaforth Highlander' rail tour from Inverness to Brora, on 21 June 2015. Completed in 2008, Tornado was the first main-line steam locomotive built in Britain since Evening Star, the last steam locomotive built by British Railways, in 1960. Dave Collier

A sub-option involved retention of the existing line from the new junction at the south end of the Dornoch Bridge to Lairg, with the railway (and the station at Rogart) closed between Lairg and Golspie. Some commentators have suggested that the lack of enthusiasm for the Dornoch routeing within the Highland Rail Partnership (and subsequently HITRANS) in part reflects Frank Roach's residence at Rogart station but, in fairness, the *realpolitik* has been that the high capital costs (by rural rail, as opposed to road, standards) have militated against progressing the new railway.

In a statement on 29 February 2008, Stewart Stevenson, the Minister for Transport, Infrastructure and Climate Change, highlighted the fact that Scott Wilson's study had assessed the benefit to cost ratio as 'at best, 0.20', although the latter figure was to prove controversial.

Campaign disagreements

FoFNL was a broad church but, after a lively AGM in November 2004, disagreements about campaigning for a Dornoch Bridge came to a head, with a significant minority of (mostly new) members keen to press for the rail link as a top priority. A majority of members and most of FoFNL's Committee doubted that in the prevailing climate this kind of investment would ever be found for a rural rail route, but agreed that a full updated study was needed. However, a rift developed between the two camps.

In January 2005, encouraged by Rob Gibson MSP and individual campaigners (including those who had become disillusioned with FoFNL's focus on more achievable short-to-medium aims), the consultants Corus – who had produced the *Delivering an innovative Borders Railway* report for the Waverley Route Trust – briefed politicians and the public on their scoping study, *A Better Railway for the North*, which set out the case for a new strategic assessment study of the Far North Line. And in October of that year The Association of Caithness Community Councils lodged a petition with the Public Petitions Committee at Holyrood:

> …calling for the Scottish Parliament to consider investment in infrastructure, rolling stock and timetabling as part of a strategic root and branch review of the provision of rail services between Inverness, Thurso and Wick, with unrestricted thinking on how best to shorten journey times and ensure the continuing future of the railway to these destinations. Thought should also be given to ensuring that the existing communities of the "Lairg loop" are provided for.

Following consultations with stakeholders and the petitioner, in October 2007 the Committee agreed to refer the petition to the Parliament's Transport,

Infrastructure and Climate Change Committee. But in February 2008 Transport Minister Stewart Stevenson responded to the Committee: 'We have concluded that the Dornoch rail link should not be progressed at this stage due to its significant cost and poor value for money'.

Following further Committee deliberations, in October 2008 it 'agreed to consider the issues raised in this petition as part of its scrutiny of the Strategic Transport Projects Review and, in so doing, to close the petition'. And that, effectively, was the end of this particular campaigning avenue.

Meanwhile, however, in December 2006, the Dornoch Rail Link Action Group (DORLAG) had been launched in Thurso, with its principal objectives being 'the strategic upgrading of the Inverness to Thurso/Wick railway line by means of constructing a new route between Tain and Golspie...whilst at the same time retaining the existing line via Lairg.' The concept of retaining all of the original line was however a fundamental problem: the increased cost to the taxpayer for supporting a deep-rural route, and its trains serving only a few bus loads a day, surely being unsustainable.

Retention of only a branch from Tain to Lairg for three passenger trains daily and one freight train a week would be more politically attractive, but could it really be financially justified, when passengers and freight could readily feed in by road to a railhead at Tain? The 'case for Dornoch' (and whether or not to retain any of the old route) was not as straightforward as some of its protagonists would imply.

However, the MVA/Corus study of the Dornoch link eventually secured funding, and the report was delivered in 2008. The consultants estimated capital costs of £118m (at 2007 prices) for the new route. In a related discussion at the Scottish Parliament's Transport, Infrastructure and Climate Change Committee on 13 April 2008, Rob Gibson took issue with a conventional wisdom which had emerged from Scott Wilson's 2006 report:

> I am concerned that the minister's argument [rejecting a Dornoch rail bridge] relies on the "Room for Growth" study, which was published by Highlands and Islands Enterprise. There is now sufficient disquiet about the curious procedures used by the Halcrow consultants in their production of the poor benefit to cost ratio. I do not know whether there is a predetermined agenda, but when you look at how the documents were drawn up, it shows that the cost benefit ratio of only one option out of the three that could have been considered was looked at.
>
> The first option was to retain the Lairg loop intact and cut across at Dornoch. The second option was to retain only the Tain to Lairg section of the Lairg loop and cut across at Dornoch. The third option was to have none of the Lairg loop served

by train and cut across at Dornoch. The cost benefit ratio was calculated only on option 1. It is clear that if one tries to make a shorter route to the north, far fewer people on the loop section will be able to use the train. The question is, why was only one option considered? It has been commented on before, but the Highlands and Islands transport partnership has somehow accepted that strange approach.

On the face of it, Gibson's question did raise a possible conspiracy theory, but the issue failed to gain enough political traction to be pursued much further.

A practical improvement to the Far North Line's service came with the 2006 introduction of a fourth daily train from Wick and Thurso. This was an early departure, giving a connection from the first ferry from Orkney to Scrabster, and providing better connections to the south and Aberdeen. With a number of intermediate stops omitted, it allowed a four-hour timing from Wick to Inverness, and 'only' 3 hours 31 minutes from Thurso.

In 2007, strongly promoted by Frank Roach, the Highland Rail Partnership (HRP) was able to announce some positive news on the rolling stock front. The Inverness-based fleet of uninspiring Class 158s – with their drab and cramped 'designer' interiors – were to be upgraded as part of a £9.1 million refurbishment programme funded by the Scottish Executive. The internal decor was improved, seats were reupholstered and realigned better to match windows, and additional space was created for luggage and bikes.

Following a campaign by FoFNL, and as specified by HRP, there was also welcome news for railway track staff on the health and hygiene front. Toilet retention tanks were to be fitted, so that the traditional flushing of toilets on to the track would at last be ended. The refurbishment of the Inverness fleet of 158s was completed in 2008, providing a much improved ambience for travellers on these general-purpose trains, but not remotely in the same league as bespoke tourist trains (with observation cars) on equivalent routes in Austria and Switzerland.

That year, commuter and shopping/leisure/educational travel opportunities were further improved, when four trains each way became the all-year pattern on both the Far North and Kyle lines. An additional early service from Ardgay began operation to improve peak hour frequencies along the southern corridor of the line, and on Fridays and Saturdays only a late evening service was introduced between Inverness and Tain.

Also in 2008, the functions of the Highland Rail Partnership were subsumed under HITRANS, one of seven Regional Transport Partnerships in Scotland which were established through the 2005 Transport (Scotland) Act. Frank Roach became Partnership Manager in the new organisation, still based at the Lairg station office which he had established in 2001.

In January 2011, the Stagecoach bus company began a consultation on revised services in Caithness, Sutherland and Easter Ross, from which it seemed obvious that Stagecoach wished to direct Orkney ferry passengers to their X99 service for the through journey from Inverness to Scrabster, rather than bus meeting train at Thurso. The long-standing connecting bus service was in due course withdrawn, but a new arrangement was put in place in summer 2011 whereby a connecting taxi service between Thurso station and Scrabster was included in the combined 'Rail & Sail' tickets to/from the Orkney ferry port of Stromness.

Also in 2011, HITRANS became concerned about suggestions from Transport Scotland (the Scottish Government agency) that the new ScotRail franchise, due to commence in 2014, might involve a 'dual focus franchise' of 'economic' and 'social' sectors, or even the creation of more than one franchise.

My Deltix Transport Consulting business was commissioned to assess the potential implications for Highland rail services of such an arrangement and the wider issue of achieving Highland policy aims, such as providing an alternative to the car, bringing tourists to the area, offering commuting opportunities and an alternative to flying, and connecting with other modes. The Deltix report in 2012 concluded, *inter alia*, that:

> The recommendations of the 2011 McNulty *Rail Value for Money* report [for the Department for Transport] and recent analysis by Paul Salveson – pioneer of the 'community rail' concept in England & Wales – point towards the possibility of a pilot 'vertically-integrated sub-franchise' [controlling both train operations and infrastructure] for the rail network north of Inverness, potentially unlocking a wide range of rail cost and revenue benefits as well as generating enhanced value from the rail system.

> As a pilot project with potentially benchmarking value for other self-contained sections of the rural network throughout Britain, this might attract additional funds for pump priming, research and development. New forms of ownership and staff involvement and flexibility could be crucial to creating (a) a better and more sustainable balance between rail costs and revenues, and (b) a business model which encourages investment and enhancement in infrastructure and rolling stock.

Unfortunately, the Scottish Government's procurement process for the new ScotRail franchise (beginning in 2015) did not embrace this kind of radical thinking, but a more modest Scotland-wide change to the 'ScotRail Alliance' (incorporating Network Rail) did emerge. However, as warned by consultants Pieda and MDS Transmodal for Highlands and Islands Enterprise in 1995, the danger remained that the Far North Line would be run as 'a poor relation of the "proper" railways operated to the south'.

An authoritative view from afar

In 2012 and 2013, *Far North Express* – Friends of the Far North Line's newsletter – featured a series of three articles by Gordon Pettitt, former Managing Director of BR's Regional Railways business sector and the last General Manager of BR's Southern Region. Regional Railways (of which ScotRail was part) was established in 1982 and operated until 1994, and was faced with arguably the hardest challenge of BR's three passenger sectors (the others being Inter-City and Network South East) – operating roughly half the national network and traffic, but generating only around a quarter of the revenue. With new rolling stock and improved marketing, Regional Railways grew passenger numbers and cut subsidies, and was one of the latter-day BR success stories.

So, although far from his home 'patch', Pettitt (a member of Friends of the Far North Line) was well qualified to comment on the railway, even if some of his more challenging thoughts were not necessarily what the Friends had been hoping for. He highlighted the difference in road and rail distances and the impact on journey times, in particular for end-to-end journeys: 'The differences between the car and train journey times are so great, that the railway must seem a total irrelevance to the majority of car owners in Sutherland and Caithness.'

Pettitt described the various investments in additional staff and rolling stock (and Beauly station) as 'a very bold initiative intended to bring about a step change in the use of the line'. Nevertheless, he had cautionary words about what had been achieved:

> In line with the rest of the United Kingdom, the number of passengers using the line has increased in recent years whilst costs have increased at a faster rate... the number of passengers joining and alighting from stations between Beauly and Thurso/Wick in the past four years (2006/7-2010/11) has increased by 54%...This increase in passengers is impressive in isolation, but must be seen in the context of the low base and the 74% increase in train miles since 1992.

Reflecting on Pettitt's analysis in 2016, Frank Roach commented that the effective increase in passengers may have been higher, since it is quite possible that, in the absence of improvements, Far North Line traffic might have decreased rather than remained static. Likely contributory factors would have been the introduction of free bus travel for senior citizens and the loss of the traditional Dounreay market, as well as the impact of internet shopping.

However, Pettitt's analysis of patronage figures did get to the heart of the growing difference between the southern quarter and the northern three quarters of this longest single-track railway in Britain:

It will be noted that 6 out of the 10 most heavily used stations are within 44 miles [Tain] of Inverness. This section of the line accounts for just over 70% of all the passengers joining and alighting from stations on the whole route.

In contrast to the relative success of the stations within commuting distance of Inverness, 10 of the 17 stations on the 130 miles of railway north of Tain are used by fewer than 35 passengers per week. At most of these, the cost of making a stop is greater than the revenue gained from the occasional user.

Nevertheless, based on his last two visits to the Far North Line, Pettitt was impressed by 'the improved cleanliness, punctuality and reliability of the trains' and by the 'smart and neatly-dressed staff, together with the clean and graffiti free stations'. In his final article for *Far North Express*, he examined some longer term options for the future, once again highlighting the disparity between the two parts of the railway, noting a 94% growth in passengers on the Tain-Inverness section over the period 2006 to 2011, but also:

> Despite an average growth of 44% [on the section north of Tain] over the last five years, the average number of passengers per train on leaving Tain is 44, reducing to fewer than 10 between Thurso and Wick. This is not the level of traffic needed to sustain a service of four trains a day in each direction and certainly not all the year round.

This was, of course, a stark contrast to the situation during the closure debate in 1963-64, when it was envisaged that a fleet of up to 15 buses would be required to cope with through rail passengers at peak summer periods. Pettitt summed up the dilemma for Transport Scotland, infrastructure providers, operators 'and indeed the Friends of the Far North Line':

> The first 25% of the route is used by more than 74% of the passengers, but the remaining 75% of the route is used by just 26% of the passengers...The current use of the line between Inverness and Tain clearly suggests that this section should be regarded as the core business of the FNL and therefore be the priority for investment, resources and timetable development.

> The challenge is to make better use of existing resources to encourage further growth over the core section.

He foresaw that future track, signalling and level crossing renewal projects would allow the Inverness-Tain journey time to be cut from 68 to 50/55 minutes. (57 minutes had been the norm throughout the 1990s and early 2000s.) Pettitt envisaged a 'total recast' and rebalancing of the timetable, creating a regular interval pattern between Inverness and Tain, in part to be achieved by switching resources away from the northern section.

Turning to the future of the three quarters of the route length north of Tain, he explicitly rejected the speed improvements at level crossings and loops mooted in previous studies, since 'the journey time savings identified were totally insufficient to justify the costs involved as the number of passengers likely to benefit would be low and there would be no measurable impact on the significant difference between road and rail journey times'. He concluded:

> ...the average train loads remain at the level of buses rather than a railway for most of the year. Journey times are long and not competitive with bus let alone car travel, primarily owing to the investment in direct road links between 1979 and 1991.

> The branch lines from Dingwall to Kyle of Lochalsh and the West Highland lines to Oban, Fort William and Mallaig all face similar problems to those outlined. The main difference is that they all have greater tourist potential. Together, these lines total up to 450 miles out of the 1,739 mile network in Scotland and represent a significant cost to the taxpayer which is out of all proportion to any economic or social value.

There were some uncomfortable truths here for rail campaigners but, as we shall see, the tourist potential of the Far North Line has long been neglected, and Pettitt did not consider the role of freight at all.

As he indicated in his analysis, journey time and frequency are crucial determinants of modal choice. Factors not mentioned by Pettit were price and quality of service, including reliability. Irrespective of rail's journey time and to a lesser extent frequency disadvantages compared to the bus, price and quality of service can give rail an important advantage for some sections of the market. For tourist and unfamiliar users, rail provides a degree of psychological assurance which the bus lacks.

In my own experience, the express bus journey from Inverness to Caithness is far from cutting-edge public transport. Outwith the realigned sections of the A9, the ride is often rough, and using the rudimentary toilet facility is a challenge even for the able-bodied. There is no opportunity to get up and stretch your legs, except an enforced one at the basic Dunbeath interchange, where Wick passengers usually have to leave the Thurso/Scrabster bus to catch a connecting service to complete their journey. And there are no refreshment facilities on the bus.

These are important considerations for many people, and most observers would agree that all the main sub-regions of Scotland deserve a decent minimum standard of public transport links to the rest of the country. The problem for rail to and from Caithness is that, in terms of subsidy, it comes at a very heavy price.

Chapter 14 considers the wider question of subsidy and value for money. In the meantime, doubtless few would have disagreed with Pettitt when he concluded his challenging and insightful 2013 analysis by looking forward to the planned 'deeper alliance' between ScotRail and Network Rail and to changes hinted for the procurement of passenger services in the next ScotRail franchise, which together meant 'that a real opportunity opens up for developing new and innovative solutions for operating and maintaining lines and also increasing revenue.' Unfortunately, by 2016, there still remained little sign that this kind of radical thinking was being applied to the future of the Far North Line.

Another station re-opening – but service quality slides

While Pettitt was making his exploratory visits to the Far North Line, the Nuclear Decommissioning Authority (NDA) was starting its programme to decommission the Dounreay complex which had promised such a golden future in the 1950s. The programme – stretching from 2012 to 2030 – also has a rail dimension. The NDA funded the construction of a bespoke terminal at Georgemas, occupying the site of the old island platform and adjacent sidings, with a large gantry crane for transferring bespoke nuclear containers from road to rail.

Trains serving the site, as is standard for nuclear traffic in Britain, are 'topped and tailed' with two Class 37 locomotives, providing a total of 3,500 horse power. In the 29 March 2016 *John o'Groat Journal*, it was reported that 99 consignments of 'breeder fuel' would be sent by rail to Sellafield by 2019, with a further 35 shipments of 'exotic fuel' between 2019 and 2021.

A nuclear waste train from Georgemas, bound for Sellafield, heads away from Kinbrace 'topped and tailed' by 37602 & 37608, on 16 May 2013. The view is looking north towards Ben Griam Mor. Peter Moore

Frustratingly for rail development advocates, the specialist crane and loading pad for nuclear flasks at Georgemas do not lend themselves to general usage, and the considerable spare traction capability on these very short freight trains cannot be utilised for other traffics, for reasons of security and the irregular pattern of nuclear demand. However, the operation of the trains to Sellafield does at least ensure the safest means of transport for a hazardous commodity, and in a modest way echoes the strategic function of the Far North Line in World War One (particularly) and World War Two.

2013 saw the second Far North Line station re-opening of the 'Frank Roach era', within the core southern corridor which Gordon Pettitt had so strongly emphasised. The success of Beauly – attracting 49,858 passengers in 2010/11 (and 57,446 in 2014/15) and becoming the third busiest station on the line, despite having the shortest platform – had encouraged the small town of Conon Bridge also to press for a station. Agreement was eventually reached for another 15 metre platform solution, and the station was re-opened at its former site, with a small adjacent car park, at a cost of £600,000. Considering that BR had managed to build a platform at Falls of Cruachan (on the Oban line) for just £10,000 in 1988, this was a shocking indictment of cost escalation since rail privatisation.

April 2015 saw the ScotRail franchise – run by First Group since 2004 – taken over by Abellio, a subsidiary of the state-owned Dutch railways. Among the attractive features of the Dutch offer – prompted by the Scottish Government in the tender process – were promotion of 'Great Scenic Rail Journeys' over six Scottish rail routes, including the Far North Line.

ScotRail was committed to marketing Scotland's scenery, its heritage and its tourist attractions to a wider audience. While there is no early prospect of the return of the 1950s-60s halcyon era of observation cars, existing trains on these routes will be modestly refurbished and there will be dedicated tourism 'ambassadors', trained by VisitScotland, to provide information on attractions, history and journey connections. The Dutch firm has also been investigating running steam-hauled trains on up to eight routes, again including the Far North Line. In theory, at least, the Highlands' most under-rated scenic railway will now be put firmly on the tourist map.

Meanwhile, train service reliability north of Inverness remained poor, and to bring matters to a head, in March 2015 HITRANS hosted a summit meeting in Dingwall, attended by Network Rail and ScotRail managers, and chaired by Iain MacDonald, the (ex-BBC) Highland broadcaster. A subsequent Friends of the Far North Line newsletter summarised some of the key contributions, perhaps the most revealing of which came from a ScotRail manager:

John Kerr [Head of Timetable Compliance and Resilience] then spoke for First ScotRail stating that they knew the timetable hadn't been working in 2014 so a "resilient" timetable was introduced in December 2014 including average 3 min journey time increases and the skipping of the Fearn and Alness stops by the 16:00 ex-Wick. He said that the opening of Conon Bridge was the straw that broke the camel's back. The Public Performance Measure (PPM) dropped to 76% when Conon Bridge was opened, having been at 90% after the massive slow-down of 2005, prior to which it had slid down to 65%. The PPM has risen from 58% to 79% in the first 10 weeks of the new timetable.

However, campaigners argued that Conon Bridge was not the root cause of the wider timekeeping problems, which long pre-dated the station's opening. Additionally, a severe and allegedly 'temporary' speed restriction at Chapelton Farm user-worked level crossing, north of Muir of Ord, had been inflicted on services for some six years, following the failure of Network Rail and the user to find agreement on sighting problems. Initially, the delay had mostly been masked by the extra time which had been added to the timetable in expectation of an earlier opening of Conon Bridge station than was actually achieved.

The initial punctuality improvements achieved by ScotRail through slowing the timetable did not last, however, demonstrating that adding time into timetables does not necessarily improve performance. Some shocking statistics were revealed for 2014-15, in response to a parliamentary question posed by Rhoda Grant MSP (also Vice-President of the Friends of the Far North Line) to Transport Minister Derek Mackay. The story was covered on 5 February 2016 by the *Inverness Courier* under the headline 'North line train service slammed as "woeful"':

> Trains arrived at their destination on time on only 49 out of 309 [operational] weekdays between December 15, 2014 and December 12 last year. It means that just 16 per cent of days passed without any disruption on the route. A service is classed as "on time" if it reaches a station within five minutes of its scheduled arrival.

> The revelations comes just a week after similar figures revealed that only 216 of the line's 309 weekday services suffered no cancellations or incidents.

> Many delays are caused by the single track line between Muir of Ord and Inverness, which forces trains to wait to let oncoming trains pass and can cause delays of up to 90 minutes. Passengers at Beauly, Muir of Ord and Conon Bridge are frequently left stranded as drivers fail to stop at these stations in a bid to make up time.

> Friends of the Far North Line are campaigning for a share of the proposed £300 million Inverness City deal to re-instate a loop at Lentran to ease congestion.

> Richard Ardern, also of Friends of the Far North Line, said he wasn't surprised at the high number of delays. He added: "We have been calling for these figures

for a long time because we know trains are late a lot. This is because we have the longest stretch of single line in the UK. If a service is provided it must be provided properly and users of the Far North Line aren't experiencing that."

Both ScotRail and its operator, Abellio, failed to respond to requests for comment.

The same day's paper also highlighted patronage statistics issued by the Office for Rail and Road (ORR) which demonstrated clearly the impact of protracted unreliability on usage of the Far North Line. Twenty-one of the line's 25 stations had suffered a drop in patronage from 2013/14 to 2014/15, and the line's nine busiest stations (those handling over 15,000 passengers annually, based on combined totals for boarding and alighting) had all seen decline.

Georgemas Junction – set in fairly bleak and treeless countryside – would never have been regarded as a rural idyll. Today it is largely industrial in character, dominated by a 110-tonne gantry crane for road-rail transfer of contaminated materials from the decommissioning Dounreay nuclear site. Seen here looking south on 26 August 2015 – framed by the A9 road overbridge – a Class 158 creeps into the station with the 10.45 arrival from Inverness. David Spaven

The biggest drops were at stations on the southern section of the line, demonstrating the particular sensitivity of commuter traffic to service unreliability, the worst cases being Invergordon (-12%), Tain (-13%), Dingwall (-14%) and Conon Bridge (-14%). In fairness, the end of the works on the Kessock Bridge, which had stimulated additional rail travel, may also have been a factor.

Bizarrely, the only station to show a significant percentage patronage increase was lonely Altnabreac, whose 240 passengers in a year demonstrated a jump of 74%; Richard Ardern later suggested this may have been attributable to 'midge fluctuations'. Underlining the deep-rural character of the Far North Line, the ORR statistics showed that Kildonan – once the scene of a 'gold rush' – was, with 96 passengers, the 11th least-used station in Britain in 2014/15, out of a total of 2,539.

Despite the disappointment around worsening reliability, Frank Roach and HITRANS could look back at generally very substantial percentage growth in patronage figures since 2002/03. Including travel by tourist pass holders (such as BritRail), which does not show up in line statistics, around half a million journeys are made on the far North Line annually.

Notwithstanding Gordon Pettitt's valid point that many of the increases started from a very low base and train miles operated had grown by a higher percentage than overall passenger growth, there were some major transformations, including three stations where patronage had more than quadrupled.

While tiny Dunrobin's jump from 191 in 2002/03 to 822 in 2014/15 at least showed some improvement in the rail tourism market, of much greater significance for the railway's fortunes were Invergordon (up from 7,069 to 31,962) and Alness (up from 3,717 to 25,934). The southern quarter of the line is now playing an important part in the everyday life of the corridor it serves.

The 2014/2015 patronage figures vindicated 'The Great Northern By-Pass' article by Adrian Varwell of SAPT 43 years earlier, as the four subsequently re-opened stations close to Inverness – Alness, Muir of Ord, Beauly and Conon Bridge – were all among the top 10 of the line's stations (based on combined totals for boarding and alighting). Alness saw 25,934 passengers over the year, Muir of Ord 66,756, Beauly 57,466 and Conon Bridge 15,510. Dingwall was the busiest station with 87,782 passengers.

The railway's 'crumbling edge of quality' (to resurrect a memorable phrase coined by BRB Chairman, Sir Peter Parker, in the early 1980s) continued to be demonstrated in 2016. By the four-weekly period 29 May to 25 June, the 'moving annual average' for the proportion of trains arriving at Wick 'right time' (ie within 59 seconds of their booked arrival time) was just 29.4%. Of 75 stations at which ScotRail services terminated, only five were performing worse than Wick and cancellations were also rife north of Inverness.[71] Coupled with already uncompetitive scheduled journey times, this was raising major question marks about the stewardship of the Far North Line.

More positively, November 2015 saw completion of Graham Rooney's 'Platform 1864' restaurant in the Grade B-listed station building at Tain, which had been empty for many years. This was just the latest in a number of initiatives to find new uses for structures which had been de-staffed in the 1980s and 1990s, encouraged by ScotRail's External Relations Manager, John Yellowlees. Other projects saw murals painted across Invergordon station in 2007, and in 2014, John Thurso, then MP and now chairman of VisitScotland, opened holiday accommodation created by Mike Willmot at Helmsdale's B-listed building.

Prior to Yellowlees' arrival at ScotRail, Frank Roach had acquired the building at Rogart as his family home – then developing the Sleeperzzz accommodation in the old goods yard – and subsequently opened the Highland Rail Partnership office at Lairg. Other station buildings on the line are mostly in residential use, but Dingwall has a tea room and a bistro bar, Dunrobin a small museum, and Forsinard houses the RSPB visitor centre (see Appendix 1). These are all part of a story which needs to be more widely told if the railway is to realise its full tourist potential.

The publication in December 2015 of Network Rail's *Scotland Route Study Draft for Consultation* – setting out options to cater for forecast demand over the next 30 years, and to provide improved resilience and performance – brought some unexpected encouragement for Far North Line campaigners. Key proposed interventions were:

- reconfiguration of Inverness platforms 5-7 to allow more frequent services

- conventional resignalling between Inverness and Dingwall to replace RETB

- an additional crossing loop between Inverness and Dingwall

- closure of level crossings between Inverness and Dingwall

- creation of a Georgemas chord

Predictably, however, when the Scottish and UK Governments' £315m City Region Deal for Inverness and the wider Highlands area was finally announced in March 2016, the transport focus was on new roads. Despite decades of world-wide evidence that these rarely solve congestion problems in the long-term – generating more and/or longer car trips on the newly-provided infrastructure capacity – funding had been found for a new 'West Link' to the A82, an 'East Link' to connect the A96 to the A9, and a flyover to take traffic up and over the Longman Roundabout at the Kessock Bridge. But the desperately needed Lentran loop/double track plan would get nothing. So much for the long-sought 'level playing field' between road and rail.

Another freight revival beckons

March 2016, however, also saw the launch of the results of a detailed investigation into timber traffic from the Flow Country, commissioned by HITRANS. In August 2015, a team of multi-disciplinary consultants had begun the 'Branchliner Plus' project (another trademark Roach branding) to assess the feasibility of regular rail haulage from Kinbrace to Inverness.

Deltix Transport Consulting was awarded the rail operations work package, and the Deltix team – comprising myself and former career railwayman David Prescott – evaluated a range of terminal and train servicing options for the movement of around 100,000 tonnes annually over a 40-week year.

With a view to minimising operating costs for substantial volumes over a lengthy (10 year) projected period, Deltix recommended that in the medium to long term, there should be bespoke sidings at a Kinbrace terminal, connected permanently to the main line by a conventional set of points controlled by a ground-frame. In the short to medium term, ideally, bespoke sidings would be connected to the main line by means of a 'semi-permanent' Non-Intrusive Crossover (NICS) connection.

Despite the protracted on-off interest in NICS within NR still not being resolved, HITRANS was hopeful that the rail company would take its cue from Transport Scotland's observation in its 2015 Rail Freight Strategy consultation document that 'innovation will be the key to unlocking transportation of timber by rail'.

A key objective of the Deltix operational analysis was to maximise payloads (and minimise unit costs) by running the longest possible trains. The maximum permitted train length on the Far North Line is 50 Standard Length Units (SLUs) – ie c. 320 metres – for normal operation of trains which are required to cross other trains *en route*. This restricts train loads to less than the maximum achievable within the line's 1,230t Gross Trailing Load limit, southbound, for a standard Class 66-hauled train. However, with Network Rail dispensation for over-length running (364-437 metres, excluding the loco), payloads of between 620t and 720t could be achieved, depending on the type of wagons used – a single train being the equivalent of 25 or more lorries removed from fragile roads.

With a view to moving the project decisively forward, Frank Roach reminded delegates at the March 2016 Timber Transport Conference in Perth, that the public sector in the shape of HITRANS had devoted considerable time and resources to developing the concept of timber by rail from the Flow Country. He was convinced that rail could deliver a solution: did forestry interests now want to 'get on track' or would they 'remain in a siding'?

The scope for innovation on the Far North Line once again made headlines, on 13 April 2016, when the *Caithness Courier* reported discussions between HITRANS and Caledonian Sleeper about the possibility of an overnight Sleeper train from Caithness to Edinburgh, utilising rolling stock displaced from Anglo-Scottish services in 2018. The suggested seven-hour service would in effect make a 'slow travel' virtue of the Far North Line's circuitous route, and haulage costs could potentially be shared with container traffic (such as supermarket supplies) from Central Scotland to Georgemas – re-vitalising the old Highland Railway practice of 'mixed' trains.

How has the Far North Line survived since 1964?

The immediate aftermath of the railway's 1964 reprieve saw sensible economies and journey time improvements place the Far North Line on a much sounder footing. However, the relentless growth in car ownership and the eventual dramatic upgrading of the A9 has put this meandering railway under increasing competitive pressure. Superficially, it is amazing that the line is still with us.

My research suggests that there have been perhaps six key factors contributing to the survival of this unique Highland railway – one of them regional, the others where nationwide factors or forces have come into play. In broadly chronological order, they are:

First: significant road improvements, which many 1963-64 opponents of closure had explicitly or implicitly assumed would eventually lead to the loss of the railway, effectively did not materialise until 1982 – when the opening of the Kessock Bridge and the A9 across the Black Isle allowed the strategic potential of the Cromarty Bridge (opened in 1979) to be realised. The

---

Dornoch Bridge did not follow until 1991. And during the period of limited change in the trunk road north of Inverness, the Far North Line enjoyed a major freight boom generated by the Invergordon smelter and North Sea oil.

Second: although the smelter closed in 1981, by this time there was growing nationwide recognition that the bus, car and lorry did not offer the anticipated transport panaceas. Traffic congestion and parking problems demonstrated the operational limitations, while increasing environmental consciousness highlighted the external dis-benefits associated with air pollution, accidents and noise intrusion.

Third: partly in response to the emerging problems of road transport, the mid to late 1970s saw the beginning of a national revival in rail's fortunes. Reflecting population growth and its geographical redistribution on the Far North Line, Alness and Muir of Ord stations were re-opened in 1973 and 1976 respectively – early examples of a trend across Britain which resulted in 1986, 1987 and 1988 being the peak years for station re-openings.

Fourth: the 1974 introduction of the nationwide Public Service Obligation funding for British Rail diverted attention away from line-specific subsidies and, as a former senior railway manager commented to me in 2016: 'A degree of lethargy, apathy, and more pressing problems [also] contributed by keeping official bureaucratic minds away from the Far North.'

Fifth: the growing spread of rail re-openings contributed to changing political and public attitudes to the rail network. The brief 1983 Serpell threat was quickly seen off, and with it, the long search for a mythical 'profitable core' was abandoned. And no public railway station has closed in Scotland since 1986, while 62 have opened or re-opened.

Sixth: privatisation has had mixed impacts but has brought one important indirect benefit to the Far North Line. On the negative side, the rail industry saw massive upheaval, and privatisation has cost the taxpayer far more than the state-owned system. It has certainly *not* unleashed transformational entrepreneurial skills on the Far North Line. But, paradoxically, its passenger franchise contracts have brought a new degree of stability. Together with the potential objections to closure by 'open access' freight and tourist charter operators, this means that closing the line – in the short to medium term – is politically unthinkable.

However, this is not the same as saying that the Far North Line will be impregnable in the longer term: once the current franchise ends and/or after nuclear traffic finishes and/or in the event of future economic recession, or even depression. The next, final chapter of this book explores the threats and opportunities.

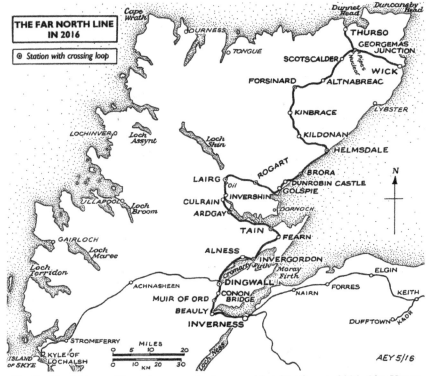

The Far North Line and its stations, crossing loops and freight sidings in 2016. Alan Young

CHAPTER 14: THE FUTURE OF THE FAR NORTH LINE

The Far North Line is a remarkable survivor.

The unprecedented 1963-64 closure threat from Beeching was seen off by an impressively united front of politicians, public, press, and key civil servants. And swift action by British Rail senior management in 1989 ensured that the collapse of the Ness Viaduct did not become an excuse to close this heavily loss-making railway.

However – having been completed through to Caithness in 1874 largely due to the enthusiasm of the 3rd Duke of Sutherland – the Far North Line's geographically idiosyncratic route has today become a particular disadvantage in the face of massive road improvements and a substantial growth in car ownership over the last 50 years. To compound the problem, the fastest trains from Inverness to Thurso in 2016 are slower than they were in 1990 (and substantially more so to Wick, due to today's enforced detour via Thurso).

1964's multi-purpose railway was central to the economic and social life of its route corridor from Inverness through Easter Ross and Sutherland to Caithness, carrying not only passengers, but also daily freight, newspapers, parcels and Royal Mail. By contrast, today's railway is a more narrowly-focused passenger operation, with just three freight flows (each less than weekly in frequency). Newspaper, parcels and Royal Mail traffic has long been lost to the roads.

Rather than being a railway of two halves, the changing Far North Line which has emerged since the year 2000 is in effect a railway of one quarter and a further three quarters (or, at best, one third and two thirds), with highly contrasting patterns of business. By far the biggest concentration of trains, the large majority of the busiest stations, and the greatest increases in passenger patronage are on the southern part of the route. However, the line's three freight terminals – at Lairg and Georgemas (two) – are all on the northern part, where most of the untapped freight potential lies. And the two largest settlements served are in Caithness: Thurso (with a population of 9,000) and Wick (8,000).

Based on analysis of official data (from the Office of Rail and Road, and Transport Scotland)[72] it would appear that rail's share of the total overland passenger transport market between Caithness and the south lies in the range 5%-10%. This is perhaps a surprisingly high figure for a railway significantly handicapped by its geography and journey times in competition with the car and the bus. But this statistic may also demonstrate the importance of factors other than journey time.

Hunters, shooters and fishers offload gear from a Class 26-hauled Inverness-Wick train at Altnabreac in the summer of 1971, doubtless heading for the up-market Lochdhu Hotel a mile across the moor. The photographer camped overnight at this isolated spot, and in the evening wandered over the then-treeless expanse (like something out of Dr Zhivago) to the hotel, to find himself in a cocktail bar full of elaborately-attired ladies and gentlemen... David Spaven

It is hard to believe that this is the same viewpoint as the shot taken 44 years earlier (see above). A Friends of the Far North Line outing is about to escape the Altnabreac midges by jumping on the 13.55 departure for Thurso and Wick on 26 August 2015. In the left foreground is former Invergordon signalman, Iain Macdonald (50 years' service on the railway). On the far right is Mike Lunan (formerly Chair of the Rail Passengers Committee Scotland), while the man in the red anorak is leading Highland rail activist Richard Ardern. David Spaven

While, in absolute terms, the southern part of the railway leading to Inverness is now much busier than the northern part, it may not necessarily have a higher share of the local transport market. The southern market is much larger, and competition at this end of the corridor is much more intense, with all of the competing roads leading to the major traffic generator at Inverness being dual-lane (and dual-carriageway on the southernmost stretch of the A9 into the regional capital), in contrast to a single-track railway with insufficient crossing loops. Fourteen trains a day from Dingwall (and stations south thereof) to Inverness is an impressive improvement on the situation 20 years ago, but an irregular-interval (and often unreliable) train service is competing daily against scores of regular-interval buses.

To bring the story of the Far North Line to a close, in this final chapter I now seek: first, to review the key characteristics of today's railway; second, to describe the major financial challenges presented by the line; third, to summarise the broader perspectives of five well-qualified observers; and finally, to set out some ideas to meet these challenges, in terms of overall management and delivery, passenger and freight market opportunities, and the resources required to match market needs.

Key characteristics

The 168-mile Far North Line is Britain's longest rural railway and its longest single-track railway. There are 11 intermediate crossing loops (varying in length from 240m at Georgemas to 466m at Muir of Ord), and the 24 miles between Helmsdale and Forsinard constitute the longest single-track 'block section' in Britain. The ruling line speed for diesel units (locomotives are generally lower) is typically 65-75 mph between Inverness and Tain and 50-70 mph north thereof – but with a short stretch of 90 mph running south of Altnabreac[73]. The maximum gradient is 1 in 60.

The rail distance from Inverness to Thurso is 154 miles; by road it is 110 miles. By rail from Inverness to Wick (with the enforced detour via Thurso), the distance is 174 miles; by road it is 103 miles.

There are four passenger trains daily (Monday-Saturday) from Inverness to Thurso and Wick, one to Ardgay, one to Tain, one to Invergordon, and five to Dingwall (of which four continue to Kyle). On Fridays and Saturdays only there is an additional late-evening train from Inverness to Tain. Six trains serve the southern section of the route on Sundays, with one continuing through to Thurso and Wick.

In the opposite direction there are four trains daily (Monday-Saturday) from Wick and Thurso to Inverness, one from Lairg, two from Ardgay, one from Tain, one from Invergordon, and five from Dingwall (of which four originate in Kyle). Six trains serve the southern section of the route on Sundays, with one starting from Wick and Thurso.

In 2015, six *Royal Scotsman* luxury land-cruise and other tourist charter train services operated over part or all of the Far North Line north of Dingwall (compared to more than 20 over the Kyle line).

There are three trainload freight flows, each on a less than weekly basis: oil from Grangemouth to the BP siding at Lairg, pipes from Hartlepool to Georgemas freight depot, and nuclear waste from the NDA siding at Georgemas. The line is currently designated 'Route Availability 5', permitting axle loads up to 19 tonnes, but with heavier weights permissible (eg in the case of the modern Class 66 loco) subject to speed restrictions. Until recently, the Inverness-Invergordon section was designated 'RA8', permitting axle loads up to 22.5 tonnes.

The financial challenges

During the brief era when line-by-line grants were provided to support unremunerative but socially necessary rail services, the Far North Line received an annual subsidy of £595,000 in 1969 and £444,000 in 1972 (the latter the equivalent of around £5.7m in today's money). This was based on the 'Cooper Brothers' formula for calculation of the deficit which would be required to be met in continuing a passenger service in the long run. From 1974, this system was replaced by a nationwide Public Service Obligation payment, with no route breakdowns.

Today, the costs and revenues of the Far North Line are subsumed within the 10-year ScotRail franchise payment of over £7 billion to operator Abellio, the biggest single contract into which a Scottish Government has entered. As a former senior railway manager commented to me in early 2016: 'At least they tried with the Cooper Brothers' formula, but no-one has any idea of costs or revenues on the system now, and because of that they do not know where and what to prioritise'. And the often-quoted business principle is 'what you can't measure, you can't manage'.

Addressing a Capital Rail Action Group meeting in Edinburgh in March 2016, Chris Green noted that a subsidy of 9p per passenger kilometre for ScotRail services in 2008 had risen to 17p in 2013, and commented that the industry in Scotland 'can't continue this way'. By 2015, the subsidy had grown to 19p per passenger kilometre, an increase well above inflation.[74]

An Aquarius road-rail permanent-way vehicle reverses north along the Far North Line at Kildonan on 27 August 2007. These vehicles provide the flexibility to reach various stretches of line where road access to the lineside is difficult or impossible. F Furnevel

While rail closures are definitely not on the current political agenda, any future period of economic recession, or even depression, will bring pressure to bear on those elements of the ScotRail franchise which appear to deliver the least value for money in terms of economic, social and environmental benefits. Arguably, the Far North Line is now playing only a marginal role in the everyday life of the corridor it serves, except over the southern part where commuter services to Inverness provide a useful and environmentally sound alternative to increasingly congested roads and parking facilities.

Based on two published documents[75], and some less formal material, an informed industry source has sought to calculate for me the cost to the taxpayer of operating and maintaining the Far North Line today, by disaggregating data for Scotland. In the case of operating costs (movement plus terminals), this has been calculated largely on the basis of train miles operated. While the Far North Line constitutes 10% of the route mileage of the Scottish rail network, the line is only single-track, it is not electrified, and it has a simple signalling system: therefore percentages significantly lower than 10% (ie 2% and 5%) have been applied to the various components of Scottish network infrastructure costs.

After allowing for revenue (fares), the net subsidy paid to keep the Far North Line in service is estimated to be between £15m and £20m annually, of which some 85% is infrastructure cost. Based on around half million passenger journeys annually on the line, this translates into a subsidy of perhaps £40 per passenger journey.

Does that represent value for money? Bus campaigners could reasonably argue that a tiny fraction of the financial support needed to maintain the Far North Line would deliver state-of-the art road-based public transport. Of course, parallel subsidy calculations are never made for maintaining specific roads (such as the A9 north of Inverness, where recent repairs to the Kessock Bridge alone cost over £13m), but there is no question that the rail subsidy is a very high figure for a not very reliable service.

Given that patronage on the line is now much more skewed towards short-distance journeys at the southern end of the route, calculation of subsidy *per passenger kilometre* would show rail in an even poorer light. These calculations exclude freight, but until such time as there is a step-change from the current one or two trains a week to an at least daily service, then freight is marginal to the calculations.

Irrespective of the fine details of analysis and argument, it seems irrefutable that if the Far North Line is to be protected against future threats, it needs to be able to demonstrate that it is (a) being run as cost-effectively as possible and (b) playing a significantly bigger transport, economic and social role, commensurate with the subsidy provided.

Of course, much has been done to reduce costs over the more than 50 years since the line was reprieved. Track maintenance has been mechanised, crossing loops have been eliminated (leaving too few for today's traffic), the signalling system has been simplified (and recently given a life extension), every station has been de-staffed (except Dingwall, Wick and Thurso) and locomotive-hauled trains were replaced by lighter-weight diesel units more than 25 years ago.

The one cost area which has worsened is train crew. The four trains each way daily between Inverness and Caithness each have a staff of three, to handle what is typically no more than a bus load for most of the journey: driver, conductor and refreshment trolley steward. ScotRail drivers are now on a basic annual salary (following a probationary period) of nearly £45,000[76], compared to £25,000-£30,000 for bus and lorry drivers[77], who bear the additional safety responsibility of steering their vehicles. All bus drivers and most lorry drivers have a customer interface, but this is only the case for train drivers in the event of very late running or emergencies.

The dramatic rise in train driver salaries has been an unforeseen outcome of rail privatisation, in particular of the competition for labour between different train operating companies. Unsurprisingly, the job has become very attractive. The *Press & Journal* of 24 March 2016 reported that: 'Scores of offshore workers are among more than 22,000 applicants for just 100 train driver jobs across Scotland.' Counter-intuitively, the enormous demand for these jobs has not led to the 'normal' market forces outcome of a consequent levelling out of pay rates.

An alternative perspective, as suggested by Frank Roach, is that eight well-paid driver jobs in Wick – part of a total ScotRail workforce of some two dozen in Caithness – have a welcome impact on the local economy. And there are a further two dozen Network Rail permanent way staff, based in depots at Georgemas and Helmsdale, contributing to rural employment and generating further economic benefits through the 'multiplier' effect.

These and other undoubted regional development benefits from the railway are not, however, any consolation for the economics of the Far North Line itself. In response to concerns about rising industry costs, in 2011 Sir Roy McNulty delivered his *Realising the Potential of GB Rail: Report of the Rail Value for Money Study* to the UK Government. The study recommended that the default position for all services on the GB rail network should be Driver Only Operation (DOO), with a second member of train crew being provided only where there is a commercial, technical or other imperative.

DOO is not currently possible on the Far North Line, as the driver is on the radio when door opening is required. Also, some low, non-compliant platforms and short platforms require the train guard to open a single door and check the platform before opening all doors (except at Beauly and Conon Bridge, where only a single door is opened). But if Driver Only Operation is not a solution for the Far North Line, with its problematic finances, should we not be expecting more input to the passenger/customer experience from such well-paid drivers?

Given that some 85% of the estimated £15m-£20m annual subsidy for the Far North Line relates to infrastructure, this in theory is a key area for cost reduction. But much has already been done to reduce such costs by mechanisation of track maintenance, simplified signalling and the deployment of light-weight diesel units – and as track is gradually renewed then ongoing maintenance costs will fall further. As suggested to me by former career railwayman David Prescott, could we learn a lesson from continental and North American experience by no longer requiring every last metre of this rural railway to be securely fenced? Legislative change would presumably be necessary, but the cost-saving opportunities would extend to many secondary railways across Scotland, England and Wales.

Overall, maximising the productivity of the line's diesel units, and increasing traffic – thus delivering enhanced economic and environmental benefits – offer a much more attractive scenario than, for example, downgrading track and structure maintenance expenditure still further, such that expanded freight and charter train traffic (with heavier axle loads) could not be readily accommodated. Could ultra-light-weight diesel units could be deployed on the Wick-Thurso shuttle service mooted by Frank Roach, supplementing the existing four trains a day to create a high-quality, but low-cost, intra-regional public transport link?

In the context of possible new forms of ownership and staff involvement to help grow the role of the Far North Line – explored under 'Realising the opportunities' below – key issues would be (a) a better and more sustainable balance between rail costs and revenues, and (b) a business model which encourages investment and enhancement in infrastructure and rolling stock. Greater staff flexibility in return for above-average salaries would be needed to make the most of a devolved sub-network more responsive to local needs and playing a bigger role in the regional transport system.

Growing revenue – and demonstrating a bigger transport, economic and social role for the railway – has to be at the heart of any development policy for the Far North Line. The basis for further enhancement of 'suburban' services into Inverness lies in building on the successes of the last 18 years. But this will not solve the financial problem of the railway north of Tain.

New markets will need to be developed, both passenger and freight. This will require innovation within and outwith the rail industry, and a closer integration of the railway into economic and social activities in the long corridor it serves.

Five broader perspectives

For all its difficulties, the Far North Line enjoys considerable goodwill from those who want it to succeed in a tough competitive environment.

The railway is fortunate to have backing from: Highland Council and HITRANS, the key statutory bodies at regional level; the well-informed and committed activists of the Friends of the Far North Line (FoFNL); senior retired railway managers who have offered the benefit of their experience and insights into options for the future; and, of course, current ScotRail and Network Rail management who are keen to make a success of this most challenging of railways.

Five different perspectives are quoted below, with the wider scene set at some length by long-standing FoFNL activist, Les Turner, from an April 2014 article in *Far North Express*:

Caithness, with a population of 30,000, is effectively an island separated from Easter Ross by 80 miles of sparsely populated country. Beyond the Pentland Firth, we have the Orkney Islands with a population of 20,000 and 800 active farming businesses. Caithness and Galloway, in the south-west, are the only mainland areas of Scotland to report a population decline between the 2001 and 2011 censuses.

(This was a timely reminder of Frank Spaven's 1994 highlighting of the much greater population along the Far North Line than those served by the other four 'peripheral' Highland lines: to Kyle, Mallaig, Fort William and Oban.)

It can be noted that the Highlands generally have not shared in the boom in rail travel experienced elsewhere, the principal reason being the lack of competitive speed over road journeys and the sparse service. However, compare this with the dramatic improvement of traffic on local services to Tain and Lairg in recent years, despite most of the stations being eccentric to the villages they serve. Dingwall now has 13 daily services instead of 5 in 1965, but journey times have extended from 27 minutes to between 31 and 37, admittedly with three new stops at Beauly, Muir of Ord and Conon Bridge. Dingwall has a half-hourly bus service taking 27 to 30 minutes via Conon Bridge.

There are numerous opportunities for additional traffic. However, in the face of the seemingly increasing centralist view covering many aspects of society, these require local management with budget responsibility, authority and accountability. Invergordon now has cruise ship landings of 90,000 annually. Coach excursions by these visitors cost over £100 each, so there must be possibilities to develop a rail option. However, the difficulties of lack of suitable rolling stock, sidings, train paths, crewing and the initial financial risk means that this is unlikely in the short term, despite success in comparative places like Skagway, Alaska or Dunedin, New Zealand, where visitors from cruise ships travel on scenic railways.

Gordon Pettitt, former Managing Director of BR Regional Railways, has taken a keen interest in the future of the line, and some of his key thoughts are worth repeating here:

> The differences between the car and train journey times are so great, that the railway must seem a total irrelevance to the majority of car owners in Sutherland and Caithness.

> While there has been a 40% growth [north of Tain] over the last five years, the average train loads remain at the level of buses rather than a railway for most of the year. Journey times are long and not competitive with bus let alone car travel, primarily owing to the investment in direct road links between 1979 and 1991.

> The current use of the line between Inverness and Tain clearly suggests that this section should be regarded as the core business of the FNL and therefore be the priority for investment, resources and timetable development.

During his presentation to the Capital Rail Action Group in Edinburgh in March 2016, Chris Green, the former ScotRail General Manager, alluded to a number of aspects of the Far North Line's prospects, in the wider context of what current rail structures do and don't allow management to achieve. Commenting that 'freedom to manage the product is what's missing today', he endorsed the idea of a sub-regional micro-franchise to deliver 'an affordable railway', with local management developing new markets such as tourism, ideally supported by speed enhancements achieved through fewer intermediate stops, upgraded level crossings and a west-to-north Georgemas chord.

Jim Summers was ScotRail's Regional Operations Manager from 1986 to 1991. In early 2016 he commented to me:

> As a former railway manager you get a 'feel' for what a railway is doing, and what it could do. I think one of the big problems is that the Far North Line doesn't do *anything* particularly well. If it was in America it would have become a 'short line' arrangement, with local management controlling track and trains, understanding costs, motivating staff, and developing new markets innovatively on the basis of strong local knowledge and a network of business contacts.

Frank Roach – the man with much of the hands-on responsibility for fostering the development of the line – reflected on the problems and opportunities during a train journey with me in March 2016. He candidly acknowledged both the weaknesses and strengths of the railway;

> On the one hand, there aren't massive grounds for optimism. We've seen the collapse of most rail freight – once seen as the potential saviour of the line – and encouraging the same levels of passenger growth as on inter-urban rail services isn't easy on a rural route where there are fewer reasons for travelling.

> On the other hand, too many people focus only on the journey time, when there are other key factors in choice of transport mode, such as service frequency, on-board comfort and facilities, and ticket prices. Smooth interchange with other services at Inverness is crucial, and even between Caithness and Inverness there are some distinctive attractions of train versus bus: for example, it can be a 'rite of passage' for young people. Groups can travel together in comfort for a trip which is price-sensitive rather than time-sensitive.

Frank's appreciation of the subtleties of the market underpins his ongoing analysis of the scope for timetable improvement, with key objectives being a better spread of trains over a longer day and an arrival before 10.00 in Inverness from Caithness. The creation of a train crew depot at Lairg would also significantly increase flexibility of operation. While welcoming ScotRail's planned introduction of on-train 'ambassadors' for tourists, like many rail campaigners he would ideally like to see bespoke rolling stock or significant modifications to existing trains to spearhead a drive to promote the under-rated scenic diversity of the line.

Based on my discussions with Frank, current and retired rail staff, railway campaigners and other protagonists – and my own perspective from a working life spent in and around the rail industry, plus some four decades as a railway campaigner – I set out below a range of ideas and discussion points on how to secure the future of the Far North Line.

Realising the passenger opportunities

In the absence of much heavy industry and major concentrations of population generating significant freight demand, the key opportunities for the railway clearly lie with the passenger market.

As Gordon Pettitt and others have emphasised, overall passenger demand within the immediate Inverness catchment, and the railway's relatively small mileage disadvantage versus road on the southern part of the route, point to it having the potential for a significantly enhanced role for **regular/daily 'suburban' traffic from Tain southwards**. For rail to fulfil its potential, the service will need to be regular-interval, faster and more reliable. This, in turn, has infrastructure enhancement implications, which are explored later.

A confusion of commercial clutter confronts the rail traveller – and obscures the original Highland Railway water tower – at lonely Altnabreac station on 26 August 2015. More sensitive management of this special location – one of just four stations in Britain with no tarred road access – would help to enhance the tourist potential of this unique section of the Far North Line. David Spaven

North of Tain, other than for a limited amount of regular traffic supported by 'short workings' to and from Ardgay and Lairg, the prognosis is more difficult. The Far North Line is routinely under-rated for **tourist traffic**, yet it enjoys probably a greater diversity of scenery than any other Scottish rail route, including the internationally-recognised Kyle, West Highland and Oban lines. There are around 20 listed buildings and structures along the length of the line, plus visitor attractions at Dunrobin Castle and the RSPB centre at Forsinard, and a stretch of railway unparalleled by any road, across the lonely moorland between Forsinard and Scotscalder. For some years, coach tour companies have organised tours with rail travel over this section of the Far North Line as a distinctive component.

Eight of the line's quietest stations – mostly on the northern section of the route – are 'request' stops. This is a sensible economy measure, designed to save fuel (and time) when there are no joining or alighting passengers. But in a small way it is also a marketable part of the journey experience. Putting your hand out to bring a train to a halt is not a personal power available to the average British (or foreign) rail traveller!

And in contrast to this quintessentially 'slow travel' experience, where can you enjoy the fastest (legal) overland transport in Scotland north of Aberdeen and Aviemore? Counter-intuitively, it's one and a half miles of 90 mph railway near the 'Fairy Hillocks' between County March Summit and Altnabreac station, on the most isolated section of the Far North Line...

Turning to potential lessons from other lines, tourist and leisure traffic is an increasing focus of the successfully re-opened Borders Railway, with integrated rail / coach packages now being strongly promoted. Scottish Government Ministers have eulogised its scenic qualities – but these are not in the same league as the Far North Line, which skirts estuaries, climbs between mountain ranges and runs along a dramatic, unspoilt coastline.

The Borders Railway has the advantage of a large city and massive tourist centre at its northern terminus. And, as Frank Roach has noted, one of the Far North Line's problems in developing day trip and leisure traffic is the sheer length of journey time from Inverness to Caithness and back. Slow travel is gaining popularity worldwide, but an eight-hour round-trip in a day has limited appeal.

The answer lies in part in identifying discrete packages which can be effectively marketed on different sections of the line. Paradoxically, the most financially challenged stretch of the railway may offer some of the best prospects. A 'unique selling point' of the Far North Line, compared to other railways focused on Inverness, is the opportunity to travel where no road goes, across the moors from Forsinard to Scotscalder, with the added historical interest of the tale of the train stranded in the snow near Altnabreac in 1978. And, of course, it is on this section of the line that there is routinely plenty of spare seating capacity to accommodate special parties on trains.

Friends of the Far North Line have highlighted the failure of the railway to tap into the cruise market at Invergordon. Yet one can envisage, for example, a coach tour from Invergordon pier depositing passengers at Dunrobin Castle, later continuing their journey inland by scheduled train to Thurso, then returning along the coast by coach to complete a circle around east Sutherland and Caithness.

'Soft' measures can cost-effectively develop such markets in the short and medium term. Guides on trains, 'window gazer' brochures (and their modern equivalents on smart phones and tablets), visitor information boards at stations, and more 'station adoptions' by local groups are some of the tried and tested ways of making the rail journey an attractive package experience for visitors. But centralised railway management structures do not lend themselves to getting the details right, nor to delivering them consistently on the day. And a big breakthrough on tourism will surely demand something special in terms of trains, as well as the level of care devoted to nurturing the heritage and other attractions of individual stations.

The potential for more tourist traffic should not obscure the opportunities for regular / daily traffic beyond the Inverness commuter catchment. The '**necessity market**', as coined by Richard Ardern of Friends of the Far North Line, includes travel from all parts of the line to Dingwall or (usually) Inverness for professional appointments for medical, legal, educational or other routine purposes. And there will always be a market for '**visiting friends and relatives**', which is less time-sensitive than, for example, business travel. As Frank Roach has pointed out, rail is also attractive for dark, early morning trips in winter, particularly when snow and ice prevail. For certain niche markets, such as Golspie, Brora and Helmsdale to Thurso (the largest service centre north of Inverness), the train is as fast – and more comfortable – than the bus, at any time of the year. From Wick to Thurso, the train is significantly faster.

Reliability is a key factor, partly determined by quality of train maintenance and also – critically – by the availability of crossing loops. Investment in more of the latter will take time, but shorter-term measures to alleviate the knock-on consequences of late-running could include re-timetabling, so that, for example, fewer than the current two out of four daily trains are programmed to cross at Forsinard loop, the meeting point of by far the two longest single-track sections of the line – 24 miles south to Helmsdale and 21 miles north to Georgemas. (Distances between all the line's loops are set out in Appendix 2.)

The B-listed station buildings at Wick and Thurso are of similar design, but different materials. This is the sandstone structure at Thurso, Britain's most northerly station, seen above in August 2007. The flagstone building at Wick – Britain's station furthest from London (729 miles from Euston) – is seen below in August 2007. John Furnevel

Management and delivery of a distinctive Far North rail service

As I identified in my *Rail 2014: potential implications of a 'dual focus franchise'* report for HITRANS, there are potential benefits in creating a North Highland focus for selected elements of possible new national rail policy directions suggested by the 2011 McNulty Report and by Paul Salveson in his thinking on development of the micro-franchising concept.

McNulty advocated devolved decision-making and experimentation with 'vertical integration' of track and train management and operation where there were appropriate operating route characteristics, notably one dominant train operator. This links to his recommendation that several routes with different characteristics be identified where the principles of lower-cost regional networks could be developed, piloted in operation and benchmarked.

Although Paul Salveson was wary at the time of the inherent limitations of franchising, and warned that if micro-franchising was pursued as part of a cost-cutting agenda it was likely to fail and confirm its critics' view as being a step towards closure, he did argue that control over infrastructure is critical if the railway is to develop to meet rising demand.

The self-contained rail network north of Inverness, ie both the Far North and Kyle lines, has (a) many of the characteristics identified by McNulty for distinctive treatment and by Salveson in his assessments of the scope for **micro-franchising** and beyond, and (b) examples of enhancements blocked by the current structure and cost base of the rail industry:

- a dominant operator – ScotRail – which provides 95% of train services over the network (others being freight and summer passenger charters)

- a natural management / operations base and principal market at Inverness

- some route infrastructure constraints on traffic growth, notably the section between Dingwall and Inverness, with just one intermediate crossing loop

- opportunities for new stations serving commuter and other markets

- substantial tourist potential.

The sub-network comprising the Far North and Kyle lines should be considered for a vertically-integrated pilot / demonstrator sub-franchise, with a view to further development towards a new model of community management. This has the potential to unlock a range of rail cost and revenue benefits, and to generate enhanced economic, social and environmental value from the entire North Highland rail system.

As a senior railway manager commented to me in 2016: 'There would be so much opportunity from a locally based, focussed team who really understood the markets, the geography and the opportunities, and were able to "challenge the norms" to get things done.'

And a retired senior railway manager echoed this sentiment, writing in *Far North Express* in May 2015:

> The idea of the Deep Alliance between Abellio and Network Rail presents an opportunity to project its logic to the situation…in our part of the network. The idea must surely be to combine the resources of the railway family in the north of Scotland to run a better service. Long and isolated single track lines need to have track and trains organised together, with a local management team in day-to-day charge, with a realistic budget and resources, including sufficient rolling stock of all kinds.

However, action is needed in advance of the likely timescale for any such major structural change, with Richard Ardern of Friends of the Far North Line commenting: 'A more senior hands-on manager with clout is required in the North, whether or not the routes beyond Inverness become a separate franchise.'

And not forgetting freight

A micro-franchise integrating track and train control need not be a barrier to the development of freight traffic, provided the appropriate safeguards are built into the new management model.

However, such a change is not in immediate prospect, and in the meantime, it is important – while the Scottish Government remains enthusiastic about the opportunities for rail freight generally – that new traffics are won to the Far North Line. There may be an opportunity for a 'short line' operator – based on the North American model – to develop peripheral rail freight services feeding into the main rail haulier networks. With local market knowledge and contacts, and utilising less costly medium-powered locos of 1960s vintage, an agile operator could open up prospects which bigger rail hauliers – with centralised management and greater overheads – might struggle to secure.

A crucial prospect, and a stepping stone for further freight development, lies in securing the 100,000 tonnes of **timber** annually from Kinbrace to Inverness and beyond. As and when a regular timber train starts operation, this would provide the scope for adaptation of the timetable to allow for extension to Georgemas (the railhead for Caithness), which already has enough facilities to accommodate extra traffic.

If a daily timber train is successful, then a second train may even be feasible, particularly if the cost can be shared with other traffics. A regular service to and from Caithness would be attractive for a wide range of commodities, including supermarket supplies, oil, compressed natural gas and cement. A spin-off from timber success at Kinbrace could be the development of timber traffic at those stations where rail sidings still survive, such as Ardgay, Georgemas and Lairg, and perhaps also at niche lineside-loading sites like Altnabreac, Borrobol and Dunrobin Glen.

The grain distillery at Invergordon was deliberately sited astride the railway in the early 1960s. Rail continues to play a major part in moving container loads of bottled spirit from Central Scotland to Britain's big Deep Sea ports, but it is now nearly 25 years since regular movement of **bulk spirit** from the north of Scotland to Central Scotland maturation plants was undertaken by rail.

The 2013 *Lifting the Spirit* trial whisky train service from Elgin to Grangemouth – backed by HITRANS, HIE, local authorities, the EU Foodport project and large distilling companies such as Diageo and Pernod Ricard – demonstrated that rail has the potential to secure a significant modal switch.

Invergordon's current capacity is 38 million litres of pure alcohol per annum, which equates to some 25 road tankers a week, a potentially important contribution to a daily trunk train service from the Inner Moray Firth and Speyside areas. Inbound grain and outbound 'co-products' (re-usable waste) may also have rail potential.

While not a major volume opportunity, mention should be made of the niche opportunities for **parcels traffic on passenger trains**. There are ample precedents on the Caledonian Sleeper, East Midland Trains and Great Western Railway, and the scope to develop this market between the staffed terminus stations at Inverness, Wick and Thurso (and possibly some unstaffed stations, using local 'agents') should be explored by ScotRail and potential partners.

Recent news that passenger sleeper services from Edinburgh to Caithness are being discussed highlights the potential for regular **intermodal traffic**, such as supermarket supplies, being conveyed in 'mixed trains'. Once again, it may be that bespoke solutions are needed for the very particular circumstances of the Far North Line, and of the peripheral Highland routes in general. If rail freight nationally succeeds in pushing its penetration of the retail market beyond 'ambient' goods to chilled and frozen, this – and logistical co-operation between the different supermarket chains serving Caithness – will create the critical mass for regular freight services.

Resources to match the markets

Any package of improvements to the Far North Line's service is likely to involve a mix of 'soft' and 'hard' measures, with finance for the latter a challenge when competing against other rail and road schemes nationwide.

I was a strong supporter of the Dornoch rail bridge in 1980s: although not, it can be revealed now, the source of the media leak. However, I have reluctantly concluded that the window of opportunity for what would have been a transformative project has probably now passed irrevocably. But I would like to be proved wrong.

Within the passenger market, the best economic, social and environmental return on any Far North Line scheme is likely to relate to enhancing speed, capacity, and hence reliability on the section between Inverness and Tain. Track speed improvements can be secured in conjunction with planned renewals (as in the case of the 90 mph section near Altnabreac), but bespoke projects will be required to tackle three other key areas:

- reinstatement of double track over all or some of the six miles between Clachnaharry and Clunes, or, failing that, a crossing loop at Lentran sufficiently long to accommodate freight and tourist charter trains rather than just the short Class 158s

- replacement of RETB signalling between Inverness and Dingwall (inclusive) by extension of colour light signalling controlled from the Inverness Integrated Electronic Control Centre

- upgrading (or closing) critical level crossings – such as that at Bunchrew, between Clachnaharry and Lentran – to remove the worst speed restrictions

As Gordon Pettitt has indicated, it will be difficult to identify a robust case for easing speed restrictions at all crossing loops and most level crossings on the lightly-trafficked line north of Tain. However, the proposed chord at Georgemas may offer sufficient time and operating cost savings to justify investment. It would also offer the useful benefit of creating a track 'triangle' to turn steam engines on tourist charter trains after their arrival in Caithness from the south.

The proposed new timber railhead at Kinbrace is likely to be based on full train-length sidings with an internal locomotive run-round, to maximise operational efficiency. Its prospects are enhanced by eligibility for Freight Facilities Grant of up to 75% of the capital cost, in recognition of the significant environmental benefits of using rail. And there may be synergies between the timber development work and the concept of a new crossing loop at Kinbrace, to break up the 24-mile single-track section from Helmsdale to Forsinard which has been a major source of knock-on delays to passenger services.

Concluding thoughts

The Far North Line has been a challenge, operationally and financially, since construction of the Inverness & Ross-shire Railway began in 1860. And following the rise of the bus, the car and the lorry in the 20th century, and the major upgrading of the A9, that challenge has grown enormously – although two major threats to the railway's existence were successfully averted in 1964 and 1989.

The current prospects for the Far North Line can be summarised in a couple of sentences: 'This is a long and unusual rural railway, which is costing the taxpayer a lot of money for a narrowly focused, and currently unreliable service. It needs much better train performance and significantly more passenger and freight traffic to strengthen and secure its role in the regional transport infrastructure network.'

If the line is to be equipped to withstand perhaps inevitable future threats to its existence, cost control – although crucial – is not enough. New ways of working, empowered local management, targeted investment and development of new markets should also be at the heart of a growth package for the railway.

One key to a positive future is recognition, based in part on the Highland Rail Partnership/HITRANS-inspired developments of the last 18 years, that this is a railway of several parts and a number of distinct potential markets. The bespoke solutions undoubtedly needed for the Far North Line will therefore not necessarily be the same across the entire length of the railway.

The southern part provides the basis for an intensive suburban-style train service, while further north, Frank Spaven's vision of 'tourists and timber' is likely to be a core focus of efforts by the rail industry and its stakeholders. However, fully realising the tourism potential will surely require new trains – not just on the line to Caithness, but for all the scenic Highland routes – with observation facilities to attract many more visitors to this very special railway.

For 142 years, the Far North Line has been a great survivor. But its fascinating history, unique qualities and considerable potential have been routinely under-appreciated. I hope that in the decades ahead it will take its rightful place as a leader in rural railway innovation, and that, once again, it will become central to the economic and social life of the 168-mile corridor it has served since 1874.

REFERENCES

[1] Neil T Sinclair, *The Highland Main Line* (2013)
[2] Neil T Sinclair (*ibid*)
[3] HA Vallance, *The Highland Railway* (1963)
[4] PJG Ransom, *Iron Road* (2007)
[5] David McConnell, *Rails to Wick & Thurso* (1990)
[6] Robin Smith, *The Making of Scotland* (2001)
[7] David Ross, *The Highland Railway* (2005)
[8] HA Vallance (*ibid*)
[9] David McConnell (*ibid*)
[10] David McConnell (*ibid*)
[11] David Ross (*ibid*)
[12] David Ross (*ibid*)
[13] John Thomas and David Turnock, *A Regional History of the Railways of Great Britain, Volume 15 North of Scotland* (1989)
[14] David Ross (*ibid*)
[15] David Ross (*ibid*)
[16] Highland Railway Society *Highland Railway Journal* (Spring 2015)
[17] Held at the Highland Archive in Inverness
[18] HA Vallance (*ibid*)
[19] HA Vallance (*ibid*)
[20] HA Vallance (*ibid*)
[21] Neil T Sinclair (*ibid*)
[22] David Ross (*ibid*)
[23] Thomas and Turnock (*ibid*)
[24] Thomas and Turnock (*ibid*)
[25] Michael Pearson, *Iron Roads to the Far North & Kyle* (2003)
[26] Neil T Sinclair (*ibid*)
[27] The Kyle Line by Tom Weir (1971), *The Skye Railway* by John Thomas (1977) and *Rails to Kyle of Lochalsh* by David McConnell (1997).
[28] HA Vallance (*ibid*)
[29] Christian Wolmar, *Fire & Steam* (2007)
[30] HA Vallance (*ibid*)
[31] Neil T Sinclair, *Highland Railway: People and Places* (2005)
[32] HA Vallance (*ibid*)
[33] Michael Bonavia, *The History of the LNER, the First Years 1922-33* (1982)
[34] Keith Fenwick, Neil T Sinclair and Richard J Ardern, *Lost Stations on the Far North Line* (2010)
[35] PJG Ransom (*ibid*)

[36] Fenwick, Sinclair and Ardern (*ibid*)

[37] PJG Ransom (*ibid*)

[38] Held in the Highland Railway Society archives; a summary is in *Far North Express* for January 2010.

[39] Neil T Sinclair (*ibid*)

[40] AJ Mullay, *Scottish Region: A History 1948-1973* (2006)

[41] As recollected by LTC Rolt, and quoted by Fenwick, Sinclair and Ardern (*ibid*)

[42] Fenwick, Sinclair and Ardern (*ibid*)

[43] Fenwick, Sinclair and Ardern (*ibid*)

[44] Fenwick, Sinclair and Ardern (*ibid*)

[45] Fenwick, Sinclair and Ardern (*ibid*)

[46] Fenwick, Sinclair and Ardern (*ibid*)

[47] Thomas and Turnock (*ibid*)

[48] Thomas and Turnock (*ibid*)

[49] Held at the Highland Archive in Inverness (Frank Spaven collection)

[50] Held at the National Records of Scotland in Edinburgh

[51] Held at the Highland Archive in Inverness

[52] Charles Loft, *Last Trains* (2013)

[53] Held at the Highland Archive in Inverness (Phil Durham collection)

[54] Held at the National Records of Scotland in Edinburgh

[55] Martech for the Scottish Vigilantes Association, *Highland Opportunity* (1964)

[56] Held at the Highland Archive in Inverness

[57] From 1969, Freightliners Ltd was 51%-owned by the state-owned National Freight Corporation (NFC) established by the 1968 Transport Act, but returned to full BR ownership in 1978.

[58] Terry Gourvish, *British Railways 1948–73: A Business History* (1986)

[59] Scottish Region Management Bulletin no 45 (September 1972) in *Far North Express* (May 2010)

[60] In a 22 June 1990 postcard from Frank Spaven to Railfuture campaigner, Ken Sutherland.

[61] National Carriers (NCL) was part of the state-owned National Freight Corporation (NFC) established by the 1968 Transport Act. NCL provided BR's road collection and delivery services for freight, sundries and parcels.

[62] www.tioatiboa.co.uk

[63] Statistics compiled by Frank Spaven (and now held at the Highland Archive in Inverness)

[64] Michael Collins, *Freightliner: the Life & Times* (1991)

[65] In a 16 June 1990 letter from Frank Spaven to Railfuture campaigner Ken Sutherland.

[66] *Hansard*

[67] Photocopied book extract supplied by John Hood, from his book on John Brown Engineering *[title and year unknown]*

[68] David Spaven, *Waverley Route: the battle for the Borders Railway* (2015)

[69] Highland Railway Society Journal (1996)

[70] The NICS kit was developed in 2004 by a Glasgow-based railway engineering company, and provides a novel lower-cost means of connecting new sidings without cutting into the existing main-line rails. An approaching train travels over 'temporary' rails raised 50mm above the height of the existing rails and then reaches the physically separate semi-permanent siding. The physical elements of NICS are, primarily, hinged temporary rail switches and crossings, and are manually controlled, accommodating rolling stock of the heaviest axleloads (25.5 tonnes) at speeds of up to 15mph. Capital costs for NICS are substantially cheaper than for conventional siding connection (primarily through avoidance of new signalling costs), and it also offers much shorter lead-times for completion than under conventional arrangements with the rail infrastructure provider, Network Rail. Potentially, the ability to relocate the kit, after weeks, months or a few years of use, has a very good fit with timber harvesting.

[71] http://www.scotrail.co.uk/sites/default/files/assets/download_ct/monthly-performance-figures-p1617-03.pdf

[72] Office of Rail and Road (http://orr.gov.uk/statistics/published-stats/station-usage-estimates) and Transport Scotland (http://www.transport.gov.scot/report/j415388-08.htm)

[73] Network Rail Scotland Route Sectional Appendix (2016)

[74] The Office of Rail and Road (ORR) 'GB rail industry financial information 2014-15' report, published on 9 March 2016: 'In 2014-15, total governments' funding varied from £1.66 per passenger journey in England to £6.70 per journey in Scotland and £9.14 per journey in Wales. The rail industry has high fixed costs, so these differences in funding are partly due to the very different average passenger densities, with 129 passengers per train in England, 81 in Scotland and 69 in Wales.'

[75] Network Rail's Strategic Business Plan for Scotland (2013) and the ORR's GB Rail Industry Financial Information 2014-15 (2016)

[76] The Scotsman, 21 March 2016 and http://www.scotsman.com/news/transport/80-people-chasing-every-scotrail-train-driver-job-1-3896410

[77] In March 2016, the Road Haulage Association advised the author a figure of £28-30,000 per annum basic salary for lorry drivers in general haulage, and the Confederation for Passenger Transport advised a figure of around £25,000 pa for bus and coach drivers.

BIBLIOGRAPHY AND SOURCES

Bradshaw's Descriptive Railway Handbook of Great Britain and Ireland (1863) Oxford: Old House Books (2012 facsimile)

British Railways Board (1963) *The Reshaping of British Railways* London: HMSO

Clarke, Reay (2014) *Two Hundred Years of Farming in Sutherland* Isle of Lewis: The Islands Book Trust

Collins, Michael (1991) *Freightliner* Sparkford: Haynes Publishing Group

Durham, Phil (2001) *Highland Whistle Blower* Aberdeen: Famedram

Faulkner, Richard and Austin, Chris (2012) *Holding the Line* Hersham: Oxford Publishing Co

Fenwick, Keith (2012) *Inverness & Ross-shire Railway* Inverness: Highland Railway Society

Fenwick, Keith, Neil T Sinclair and Richard Ardern (2010) *Lost Stations on the Far North Line* Inverness: Highland Railway Society

Hamilton, Bill (2010) *Man on the spot: a broadcaster's story* Kibworth: Book Guild Publishing

Hardy, RHN (1989) *Beeching: Champion of the Railway?* London: Ian Allan

Harvie, Christopher (2001) *Deep Fried Hillman Imp* Glendaruel: Argyll Publishing

Jones, Robin (2012) *Beeching: the inside track* Horncastle: Mortons Media Group

Loft, Charles (2013) *Last Trains* London: Biteback Publishing

McConnell, David (1990) *Rails to Wick & Thurso* Dornoch: Dornoch Press

Nolan, Mark http://tioatiboa.co.uk/travel-and-transport/a-railman-remembers/

Pearson, Michael (2003) *Iron Roads to the Far North & Kyle* Wayzgoose

Ransom, PJG (2007) *Iron Road* Edinburgh: Birlinn

Ross, David (2010) *The Highland Railway* Catrine: Stenlake Publishing

Simmons, J and Biddle, G (ed) (2003) *The Oxford Companion to British Railway History* Oxford: Oxford University Press

Sinclair, Neil T (2005) *Highland Railway: People and Places* Derby: Breedon Books Publishing

Sinclair, Neil T (2013) *The Highland Main Line* Catrine: Stenlake Publishing

Smith, Robin (2001) *The Making of Scotland* Edinburgh: Canongate Books

Spaven, David and Holland, Julian (2011) *Mapping the Railways* London: Times Books

Spaven, David and Holland, Julian (2012) *Britain's Scenic Railways* London: Times Books

Spaven, David (2015) *Waverley Route: the battle for the Borders Railway* Edinburgh: Argyll Publishing

Spaven, David (2015) *The Railway Atlas of Scotland* Edinburgh: Birlinn

The Stephenson Locomotive Society (1955) *The Highland Railway Company and its constituents and successors* London: SLS

Thomas, JA and Turnock, D (1989) *A Regional History of the Railways of Great Britain, Volume 15 North of Scotland* Newton Abbot: David & Charles

Vallance HA (1963) *The Highland Railway* Dawlish: David & Charles

Wolmar, Christian (2007) *Fire & Steam* London: Atlantic Books

Public archive sources:

The principal source is Highland Council's **Highland Archive** in Inverness, and in particular the following collections: D113 JK Forsyth papers; D285 Frank Spaven papers; D531 Phil Durham papers; D696 Sir Robert Reid papers.

Archive copies of the *Inverness Courier, John O'Groat Journal and Ross-shire Journal* are held in, respectively, Highland Council's **Inverness, Wick and Dingwall public libraries**.

The other main public archive source is the **National Records of Scotland** in Edinburgh, and in particular the following collections: BR/RSR British Railways (Scottish Region); DD17 Scottish Office Development Department; SEP4 Scottish Economic Planning Council.

APPENDIX 1:

SELECTED 'LISTED' STRUCTURES, FEATURES AND ATTRACTIONS

Inverness – Inverness & Aberdeen Junction Railway 1858 commemorative plaque; Frank Spaven memorial seat on Platform 2; original Highland Railway Lochgorm Works building in the track 'triangle' beyond the station

Clachnaharry – B-listed canal swing bridge and signal box (and nearby lineside view from the Clachnaharry Inn beer garden)

Beauly – Britain's smallest station (only one door on the train is opened)

Dingwall – B-listed station building; The Mallard bistro bar (www.the-mallard. com/); Tina's Tearoom (www.tinastearoom.com/) on the station platform

Invergordon – station murals

Fearn – B-listed station building and C-listed station cottages

Tain– Platform 1864 restaurant (www.facebook.com/ Platform-1864-394867740704091/) in B-listed station building

Ardgay – B-listed station building

Culrain/Invershin – A-listed Oykel (or Shin) Viaduct; one of the shortest distances between two stations on the British rail network, which can now also be walked on a footbridge beside the viaduct

Lairg – Frank Roach's HITRANS office in the station building, adjacent to the small oil terminal (the only freight facility along the first 147 miles of the railway)

Rogart – holiday accommodation (www.sleeperzzz.com) in historic railway coaches in the former goods yard

Golspie – B-listed station building

Brora – B-listed station building

Dunrobin Castle – B-listed Arts & Crafts station building (with museum) and nearby Dunrobin Castle (www.dunrobincastle.co.uk)

Helmsdale – holiday accommodation (www.helmsdalestation.co.uk) in B-listed station building

Forsinard – RSPB reserve visitor centre in the original station building (www. rspb.org.uk/discoverandenjoynature/seenature/reserves/guide/f/forsinard/ directions.aspx)

Altnabreac – original Highland Railway water tower at one of just four stations in Britain with no tarred road access

Wick – B-listed flagstone station building at Britain's station furthest from London

Thurso – B-listed sandstone station building at Britain's most northerly station

Additional information on many aspects of the railway (including archive copies of *Far North Express*) can be found on the **Friends of the Far North Line** web site: http://www.fofnl.org.uk/index.html

Train timetable details are on the **ScotRail** web site: http://www.scotrail.co.uk/plan-your-journey/timetables-and-routes

Details of the **Highland Railway Society** are on http://www.hrsoc.org.uk/

APPENDIX 2:

RETB TOKEN EXCHANGE POINTS, AND CROSSING LOOPS

	Token exchange point (miles and chains)	Loop length (metres)
Inverness	0.00	n/a
Clachnaharry (signal box)*	1.50	-
Clunes	7.51	-
Muir of Ord	13.04	466
Dingwall	18.58	410
Evanton	25.00	-
Invergordon	31.37	395
Fearn	40.60	-
Tain	44.23	255
Ardgay	57.70	435
Lairg	66.78	302
Rogart	77.01	330
Brora	90.48	330
Helmsdale	101.40	255
Forsinard	125.69	250
Halkirk	146.53	-
Georgemas Junction	147.20	240
Bower	147.56	-
Wick	161.35	out of use
Thurso	6.50 (from Georgemas)	out of use

* not an RETB token exchange point: controlled from Inverness RETB signalling centre with local manual control of canal swing bridge

Source: Network Rail Scotland Route *Sectional Appendix* (2016)

INDEX

Highland Survivor *is written for the general reader as much as for the railway enthusiast. This Index is a relatively brief list of events, places and organisations which have arisen from and defined this railway line throughout its frequently problematic yet proudly stubborn existence.*

The Index includes some technological references. eg locomotive classes from the past 60 years, but it does not pretend to be a technical index. Also, it does not list the names of the existing Far North Line stations, nor does it contain any personal names. The former, obviously, are spread profusely throughout the book, while the principal protagonists appear within well-defined periods of this largely chronological history.

However, the entries herein will, we feel, serve as sufficient signposting to the key components of the fascinating history of this most unusual railway.